Knowledge and Discourse

Towards an ecology of language

Edited by
Colin Barron
Nigel Bruce
David Nunan

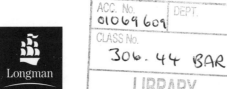

Longman

An imprint of **Pearson Education**

Harlow, England · London · New York · Reading, Massachusetts · San Francisco
Toronto · Don Mills, Ontario · Sydney · Tokyo · Singapore · Hong Kong · Seoul
Taipei · Cape Town · Madrid · Mexico City · Amsterdam · Munich · Paris · Milan

Pearson Education Limited
Edinburgh Gate
Harlow
Essex CM20 2JE
England

and Associated Companies throughout the world

Visit us on the World Wide Web at:
www.pearsoneduc.com

First published 2002

ISBN 0-582-32880-2 PPR

British Library Cataloguing-in-Publication Data

A catalogue record for this book is available from the British Library

Library of Congress Cataloging-in-Publication Data

A catalog record for this book is available from the Library of Congress

Set in 10/12pt Janson by Graphicraft Limited, Hong Kong
Produced by Pearson Education Malaysia, Sdn Bhd
Printed in Malaysia, PJB

LANGUAGE IN SOCIAL LIFE SERIES

Series Editor: Professor Christopher N Candlin
Chair Professor of Applied Linguistics
Department of English
Centre for English Language Education & Communication Research
City University of Hong Kong, Hong Kong

Contents

Coda

List of contributors

Colin Barron teaches communication skills to science and engineering students and sociolinguistics on the Masters course in applied linguistics at the University of Hong Kong. He has also taught in Saudi Arabia, Iran, Jordan, Nepal and Papua New Guinea. His research interests are in the analysis of the discourse of engineers and scientists, and culture in applied linguistics. He recently completed his doctoral dissertation at Lancaster University, entitled *On the way to being an engineer: An analysis of time and temporality in mechanical engineering discourse.* csbarron@hkusua.hku.hk.

Kingsley Bolton teaches sociolinguistics, the history of linguistics and varieties of English in the English Department of the University of Hong Kong. His research interests include the sociolinguistics of Asian societies, English in Asia and Hong Kong, and the history of western language scholarship in Hong Kong and China. Publications include *Sociolinguistics today: International perspectives* (edited with H. Kwok, Routledge, 1992). Together with Christopher Hutton, he has published on taboo language and criminal slang, including 'Bad language and banned language: triad societies, the censorship of the Cantonese vernacular and colonial language policy in Hong Kong', in *Language in Society*, Vol. 24 (1995); and 'Bad boys and bad language: *Chou hau* and the sociolinguistics of swearing in Hong Kong', in Grant Evans and Maria Tam Siu-mei (eds), *Hong Kong: The anthropology of a Chinese metropolis* (London: Curzon/The University of Hawaii Press, 1997). hraeklb@hku.hk

Nigel Bruce has taught English in France, Mongolia and Kuwait, and has spent the last 14 years at Hong Kong University teaching academic communication skills. He currently teaches students of law, dentistry, social sciences, arts and applied linguistics. His research and development interests are in constructions of knowledge and practice, academic writing, and the potential of the Internet for promoting autonomous learning and enriching writing response practices across the academy. Recent publications include

'Integrating computers into teaching practices: The value of a broad-based approach', in J. Gassin *et al.* (eds) *Proceedings of the 1998 WorldCALL Conference* (1999), and 'Classification and hierarchy in the discourse of wine: Emile Peynaud's *The Taste of Wine*', in *ASp*, journal of GERAS [ESP study and research group], University Victor-Sigalen, Bordeaux 2. njbruce@hku.hk

Christopher Candlin is Chair Professor of Applied Linguistics and Director of the Centre for English Language Education & Communication Research at the City University of Hong Kong. Formerly Professor of Linguistics and Executive Director of the National Centre for English Language Teaching & Research (NCELTR) at Macquarie University, Sydney, he has taught in the UK, the USA, Germany and Australia. His research and teaching interests are in professional–client discourse, especially in the fields of healthcare, medicine, law and business studies; in workplace communication; and in the application of pragmatics and discourse analysis to the understanding of social and institutional practices. He is a member of the Editorial Boards of several international journals and has managed a number of funded research projects in his fields. His most recent publications are: *Sociolinguistics and Social Theory* (edited with Nikolas Coupland and Srikant Sarangi, London: Longman, 2001); *Writing: Texts, Processes and Practices* (edited with Ken Hyland, London: Longman, 1999); and *English Language Teaching in its Social Context* (edited with Neil Mercer, London: Routledge, 2000); and with Sally Candlin is guest editing an issue of *Research on Language and Social Interaction* on the topic of Expert Talk and Risk (2002). He edits or co-edits six international book series for major publishers and is currently President of the International Association of Applied Linguistics (AILA). enopera@cityu.edu.hk

Chng Huang Hoon teaches critical discourse analysis and feminist theories and discourse at the Department of English Language and Literature, National University of Singapore. In addition, she teaches a course on law and gender at the American Studies Centre at the National University of Singapore. Her main research interests are in issues of language, law, gender, ideology and power. Her publications include a monograph entitled *Towards multidisciplinarity: The case of judicial language* (1996), a 1996 article review of Norman Fairclough's book, *Critical Discourse Analysis*, published in the *Journal of Pragmatics*, Vol. 26, and an article entitled 'In the beginning there was Myra: The role of language in the construction of gender and power relations in the judicial setting', published in *Text in Education and Society* (Singapore University Press, 1998). ellchh@nus.edu.sg

Gail Forey is an Assistant Professor in the Department of English at the Hong Kong Polytechnic University where she teaches both undergraduate and postgraduate courses in applied linguistics, and English language professional development workshops and other types of support to academic staff.

She has taught in England, Hungary, Australia, Japan and Hong Kong. Her research interests are discourse analysis, English for specific purposes and systemic functional linguistics. She is currently enrolled for a PhD at Glasgow University and her working title is 'Text and context of written business discourse'. Her recent publications include 'Exploring aspects of context: selected findings from the Effective Writing for Management project' (with F. Davies and D. Hyatt), in F. Bargiela-Chiappini and C. Nickerson (eds) *Writing business: Genres, methods and language* (London: Longman, 1999); and 'A cybernetic musing: Language and science in the language of science' (with R. Glanville and S. Sengupta) in *Cybernetics and Human Knowing*, Vol. 5, No. 4 (1998). eggail@mail.polyu.edu.hk

Tara Goldstein currently teaches in the Initial Teacher Education and Graduate Education Programs at the Ontario Institute for Studies in Education at the University of Toronto (OISE/UT). Her research and teaching interests include dilemmas and practices in critical ethnography; the education of immigrant learners; policies practices and politics associated with linguistic diversity in multilingual secondary schools and workplaces; and working towards equity in public education. Tara recently won a teacher of the year award from the University of Toronto for her work in OISE/UT's Initial Teacher Education Program and has been recently appointed Academic Director of Student Services at OISE/UT. She has had articles and book reviews published in *TESOL Quarterly*, *TESL Canada* and *Canadian Modern Language Review*, and is the author of *Two languages at work: Bilingual life on the production floor* (Berlin/New York: Mouton de Gruyter, 1996). tgoldstein@oise.utoronto.ca

Gu Yueguo, PhD at Lancaster University, UK, is a research professor of linguistics at the Institute of Linguistics, the Chinese Academy of Social Sciences, and a British Academy K. C. Wong Fellow. His research interests include pragmatics, discourse analysis, and corpus linguistics. He has contributed to the *Journal of Pragmatics*, *Text*, and *Journal of Asian and Pacific Communication*. He is co-chief-editor of *Journal of Contemporary Linguistics*. He is currently working on a Spoken Chinese Corpus and is Director of the National Distance Education for In-Service Teachers of English. guyg@hns.cjfh.ac.cn

Po-keung Hui received his PhD in Sociology from the State University of New York at Binghamton in 1995. His first degree is in Mathematics and his Master's degree is in Economics. He is now assistant professor with the newly established Cultural Studies Program under the School of General Education at Lingnan University, after teaching at the Translation Department of the same institution for four years. His main research interests are cultural and translation studies, political economy, and development studies.

He is one of the editors of the *Cultural and Social Studies Translation Series* (in Chinese), published by Hong Kong Oxford University Press. pkhui@ln.edu.hk

Christopher Hutton teaches sociolinguistics, semantics and the history of linguistics in the English Department of the University of Hong Kong. He previously taught Yiddish studies at the University of Texas at Austin. His main research interests are in the politics of language and the politics of linguistics. Recent publications include *Linguistics and the Third Reich: Race, mother tongue fascism and the science of language* (London: Routledge, 1999), a study of the contribution of linguistic theory to Nazi ideology, and a series of articles on taboo language, language policy and colonialism in Hong Kong (with K. Bolton). chutton@hkucc.hku.hk

Allan Luke is Dean and Professor of Education at the University of Queensland, where he teaches sociology of education, discourse analysis and literacy studies. He is author and editor of numerous books and articles, the most recent of which is *Constructing Critical Literacies* (with Peter Freebody and Sandy Muspratt). He is currently completing a three-year study of interracial Asian/Australian families and a large-scale government study of school reform and pedagogy in Queensland schools. He is editor of the *Journal of Adolescent and Adult Literacy* and an ongoing series of monographs published by Taylor & Francis: *New Critical Perspectives on Literacy and Education*. a.luke@mailbox.uq.edu.au

Minna-Riitta Luukka is Professor at the Centre for Applied Language Studies and the Department of Finnish at the University of Jyväskylä, Finland. Her main research interests are in various kinds of institutional discourse and the interpersonal and functional nature of language, especially Finnish language. She has published on metadiscourse and hedging in scientific texts, classroom interaction, university level seminar discourse, popularized science in newspapers, scholarly e-mail discussions and institutional texts dealing with information society. Her theoretical interests are found in critical discourse analysis, social constructionism, dialogism, gentre theory and systemic-functional linguistics. She is currently working on constructions of psychiatry and mental health in Finnish newspapers and is in charge of a multidisciplinary project called '(E)merging Finnish Media Culture: Encounters between Authors, Texts and Youth at the Millennium'. luukka@cc.jyu.fi

Ian Malcolm is Professor of Applied Linguistics and Co-Director of the Centre for Applied Language and Literacy Research at Edith Cowan University in Perth, Australia, and is Vice President of the Australian Linguistic Society. He teaches and coordinates courses in applied linguistics at ECU, and has carried out research into classroom discourse, second language learning and teaching, cross-cultural communication and Aboriginal English. He is currently researching Aboriginal English genres among the Yamtji people. Among recent publications are *Aboriginality and English: Report to the Australian Research Council* (with M. Koscielecki, 1997); *Australian Aboriginal Students in Higher Education* (with J. Rochecouste, 1998); '"You gotta talk the proper way": Language and education', in G. Partington (ed.) *Perspectives on Aboriginal and Torres Strait Islander education* (Katoomba, NSW: Social Science Press, 1998); and 'Writing as an intercultural process', in C. Candlin and K. Hyland (eds) *Writing: Texts, Processes and Practices* (London: Longman, 1999). i.malcolm@cowan.edu.au

David Nunan is Director of the English Centre and Chair Professor of Applied Linguistics at the University of Hong Kong where he teaches undergraduate courses in English for Academic Purposes as well as graduate courses in Research Methods and Curriculum Development. His research interests include classroom discourse, learner-oriented curricula, and task-based learning. Recent publications include *Second language teaching and learning* (Heinle & Heinle, 1999), and (with Ron Carter) *The ELT Companion* (Cambridge: Cambridge University Press, 2000) dcnunan@hku.hk

Alastair Pennycook is Professor of Language in Education at the University of Technology, Sydney. Formerly at the University of Melbourne, he has also worked in Japan, China, Hong Kong and Canada. His interests include ethics, culture and difference in language and teacher development projects; plagiarism and intertextuality; colonialism and language policy; and implications of the global spread of English. He is the author of *The Cultural Politics of English as an International Language* (London: Longman) and *English and the Discourses of Colonialism* (London: Routledge). He was guest editor of a special edition of *TESOL Quarterly* in 1999 on Critical Approaches to TESOL. alastair.pennycook@uts.edu.au

Guenter A. Plum has researched academic literacy, doctor-patient communication, genre/register variation, and L2 learning, and taught systemic-functional linguistics. For the past two years he has been part of a team at Hong Kong University developing a web-based functional grammar of English for primary teachers in Hong Kong.

Kalpana Ram is a Research Fellow of the Australian Research Council, at the Anthropology Department of Macquarie University. She is author of a full-length monograph, *Mukkuvar women. Gender, hegemony and capitalist transformation in a south Indian fishing community* (London: Allen and Unwin, 1991); and editor (with Margaret Jolly) of *Colonial and postcolonial experiences in Asia and the Pacific after Maternities and Modernities* (Cambridge: Cambridge University Press, 1998); and (with J. Kehaulani Kauanui) of *Migrating feminisms. The Asia/Pacific region*, a special issue of *Women's Studies International Forum*, Nov.–Dec. 1998 (Oxford: Pergamon). She is also the author of several papers on feminist theory, anthropology and gender. The book she is currently writing is on discourse and lived experiences of the female body in south India. kram@bunyip.bhs.mq.edu.au

Joseph Schneider is Professor and Chair in the Department of Sociology, Anthropology, and Geography at Drake University in Des Moines, Iowa, USA. He teaches courses in social constructionism and poststructural theory, masculinity and popular culture, morality, and the Cultural Revolution. Past work has focused on the medicalization of deviance, the experience of chronic illness, and social problems theory. **Wang Laihua** is an associate professor and Director at the Tianjin Academy of Social Sciences in Tianjin, China. His research has focused on aging and the elderly, caregiving, family, and social services in a changing economy. Wang and Schneider have published a manuscript in Chinese based on their collaborative research in Tianjin, Loudou: *Yi Xiang dui Laonian Ren Jiating Zhaogu he Jiating Guanxi de Shehuixue Yanjiu (Funnel: A sociological study of family caregiving for the elderly and of family relationships)*, (Tianjin People's Press, 1998). A second book by Schneider and Wang based on this project, *Giving care, Writing self: A new ethnography*, is forthcoming from Peter Lang, Inc., New York. joseph.schneider@drake.edu

Ron Scollon is Professor of Sociolinguistics at Georgetown University in Washington, DC, and Adjunct Professor in the English Department of City University of Hong Kong. He teaches courses in public discourse, mediated discourse and intercultural communication. His current research interests extend earlier 'new literacy studies' work in the ethnographic study of literacy and technology to the study of identity in transnational and national environments undergoing sociopolitical transformation, with a particular focus on problems of intellectual property and technological mediations of power. At Georgetown University he is the Director of the Asian Sociocultural Research Projects Group. His several books include the recent *Intercultural communication: A discourse approach* (Oxford: Blackwell, 1995) and *Contrastive discourse in Chinese and English: A critical appraisal* (Foreign Language Teaching and Research Press, Beijing, in press), both co-authored with Suzanne Wong Scollon, and *Mediated Discourse as Social Interaction* (London: Longman, 1998). scollonr@gusun.georgetown.edu

Dorothy E. Smith is a professor in the Department of Sociology and Equity Studies in Education at the University of Toronto. She has been preoccupied for the past 25 or so years with developing the implications of women's standpoint for sociology, problematising the objectified forms of organisation and social relations characteristic of contemporary society, and focusing more recently on the significance of texts for the organisation of power. In 1975, with Sarah David, she published a ground-breaking collection of essays by feminists called *Women look at psychiatry: I'm not mad, I'm angry*. Since then she has published numerous articles and books, including *The everyday world as problematic: A feminist sociology* (1987), *The conceptual practices* *of power: A feminist sociology of knowledge* (1990), *Texts, facts, and femininity: Exploring the relations of ruling* (1990) and *Writing the social; Critique, theory and investigations* (1998). With Susan Turner, she has also edited Sally Hacker's papers for publication, combining them with extensive materials drawn from interviews with the sociologist and activist, then suffering from a terminal cancer. dsmith@oise.utoronto.ca

Graeme Storer is completing a doctorate in sociology at the University of New South Wales, Australia. His research is concerned with the discursive and sexual interactions between bar-based male sex workers and their clients in Bangkok, Thailand. Graeme also works as a freelance consultant, advising non-government organisations in Asia on management development and organisational change processes. Related publications include 'Performing sexual identity: naming and resisting "gayness" in modern Thailand', *Intersections*, Vol. 2, May 1999; 'Bar talk: Thai male sex workers and their customers', in Peter Aggleton (ed.) *Men who sell sex – international perspectives on male sex work and HIV/AIDS* (London: UCL Press, Taylor and Francis, 1999); and 'Rehearsing gender and sexuality in modern Thailand: Masculinity and male–male sex', in Peter Jackson and Gerard Sullivan (eds) *Lady boys, tom boys, rent boys: male and female homosexualities in contemporary Thailand* (New York: Haworth Press, 1999) graemestorer@ozemail.com.au

Zhu, Weifang, MA at Warwick University, UK, and associate professor of applied linguistics, is deputy dean of the School of English Language Communication, Beijing Foreign Studies University, Beijing. She is interested in ELT, language communication and culture, and cultural studies through films. She was a Fulbright Scholar at Yale University in 1997–98. Her publications include, among others, 'Politeness phenomena in epistolary discourse', 'Managing multi-culture miscommunications', and 'Ripples of American culture in Chinese students' minds', all in the *Journal of Foreign Language Teaching and Research*. Her textbooks include *English through movies*, *Culture through movies*, and *Cross culture through movies*, all published by Foreign Language Teaching and Research Press, Beijing. guyg@hns.cjfh.ac.cn

Publisher's Acknowledgements

We are grateful to the following for permission to reproduce copyright material:

Young Best Development Limited for Figures 9.1 and 9.2 from the triad comic *The Black Way and the White Way*, 1995.

Introduction: Knowledge and discourse: towards an ecology of language
Colin Barron, Nigel Bruce and David Nunan

The papers in this collection owe their genesis to an innovative conference held at the University of Hong Kong in June 1996. The International Knowledge and Discourse Conference brought together a wide range of scholars from every continent and from a variety of disciplines — sociologists, philosophers, linguists, geographers, economists, lawyers, and architects. We owe the book to the range of perspectives shared in a particular time and place. While the conference may have been innovative in 1996, the perspectives of the articles in this book are particularly timely now as linguistics and applied linguistics increasingly embrace heterogeneity and interdisciplinarity in their practices and in their institutions.

The title of the conference, Knowledge and Discourse, indicates that we were concerned to problematise the relationship between beliefs and practices, whether in our academic disciplines or in broader social and political contexts. Many participants questioned traditional views of disciplinary knowledge and the role of discourse in the pursuit, construction and compartmentalisation of knowledge. We use the term 'discourse' here to look beyond the communication of intentional meaning to all those practices that shape our social behaviours and beliefs, whereby discourse is more than just shared texts and shared utterances, as traditional linguistics proposes. Participants came from different places and with different histories of their disciplines. The convergence of their different space–time perspectives on knowledge points to a notion of discourse as an underlying network of paths and nodes which make up a relational world of significances bound by space and time. This Foucauldian notion of discourse, which has its own rules governing discursive activities and objects within a particular background of practices, is not reducible to language. '[T]he ordering of objects' (Foucault 1972: 49) suggests that knowledge is constituted through discourse, is understood through a particular configuration of time and space, and may be realised as more than just language.

Knowledge and discourse, then, are not separate entities, but relational twin poles which brought the participants to the conference, drawn together by a concern with releasing discourse from the margins and reflecting their shared interest in the discoursal foundations of knowledge. The writers of the papers in this collection are investigating the interconnectedness of the structures of knowledge and discourse in ways which we suggest are ecological. The ecological perspective to language can be described as the interplay of multi-dimensional networks extending along both temporal and spatial directions which underlie social action. In response to charges that such ecological systems are too complex for adequate analysis, the array of methods used by the authors show that much is missed if a single method of enquiry is used. In employing more than one method of enquiry — an ecology of methods — they help to establish the integrity of discourse in the wider world of human conduct, and in the analysis of social interaction in particular. They are concerned with contingency, change and connectivity within both their embodied selves as active language users and their disciplinary spaces. These three pillars of language ecology — connectivity, contingency and change — are themes that echo throughout the papers in this collection.

The three pillars are not bridges to enable us to gain access to transcendental or superordinate entities of the kind that structuralism offers with structure, or that functionalism offers with system. They are paths in networks of multiple local worlds of significances, in which knowledge is a particular configuration of time in a particular time–space (or chronotope in Bakhtin's (1981) terms) and discourse is the force field of tactics and strategies which realise this knowledge. Time, via chronotope, makes the connections between discourse and language. As Bakhtin (1981: 251) states, 'language . . . is fundamentally chronotopic'; it is historic (it changes over time), it is contingent on particular configurations of people and things in the world, and it connects people and things in a local world of significance. Time then becomes a fundamental element in a theory of language, and an ecology of language is the study of intermeshing temporal networks.

The study of ecology of language, as a theoretical perspective, is still very much in its infancy. The papers in this collection differ in their topics, methodologies and theoretical backgrounds, yet they all have a common concern with language in real time and in real space. They examine how language makes connections between subjective experiences as people move through events and construct meaning and action, knowledge and discourse, together in real time. In linguistic terms the writers are expressing a dilemma that de Saussure initiated, a dilemma that he realised as dichotomies — message and code, *parole* and *langue*.

1 Historical background

Many linguists and applied linguists are coming to recognise that the dilemma created by Saussure's dichotomy of *langue* and *parole* is historical.
Bronislaw Malinowski addressed this dilemma in 1937 as both an epistemological and a methodological problem. Stating the problem epistemologically,
he asked:

> Can we treat language as an independent subject of study? Is there a
> legitimate science of words alone, of phonetics, grammar, and lexico-
> graphy? Or must all study of speaking lead to sociological investigation, to
> the treatment of linguistics as a branch of the general science of culture?
> (Malinowski 1937: 172)

Malinowski's anthropological linguistics took the route of sociological investigation, establishing in the British tradition of linguistics the 'context of
situation' (Malinowski 1923: 306), which eschewed completely Saussure's
mental mapping. According to Malinowski, 'the main function of language is
not to express thought, not to duplicate mental processes, but rather to play
an active pragmatic part in human behaviour' (Malinowski 1965 [1935]: 7).
Malinowski's context of situation is heterogeneous, a 'context of cultural
reality', by which he meant 'the material equipment, the activities, interests,
moral and aesthetic values with which the words are correlated' (Malinowski
1965 [1935]: 22). His anthropological linguistics is both temporal and spatial
because it 'will force us to define meanings in terms of experience and
situation' (Malinowski 1965 [1935]: 9). Malinowski's sociological route is
similar to the one taken by Boas and Sapir in the USA, with their emphasis
on analysing language to investigate the mental habits and social life of a
people (Schegloff, Ochs and Thompson 1996: 4). And it is similar to the
Prague School's functionalism, in which language is at the same time embedded in, and an instrument of, human activity (Vachek 1964: 33). All three
linguistic traditions acknowledge the dialectic of time and space in language,
through the temporal horizon of past, present and future of experience and
the spatial material environment.

 This historical perspective enables us to see how all three traditions have
converged along a single route. While some linguists of the Boasian school
took the route of the Sapir–Whorf Hypothesis of linguistic relativism (e.g.
Hoijer 1951; Goodenough 1956), most travelled along the route of language
as an independent subject of study, as they became concerned with Universal
Grammar and with syntactic structures rather than semantic categories, concerned with *langue* rather than *parole*. It would seem that Saussure's objective
for linguistics to become a science was being realised. It is ironic to note that

had relativist linguists followed Whorf to his ultimate end, they too would have ended up at the same place as the linguists of the Universal Grammar school because Whorf's objective was a universal linguistics. '[H]e stressed linguistic relativity so that it might be transcended' and take linguistics to 'a common picture of the world' (Hymes 1964: 119).

The British linguistic tradition followed the route to a universal grammar more gradually. J. R. Firth, Malinowski's student, turned his context of situation into a series of concentric rings in which language events are 'at a different level from grammatical categories' (Firth 1957 [1950]: 182), bringing it closer to the notion of language as a bounded, isolated entity. Firth's direction suggests that, once linguists have isolated the alternatives of objects of social investigation and linguistic categories, they can treat language as an independent object of scientific study, 'rather like the dispersion of mixed wave-lengths into a spectrum' (Firth 1957 [1950]: 183).

M. A. K. Halliday, addressing the problem of 'How much do linguists include in their analyses of discourse?', privileged the homogeneity of text over Malinowski's heterogeneity of context by taking out 'the bits and pieces of the material environment such as might appear if we had an audio and video recording of a speech event with all the sights and sounds surrounding the utterances' (Halliday 1978: 29). The context of situation then becomes a device for predicting 'the linguistic features that are likely to be associated with it' (Halliday 1978: 33). In his functional approach discourse is 'what people say and write and listen to and read' and '[d]iscourse analysis has to be founded on a study of the system of the language' (Halliday 1994: xxii).

This move from the dialectic of time and space of the context of situation to the primacy of presence as a mapping of discrete linguistic items on forms of participation, at a single point in time and in a particular place, is one that was also followed by functionalists of the Prague School (Jakobson 1971; Firbas 1992). From the scientism of Firth's linguistic code as a spectrum and Firbas's direct mapping of linguistic items onto functions, it is only a short step to an atemporal *langue* in which 'succession in time does not exist' (Saussure 1974 [1915]: 81). *Langue* rather than *parole* becomes the appropriate object of study because the stability of the language system is more solid, and therefore more amenable to analysis, than the transitoriness of discourse.

There is perhaps an irony in that, when creating a 'scientific', atemporal linguistics, linguists tacitly acknowledged the priority of time by drawing their inspiration from the scientific and technological innovations of their day. These innovations are temporal because they represent both succession and duration, and are representatives of a Western temporality. But linguistics turned the actuality of their temporality into virtual temporality and placed itself outwith time. Firth's language spectrum, Halliday's network of systemic linguistics and the Prague School's mapping all converge with Saussure's telephone and electric circuit models of language (Saussure 1974

[1915]: 11–12) to turn the temporal existence of technological innovations as succession and duration into atemporal *langue* by giving priority to system over event through the stability of the code and the presence of function. Here the British and American routes approach each other, not merging but becoming parallel, as American linguists coming from the Boasian tradition who are concerned with Universal Grammar (for example Hockett) deny the succession of time and give priority to syntactic structures. Chomsky's tree diagrams emphasise the supremacy of space over time in linguistics by digging deeper and deeper into the structure of language, a spatial practice that reinforces the elimination of time by using invented examples that make no connection with experience and event.

Having outlined the epistemological consequences of the dilemma that Malinowski stated, we can now turn to the methodological implications of the dilemma in linguistics, which Malinowski expressed as:

> The dilemma of contemporary linguistics has important implications. It really means the decision as to whether the science of language will become primarily an empirical study, carried out on living human beings within the context of their practical activities, or whether it will remain largely confined to deductive arguments, consisting of speculation based on written or printed evidence alone.   (Malinowski 1937: 172)

Malinowski had no answer to the methodological implications of the *langue–parole* dilemma because he did not develop 'a conceptual framework for analyzing different functions of speech or different types of relations between utterances and social acts' (Duranti 1997: 218). But we are now starting to see answers to his methodological dilemma as linguists and applied linguists apply more than one different method of enquiry in their analyses. One example is the way in which Ochs's ethnography, Schegloff's conversation analysis and Thompson's functional grammar come together in a single volume to provide insights on spoken language (Ochs, Schegloff and Thompson 1996). Grammars of spoken language from interactions in real time are changing both the kinds of questions linguists ask and their understanding of what grammar actually is (for example McCarthy 1999). Prior's (1998) sociohistoric approach challenges the linear temporal representation of the empirical methodology and argues for a heterogeneity of methodologies in applied linguistics.

These are three instances of how linguistics and applied linguistics are beginning to be informed by a convergence of methods of enquiry. The authors in this collection provide contributions to the analysis of discourse with a variety of methods of enquiry, including ethnography in Thailand, China, Australia and Canada, actor–network theory in Papua New Guinea, social constructionism in Finland and frame analysis in Australia. We do not claim to provide either a complete or systematic set of possible methods of enquiry in this book, but we do claim to provide a rich analysis of discourse and a sense of the direction in which linguistics and applied linguistics are heading.

2   Towards an ecology of language

The different combinations of methods of enquiry of the authors in this collection reveal the kinds of questioning that evolve when linguists connect presence and absence by retracing a historical route back to the past of linguistics and applied linguistics, locating it in the present to proceed to the future. In so doing they re-unite knowledge and discourse, message and code, in their various ways. They illustrate how discourse discloses knowledge in a dialectic of contested and evolving institutions, contingent on ideology, tradition, convention, consensus and colonialism. We want to show in this book how discourse establishes, dismantles, denies, excludes. But that is only part of the story. The dichotomy is not just about *langue* and *parole*. If it were, we would be concerned only with the epistemological problem of how to combine the multidisciplinarity of *parole* with the mono-discipline of *langue*. The fact that unity of *langue* and *parole* has proven to be so difficult to achieve is an indication that it is more than an epistemological problem.

Knowledge and discourse are mirror images of the same entity — message. Message correlates with *parole* in that both are moments in a succession of events and thus constitute the diachronic dimension of time. Message's dialectic opposite is code, which correlates with *langue* in that they both exist in time and thus constitute the synchronic dimension of time. Like Einstein's mirror, knowledge and discourse both have to be in the same space and time. Knowledge, then, is not the mirror of reality, but the realisation of socially-established discoursal conceptions of temporality. Time is the key to understanding the struggle between *parole* and *langue*, between message and code, and ultimately between the modernist project and its post-modern critics.

The papers in this book offer an initial exploration into the ontological foundations of knowledge and discourse and the beliefs driving their definitions and their active pursuits. A number of them question the dominant Western paradigm that privileges ideas over their construction, that pursues the rational, modernist project of the mastery of nature. Zygmunt Bauman (1992) described modernism as Western man's mission, his thrust for power, founded on a desperate search for structure. From him we get a picture of the zeal and ethos of the mediaeval Catholic Church transferred to the cumulative search for and protection of another secular set of truths, but this time based on empiricism. Zygmunt Bauman sees post-modernism as seeking to define and expose the 'legislative' and controlling power of modernism as it established its own orderly hierarchical universe, its pronouncements 'adorned with the badges of reason, uncontested and uncontestable'. The resulting 'obsessively legislating, defining, structuring, segregating, classifying, recording and universalising state reflected the splendour of universal and absolute standards of truth' (Bauman 1992: xiv).

Linguistics takes up the modernist project of universal and absolute standards of truth through its concern with syntactic, morphological and phonological contrasts, a project which, according to Deleuze and Guattari, confirms *parole*'s marginal existence in linguistics.

> As long as linguistics confines itself to contrasts, whether syntactical, morphological, or phonological, it ties the statement to a signifier and enunciation to a subject and accordingly botches the assemblage; it consigns circumstances to the exterior, closes language in on itself, and makes pragmatics a residue.   (Deleuze and Guattari 1987 [1980]: 82)

Deleuze and Guattari's description of modern linguistics is a cry of concern over the Chomskyan imperative of digging ever deeper and deeper into the structure of language. Linguists have erected an idealised structure, throwing out 'all knowledge of everything that produced it and ignoring diachrony' [time] (Saussure 1974 [1915]: 81), a structural void where meaning is that which pertains between items in an autonomous code, rather than the totality of significances of discourse in a material world. Modern linguistics has created a vacuum — a vacuum which Deleuze and Guattari, among others, are eager to fill by calling for a return to the essentiality of language, and to the dialectic of presence and absence that makes up the systematic ambiguity of language. That is, 'we use a word so as to allow the context to determine what it is we mean' (Heim 1999: 35). Linguistics has to take systematic ambiguity into account because it allows for a diversity of perspectives, connections through time and space, contingency and change.

The authors of the papers in this book echo Deleuze and Guattari's call to fill the vacuum created by modern linguistics as their voices express the different ways in which either personally or as observers they have experienced Otherness. The papers have been arranged in this book to help the reader make the shift from exclusive to inclusive notions of language. Alastair Pennycook sets the scene by offering a critique of the modern linguistic project in the prologue. We then offer a tour through various personal, social, academic and professional worlds so that readers may see how discourse constitutes these worlds.

We suggested earlier that the themes of connectivity, contingency and change pervade the three sections in this book. The first section presents textual autobiographies and biographies to show how the subjects have not accepted the socio-rhetorical and discoursal restrictions imposed by society and have changed their careers (Ram and Smith), their discipline (Schneider and Wang) and their views of their identity (Luke). The second section has a strong theme of connectivity, realised through the notion of networks, both dominant and overlapping, temporal and spatial. 'Guan' in China (Gu and Zhu) is a dominant and spatial network. European colonialism (Barron; Bolton and Hutton) is a dominant and temporal network, and globalisation is dominant, spatial and temporal (Storer). These networks spread capillary-like through societies, with language as the contingent indicator, charting the progress of events and objects through the networks. The third section on academic and professional practices suggests familiar territory to the applied linguist. Here the emphasis is on contingency, as the papers chart how language constitutes conceptual frameworks in disciplines and professions as varied as the law, accountancy, psychology, education and applied linguistics itself. An important theme running throughout the papers in this book is that of the technologisation of the world and how people in both 'developing' and 'developed' countries respond to it (Storer, Barron, Hui, Luukka, Goldstein), sometimes expressed as a struggle against rationalisation (Chng, Malcolm, Scollon), sometimes expressed as a struggle to maintain one's identity in a male-dominated Western world (Smith, Luke), or how to juggle the requirements of academia while maintaining a personal history (Plum and Candlin). The interplay of different voices in the three sections of the book connects language to contingency and change. This triple conjunction of contingency, connection and change forms the project of an ecological linguistics.

This collection aims to open up a new horizon for linguistics and applied linguistics in which language is no longer a world on its own, or seen as a self-sufficient system. We are concerned to portray language, in Heidegger's terms, as the expression of discourse, and 'discourse must also essentially have a specifically *worldly* mode of being' (Heidegger 1996 [1953]: 161/151; emphasis in original). In this view, language is not self-sufficient because it has an ontological foundation — discourse (Heidegger 1996 [1953]: 160/ 150). This totality of language and discourse is always already in-the-world, 'like something at hand' (Heidegger 1996 [1953]: 161/151). Language in-the-world is always 'our' language, never 'my' language, because it is an activity in which 'we' are always involved, always inclusive. This view leads us to a holistic perspective whereby human life cannot be conceived without language (Taylor 1992: 248). This is a constitutive view of language-with-discourse which dissolves dichotomies of *langue* and *parole*, code and message, knowledge and discourse. At the same time it dismantles mechanistic, objective analyses of language and makes neutral, atemporal language a thing of the past.

The implications of this perspective are that discourse is already contextually situated, already partial, already selective and already contestable. Here we can make the direct link between discourse and knowledge, a link that makes a difference to our understanding of knowledge, whether it be knowledge of AIDS constructed in Thailand (Storer), knowledge of applied linguistics in Finland (Luukka), knowledge of economics in Hong Kong (Hui), knowledge of the law in Singapore (Chng), or knowledge of psychology in Australia (Plum and Candlin).

This leads us to a specific understanding of knowledge and discourse in which discourse is the fundamental way in which patterns of meaning are manifested to us (Polt 1999: 74). Many of the papers in this book acknowledge the priority of discourse over knowledge. We see a recognition of the Wittgensteinian notion of language as forms of life and an acknowledgement that social life is constituted by more than language (Adam 1995: 163). This struggle between modernist views of language that separate it off and post-modern ecological views of language that acknowledge the heterogeneity of entities constitutes the dialectic of this book and is what makes it a novel contribution to applied linguistics in relation to linguistics.

The papers in this book suggest far-reaching changes to taken-for-granted linguistic assumptions. They confront the reader with dynamic frameworks that have pasts, presents and futures, rather than the static structures of grammars and dictionaries that are rooted in the past. The basis of the frameworks is the context, each a particular world of heterogeneous entities, material, human and abstract, all of which are interrelated. The framework requires us to shift our concern from a static space to a dynamic space–time or *chronotope* (Bakhtin 1981). Neither is the authors' concern any longer exclusively with the temporal short-term, as represented by the here and now of standard languages and learners. Instead, we should shift our attention to dynamic temporal networks that historically situate the interlocutors, a concern shared by Prior with his sociohistoric project. This offers a theory of language as history rather than system (see Prior 1998: 247). The contexts in the papers invite the reader to venture beyond the individual language and individual learner/speaker to a concern with the histories of people, forms of life, things — a move that requires a shift from the exclusive to the inclusive.

3 Language and ecology

Ecology is one of those concepts that has been borrowed by a wide variety of disciplines and as a result changes its meaning as it crosses disciplinary boundaries. In linguistics, ecology has been defined as 'structured diversity, i.e. diversity defined not so much in terms of numbers, but in terms of the quality of meaningful interrelationships. A plural society with many species of different languages that do not interact is not a proper language ecology' (Mühlhäusler 1996: 206). However, Mühlhäusler's language ecology is a 'shallow' one, 'grounded ultimately on human purposes' (Taylor 1992: 267).

We are not talking of a world 'out there' in which relationships take place, one which is indifferent to us, but a world of our involvements. Everything around us becomes a potential bearer of meaning for us. Language ecology is more than the two-dimensional network of interacting languages — it acknowledges an infinite world of possibilities. The network thus has to be multi-dimensional; it has to have depth, a seamless web of relations extending in all directions. What we were looking for in our conference was a 'deep' ecology, a constitutive perspective on language that would turn 'toward the creative dimension of expression in which, to speak paradoxically, it makes possible its own content' (Taylor 1992: 252). This is normally screened out in analyses of discourse. The papers in this book illustrate this constitutive perspective.

The linguistic turn which Alastair Pennycook discusses in the first paper in this book constructs a very different world. This suggests an ecological world in which 'every language is a world-view and is, therefore, not a mere *tool* for expressing preexisting significations but instead *constitutes* them' (Dastur 1998 [1990]: 71; emphases in original). In this world 'the epistemological project is to show that thinking is possible only in language and, consequently, that every object that can be given to us in experience is capable of existing for us only through language' (Kögler 1996 [1992]: 63). This is the first person perspective. We know the subject of the narrative because the subject, 'I', is allowed to speak. There is no Us and Them, only We, the unique subjects at the instance of discourse (Benveniste 1971 [1966]: 218).

Ecology provides us with a metaphor of creativity and evolution in the making of meaning. This has echoes with Bakhtin's notion of texts and works as the focus of an author's interpretation, but we can extend his constructionist perspective to the interpretation of the world around us — the worlds being written about in this collection of papers. Here we have a picture of a world being continually renewed through our own creative construction. Bakhtin proposes a dynamic, reciprocal dialogic process whereby our constructions, given expression in our discourses, enter and enrich the world, while the world enters the 'work' as part of the process of its creation and its subsequent life (1981: 254). Gadamer, in his hermeneutic model, similarly argued that our relationship to a historic tradition is not a dissociated but a creative one. Language is more than a system of symbols for labelling the external world; it becomes an expression of the human mode of 'being in the world', where in effect, 'being is manifest in language' (Gadamer 1997: 362).

Language ecology enables us to understand the discourse of difference where each voice is respected and allowed to speak for himself/herself. In this difference we learn from each other and come to know each other. This raises the question, 'how do we understand one another in a language ecology if everything and everybody is different?' Understanding in this perspective consists not in understanding what people say, but in grasping what it is possible for others to be, that is, understanding the temporality of others. A persistent and systematic tendency of linguistics has been to place the referents in a time other than the present of the producer of the discourse. Sociolinguistics, for example, has been criticised for its unequivocal acceptance of Western models to explain language use, which 'rests on the unquestioned adoption of a specific conception of society by what are either naïve or politically motivated practitioners' (Williams 1992: 240). The specific conception is that of the Western temporality, which divides time into equal quanta (Crosby 1997). Once it has been made divisible and measurable, time becomes a 'neutral' technology with a definite direction — it 'flows equably without relation to anything external' (Newton 1989 [1687]: 20). Within applied linguistics, the few programmes in English language teaching which deliberately set out to include culture either promote the culture of the target language, that is, British or American culture (see for instance Valdes 1986; Jacob 1987), or contrast cultures as unchanging and homogeneous monoliths (for example Hinkel 1999). Dominant groups consign the students' cultures to an ethnographic present where time is lost and open resistance is futile (see Canagarajah 1999). The students are directed to a future that is dominated by a Western temporality, a chronocentrism that is notable for the complete neglect of the students' individual and cultural pasts. The connection between the students' past and present, absence and presence, is severed, so students are condemned to wander in a linguistic no-man's land.

In contrast to sociolinguistics, linguistic anthropology's project has been to connect 'people to their past, present and future, language *becomes* their past, present, and future', and to accept that 'linguistic communication is part of the reality it is supposed to represent, interpret, and evoke' (Duranti 1997: 337; emphasis in original). In applied linguistics, Barron's (1991) course for engineering students in Papua New Guinea resonated with each of the students' cultures and temporalities by asking them to make and present examples of artefacts from their villages. This project linked temporal absence and temporal presence by recalling past technological activities and bringing them into the students' present. Temporality is a necessary condition of mutual understanding between actors because it opens up the boundaries of linguistics by not relegating the problem of time to philosophy or psychology, and permits creativity and dynamism between languages and with other disciplines.

An ecological approach to language, then, offers us challenging alternatives to static, backward-facing approaches to language description, and to forward-looking prescriptive approaches to language in which the past directs the future. It is on the one hand dynamic, concerned with exploring how language manipulates time (Barron 1999; Higginbotham 1999), and with revealing how the past, present and future 'question and illuminate one another'

(Mulhall 1996: 177). It is also creative, rejecting a political or veridical stand-point by which to interpret meanings, and opting for multi-dimensional frameworks that situate the linguist in networks within which meanings are constituted and negotiated. An ecology of language asks us to recognise that the task of understanding the roles of language, discourse and knowledge in our lives requires a radical revision of the linguistic discipline, both of the premises that underpin much of linguistic study, and the ramifications of taking a more holistic and network-oriented view of the study of language. We hope that readers will find, in the papers in this book, illustrations of an ecological approach to applied linguistics.

1

Prologue: Language and linguistics/ Discourse and disciplinarity
Alastair Pennycook

Introduction: caught in the crossfire

In his popular book *The Language Instinct*, Steven Pinker (1994) argues against a view that language might play too large a role in how we think or behave. Rather than viewing language as a system of meanings that influence, construct or determine the way we think, he argues that language, while interesting as a structured, biologically-based system, is ultimately only a medium into which we translate the all-important 'language of thought ... mentalese' (1994: 81). Acknowledging a certain smugness derived from his scientific knowledge of how language really works, however, he is prepared to forgive people for considering language to be more important than it really is: 'People can be forgiven for overrating language' (1994: 67). By contrast, Chris Weedon — someone whom I presume Pinker is going to have to forgive for her misguided over-evaluation of the importance of language — argues in her slightly less popular book, *Feminist Practice and Poststructuralist Theory*, that 'the common factor in the analysis of social organization, social meanings, power and individual consciousness is *language*. Language is the place where actual and possible forms of social organization and their likely social and political consequences are defined and contested. Yet it is also the place where our sense of ourselves, our subjectivity, is *constructed*' (1987: 21).

This paper sets out to explore some of the implications of this divide between the so-called linguistic turn in the social sciences — a shift that allows for statements such as Weedon's, and which may be seen generally as poststructuralist — and the concept of language in the so-called linguistic sciences — which allows for such warnings as Pinker's. Of course, it might be argued that these are simply looking at different aspects of language: linguistics is concerned with the analysis of language as a system, while poststructuralism, coming from a tradition of literary criticism, has to do with interpretation, and therefore takes representations in language as primary.

And yet, I want to suggest that there is far more going on here than simply two different approaches to language, in part because of the very large claims each makes about the importance of its own position. This discussion, then, concerns issues to do with language, discourse, science, power, and disciplinary knowledge, issues that go to the heart of the concerns of this book.

There are also for me more immediate concerns to do with my work as an applied linguist, since we now seem to find ourselves sandwiched between these two positions on language. To our right stands the threatening presence of linguistics. As applied linguists we are continually encouraged to see ourselves as simply applying the 'scientific knowledge of language' to particular contexts. As our own (University of Melbourne) Linguistics and Applied Linguistics Department handbook recently put it, 'Linguistics is the scientific study of language in all its aspects [sic!]. Applied linguistics is the application of linguistic knowledge to real-world issues having to do with language . . .' In this role we are but the appliers of scientific knowledge about language to 'real world' contexts. Looming up on the left, however, is the vibrant domain of poststructuralist work, with questions of language and representation pervading everything. Seductive though such work may be, it also presents us with a dilemma, for surely in this view everyone is an applied linguist, everyone is dealing with language in real-world contexts.

There are, therefore, a number of very serious issues here. As an applied linguist concerned with understanding the political contexts of language education, I am confronted on the one side by a seductive but all-embracing version of poststructuralism that threatens to engulf applied linguistics, and on the other side by an intimidating body of 'scientific knowledge' that I am supposed to be able to apply. These issues here, then, are far more than abstract speculations about language, discourse and knowledge: they have major implications for how we think about language, literacy or language teaching. Are these simply different paradigms, or can they perhaps learn from each other? In the rest of this paper I shall explore, first, the construction of linguistics as a science of language; second, the evolution and implications of poststructuralist thinking; and, third, possible ways forward via 'postlinguistics'.

Linguistics and language: full of sound and science, signifying nothing

We may, fairly uncontroversially, turn to Saussure to see the origins of the particular view of language that holds sway in modern linguistics.[1] Of course, there have been lots of 'advances,' even the so-called Chomskyan revolution in linguistics, but looked at from the outside it generally appears more consistent than disjunctive. The important thing to understand here is the very particular move made by Saussure in order to establish linguistics as a discipline. 'In the whole history of science,' according to the philosopher Ernst Cassirer, 'there is perhaps no more fascinating chapter than the rise of the new science of linguistics. In its importance it may very well be compared to the new science of Galileo which in the seventeenth century changed our whole concept of the physical world' (cited in Culler 1976: 114).

The intellectual climate of the nineteenth century made claims to scientific knowledge almost obligatory, and indeed, as Crowley (1996) points out, Saussure's move to define linguistics as a science was made in an attempt to overcome the claims already being made to scientific status by historical–comparative linguistics. With Saussure came a dramatic narrowing of the scope. Saussure's definition of language 'assumes that we disregard everything which does not belong to its structure as a system; in short everything that is designated by the term "external linguistics"' (1983: 21). Among these exclusions were the relations between the history of a language and the parallel history of a cultural or national group; relations between languages and political history (which include 'colonization', the internal politics of a country, and the development of specialised vocabularies within modern nations); relationships between languages and social institutions such as church, school, etc., and the relationship between these and the development of a literary language; and finally relationships between language and geographical spread and variation (Saussure 1983: 20–21). This is a pretty interesting list of things to cast aside.[2]

Saussure also made a number of other crucial moves. As can already be seen, the development of structuralist linguistics involved a major inward turn, a move to define language and linguistics in a very particular way. One of the most significant aspects of this was to develop a view of meaning that suggested that meaning was not to be sought in any relationship between language and the world but rather was a product of the relationships between signs within the system of language. This was a crucial and radical step. Instead of the earlier 'God-given' views of meaning (still prevalent in Christian, Muslim, Hindu and other fundamentalisms), or the 'humanist' version of meaning brought about by the so-called Enlightenment (in which 'man' became the guarantor of meaning), this new view was what Taylor (1990) calls an 'institutional' view of meaning, whereby language comes to reside in a fixed, institutionalised system.

According to Crowley (1990), the significance of Saussure's move to show that words do not stand for objects or ideas, that they were part of a system of signs whose meaning was constructed by their relationship to each other, was that he was then able to argue that rather than words being a pale reflection of reality, a second cousin to the real world, they were in fact part of reality, that is, language was an objective fact and thus could be studied according to the same scientific principles as other objective domains of the real world: 'Once liberated from its status as but a pale shadow of the world of things into its proper place standing alongside those things, then language could join those other items of reality in the privileged status of scientific object' (Crowley 1996: 18). Thus, as Taylor (1990) suggests, access to an understanding of the meaning of words was only to be had through the institutional construction of language as described by experts. Meanings in this view are facts that can be understood by the linguist but are not accessible to the rest of us; they cannot even be influenced by the rest of us.

Thus, by defining the structuralist notion of the sign as part of the linguistic system itself, as part of *langue*, Saussure and subsequent linguists have been able to argue that the only scientific (the only true) way to understand language is through versions of the 'scientific study of language' as defined from within the discipline of linguistics. Indeed, the *langue / parole* distinction of linguistics has come to suggest not only a division between system and use but also between on the one hand methods of analysis and objects of study (*langue*/linguistics) and, on the other, all the trivial, non-scientific interests in language (*parole*/everyone else). With a few quick moves, therefore, Saussure managed to construct a linguistics that relied on a massive set of exclusions. It was able to claim scientific status and thereby to deny that other approaches to language had anything useful to say. As Harris (1981) explains, 'The version of the language myth propounded by modern linguistics has it that there is only one descriptive standpoint which allows us to proceed to a systematic analysis of linguistic phenomena' (1981: 35). He goes on to explain that 'A study of the development of modern linguistics makes it clear that the entrenchment of the language myth as a basic theoretical assumption arose from the need to establish for linguistic studies respectable academic status as a "science"' (1981: 37). It is indeed interesting to note that, as Derrida (1974) points out, of all the human sciences, 'linguistics is the one science whose scientificity is given as an example with a zealous and insistent unanimity' (1974: 28).

With the coming of the so-called Chomskyan revolution, the scientific status of linguistics was even further emphasised. 'Academic prestige is dependent on various factors, but one of them is *scientific status*: a prestigious discipline will tend to possess qualities associated with science (however erroneously) such as theoretical and methodological rigour, "objectivity", abstraction and so on. One achievement of the so-called Chomskyan revolution has been to appropriate this sort of status for linguistics more successfully than previous or alternative paradigms' (Cameron 1990: 83–4). Whereas, as I suggested above, the construction of the sign-as-fact enabled Saussurean linguistics to constitute its study of language as a study of linguistic facts, the Chomskyan move to construct language as a biological fact in the brain allowed for even greater claims to scientificity, moving through the mechanistic and computer modelling world of cognitive science into biological reality. Robinson (1975) suggests that this Chomskyan move will in time be recognised as 'only another episode in the history of the long and desperate effort to reduce thought about language to an exact science' (1975: 124).

There are several upshots of this claim to scientific status. First, it has given this particular approach to language immense power relative to others. This has been even further increased by the influence of structuralist linguistics on other areas in the social sciences. For a time linguistics was able to look at itself as some sort of central founding discipline in the social sciences, the scientific basis of knowledge about language from which all other possibilities flowed. This has clearly had a rather sad, inhibiting effect on the possibility for change in linguistics. Second, it has meant that linguistics has as another of its founding dogmas the belief that it is engaged in a descriptive rather than a prescriptive enterprise. As Pinker (1994) explains, 'The rules people learn . . . in school are called *prescriptive* rules, prescribing how one "ought" to talk. Scientists studying language propose *descriptive* rules, describing how people *do* talk' (1994: 371). Such claims to being engaged in objective description with no normative effects are clearly naïve.

As Taylor (1990) argues, linguistics is a fundamentally normative discipline in that while purporting to describe facts about language, it is laying out normative principles: 'If purportedly descriptive discourse on language is best reconceived as a (covertly authoritarian mode of) normative discourse, then the assertion of the political irrelevance and ideological neutrality of linguistic science can no longer be maintained. Descriptive linguistics is just another way of doing normative linguistics, and an ideologically deceptive one at that' (Taylor 1990: 25). Similarly, Parakrama (1995) points out that so-called descriptive work always focuses on certain forms of language at the expense of others. 'This unequal emphasis,' he goes on, 'is not so much the fault of individual descriptivists as a problematic of description itself, which can never be a neutral activity. In other words, description is always a weak form of prescription' (1995: 3). As Harris (1981) puts it, 'the linguistics introduced by Saussure placed theoretical constraints upon the freedom of the individual speaker no less rigid than the authoritarian recommendations of the old-fashioned grammarian–pedagogue. But instead of the rules being imposed by educational pedants, they were envisaged as being imposed from within the language itself' (1981: 46).

The third effect of linguistics creating itself as a science has been a constant tendency to seek so-called universal aspects of language. This is of course a fundamental aspect of Chomskyan transformational grammar, since the whole project presupposes and simultaneously claims to be searching for aspects of a Universal Grammar. But this is also an aspect of other forms of linguistics; like science, it claims that what it finds are culture-free, universal laws of nature. One of the effects of trying to make this claim is that culture, as the local, the different, the incommensurable, inevitably becomes detached from language: culture is difference, language is similarity. Finally, the linguistic claim to scientific status means it must also be answerable to the question posed by Foucault: 'What types of knowledge do you want to disqualify in the very instant of your demand "Is it a science?"' (1980: 85). Of course, as we have already seen, the lists of types of knowledge that linguistics sought to *exclude* were long. But perhaps even more significant were the types of knowledge it sought to *disqualify*: all those non-scientific, interpretive, exploratory, open-ended questions about language and life.

The disciplinary boundaries, the lists of exclusions, the claims to scientificity made by linguistics, therefore, lead to the dismissal of many other possible interests in language. As Poynton (1993) observes, even an interest in fairly uncontroversial aspects of 'external linguistics' is often 'characterised as not sufficiently linguistic, providing the perfect excuse for "real" linguists not to engage seriously with it. There is a particular arrogance about most linguists concerning what it is necessary to know about language, so that only those who "really know" are regarded as having proper authority' (1993: 4). And meanwhile, the great misfortune for applied linguistics is that in order to attain academic credibility it has desperately sought to be as scientific as linguistics and has celebrated its increasing scientificity.

For applied linguists, questions of language learning, education and literacy came to be seen as centrally cognitive issues to do with the acquisition of a system — how people master the morphemes, syntax and phonology of a language; how a reader decodes words — rather than with how language learning is almost inevitably a process of socialisation into a culture, or how literacy is embedded in cultural politics, in who has access to whose knowledge. Recent acrimonious debates around the hardcore 'scientific' study of second language acquisition (see Block 1996; Firth and Wagner 1997; Gregg *et al.* 1997) have shown how steadfastly the conservative disciplinarians will battle to hold their ground. The problem for many of us who work in areas such as applied linguistics, then, is that in trying to develop more critical, more political analyses of language as it is used, learned, and taught, we find ourselves caught between a linguistic model of language that offers little hope for developing such an analysis and a poststructuralist view that sits at odds with the disciplinary pulls of our work.

The model of language developed in linguistics and adopted by applied linguistics offers little prospect for an understanding of the non-autonomy of language. As Bourdieu puts it, 'As soon as one treats language as an autonomous object, accepting the radical separation which Saussure made between internal and external linguistics, between the science of language and the science of the social uses of language, one is condemned to looking within words for the power of words, that is, looking for it where it is not to be found' (1991: 107). For a more critical approach to language, we are confronted by two main options: a plunge into poststructuralism with the possible dangers that we then just disappear amid a sea of poststructuralists;

or some sort of marriage between linguistics, politics and poststructuralism. Before I explore these possibilities, I shall look in greater depth at the linguistic turn of poststructuralism.

The linguistic turn

While the linguistic version of language has been continuing on its way, isolated from outside changes by the solidity of its disciplinary knowledge (and it is interesting to note here the extent to which its disciplinary boundaries appear to have isolated linguistics from the poststructuralist challenge while other disciplines such as anthropology and sociology have been far more permeable), developments in the understanding of language elsewhere have taken a different track. At some levels, there is an interesting irony here in that it was exactly the radical potential of Saussure's linguistic sign that gave the impetus to poststructuralist thought. Nevertheless, a great deal of the work in language that clusters around the term poststructuralism is more directly opposed to the very forms of structuralism that originated from Saussure's linguistics and spread to other domains of the social sciences. As Poynton (1993) explains,

> From the poststructuralist side, linguistics as a profoundly structuralist enterprise has been trenchantly critiqued or marginalised as of no conceivable interest. In significant respects, linguistics as the founding structuralist enterprise has come to signify what post-structuralism is 'post' in its radical critique of the structuralist project. Conversely, linguistics itself . . . has been so seduced by its standing as senior technicist discipline within structuralist conceptions of the humanities and social sciences as to fail to register that the 'linguistic turn' of the last twenty or so years within these areas was not only asking different kinds of questions about language as a social phenomenon but was calling into question the premises of established ways of 'knowing about language' within disciplinary linguistics itself.
> (1993: 3–4)

Parakrama (1995) makes a similar point when he suggests that 'much of the most exciting work in poststructuralism has gone unnoticed' in linguistics because of 'the conceptual framework of linguistics as a *science* which still remains in place even with the sub-disciplines of sociolinguistics and applied linguistics; and the historical complicities between linguistics and colonialism (both "internal" and "external") which still pervade its "neutral" systems of classification and nomenclature' (1995: 3). In many ways, then, the view of language that underlies the linguistic turn is vehemently opposed to the view of language constructed by linguistics. It is important, therefore, to

observe not only some of the common origins here but also the fundamentally different questions being asked.

This more radical view that allows us to think of language as constructing
reality comes via the poststructuralist turn. This line of thinking represents
a coming-together of a wide range of philosophical and political thought
that has sought to challenge both the notion of the autonomous rational
individual and the fixity of institutionalised meanings held in place by linguistics. Drawing on the lessons first of Marx and Freud, which greatly
eroded the centrality of rational thought as guaranteed by the human subject, and later of Nietzsche, Wittgenstein, Heidegger and others, this line of
thought has shown the impossibility of maintaining a belief in rational autonomous action: our lives are governed by the unconscious, the 'irrational',
wills and desires. In this view, our subjectivities do not preexist the cultural
worlds we live in: we are formed, produced, made subjects amid complex
cultural relations. This decentring of the subject and rationality in a sense
leaves something of a void to be filled. If our lives are not governed by
individuals thinking rationally, what then is it that runs our lives? Where
Marx was to answer ideology and the class system, and Freud to answer
the subconscious, the importance of language in the construction of ideology and the subconscious was already starting to emerge. Thus, in a shift
away from a view of enlightened rationality and individual autonomy, the
question turns towards the cultural and linguistic ways in which our worlds
are constructed: rather than our subjectivities guaranteeing meaning, they
are produced by it; we are not so much authors of our worlds as authored by
them.

From this point of view, we cannot access a real knowable world as some
form of objective reality, since language always intervenes in our interpretations. There is no possibility of a 'linguistically naked "given"' (Baynes,
Bohman and McCarthy 1987: 5) that is then open to varied interpretations,
but rather a series of differently constructed understandings. As Rorty (1987)
suggests, a 'bedrock metaphilosophical issue' is now the question: 'Can one
ever appeal to nonlinguistic knowledge in philosophical argument?' (1987: 53).
From Lyotard's postmodern language games, Habermas's 'communicative
action', the philosophical hermeneutics of Ricoeur and Gadamer, and Rorty's
pragmatics, to the deconstruction of the 'logocentric' core of Western meta-
physics by Derrida, or Foucault's politics of language in his genealogies of
power/knowledge (discourse) relationships, language is no longer a transparent medium of knowledge transaction, but rather becomes the central part
of the problematic.

Thus, for example, Foucault's broad genealogies of madness, punishment
and sexuality reveal how tied up with language are our inclusions and exclusions, what counts as knowledge and what is to be deemed as unworthy,
what is to be normal and what abnormal, how the construction of disciplines
has been a process not of the ever greater advance of scientific thinking but

rather of naturalisation and exclusion. As we saw above, Saussure's move to construct linguistics as a discipline was a move coupled with a vast list of exclusions. The scientific study of language was no longer to be about language and historical change, language and colonialism, language and politics, language and society, language and culture. The project of writers such as Foucault has been to examine how particular *epistemes* — particular regimes of truth — have been historically constructed and what, in so doing, they have left out.

If this is the philosophical background to this linguistic turn, this belief that it no longer makes sense to appeal to some reality outside language, there has also been a connected shift in thinking about language itself. From Barthes's (1972) consideration of how in the semiology of myths one sign can become the signified of another sign, or Baudrillard's (1983) postmodern construct of the simulacrum, in which signs refer to nothing but each other, and 'the principle of simulation wins out over the reality principle' (1983: 152), to Derrida's argument that the assumption is untenable that stable and agreed-upon signifieds can hold the system in place, since it implies a 'transcendental signified', we see a pulling apart of the stable system of signs posited by Saussure and adopted by linguistics: 'The plurality of language and the impossibility of fixing meaning once and for all are basic principles of post-structuralism' (Weedon 1987: 85).

In this deconstructive position, both the arbitrariness and the autonomy of Saussure's sign are retained, at least to the extent that language is seen as prior to reality: we live in a world of signs that construct our meanings. Having arrived at this version of unstable meaning, however, we seem to be left nowhere to stand. But here we come to another important move made by the more politicised versions of post-structuralism (as opposed to some versions of deconstruction) as it took on board the radical implications of the linguistic turn in philosophy: it questioned the way in which structuralism had assumed that although meaning was not guaranteed by an external world, it was nevertheless held in place by the consent of a speech community. As Gee (1993) puts it, 'A sign system operates not because it is inherently natural or valid, nor because it is universal, but simply because some group of people have engaged in the past and continue to engage in the present in a particular set of *social practices* that incorporate that sign system. . . . These practices have often evolved in order to claim authority and privilege for one group against other groups. The sign system is a social and historical tool in terms of which groups of people carry out their desires and claim and contest power. It is not a disinterested reflection of a historical and a social reality' (1993: 281–2).

The radical potential of the idea that language structures the world is given full play, but this is now seen not in terms of *a* language and *a* world but rather in terms of worldviews and interests. To Derrida's view of a sliding signifier we need to add a view that brings certain stabilities to this moving sea of signs, but this is no longer a stability guaranteed by a language, but multiple and competing stabilities put in place by discourses. 'Whereas in deconstruction language is an infinite process of play and the deferral of meaning, feminist poststructuralism, concerned as it must be with power, looks to the historically and socially specific discursive production of conflicting and competing meanings' (Weedon 1987: 86). Of course, what is meant by discourse here is very different from the version in more mainstream linguistics. Indeed, as Poynton (1993) suggests, it is a paradigmatic example of the difference. On the one hand, in linguistics, discourse is used to refer to language used beyond the level of the sentence, to real language use. In this version, language is the more significant category, with discourse a manifestation of its contextual use. On the other hand, in poststructuralist use, discourse refers to conventionalised or institutionalised organisations of meaning, akin in some ways to the notion of ideology. Discourses, in this sense, may constitute meaning, and may often be realised in language, but are not produced by language (see Pennycook 1994).

While certainly not all people who have taken the linguistic turn also take a poststructuralist stance (Habermas, for example, still maintains a faith in the enlightenment ideals of rationality and modernity), it is the more politicised end of poststructuralism that has given this view probably its strongest direction. Drawing on the earlier Marxist-based thinking on hegemony (Gramsci), or how we are 'interpellated' by ideology (Althusser), and taking on board Derrida's attack on the logocentricity of Western thought and Foucault's interest in the discursive production of truth, it has become a powerful and political mode of understanding most particularly through its adoption by feminist (Weedon 1987; Butler 1990) and postcolonial scholars (Said 1978, for example). Instead of asking how the structure of language may affect the way we think, the question becomes how language as a social practice is involved in the social construction of our realities.

The important shift here has been away from a view of language as a transparent medium that represents reality, to a view of language as an opaque medium that constructs what can be said and thought. As Shapiro puts it, 'once the transparency metaphor for language is exchanged for the opacity metaphor, analysis becomes linguistically reflective' (1989: 23). Similarly, arguing from a poststructuralist feminist point of view, Weedon (1987) suggests that 'Once language is understood in terms of competing discourses, competing ways of giving meaning to the world, which imply differences in the organization of social power, then language becomes an important site of political struggle' (1987: 24). Here, then, is the crucial insight. By maintaining the radical anti-humanist insight of structuralism, by leaving the arbitrariness but not the autonomy of the sign intact, and by taking up this liquid view of language from a strong political standpoint, it becomes possible to explore how language constructs our worlds, and how language is a crucial site of struggle.

Language, politics and anti-disciplinary knowledges

Where, then, does this leave us? As I said earlier, one of my interests lies in working towards an understanding of language that can link concerns in applied linguistics — language education, discourse analysis, translation, and so forth — to broader social, cultural and political analyses. Broadly speaking, there are two possible directions here: on the one hand, we can attempt to link work in linguistics to a broader politics; on the other hand we can attempt to link poststructuralist work to an applied linguistic agenda. In this section I shall look, first, at what tends to happen to language if the first option is taken up — what I shall call here a materialist approach to language — and, second, at possible ways of melding poststructuralism and linguistic analysis.

A critical materialist approach to language

If, then, we wish to develop a more critical, a more political, version of language than the autonomous version of mainstream linguistics, some of its central notions need to be dislodged. As I suggested earlier, two principal tenets of structuralist linguistics are the arbitrariness of the sign and the autonomy of the sign system. This allows linguistics to claim to have a theory of meaning interior to its own discipline. But this disciplinary autonomy is won at some cost, since it constantly raises the possibility of the fairly radical implication that language in a sense comes before 'reality'. It is not uncommon, in fact, to be quite contradictory about this. Thus Pinker (1994), for example, on the one hand maintains that 'Words have stable meanings, linked to them by arbitrary convention' (1994: 237) — the structuralist argument for the stability of the institutionalised meanings maintained by a speech community — and on the other hand suggests that 'there really are things and kinds of things and actions out there in the world, and our mind is designed to find them and to label them with words' (1994: 154) — the materialist position that meaning is in fact determined by a 'real world' external to language.

Of significance here is the stability of meaning suggested by both views on language, either guaranteed by the social convention of a speech community or by a real world: 'Language becomes a collection of signs whose nature is dependent upon relation to extra-linguistic phenomena. It is the conscious, thinking subject who gives meaning to words and ensures that they are correctly employed' (Williams 1992: 251). It is precisely against such stability that a critical approach to language must take a stance, since this linguistic view of language acknowledges instability and change only as a 'natural' process over time that is part of external linguistics, rather than an inherent aspect of the ongoing struggle over meaning. Second, in taking such a stance, it will be crucial to establish whether one is arguing for a different reality that will make language look different, or a different version of language that will make reality look different. This, I would suggest, is the difference between a critical materialist approach to language and a poststructuralist approach. The former seeks to critique a notion of autonomous language by locating it in material conditions; the latter makes its critique not through material relations but through discursive constructions.

Now there has clearly been a lot of useful work done from the critical materialist perspective, but I want to point here to one of the ways in which it too misses the more radical potential of poststructuralism. One line of attack from the materialist perspective has been to critique the arbitrariness of the sign: according to Kress (1994), 'The relation of signifier to signified, in all human semiotic systems, is always motivated, and is never arbitrary' (1994: 173). Kress suggests that signs 'reflect in their construction that relation of signified to signifier' that expresses the particular interests of the user of the sign. And, 'if the notion of "interest" is extended to the making of signs by the fully acculturated, fully socialised individual, we will have to take into consideration the individual's social and cultural histories, and her or his present social positioning in the whole complex of social structures which make up an individual's social life' (1994: 174). What Kress is arguing here is that we choose to represent certain aspects of the world with certain signifiers, and the ways we make those choices are not arbitrary, but are bound up with social, cultural and political relations. All signs therefore 'code ideological positions in that they realize the social, cultural and therefore political position of their producer' (1994: 174).

This argument has been taken up by Fairclough (for example 1992: 75) who suggests that the signifiers 'terrorist' or 'freedom fighter' are summoned up by a non-arbitrary signified. Now, on the face of it, this might seem a useful way forward; it certainly appears to challenge both arbitrariness and autonomy. Unfortunately, however, in this attempt to meld together 'external' and 'internal' linguistics, this argument falls into the trap of trying to rescue the sign from the clutches of apolitical linguistics by reconnecting it to the referent, since in arguing that the sign is not arbitrary, they appear to confuse signified and referent. Of course, Fairclough is making a useful point here — it is important that a particular referent (say, Che Guevara) may be a freedom fighter to some and a terrorist to others — but this is not a question of the arbitrariness of the sign (the relationship between signifier and signified) but of the social and political non-autonomy of the sign. What I think Fairclough and Kress are really objecting to, therefore, is the autonomy of the sign system, not the arbitrariness of the sign.

The Saussurean argument makes signs arbitrary and autonomous, meaning being held in place by social consensus. Critical linguistics is quite right in questioning this and asking in whose interests signs are used and constructed, but they back away from the more radical step of keeping the sign arbitrary (and thus disavowing the need for a prior reality) while at the same time looking for ways to understand the social organisation of the sign. What I am suggesting, then, is that this form of critical linguistics has unfortunately confused the issues of arbitrariness and autonomy by confusing signified and referent, and in doing so has left us not with a radically politicised version of language, but rather with the more conservative view of a stable, material world of referents that may be represented differently. In trying to make language matter, they have put matter first and language after it. What this approach to language avoids is the more radical step of keeping language first and making matter a product of it. Such a position is poststructuralist.

Towards a postlinguistics

As Fairclough (1992) and others (such as Poynton 1993) have suggested, however, while poststructuralism can provide crucial anti-essentialist insights into the construction of reality, it generally lacks the tools that can engage in close textual analysis. If, then, as I suggested above, critical linguistics may have the linguistic tools but fails to engage with a more radical theory of meaning, we need to ask if poststructuralist thinking can be linked to linguistic tools of textual analysis. This is a challenge that has been taken up by Lee (1996), Poynton (1993, 1996) and Threadgold (1997), who argue for the possibilities of doing feminist poststructuralist work while using linguistic tools, particularly from systemic functionalist linguistics. According to Poynton (1993), there is 'a need for the recuperation within poststructuralist theory of certain kinds of linguistic knowledge, considered as technologies for understanding how the representations constituting discourses are actually constructed and the linguistic means by which subjects come to be constituted in terms of specific power/knowledge relations' (Poynton 1993: 2). Similarly, Lee (1996) argues for the use of linguistic analysis as a way of 'engaging with the density and specificity of texts' (1996: 5). Poynton (1996) and Lee (1996) therefore propose a 'feminist (post)linguistics' (Lee 1996: 5), a term that hopes to blend poststructuralism and linguistics, but also a term which seems to imply the need to go beyond linguistics, even to suggest the need to consign it to an era that we are now 'post'.

Such a position is not without difficulties, however. First, there is the question of whether grammars are simply neutral technologies that can be used for any purpose. Lee, Poynton and Threadgold use systemic functional linguistics for two main reasons: it is the approach to linguistic analysis with which they are most familiar, and it at least has a far greater social orientation than other approaches to grammar. They are also very wary of the problem raised by Luke (1996) that the technical manipulations of systemic functional grammar often lead to the conviction that what they produce is worthwhile in itself. Thus, Lee's (1996) critical reading of this tradition points to its 'fetishization of technicism and a celebration of a masculinist mode of knowledge production' (1996: 98). Nevertheless, the question remains as to whether what Corson (1997) perceives as the 'unwitting conservativism in systemic linguistics that makes it politically reactionary at the applied level' (1997: 175) can simply be erased when one uses the tools without the underlying philosophy.

This leads to the second problem: what to do about linguistics? Harris argues that linguistics 'will not be an academic discipline worth preserving' if it continues to shirk broader political questions (such as freedom of speech) by appealing to naïve notions of linguistic communities conferring equal linguistic rights, and attributing any departure from this state of affairs to 'external, pragmatic factors which are by definition non-linguistic' (Harris 1990: 160). Poynton (1993) has similarly challenged linguistics to deal more adequately with language: '. . . no linguistics that does not and cannot engage with central issues of feminist and poststructuralist theory concerning questions of subject production through discursive positioning can be taken seriously as a theory of language' (1993: 2). The problem remains, however, that linguistics takes itself very seriously indeed as a theory of language.

My argument here, then, is that not only do we need to find linguistic tools for use in poststructuralist analysis, but that we also need to engage in anti-disciplinary action against linguistics in order to make its boundaries more permeable. The problem with linguistics, as I have been suggesting, is that it has constructed its own hermetic cosmos, a world of science about language, a discipline with a whole language of its own and yet no element of self-reflexivity that can help it understand its own construction of itself. As Elinor Ochs (1993: 302) has observed, 'Just about the only social science that has not developed a social constructivist paradigm is linguistics'. Thus, one of the great ironies of linguistics is that its view of language gives it no self-reflexive element with which to consider the linguistic construction of its own disciplinarity. Thus, to paraphrase Brantlinger's (1990) argument with respect to the discipline of literary studies, in order for linguistics 'to matter in the world, the very processes which caused its emergence as a separate, seemingly transcendent . . . category must somehow be reversed or resisted' (1990: 72).

I am convinced that language learning, literacy, language use in professional settings, discourse analysis, translation, and so on, are matters of cultural politics, and I would like both poststructuralist understandings of knowledge, power and discourse, and linguistic tools to deal with them. This, then, is the challenge we are left with: to use poststructuralist thought about language in order to engage in a form of anti-disciplinary action that can shift linguistics from a self-satisfied discipline with rigid rules of inclusion and exclusion and render it more self-reflexive about its own construction of itself; to develop a form of 'postlinguistics' in which linguistic tools are freed up for use in a poststructuralist enterprise that can make poststructuralism the driving theory and linguistics the provider of tools; to use such a postlinguistics in combination with a broader politics, such as the feminist postlinguistics suggested by Lee (1996), Poynton (1993, 1996) and Threadgold (1997); and to work towards similar conjunctions, such as postcolonialism as a form of 'postlinguistic rewriting of colonialism' that could address ways in which language, the construction of 'race', colonial history, and forms of postcolonial resistance operate.[3]

Notes

1. I am of course aware that Linguistics is a far broader and more complex discipline than I am here able to describe. I am trying here to account for central themes and tendencies as I observe them; this is by no means a claim to describe Linguistics in its many different forms.
2. It is nevertheless important here to acknowledge that 1. Saussure did not cast these aside as irrelevant but rather as a necessary move in order to construct a science of language. For Saussure at least these remained issues of interest (see, for example, Crowley 1996); and 2. This limitation on the scope of language has clearly led to advances in our knowledge about how languages as systems work. The problem here is the dominance of this particular take on language as a science of language.
3. I have tried (Pennycook 1998) to formulate something along these lines, though this attempt has lacked the closer linguistic analysis called for in this model of postlinguistics.

Part

I

Reflexive Practices

Introduction to **Part I:**
The **discourse of selfhood**

Who is speaking of what? Who does what?
About whom and about what does one construct a narrative?

(RICOEUR 1992 [1990]: 19)

In a male-dominated, objective world the answers to these questions are all prescribed. Only certain people, usually male, have the right to speak, and they are far too removed from the events to construct a narrative about themselves. Narratives are for the 'Other', inhabiting a different time–space from those concerned with the objective world. The actors in the objective world somehow maintain the fiction that language can blur the distinction between past, present and future. There is only before and after. In an ecological world anybody has the right to speak; anybody can act; and anybody can construct a narrative about themselves. Actors are first-person participants in their own and others' texts and not third-person manipulators of puppet strings in a real world.

In this section we do not have what Schneider and Wang call 'readerly texts', that is texts that 'contain Truths to be obtained, consumed; capitalised upon' (p.75). Instead we have what they call 'writerly texts', 'wherein readers are regularly encouraged in the very reading to become writers, or, readers/writers. Such a text is full of marked "seams," "rough spots," aporias; it makes the reader more rather than less aware of how writing can be a technology for producing closure and smooth, tidy surfaces; the cleaner the better' (p.75).

The authors in this section present writerly texts written from the first-person perspective. This alone challenges the dominant discourse of the objective text. They are all examples of the new genre of auto-ethnography, narrating from the 'I' perspective. All are crossing boundaries, both physical and personal.

The themes running through all the texts are those of displacement, both physical and of identity, of otherness, and of identity. Kalpana Ram moves from India to Australia and finds there that the discourse of otherness does not recognise Indian philosophers. Ram describes how identities ascribed to the non-western Other clung to her as she sought a disciplinary domicile in

Australia: 'My attempts to undertake scholarship on India in Australian academia resulted in a steady series of disciplinary referrals that propelled me from my original discipline of philosophy, to sociology, until I was finally placed in the slot explicitly set aside for the study of the non-westerner: anthropology' (p.35). Kalpana Ram finds her identity in Indian dance, which was 'the trigger for a whole rush of access to forms of reflexivity' (p.40).

Dorothy Smith moves from Yorkshire to Canada, and from student to housewife to academic, discovering early on that the institutionalised discourse of culture, science, politics and religion required women to be silent. She discovered that texts, although written by the ruling class, are in language, which happens only in the present. Therefore, texts are indifferent to who reads them, and indifferent therefore to the reader's gender. This leads to the realisation that 'women's experience [has] an authority equivalent to knowledge vested in the institutional forms that have been created under a system of male dominance' (p.49). Dorothy Smith voices a writerly text that invites you to question issues of power and representation.

Joseph Schneider and Wang Laihua articulate all the aporias of moving to a different genre. Their text may appear to be 'disingenuous,' 'rough,' 'fragmentary,' even 'naive,' but this is inevitable if we are to challenge the dominant scientific paradigm which condemns error and the subjective, and which produces prose that is 'clean and sleek; penetrating and powerful' (p.65). As Joseph Schneider moves back to the USA from China he reflects on himself and his Chinese colleagues. He realises his position in China has changed. Just as Kalpana Ram finds herself manoeuvred into anthropology because she is the 'Other' in Australia, so Joseph Schneider discovers he is in danger of being manoeuvred into the objective world because he is the 'Other' in China.

Allan Luke's family went the other way — from China to the USA. In the narration of his personal odyssey from California to Australia, Allan Luke shows how even being male is not enough. Those who can speak are not just males, but Western males. Chinese males in the USA and Australia are narrated in terms of absence because of their difference; 'we are invisible — not present, without a place or "name" in the discourses and practices of white male sexuality.' These discourses construct Chinese males as either faceless servants or evil villains; timeless, silent, invisible images in Hollywoodised societies where the present image is everything. In order to articulate Chinese identities, Chinese temporalities, Luke shows that 'being "not a white male"' is a strength because it establishes a gap. That gap can be bridged. On the other side of the bridge (*qiao*) Luke finds anti-racist and feminist movements who help him to deconstruct 'archetypal Asian and Anglo–European masculinities' and then reconstruct his own and others' Chinese identity. The gap becomes 'an opportunity for finding other ways of being and expressing ourselves as men and partners, as fathers and sons'. With an identity that explores 'new kinds of masculinities', Chinese males in the USA and Australia enter the present and can have a future. Allan Luke's narrative shows us how 'time becomes human to the extent that it is articulated through a narrative mode, and narrative attains its full meaning when it becomes a condition of temporal existence' (Ricoeur 1984 [1983]: 52). Allan Luke's personal narrative achieves its full meaning when he finds his temporality.

What we have here is a profusion of proper times (Nowotny 1994) struggling to express their voices in discourses which try to deny them this right. What we are seeing is 'the dialectic of self and the other than self' (Ricoeur 1992 [1990]: 3). As long as one remains within the same identity, within the self, the other has nothing to offer. But if that identity is constructed by others, then a change of identity is necessary in order to assert one's selfhood, to be a subject and not subjected, in the Foucauldian sense (1977, 1978). This selfhood implies an otherness that requires a reflexive search for the self. So self and other are in a dialectic intimacy to such an extent that one cannot be thought of without the other.

The papers in this section question the modernist discourse of displacement, otherness and identity and try to break down the dualisms of insider/ outsider, us/them and self/other through the discourse of ecological harmony. In these four auto-ethnographies the authors demonstrate the 'ability to transcend everyday conceptions of selfhood and social life . . . This is a postmodern condition' (Reed-Danahay 1997: 4). The four auto-ethnographies establish the epistemic presuppositions of a postmodern, ecological world; where there are no facts, only interpretations; where individual and cultural differences are respected, and where the ontological presupposition is that of the co-evalness of all the actors and the authenticity of all voices.

2

Stranded between the 'posts': Sensory experience and immigrant female subjectivity
Kalpana Ram

This paper[1] is the by-product of my attempts to write ethnographies that deal with the relationships that obtain between female subjectivity and social location. My ethnographic work on gender has been located in two kinds of socio-historical contexts: the first is the Tamil-speaking region of south India, where my enquiries have, over the last ten years, focused particularly on subaltern labouring castes (Ram 1991, 1998); and the second is the Indian diaspora in Australia (Ram 1995). In this paper, I wish to draw particularly on both research and experience of Indian immigrant life in Australia. My purpose here is to highlight some of the ways in which postcolonial displacement and its corollary, minority status, can produce specific ways of knowing. However, these ways of knowing lack any real acknowledgement or affirmation in the available frameworks of theory, whether poststructuralist or postcolonial. In this paper I use just one kind of experience in order to show how an immigrant woman who seeks to locate her ways of knowing in a wider theoretical framework runs into enormous difficulties in doing so.

The academic division of labour and the production of 'difference'

The first problem in pursuing these intellectual goals arises in the construction of 'difference' in academic social theory. In the flurry of theoretical excitement over the efforts of poststructuralist social theory to de-centre the subject, it is easy for poststructuralism to overlook the realities of colonial subject construction as this is played out by the very disciplinary divisions within academia. For away from the departments of philosophy, in the domain of anthropology and comparative sociology, the view of the *non*-western subject permitted by social theory has never been anything *but* de-centred. Certainly it is hard to think of any lay figure which has served comparative sociology as well as the Indian Homo Hierarchicus, apparently the perfect creature of hierarchy, holism, and collectivity. Anthropological constructions of Indian identity have contributed to a process whereby 'Indianness' becomes locked into immutable categories of social collectivity, a problem I have examined in some detail elsewhere (Ram 1994). Such problems run wider than Indology, of course. In 'East Asian studies' Rey Chow writes (1993) about Sinology as exemplifying an Orientalist melancholia, which, in mourning for the grandeur of a cultural past, is unable to admit the centrality of modernity and colonialism to contemporary Chineseness. In the 'Middle Eastern' field of area studies, Abu Lughod (1990a) has described the suppression of subjectivity in the name of a different array of sociological designations: 'segmentary lineage theory', 'harem theory', and Islam. In response to this suppression, Abu Lughod feels impelled to reassert the value of 'extraordinary individuals' through her ethnographic skills of description (1990a: 116).

The contrast between the western 'individual' and the non-western 'collectivity' is just one of many forms of the opposition between the modern and non-modern which underlie the basis of social theory's constructions of difference. Other distinctions constitutive of social theory include market versus kinship, exchange versus use value, commodity versus gift, rationality versus religion. Of these interlocking antinomies, the polarity that opposes the subject (the Western enquirer) to persons regarded as mere sociological subject-effects is the one I wish to explore, since its effects extend well beyond academia. It is writ large as the very common sense of modernity, and shapes the version of difference which occurs 'spontaneously' in the logic of multiculturalism in Australia. The identities ascribed to the non-westerner travel with and continue to cling to immigrants who come to Australia from those parts of the world which are deemed to be fitting objects for anthropology, but not for sociology, and certainly not for philosophy. My attempts to undertake scholarship on India in Australian academia resulted in a steady series of disciplinary referrals that propelled me from my original discipline of philosophy, to sociology, until I was finally placed in the slot explicitly set aside for the study of the non-westerner: anthropology. In this new environment I found that the currents of critique transforming philosophy had not been allowed to disturb the construction of 'the westerner' that implicitly underpinned the 'comparative method' used in anthropological constructions of 'Indian identity' (Ram 1994).

The self-construction of postcolonial subjects

Such antinomies also have consequences for the self-construction of postcolonial subjects. Quests for individual autonomy become 'Western', 'modern' and at odds with nationalist claims to superiority or at least equality in relation to the West. Such a consequence is particularly disastrous for those who might have more than a purely intellectual stake in pursuing such quests: subordinate groups in the immigrant collectivity, such as women, or groups subordinated by class and caste relations. Within India and other parts of the postcolonial world, a range of subaltern groups can easily have their struggle for greater autonomy redefined as so many instances of a 'western consciousness' and rendered illegitimate. We encounter the same logic in the way in which a celebration of ethnic difference and identity in Australia leaves immigrant women with little way of claiming feminism for themselves without seeming to have betrayed their collective identity and acceded to assimilation. Further ramifications of the opposition between hierarchy as Eastern and egalitarianism as Western are constantly felt in the crippling association between democracy and western political traditions.

Yet there is no valid reason to assume that the values of humanness can only be expressed in terms of western humanism, that the value of rationality is entirely subsumed by western philosophical concepts of Reason, that expressions of aspirations to equality occur only in the form of western Egalitarianism, or that a critical tension between individual subjectivity and social locations occurs only in western Individualism. Themes of equality and a common humanity are recurrent themes in dissident movements within major world religions, such as Sufism in Islam, and Bhakti movements in Hinduism.

The charge of 'nostalgia'

The problem goes deeper than the construction of certain select elements of modernity as 'western'. As postcolonial subjects we have also deeply internalised colonial modernity's construction and adjudication of our own cultural practices and embodied ways of being. For example, British colonial adjudication of caste and forms of labour encountered in India designated them as so many forms of 'bondage', 'representing history as a progression from unfreedom to freedom, as a process of restoring the loss of natural rights to liberty' (Prakash 1990: 2). Today, such colonial representations of modernity and of Indian tradition continue to play a formative role in the way Indians represent their past to themselves. In a milieu shaped by this history, every attempt to represent the non-modern lays itself open to the charge of neglecting to understand power relations, and possibly even to the charge of reproducing oppressive relations. The following evaluation by Nair (1993) is a case in point, aimed specifically against appreciative reconstructions of Indian female culture in the colonial period:

> The attention paid in these works to the appropriation of popular/lower caste cultural practices by an increasingly hegemonic nationalist culture is noteworthy. *Yet such an approach also displays a marked nostalgia similar to the conservative longings for an idealised pre-capitalist / pre-colonial social order*. The 'autonomous' cultural domain itself was an expression of a sexual division of labour appropriate to the socially, economically and politically dominant groups in these societies. The refusal to engage with the ways in which material inequalities were masked by cultural compensations is problematic. (1993: 88, emphasis added)

The charge of 'nativism'

Equally, certain variants of postcolonial theory, fearful of the charge of 'nativism' that it has itself helped to produce, too quickly dispense with the possibility of non-western ways of being and knowing. A notable example occurs in an interview with Spivak by Indian feminists in Delhi (Spivak 1990). The latter articulate an unease with transposing western models onto their own context, and enquire about the possibilities of discovering and promoting indigenous theory. Spivak responds by stating:

> I cannot understand what indigenous theory there might be that can ignore the reality of nineteenth-century history. (1990: 69)

For one of the Delhi-based interlocutors at any rate, Gandhism provides an example of indigenous theory — *'even though it is a highly synthesised model'* (1990: 69). In other words, the model of indigenousness being advanced here does not involve a simple claim for an a-historical native essence. Yet Spivak's response fails to recognise any distinction between the two:

> As for syntheses: syntheses have more problems than answers to offer. To construct indigenous theories one must ignore the last few centuries of historical involvement. I would rather use what history has written for me. (1990: 69)

However, the issue here is precisely the question of what, exactly, history *has* 'written for' postcolonial subjects. Colonial western domination is historically a contingent factor and has been highly variable where it has occurred, both in the intensity and in the scope of its impact. Nowhere does it represent the horizon of all understanding. Instead dominance is often exercised at a distance, as in the requirement that all alternative understandings have ultimately to be translated into western discourse in order to receive global acceptance. The existence of different languages, different embodiments, different ways of becoming cultural subjects will necessarily make available a variety of different strategies of resistance besides the deconstructive strategy.

The indiscriminate use of the same critique against very differently-situated theorists shows up sharply when we compare Spivak's (1988) criticisms of Kristeva with her criticisms of the Delhi feminists (Spivak 1990). Both, it would seem, are guilty of the same error: of attempting to retreat to an originary space before the sign, the former in her notion of the semiotic, the latter in their notion of indigenous theory and identity. But are the Delhi feminists appealing to a space before the sign and outside of language? Or are they rather appealing to a space available to most postcolonial subjects, namely a space outside the *dominant* language? The potentialities of this space should not be romanticised, but to those interested enough to investigate this space, there are discursive histories and rich resources for alternative understandings to be found. The concept of an 'indigenous synthesis' may therefore be more sympathetically interpreted not only as an attempt to acknowledge the transactional quality of postcoloniality, but also as an attempt to render more accessible to intellectual reflection submerged but nevertheless vibrant ways of being.

Nostalgia as 'unreconciled historical experience'

Neither the charge of being 'western' nor the charges of 'nativism' or 'nostalgia' are entirely able to suppress the complexity of postcolonial experience. Instead, images of doubleness, hybridity, and multiplicity reverberate in the recent writings of postcolonial intellectuals. Within India, for example, Veena Das has argued (1995) that postcolonial institutions and social relations in India are now subject to a 'double articulation' — even caste and religion, usually designated as traditional institutions, are now re-articulated through institutions as modern as the bureaucracy and the law.

Such 'doubling' is not confined to institutions. It has enormous implications for postcolonial subjectivity. In the immigrant context, doubleness works through the submergence of a whole way of being. What is submerged is not primarily a matter of what is commonly called 'subjectivity', in the sense of conscious beliefs, hopes, aspirations, reasoned reflection, or even the creation of intersubjective meanings in social interaction. Rather, it includes, besides language, styles of embodiment, of affect and emotion, modes of relating to other people and also to the whole range of categories constructed by a culture, such as objects, animals and deities. Yet access to this submerged domain can re-emerge. In immigrant and postcolonial life it does not only re-emerge as a way of being, but, because of its submergence in everyday life, it re-emerges as a heightened form of reflexivity.

An attempt, unusual in contemporary theory, to creatively re-think the value of sensory experiences from the perspective of those on the periphery of western modernity occurs in the work of Seremetakis (1994). Introducing a distinction, if not a downright opposition, between what she calls 'depth' and 'dust', she argues:

> Sediments of sensory memory stratify the artifact as depth, forming a diachronic volume, from which all historical matter, valued and devalued, may seep as expressive material culture. The memory of the senses runs against the socio-economic currents that treat artifacts and personal material experiences as dust. Dust is created by any perceptual stance that hastily traverses the object world, skims over its surface, treating it as a nullity that puts no meaning into our bodies, or recovers no stories from our past. (1994: 12)

Seremetakis's contrast between depth and dust begins to restore a distinction which has fallen into disrepute along with scholarly adjudications of authenticity as 'invented' (Hobsbawm and Ranger 1983), 'constructed' (Schechner 1985), and 'colonialist'. Yet this is precisely the distinction Seremetakis needs in order to enable her version of hybridity and post-modernity to recover a critical edge.

In Seremetakis's exploration of sensory memory, the sentiment of nostalgia, so central to immigrant experience, is rendered in new terms. Nostalgia is a difficult experience to explore, let alone to defend. Its English meanings denote little more than trivialising sentimentality. Within traditions of modernity, as I have indicated earlier, it acquires the additional meanings of concealing, perhaps the better to covertly reproduce, practices that are old, outdated and, by the standards of modernity, quintessentially oppressive. Yet in the hands of Seremetakis, who employs etymology as a methodology with which to 'capture the uneven shifts of semantic history that may be present at any given moment in a society' (1994: 17), the Greek meanings of 'nostalgia' open up a new way of understanding. The term now invokes the sensory dimension of memory in exile and estrangement, the mix of bodily and emotional pain — but it also has the capacity to 'evoke the transformative impact of the past as *unreconciled historical experience*' (1994: 4, emphasis added).

Seremetakis's notion of the past as *unreconciled* experience contains profound possibilities not only for exploring immigrant life, but also for the evaluation of postcolonial subjectivity in countries like India, where the synchronic coexistence of modern along with non-modern discourses creates, not hybridity *per se* — a concept which in itself equalises all dimensions of experience and discourse — but rather subjects who have zones of experience for which no official place is provided in the dominant language.

Sensory experience and immigrancy: the dancer

In my own case, learning classical dance, and thus renewing an integral part of the experience of socialisation within a Tamil Brahman habitus in India, has functioned as the trigger for a whole rush of access to forms of reflexivity. Reflexivity normally conveys a subjectivity capable of turning back and reflecting on itself. The experience I wish to convey is not based on this model of consciousness but rather one in which embodiment cannot be separated from conscious subjectivity. I present this experience as ethnographic self-reflection, supplemented by interviews with other Indian women students of dance:

A moment of stillness, in which the past rushes in it occurs the first time I resume the basic stance of all Indian dance: the ardhamandali or the turned out knees, the feet turned out, arms clasping the waist. Even basic bodily schemas and the kinetic hypotheses based on them are already culturally informed. This would help to explain the feeling of 'recognition' that I experience as soon as I take up the basic stance and begin the preliminary steps. The basic posture of the ardhamandali is a stylised form unique to the dance genre. Yet it exists in a continuum with basic cultural forms of embodiment in everyday life in India — the emphasis on striking up a fundamental relationship to the earth, feet flat on the earth, so unlike the ballerina's standing on points. The very next move emphasises the relationship to the ground — feet flat, we stamp the earth in rhythms in response to the syllabic call of the teacher: ta thai tom thakka.

Already, I renew an orientation to the earth missing here in Australia. When I do rural field work in south India I find myself wondering why I spend so much of my time in Australia separated from the ground. It has everything to do, of course, with the way the social environment is organised in terms of relations between humans and objects: perched on chairs, seats, beds. For the orientation to the ground is not an isolated practice — in turn it fits in with the very way in which space is organised. In the village, I sit and eat on the floor, I sleep on an unrolled mat, I sit on the ground to write. One practice leads to the other. The way I was lulled to sleep as an infant, and the way women still do in India — sitting cross legged and placing the baby in the lap, shaking one leg, and striking it on the back with the flat of the hand. The nonsense rhythms called out aloud are in a continuum with what the dance teacher calls out — Ra Ra Ro! But how would this practice be possible if it were not for the clothes women wear? Where would the infant nestle in the lap if the sari did not form a comfortable hammock between the cross legged mother's thighs? How would the mother sit on the floor except with such a garment? I think of my discomfort recently in Australia caught having to sit on the floor in an Indian gathering wearing a dress and wrestling with the requirements of female modesty at the same time. Basically an impossible task.

There is a holism here which is inescapable. One cultural practice seems unima-ginable without its place within a whole ensemble. Even before I have begun the dance I have struck a point of entry into this whole bodily orientation.

But the dance insists on these cultural references in much more explicit ways. Already, before taking up the ardhamandali stance we have rendered the space sacred by giving the ritual apology to the earth for stamping on her. Simultane-ously, I have renewed a forgotten and rejected relationship: of reverence and submission to the authority and knowledge of the guru, who sits calling out the syllables, hitting the rhythm out with her wooden stick:

thadi . . tha naka dinda, thadi tha na dinda, tharikitta thom, tharikitta thom.

As we respond by stamping out the rhythms with our feet, the sensory experience is already informed by submission to power, first to the power of the guru, but then to the power of the deity, and to the absent figure of the lover. We go on to explore the intricacies of submission to the Other in minute figurations and nuances of gesture and emotion. The dance elaborates, in accordance with the Indian aesthetic of viraha bhakti, the sentiments of an identity which is constructed centrally in the absence of the loved deity, lover, husband. It seems perfectly fashioned to resonate with immigrant experiences, where a whole background fundamental to one's being is absent. Can this vast reservoir of an aesthetics of absence teach the immigrant Indian how to turn the loss of the beloved (India) into a creative source of energy?

A fellow learner, another Indian immigrant, reflects on learning to per-form an erotic dance piece in the Kuchipudi genre:

Kuchipudi has made me aware of eroticism in Indian culture. The Aus-tralian girls in my dance class found the kind of flirting seduction in Krishnasabadam very hard — they had problems with that behaviour. The seduction is less open, covered with so many layers of games. Maybe Indians are still hung up about women openly seducing, so they have to cover it up? But it is much more complicated than western seduction. There is a lot of teasing in it which I found fascinating. But I was myself much more comfortable with that mixture of shyness and really quite open sexuality.

This sense of being inducted into another embodiment, another con-struction of sexuality and a whole style of being with which one feels a certain cultural affinity, requires fuller exploration. In particular, it requires us to reconsider the nature of embodiment when embodiment is fashioned not by one but by several languages and cultures. It has become easy, even a matter of course in discussions of immigrant and postcolonial identity, to use the language of 'fragmentation' and 'discontinuity'. This language is, in a sense, pre-given; it is provided by western auto-critiques of the unitary subject. What needs equally to be remarked on, however — for it is too often overlooked — is the endurance of sensory continuities *across* processes of cultural fragmentation. Deprived of context, deprived of their material props such as saris and ways of building houses without much furniture, these ways of being become, not forgotten, as the language of consciousness and memory implies, but unused, overlaid and dormant.

In considering the remarkable efficacy of dance in providing the trigger to this submerged way of being, we must consider not only the nature of embodiment in cultural transmission, which I have already characterised in holistic terms, but also the holism of aesthetic experience. Dance exercises a particularly potent force in the transmission of sensory continuity, bearing within it an internal coherence, so that the subject cannot choose to adopt one component without adopting the whole that informs the aesthetic. Temple dances rely heavily for their transmission on certain specific interlinkages between the body and the memory. They rely in particular on the body's capacity to develop habituated forms of knowing, which can enable it to perform highly skilled actions without conscious reflection being involved. The kinesthetic link between an inner being and the felt movements which are reinstated allows memory to take the form of re-enacting rather than of re-presenting the past.

This capacity of the body is aided and synthesised in the case of Indian classical dance by virtue of the integral place given to the voice, which brings with it melodic, rhythmic and narrative structures and patterns. The musician who accompanies the dancer gives the dancer her mnemonic devices. The voice sings, and narrates a story, as well as breaking periodically into the *jatis*, according to a process of mimetic interchange between the voice, the rhythm of the feet and that of the drums. The confluence of voice, language, melody and rhythm lays an extremely rich base for the aesthetic experience of coherence, forming a network in which signs and semiosis play as important a part as embodied ways of knowing. Such an aesthetic must be learned, through an arduous apprenticeship, but it is precisely its internal coherence which makes such an apprenticeship necessary and, indeed, desirable to the apprentice.

Indian aesthetic theories of *rasa* offer an explicit account of the relation between the everyday and the stylised representations of art in Indian performative genres, in which theatre and dance are inextricably intertwined. They view the modes of stylisation as the effort to extract the very essence, flavour and taste (i.e. the *rasa*) from everyday experiences of emotions, styles of embodiment and particular kinds of relationships. Seremetakis has referred to the transformative potential of unreconciled experience. In a small way, this is what occurs with Indian aesthetics in an immigrant context. The aesthetic imperative of exaggeratedly representing the quintessence of what is everyday in India allows the dance to illuminate that which is *not* everyday as a taken for granted background. Instead, it illuminates a background which can no longer be taken for granted, that which is unimagined and unimaginable by the dominant culture we live in. Participation in aesthetics comes to offer the fragmented postcolonial subject a powerful discourse within which to come to 'recognise' styles of embodied expressivity that lack affirmation and therefore become inaccessible. As one immigrant spectator put it when viewing a scene between mother and daughter in a dance performance of Tagore's *Chandalika*:

> The gestures are so familiar — that scene between the mother and daughter . . . It's like travelling somewhere and seeing points of reference, and saying *Ah! that's me!* (Interview)

At the same time, not everything that is so illumined is palatable or acceptable to the immigrant women dancers, particularly to the highly educated, professional Indian women with whom I learned the dance. Just as the dance illuminates styles of intimacy and affect, it makes larger than life the hierarchical gender relations of Indian social life. For in Kuchipudi, the relationship between devotee and deity is not only modelled on the relationship between female and male lover, it forms the very basis of the dancer's subject position as she shifts from the flirtatious, to the coy, to the arrogant tease, to the suddenly serious and pious *bhakta* or devotee. If it highlights the variety of intimate modes that are possible between women and men, it nevertheless clearly elaborates them as possibilities within a hierarchical modality. For women who have experienced, since their grandmothers' generation, the enormous historical shifts in gender relationships among the Indian elite over the colonial and postcolonial periods in India, the modality elaborated by the dance is a disturbing anachronism. This too is part of its transformative potential, which is obscured by the discourses of Indian nationalism which seek to harness the dance as a simple expression of Indian spirituality.

Sensory experience and contemporary theory: Bourdieu

The power of unreconciled historical experience can easily be squandered by theoretical mischaracterisations. I have examined examples of this in relation to postcolonial theory's over-hasty resort to charges of nativism and nostalgia. In this section and in the next, I wish to consider, too briefly, some examples of how poststructuralist theory would also bypass much of what is distinctive about postcolonial experiences. Instead of allowing us to validate and sympathetically enlarge on the kinds of complex reformulations of ways of being and ways of knowing under immigrant conditions, we find a legacy that encourages suspicion, if not downright denial, of the possibility of certain kinds of manifest experience.

The work of Pierre Bourdieu is often cited as an example of someone who has successfully negotiated and transcended the limitations of structuralism, and in this sense has constituted through his corpus of work a striking example of *post*structuralism. His concept of practice is widely understood to have allowed greater initiatives for the cultural subject than was possible within a rule-oriented description of cultural formation.

If I investigated the immigrant dance world in terms of his theory, particularly in terms of his notion of class as based on a set of culturally defined predispositions which form a 'habitus', I would be enabled to produce a sophisticated sociological account of the way in which a bourgeois nationalist habitus provides a framework for the transmission and shaping of Indian temple dances. The temple dances of south India have earned a special place in the aesthetics of nationalism both in India and in the diaspora. As the value and uniqueness of India as a nation came to be located in the sphere of its religious spirit, the dances of the temple–court nexus in south India became one of the key sites in which to elaborate this claim. The characteristic impulses of Indian nationalism involve two tendencies: first, the advocacy of a break with the past; and secondly, the elaboration of an emotional yearning for the re-discovery and revival of the past. The two often coalesce around the notion of reviving a *reformed* past. In the case of temple dances, this notion took the form of breaking with the dances as danced by an elite but non-Brahman group of women known as *devadasis*, to be reformed and revived under Brahman leadership. It is this habitus which is reproduced in Australia, where the Australian state policy for Asian immigration — even after the 'White Australia' policy was officially relaxed in the late sixties — continued to emphasise professional middle-class immigration. The practice of enrolling oneself or one's children in a dance school for classical dance takes its meaning not only from an immigrant imperative to transmit and reproduce cultural forms, but from the version of cultural modernity constructed through the interaction between nationalism and colonialism.

Nor does Bourdieu's sociology require us to ignore the realm of the body. Quite the opposite, for he has harnessed the work of phenomenology as the support of his sociology, making the body one of the prime sites in which the habitus is fashioned, out of the reach of conscious discourse or reflection. An immigrant whose primary habitus has been formed under conditions other than those prevailing in her new country experiences a different embodiment. Bourdieu's notion of symbolic capital will explain why this embodied habitus brings with it little cultural prestige or power in the immigrant situation. Australian theorists of immigrant experience such as Bottomley (1992) have drawn upon Bourdieu's work on the relationship between symbolic capital and objective relations of power in order to reinterpret Australian multiculturalism. Instead of 'differences in life style', we come to perceive multiculturalism as a matter of different 'positions in the field of power' (Bottomley 1992: 13). Bottomley has recently drawn attention to the fact that Bourdieu first developed his notion of the habitus in the study of peasant men in the Pyrenees who were increasingly marginalised by the gradual incursion of urban cultural practices such as new forms of dance (chacha, the twist), leaving the peasant men to carry their habitus like a burden ('heavy, bowlegged, knock-kneed, with bent arms') (Bottomley n.d).

Bourdieu's notion of habitus therefore helps us to specify the class and historical components in the shaping of immigrant sensory experience. Can it also illuminate aspects of experience that are in conflict or in tension with the dominant habitus? Bourdieu certainly refers to such subordinated experiences in class society:

> The universe of discourse . . . is practically defined in relation to the neces-
> sarily unnoticed complementary class that is constituted by the universe
> of that which is undiscussed, unnamed, admitted without argument or
> scrutiny.   (1992 [1977]: 170)

However, the very yoking of embodiment into Bourdieu's social theory of class leaves the body in the passive role of reproducing class inequalities. Read in his terms, the immigrant dancer emerges as a carrier of middle-class cultural capital, once valuable in India, now devalued by immigration and the consequent reduction to a minority culture. Either the body carries in it a ruling class culture, or it embodies a marginalised and displaced habitus. The phenomenological experiences I have described, of suddenly moving between the dominant and the marginalised forms of embodiment, of the capacity of an aesthetics that is 'upper class' in India to acquire new illuminating capacities in the immigrant context, all these dimensions become minimised by Bourdieu's discourse. One of the key dimensions which is striking about the Indian Australian women involved in dance is the sense of discovery and excitement they derive from their explorations:

> Dancing itself is liberating. I've always been ladylike, not wanting to leap
> around too much. I always thought of Indian dancers as conservative. I
> suppose because of the way they dress, and the Hindu framework. So this
> particular teacher and group of women dancers have been a revelation
> to me. The dancers are incredible women. If an outsider looked at them,
> they would think: 'Indian traditional women', but there is so much there
> of themselves, and an expression of their own freedom there. It is a self-
> expression of their freedom. (Interview — *with the reference to 'Hindu'
> framework, the speaker is positioning herself as a member of an Indian Christian
> community.*)

Migration *should* offer a classic example of the kind of 'objective crisis' which, according to Bourdieu, permits 'the practical questioning of the theses implied in a particular way of living'. Indeed, 'culture contact' is one of the examples he gives of such an enabling shift in objective conditions (1992 [1977]: 168). The relationship between the immigrant's embodied habitus and the aesthetic discourse of dance is, moreover, one which could well be understood in terms provided by Bourdieu himself of the transformation which occurs when unnamed experiences acquire access to language:

> 'Private' experiences undergo nothing less than a change of state when they recognize themselves in the public objectivity of an already constituted discourse, the objective sign of recognition of their right to be spoken and to be spoken publicly.   (1992 [1977]: 170)

It is, however, characteristic of this theorist that even when Bourdieu concedes that such transformations can trigger off a crisis in the everyday order, he will permit nothing of utopian significance to occur. We may expect only the production of another order of legitimacy and authority, another form of 'logotherapy' (1992 [1977]: 171).

The attenuated female subject of contemporary feminist theory

In the face of some of the dominant tendencies of contemporary theory, which overwhelmingly underestimate the complexity of experience, attempts to rescue some sphere of human agency remain weak, under-formulated, and hard to reconcile with the prevailing tenor of argument. Feminists, who have a particular stake in preserving the possibility of emancipatory action, have repeatedly seized upon Foucault's notion that power itself generates resistance (McNay 1992; Diamond and Quinby 1988). This notion, under-developed in Foucault's own work, has resulted in an effort among social theorists to identify elements of the now fragmented human subject in an 'agency' which seems to be exercised exclusively in moments of resistance. Resistance, choice and subversion in turn are located in more and more exiguous nuances of cultural life. Judith Butler (1990), for example, locates resistance in the parody and mimicry of gender in drag and cross-dressing. Having resolutely undermined the viability of the subject, of identity, and of representation, Butler seeks to locate the agency requisite for feminist politics in the contradictions and incoherencies of the multiple injunctions that face a contemporary woman: to be a good mother, a heterosexually desirable object, a fit worker, etc. The conflict of the objectives produces dissonance and enables subversion.

But this argument is inadequate. Dissonance can only be experienced as dissonance if the subject knows or at least aspires to what it is to experience a more harmonious mode of existence. At the very least the idea of dissonance *presupposes* a subjectivity which overarches and attempts to provide continuity and coherence between the different contradictory constellations of identity.

In India, surrounded by far grimmer circumstances — increasing communal tensions, increasing poverty and inequality — the attempt to re-locate elements of the attenuated female subject in fragments of 'agency' has had even bleaker consequences. At least two Indian feminists have, in influential articles, been able to locate female agency only at the very limits of human endurance. Reacting, quite justifiably, to an earlier feminist emphasis on women as victims of larger social collectivities (caste, religion, nation), Bhutalia writes on women's agency during the massacres, rapes and forcible religious conversions of the Partition of India and Pakistan. She locates the agency of some women at least, in female suicides that occurred on a mass scale:

> But what of the women who took their own lives, or who 'offered' themselves up for death? Can we see them only as victims? Or did they play some part in the decision to take their own lives? The women could well have consented to their own deaths in order to preserve the honour of the community.   (1993: WS15)

Sundara Rajan (1993) pushes matters to an even greater extreme when she seeks to locate female subjectivity in pain. She is referring to the pain of the fire that engulfs the burning widow. In a lucid effort to avoid the methodological impasse — is sati freely chosen or is it imposed on the passive woman as victim? — she decides instead to locate female agency at the point of no return, in the aversive flinching away from the fire by the dying woman.

First, subjecthood is located exclusively in agency; then, agency can be found only in such extremes. What have we come to that we must find 'female subject-constitution', to use Rajan's terms, in the extraordinarily diminished or attenuated vision of the last moments of a dying woman?

The 'romance of resistance' (Abu Lughod 1990b) that flourishes in contemporary oppositional writing is itself a symptom of the impoverished half-life within which the regulative principle of hope survives. If feminism and other oppositional social movements are to replenish their utopian imaginings, we need to expand our vision of subjecthood under modernity. Subjecthood includes not only our conscious acts of resistance, but embodied ways of being that are not accessible to consciousness, particularly when some of those ways lie submerged under the weight of the dominant culture. Embodiment in turn is not *only* a support for reproducing dominant relations of power — it includes within it the capacity to sustain these marginalised ways of being which occasionally find their way into critical discourse.

Note

1. I wish to thank Ian Bedford for his unfailing editorial reading.
    The structure of this paper is in part envisaged as a sequel to 'Too Traditional Once Again' (Ram 1993). Parts of this paper have benefited from their presentation in conferences. The segment on the female subject was presented in Melbourne, 1994 at the conference *Identities, Ethnicities, Nationalities in Asia and the Pacific*, La Trobe University. Ongoing work on dance and diaspora was presented at Melbourne University in 1995, at the conference *Linking Our Histories: Women and Migration in Asia and the Pacific*. Finally, the present version was presented at the conference *Knowledge and Discourse 96*, at the University of Hong Kong, 1996. I wish to thank the organisers for their invitation, and participants for their comments and discussion. Finally, I wish to thank the Australian Research Council for its financial support in undertaking this scholarship.

3

Feminist consciousness and the ruling relations
Dorothy Smith

This paper locates a distinctive moment in the women's movement that opened in Western Europe in the late 1960s. The organisation of this movement, particularly in English-speaking North America, has accorded special authority to the speaking of women's experience. Concepts such as 'being silenced', 'exclusion', 'voice', became central to the movement's critique of the world of established knowledges, politics, and culture. They also became central to its internal organisation and its often contentious expansion. Consciousness-raising was a foundational organising device, assembling women *as women* to explore, discover and recognise a community of experience. The institutionalised languages of culture, politics, science, and religion had been developed under male dominance and took for granted the experiences and interests of men. They were not made for women and did not speak of our situations or experience. We had to begin without a language, culture, politics, theory, literature which could speak of the issues and experience around which we assembled. In our dialogue with the massively masculinist order we both discovered and confronted, we had to find a resource that was not already appropriated and spoken. Consciousness-raising or related practices that drew on our experience were ways of working together to discover, in the category 'women', a political community. Recourse to experience has been the basis of the distinctive political organisation of the women's movement, creating the potentiality for women coming from somewhere else to challenge and disturb apparently established positions. Thus it became at once a basis on which women came together for what we discovered we had in common and on which women found difference and questioned nascent hegemonies within the movement itself. Afro–North American women, for example, drawing on their own experiences as women and of racism, have challenged the hegemony of white feminists. Some feminists have claimed for women's experience an authority equivalent to knowledge vested in the institutional forms that have been created under a system of male dominance.

Here was the site of what, at least as I experienced it, became an extraordinary transformation of consciousness unlike anything I'd known before, the shrugging off of a gender hegemony, a giving birth — slow, remorseless and painful — to a new self, a peeling away of imbricated layers of the taken-for-granted learned, known and performed. My own experience was as an academic already committed to a discourse in which the intersecting hegemonies of class, race and gender worked their synergy.

Feminist consciousness, in all its varieties and contentions, broke away along the line of fault created historically by the male monopoly of the objectifications of consciousness and agency in ruling relations. This paper explores the geology of those social relations to display the peculiar conformation of the terrain where women faulted into consciousness. I am interested in locating that moment in the first stages of this round of the women's movement when we discovered in speaking our experience that we were in exile from the dominant discourses of our societies in an historical trajectory, a narrative of changing forms of dominance in Western Europe and North America.

Thinking back over my own past experience, I can trace a segment of this trajectory. I went to a school for girls, eventually trained as a secretary and did secretarial work, got fed up with that and was encouraged by an academic couple who befriended me to go to the university, married when I graduated, went into graduate school working as a housewife and mother at the same time, ended up as a single parent and eventually got an academic job. My life wove in and out of situations preserving traditional gender relations (secretary, housewife and mother) and others in which I participated as a subject in the formally impersonal and neutral discourses of the academy. That personal history was embedded in the trajectory of the relations I want to uncover here. The secretarial/clerical work, in which women were and are so very generally employed, translated the thoughts and spoken words of male managers, professionals, academics, authors, and so on, into the material forms of the texts through which they became communicative to others elsewhere. The bureaucratisation of the state and the advancing organisation of corporate management created a demand for workers who would play no part as subjects or agents, but would be in charge of the material side of texts and documents, transforming words into texts, texts and documents into records, filing, finding files, doing the work of producing and organising the memory of the firm, and so on. In the academic setting I worked first as a graduate student and then as a faculty member and at the same time I was mother to two kids, playing at first a traditional role of housewife vis à vis my husband and then a less traditional role as a single parent. My household work and childcare freed my husband to engage in his own studies but did not, of course, similarly facilitate my own.

As I became involved in the women's movement, my double life of household/mothering and the university became a discovery of a daily traverse across the line of fault between a woman's life in the particularities of home and children and the impersonal, extra-local relations that the university sustains. Here, in these two work situations, were radically different modes of consciousness. Household work and childcare are highly attentive to the particularities of the local setting — the physical layout of the household, taking in the state of the floors, putting clean sheets on the beds, checking the refrigerator to see what's there for supper, calling the kids in from play to get ready for school. It is a consciousness coordinating multiple particular details, cues, and initiatives, involving relationships with particularised others — children, partner, neighbours, and so on. The consciousness that organises and is organised in the university setting and in relation to academic work is entirely different. It participates in a discourse in which particular others appear only as their printed names in texts, or positioned as members of definite classes of others — colleagues, students, supervisors, administrators, etc. Here the subject participates in relations that extend beyond the local and particular, connecting her or him with others known and unknown in an impersonal organisation, both of the university and of the extra-local relations of academic discourse. Passing between these two modes is a reorganisation of relevances and memory, a reconstitution of self in modes incompatible with one another.

The women's movement endowed the experience with authority. Here was a place to start, from which the forms of exclusion, silence, and absence vested in the institutional order became visible and could be subjected to critical examination.

Between women's experience in its varieties and the established order of culture, politics, and knowledge a great cleavage appeared. Whole areas of the society that had been marginalised or totally excluded (women's lives as workers in the home, for example) were opened up within political and academic discourses. In academic contexts, women began to challenge the established discourses. Women's experience became a method of testing the texts of various disciplines for what was missing. The women's movement brought women together in creating knowledge, theory, understanding, art, and an active politics at work in multiple institutional settings, by examining our own lives as women.

Taking the standpoint of women is a political move in settings, such as the academic, that claim indifference to power. What would be seen if we did not take for granted the opposing modes of consciousness, the sites of women's experience and of the universalised discourses of the academy, but took the former as a basis for critical examination of institutional processes including academic discourses and, beyond that, a new grounding for exploration and discovery? Taking the standpoint of women made it possible to resort to the embodied sites that defined what was distinctively *of women* and to create from such modes of consciousness an authoritative ground from which to criticise, examine, and explore. From women's standpoint, the peculiarities of the abstracted extra-local organisation of the academic was brought under critical examination. A distinctive body of theory began to emerge in which philosophers such as Genevieve Lloyd and Sandra Harding questioned the masculine subject of reason and objectivity. While postmodernist feminism has challenged the women's movement's reliance on the authority of experience, it has also questioned the unified subject of truth, objectivity and reason.

Of course, as Alfred Schutz (1967) has insisted (though not quite in this language), the embodied consciousness is primary and foundational. He envisages consciousness switching effortlessly from one cognitive mode to another, from a consciousness structured by the temporal and spatial coordinates of bodily being to the theoretical mode in which those particularities are set aside in favour of a subject attentive to an impersonal realm. Taking women's standpoint proposes that the latter can only be resumed in settings of people's practices that do not replace but, rather, are built upon embodiment and provide for body's forgetting. That is inescapable. What then were the distinctive forms of people's local practices that objectified and abstracted and made it possible for people to enter into and be active in relations that did not begin and end in the local and particular? The academic was not the only form of these relations. Other extra-locally structured relations entering into and organising the local and particular were a general institutional form in the kind of society in which I/we lived and live. The ruling relations came into view from women's standpoint not as discrete and problematically-related entities such as the state, corporation, profession and so on, but as a general field of relations and organisation constituted extra-locally, external to particular persons and places, and organising and regulating people's activities in multiple local settings.

The concept of ruling relations identifies an historical development that can no longer be adequately conceived as arising in the life conditions of particular individuals. It directs investigation to a complex of objectified relations, coordinating the activities of many, many people whose consciousness as subjects is formed within those relations. Conceptions such as Louis Althusser's (1971) of the ideologically constituted subject, or Michel Foucault's (1972) of discourse without authorial intention, or poststructuralism's adaptation of de Saussure's theory which construes the subject as a function of a symbolic order that determines rather than being determined by the individual's intentions, or, in the very different tradition of organisational theory, a theory of institutions and institutionalisation as cultural rules constructing the 'existence' of actors and viewing action as enacting institutional scripts (Meyer *et al.* 1994): these and other related theoretical discoveries are some of the complex of relations I'm indicating by the term 'the social relations of objectified consciousness'. They mark a transition from the social conditions of Marx's theorising of consciousness as an attribute of individuals, to 'consciousness' as the workings of objectifying organisation and relations mediated by texts and computer technologies. Information, knowledge, reasoning, decision making, 'culture', scientific theorising, and the like become properties of organisation grounded in and relying on the materiality of the text and its increasingly complex technological expansions.

The objectified relations of ruling

The notion of the social 'relations' of objectified consciousness is analogous to Marx's (Marx and Engels 1973) specification of the 'object' of his investigations of capital as the specialisation and differentiation of relations of dependence. Relations of dependence were originally relations between persons.

When we look at social relations which create an undeveloped system of exchange, of exchange values and of money, or which correspond to an undeveloped degree of these, then it is clear from the outset that the individuals in such a society, although their relations appear to be more personal, enter into connection with one another only as individuals imprisoned with a certain definition, as feudal lord and vassal, landlord and serf, etc., or as members of a caste, or as members of an estate. In the developed system of exchange the ties of personal dependence, of distinctions of blood, education, etc., are in fact exploded, ripped up. So far from constituting the removal of a 'state of dependence', these external relationships represent its disintegration into a general form, or better, they are the elaboration of the general basis of personal states of dependence. Here too individuals come into relation with one another only in a determined role. These material states of dependence, as opposed to the personal states, are also characterised by the fact that individuals are now controlled only by abstractions, whereas earlier they depended on one another (Marx and Engels 1973: 164). With the full development of the market as relations of exchange between people mediated by money and commodities, relations of dependence become differentiated and specialised as those relations we know as the economy. They come to have an autonomous status and dynamic.

I envisage the relations of ruling and the historical trajectory of their development as an analogous process of differentiation and specialisation, but in this case of the relations of consciousness (in Marx's sense of 'social consciousness'). The social relations of objectified consciousness, the organisers and regulators of our contemporary world, supplant particularised and territorially-based forms of social organisation. Marx describes how the functions of knowledge, judgement and will are transferred from the producers to capital. These functions of consciousness become transferred not simply to the individual capitalist, but to organisation that creates new and objectified forms of agency, knowledge and decision. Organisation, as such, becomes differentiated as a focus of technical and rational refinement and elaboration. An order of social relations emerges that 'extracts' the coordinative and concerting of people's everyday/everynight activities from relations between particular persons. It becomes, as a complex of ruling relations, independent of particular individuals; individuals participate in them through the forms of agency and subjectivity they provide. Organisation is produced as a differentiated function, subjected to specialised and technical development.

The ruling relations are modes of action, not merely of objectified consciousness. Subject *and* agency are constituted within them. A medium of action is brought into being which subsists and is organised externally to the local sites of the necessarily embodied people who bring them into being. Subjectivity and agency are 'effects' of discourse, bureaucracy, and other objectified forms. People may be at work within this form without capacity as agents: for example, one study (Reimer) found executive secretaries in a Canadian provincial government service doing work that overlapped with and was in many ways the same as their executive or administrative bosses. Their work, however, was not counted as executive or administrative work and was not attributed to them as agents. Rather it was held to be delegated to them by the executives or administrators for whom they worked.

While the relations of ruling are an organisation of power, it is misleading to reduce them to relations of domination or hegemony, or to view them as monolithic or manipulated. Forget crude and reductive notions such as 'superstructure': the term 'relations of ruling' points to modes of organised action, not merely to thinking, feeling individuals, getting together or otherwise. They form a complex field of coordinated *and coordinating* activities mediated by texts.

The materiality of the text and its indefinite replicability creates a peculiar ground in which it can seem that language, thought, culture, formal organisation, have their own being, outside lived time and the actualities of people's living — other than as the latter become objects of action or investigation from within the textual. A sociology from women's standpoint insisting on beginning in the actualities of everyday/everynight experience problematises relations coordinating people's work in many such local sites, organising them extra-locally. Texts that are indefinitely replicable have the miraculous effect of creating a join between local and particular, and the generalising and generalised organisation of the relations of ruling. Here on the one hand, just where she is, is the reader of the text; here is each such reader, reading the same text. Through the text each participates in a discourse in which many others are active; or through the text (entering information into a computer, filling in a form, or a set of fields on the monitor), her work is coordinated with others' work in a large-scale organisation that has manufacturing plants in many regions and business offices in major financial centres. Though texts are always read and written in definite local settings of people's work, they coordinate people's work with that of others elsewhere and at other times. The ruling relations organise extra-locally.

The ruling relations are characterised by a capacity to realise the same forms, courses of action, relations, etc. in the varieties and multiplicities of the local settings in which they operate and which they regulate. Indeed it is their capacity to reproduce standardised forms of control, management, communication, etc., across multiple local sites and at different times that distinguishes them from other forms of organisation or ruling. The textual bases that objectify knowledge, organisation and decision processes are essential to this ubiquity. They distinguish what individuals are in themselves from what they do organisationally, professionally or as participants in a discourse, thereby constituting objectifying properties of formal organisation, profession, or discourse. Thus progressively over the last two hundred years in Western Europe and America an order of 'consciousness' has been institutionalised, constructing knowledge, judgement and decision in a textual mode and transposing what were formerly individual and subjective judgements, hunches, guesses, observations, opinions, stories, and so on, into objectified social forms vested in texts and textual practices. While postmodernity may reject the unitary subject, it takes for granted, as the fish takes the water in which it swims, the text-based and mediated objectifications of this complex of relations and its construction of out-of-body modes of being and acting as subject and agent.

The standpoint of women, locating the knowing and inquiring subject in the site of her/his bodily site of being in its ineluctable particularities throws into relief these objectified relations. The experience of such radically different modes of consciousness as that located in the work of mothering and the household, oriented towards the particularities of setting and of others, and that located in extra-local relations mediated by texts of one sort or another (including, of course, the computer) becomes a point of entry into what Foucault calls an archaeology, the exploration of that past (that trajectory from the past) that situates that experience.

Gender and the ruling relations: an historical trajectory

The social relations organising the site of a woman's consciousness, my own as well as that of others, in the early days of this phase of the women's movement are embedded in this historical trajectory emerging with industrial capitalism in Europe and North America in the seventeenth and eighteenth centuries. Capitalism both is and drives a displacement of social organisation integrated with particularistic relationships, particularly of kin and household, and with land. When the trajectory of the developing ruling relations is described or explored from a standpoint which we might think of as the standpoint of a middle-class man, gender does not appear, and nor does race. Yet from a woman's standpoint, such as that I have located, the intertwined trajectories of capital and the ruling relations appear as fundamentally gendered. It is a short step from there to recognising their racial organisation in the imperialist projects of Western Europe and North America.

With the accelerating growth of the social relations of capital, households became increasingly separate from manufacturing and places of business. Middle-class women and men came to inhabit largely different worlds of work, knowledge and culture. The everyday work lives of middle-class women and men came to be situated very differently; they participated in diverging relations, women in the domestic sphere, men in relations that hooked them into an economy organised extra-locally and connected them with news of the world, with scientific and technological developments, with politics and government, and with the wider public world in general. Over a period of 200 years men's work in the middle classes was more and more implicated in the commercial and manufacturing enterprises which caught them up into the relations Marx characterises as 'material states of dependence' in which 'individuals are now controlled only by [the] abstractions', that is, by relations between money and commodities, rather than the direct person-to-person control of, say, lord over vassal (Marx and Engels 1973: 164). As men were pulled more and more into an engagement in the social relations of an economy no longer organised locally, but extensively and in accordance with developing markets, their work lives became increasingly extra-domestic.

Over time a distinct domestic sphere was constituted, at first a physical separation of household from plant, shop or workshop, associated with the emergence of systems of accounting which separated the affairs of household and business (Davidoff and Hall 1987). Owners no longer directed their enterprises from their households and their wives no longer managed a household serving a business or craft or acted as their husbands' agents in their absence. Management of the household became increasingly distinct from management of the business or workshop. Men could therefore develop a specialisation of subjectivity in activities articulated to the extra-local organisation of capital while women's was correspondingly focused within the domestic sphere.

The worlds of men and women diverged. Men participated in extra-locally organised relations, both those of capital and market and those of new text-mediated discourses of the Enlightenment. They associated with other men of the bourgeoisie in coffee houses, clubs, societies, and the like where current events, state policies and practices, new scientific knowledge, were discussed (Habermas 1992; Eley 1994: 327). They read journals in which the latest scientific developments and their relevance for manufacture were discussed. There was a redefining of civil society (Davidoff and Hall 1987), creating an hegemony of the bourgeoisie and bringing into being a 'public sphere' dominated by men from which women were largely excluded (1987: 416). The domestic became correspondingly insulated from the expanding and more and more exclusively male world of business, politics and science outside the home as the ruling relations evolved.

The forms of consciousness represented and ascribed to women came to be seen as incompatible with the objectified and universalised modes of the ruling relations. The constitution of universality as a property of these relations had as its necessary supplement the active exclusion of women as representing subjectivities embedded in particularity. There is an old saying from the Yorkshire of my youth: A whistling woman and a crowing hen let the devil out of his pen. Masculinity, and the social order with which it was identified, relied on excluding women. The importance to moral order of women's avoiding encroachments on male territory expresses almost formulaically the gender order substructing the emerging ruling relations. Carole Pateman (1988) argues that 'civil society' was constituted through women's exclusion and the denial of the embodied sphere of women's do-mestic work. Rationality and its claims to universality came to be identified with the male sex. Joan Landes (1995) suggests that women's exclusion from public discourse was essential to men's capacity to sustain what she calls 'the masquerade of universality'. She argues indeed that a gender order was constitutive of the public sphere (Habermas 1992) that was established in the seventeenth and eighteenth centuries. During the French Revolution and later, women's attempts to organise in public 'risked violating the constitut-ive principles of the bourgeois public sphere . . . [they] risked disrupting the gendered organisation of nature, truth, and opinion that assigned them to a place in the private, domestic but not the public realm' (Landes 1995: 97–8). Men confronting men did not raise the spectre of particularity, whereas women bore particularity, as their social being. Hence men associating exclusively with men could miss 'the masquerade through which the (male) particular was able to posture behind the veil of the universal' (Landes 1995: 97–80).

In the early days of the Enlightenment rationality was vested in the male body; the individual subject undertook the discipline of the fully rational Cartesian consciousness; as a subject he claimed freedom to participate in relations, whether of commerce or science and philosophy, as an individual, implicated in and constituting their increasing differentiation from the particularistic claims of kin, family and locale.

The work of housewifery and the working consciousness of housewives was, of course, what enabled philosophers to avoid the distractions of think-ing about the pragmatics of the working world (Schutz 1962), so far, at least, as their personal needs were concerned. Indeed Schutz's account of the form of consciousness that is a condition of entry to the domain of scientific theorising identifies as a necessary corollary of participation in that domain the exclusion from consciousness of the personal and of the pragmatics of the everyday world — indeed precisely those encumbrances of conscious-ness from which women could not divest themselves unless by becoming unwomanly (or possibly mad). Kant prescribed a specialised education for women, differentiating them from the masculine. 'Deep meditation and a long-sustained reflection', 'laborious learning or painful pondering . . . destroy the merits proper to her sex' (Agonito 1978: 131). Sustained reflection and painful pondering are incompatible with the consciousness that inhabits and sustains the pragmatic domain of the everyday world of housewifery. Correlatively, the function of housewifery on which masculine freedom to engage in extra-local relations depended required a consciousness continually attentive to the multiple minute-by-minute demands that bring an orderly household into daily being. Of an eighteenth-century housewife, Lee Davidoff and Catherine Hall write: 'With water to carry, a house to keep clean, meals to prepare, servants to supervise, clothes to make and mend, apprentices to keep in line, little children to nurse and teach and a watchful eye required for the business' (Davidoff and Hall 1987: 52). Though her duties were undoubtedly not so intimately tied to physical labour, Elizabeth of Bohemia complained to Descartes (who was unusually conscious of the situated character of doing philosophical work) that what we might describe as her work at court inhibited her ability to sustain the kind of consciousness needed for philosophical thought.

The barriers were not set up all at once. In principle, print enabled anyone who could read to learn from books, journals, newspapers and magazines. Both Londa Schiebinger (1989) in her tracing of women in science, and Landes (1995) in her exploration of women's relation to public discourse, describe women as participating actively in the intellectual, scientific and political life of pre-revolutionary France. Schiebinger (1989) suggests that in the first years of the Enlightenment rationality was indeed a discursive terrain shared by women and men. She describes salons in France where both women and men participated in scientific discourse. Landes argues that it was the French Revolution which brought a halt to the salon-life in which both women and men participated in political and literary discussion. Susan Okin's (1981) account of the seventeenth- and eighteenth-century emergence of what she calls 'the sentimental family' presents the work of philosophers designing the discursive positioning of the transcendent subject of rationality so as to segregate it from forms of subjectivity identified with women. Kant puts women firmly outside the discourse of the transcendent subject: 'Her philosophy is not to reason, but to sense' (Kant in Agonito 1978: 132). The 'sentimental family' designs a role for women which is complementary to the masculine appropriation of reason: 'women increasingly come to be characterized as creatures of sentiment and love rather than of the rationality that was perceived as necessary for citizenship' (Okin 1981: 74). The gender boundaries of public discourse were actively policed by parents, educators, and the spokesmen of the public sphere. Shevelow (1989) describes an increased 'containment' of women with the emergence and development of the periodical (Shevelow 1989: 24). It 'became a key participant in the reification of new conceptions of gender relations, conceptions that expressed the cultural shift through which individualism joined with natural law to institutionalize the household as the natural and valorized realm of women' (Shevelow 1989: 192).

As the ruling relations extended their scope and organisation, becoming increasingly objectified, their segregation from the domestic sphere became more marked. Theodore Porter (1995) describes an historical shift from familial and personal relations as sources of information, to impersonal and objectified. He describes the earlier personalised forms of relations as follows:

> Public affairs . . . were kept largely private until at least the late eighteenth century. This did not require elaborate mechanisms to preserve secrecy, though public as well as private institutions often had good reasons to maintain secrets. It reflected, rather, the weakness of institutions promoting public knowledge. Political and business information alike was spread mainly through networks of personal acquaintances. Indeed, political and business connections were often inseparable, and neither could be readily distinguished from friendship. Eighteenth-century Americans treated private letters as public business, and a letter might be opened and read several times as it made its way along a chain of acquaintances from sender to recipient. Family was central to much information exchange, and letters within elite families often mixed family and public news. Those who lacked the connections to learn of political affairs informally were assumed to have no real need to know. Elites viewed local newspapers as an extension of personal knowledge. Only newspapers from abroad were experienced as something like pure information. Even printed material often bore a personal stamp, and some one arriving with a newspaper or proclamation from afar would be expected to interpret and explain its contents.
>
> (Porter 1995: 46)

Max Weber's account of rational legal authority is part of a typology of forms of imperative coordination that mark an historical shift from forms of authority knitted intimately to relationships of kin, family and locality to the rational organisation of bureaucracy constructed on a system of offices. Bureaucracy as a form is distinct from the private and personal and, by implication, from the domestic and familial; 'the modern organization of the civil service separates the bureau from the private domicile of the official and, in general, segregates official activity from the sphere of private life' (Weber 1968: 957). The segregation of 'the sphere of private life' is the complement of objectified organisation in which activities 'are assigned as official duties', and the capacity to act is defined by 'official *jurisdictional areas* . . . ordered by . . . laws or administrative regulations' (Weber 1968: 956). Michel Foucault's (1972, 1981) theorising of discourse implies an analogous differentiation of the field of relations constituting a discourse from the actual person who wrote or writes the text. He makes a decisive move away from a tradition of intellectual history that returned to the author, his intentions and the part he played in a particular tradition. The concept of discourse introduces an order existing independently of particular speakers or writers and transcending language and speech (Foucault 1972). Discourses have their own rules governing discursive practices (1972: 49). Who enters the 'society of discourse' [Foucault 1981: 63] as speaker or writer enters not as herself or himself, but in an 'author-position' defined by its conventions. Like Weber, Foucault marks an historical transition in the exercise of power. In Weber it is a transition from authority vested in persons to authority vested in offices; in Foucault the transition is from the exercise of power upon the individual body to the exercise of power through the diffused and decentred order of discourse (Foucault 1979). Furthermore, from the end of the eighteenth to the end of the nineteenth centuries, there was an extraordinary development of new financial and economic institutions, including life insurance, stocks and stock markets, joint stock companies and limited liability which protected family from commitments incurred in business, and, in the United States the invention of the corporation as a unitary organisation capable of owning property and acting independently of those owning shares in it. With these went the development of sophisticated accounting practices (Chandler 1977) separating the ownership of business from private wealth (Berle and Means 1968), the invention of new forms of management based on new textual technologies (Yates 1989) substituting record keeping and feedback through systems of reporting for direct lines of command, the associated developments of professions, such as law, engineering as a profession (Noble 1979), land surveying (Davidoff and Hall 1987), and so on, that required post-secondary training, the training in England of public servants and colonial administrators, involving not only the learning of skills but the changing of the subject (Henriques *et al.*), that is, the acquisition of 'character'. These and related developments transform the world known to and open to men of the middle classes, creating expanding regions of action increasingly dissociated from the particularisms of the family/household and personal relationship formed through family connections. The lineaments of the great divorce of men's and women's consciousness registered in studies like William H. White's *Organization Man* and John Seeley's *Crestwood Heights* resides in the dynamic that (particularly in the middle classes) expands the sphere of activity appropriated by men while diminishing that of women.

The contradiction

This archaeology uncovers the historical trajectory within which my own experience of a double consciousness was embedded. Here, in an historical trajectory in Western Europe, bound up with the dynamic generated by capitalism, emerged a distinctive organisation of the society: an expanding and technically elaborated complex of objectified relations, progressively expropriating organisation embedded in the family, kin and localised forms of producing subsistence, that is also an organisation of gender. At the same time, a contradiction emerges. The relations of ruling are mediated by texts; texts are indifferent to who reads them, and indifferent therefore to the reader's gender. Women came to have a subordinated and in a sense concealed access to and participation in the ruling relations. They were scientists through brothers or husbands; they were secretaries to executives and administrators; they did the laborious calculations of astronomy and went unmentioned in its journals; they worked as laboratory assistants; they wrote on policy in books published with or under their husbands' names; they were the wives and sometimes accountants for their businessmen husbands. And piece by piece through a century of struggle, they gained access to forms of education that equipped them to participate in the text-mediated relations of ruling. At earlier stages and particularly in association with imperialism, the order of ruling had relied heavily on the education of the masculine body and subjectivity. Young men were inducted into a shared class-culture at class- and gender-segregated schools and universities where, in addition to the promotion of team sports, they were taught a literary canon of (male) authors, histories of heroic wars, and the line of the nation's monarchs. As the relations of ruling became more technologically elaborated, they relied less on individual 'character' and on a specifically masculine ethos. Barriers against women that had formerly been so massive became attenuated and arbitrary. Women like myself, who could participate in the same discourses as men, came to sense the arbitrary nature of our exclusion. So did those excluded on racial grounds.

Here is the juncture, shaped by the historical trajectory of the ruling relations described above, that situates my, and other women's, experience of a dual subjectivity and defines the absence that the women's movement has turned over into an active presence, as a newly constituted base within these relations that is fundamentally at odds with its objectifications. This, I suggest, is the force of the theorising of 'women's standpoint' and of the claims of 'experience' to knowledge.

In the context of my own discipline of sociology, women, or rather feminist sociologists, sought ways of speaking from the local and particular without adopting the objectifying practices of established sociologies. We were not ashamed to be partial and interested. We sought new relations of knowledge that relied on, rather than repressing, the subjective. Our reading of the texts of the discourse has taught us that indeed universality is a masquerade concealing a substructure of racial, class and gender domination. And in my own work as a sociologist, I have wanted to work from the local actualities of a consciousness embedded in the everyday, to discover the everyday local practices that produce the generalising and universalising relations of which I have sketched the historical trajectory above. I am interested in investigating the ordinary, everyday ways in which the ruling relations as practices of power insert their generalising and standardising organisation into people's everyday/everynight lives, bringing us into relations at the extra-local level of the organisation of society. And I have sought to make such investigations not as a service to the rulers, but from the standpoint of people's actual experience of the extended relations of capital and of ruling. Their aim is to discover just how what we are doing, thinking, speaking of, articulates to social relations that extend beyond the reach of what we can know directly and how, therefore, we participate unwittingly in the massive powers that stand over against us and overpower our lives.

4

Telling true stories, writing fictions, doing ethnography at century's end: Stories of subjectivity and care from urban China[1]

Joseph Schneider and Wang Laihua

Given the criticism of representation and of the idea that knowledge and truth are distinct from relations of power and desire, just what the work of the social sciences might be read to be and to do have become opening questions. Taking these critiques seriously is surely part of what occasions the so-called crisis in the social sciences about which Charles Lemert has written with particular (but not exclusive) relevance for sociology.[2]

This crisis — or opportunity — may be considered in terms of the disciplines as professional enclaves in and outside the academy. But it also may be addressed for individuals who write in the names of these disciplines (or, who help effect a discipline in their writing accordingly). While the former question may be addressed in terms of institutional and/or professional organisation and politics, we want to direct attention to the promise of this opportunity in the more embodied space of the latter: in the practices of writing and subjectivity that constitute ethnography and related scholarly work.

For if we decompose the term 'ethnography' we sense just how fundamental writing — in diverse 'fields' — is to its production. And while writing is hardly central only to ethnography and the social sciences, the extent to which those of us who do this kind of work have appreciated and/or been interested in and willing to talk about writing as a core ('methodological'?) practice has been, until quite recently, limited. This focus on writing is part of a more widespread (some might say paradigmatic) shift in the academy sometimes referred to as the 'linguistic' or 'interpretive' turn toward a critical awareness that language use and the creation of meaning are at the very heart of the activities by and in which knowledge and the social are produced and held in place. Instead of being thought-transparent, these practices are seen increasingly as opaque, themselves a proper object of critical analysis. Some of the reaction against this attention to writing and 'the literary', as importantly if not primarily what 'doing knowledge' is, would itself seem to endorse critics' attention.

Some of this reaction against may be a result of the criticism this scrutiny brings of the usually unexamined ways that writing, the real, and subjectivity are linked and embedded in ethnography, sociology, and the human sciences more generally. While realism and its critique have a history, so to speak, in literature, literary studies, and the arts (as does representation), in general they have rarely been topics of critical examination within modern(ist) sociology and the social sciences. Given this, it is perhaps not surprising that the plausible links between writing, realism, and subjectivity and their implications for understanding how knowledge and truth are produced and sustained have also been little (even less) discussed there.

Of course, we sociologists and social scientists have been trained in 'methods' intended to contain what are seen to be diverse sources of distortion threatening our scientific vision of the natural world, in this case that it is the society discursively cast as separate and distinct from us as observers. Some of the most contaminating sources of this 'error' are believed to come from the very person(a) of the scientist; from the fact that the scientist/analyst, like those being studied, is a person too. The 'personal' is not to loom too large, if at all, in scientific work.

We speak about 'collecting data', so defined by research questions that we teach students must be located appropriately within and relevant to a canon. We seek to tell true stories both about particular people in this world (although just who those particular people are has been thought irrelevant according to conventional wisdom) and about larger, more abstract questions deemed theoretically worthwhile, aiming to make a 'significant' contribution to an accumulating body of knowledge. In short, we seek to get somewhere, to offer compelling arguments; to be definitive in what we say and write, and to set our contributions apart from and as more notable than those made by others. And of course we seek to know; and to know more; and more.

But poststructuralist critics note that these ends are accomplished only through a good deal of what Erving Goffman called back-stage management work. That is, in order to produce the reasonable, logical, compelling, and impersonal 'front-stage' analysis and argument that realist sociology and social science require — the science that seeks to tell True stories about others — our writing practices must be properly disciplined to deny and displace a variety of things that complicate those stories. In effect, we fabricate a world, the real world, about which we then speak seriously as though this world, as described/inscribed, exists as fully independent of these writing/speaking practices and, to the point, the subjects who create and recreate and depend on it. The result of this disciplinary work is a scientific discourse that is well-ordered. It is hard and smooth; the prose is clean and sleek; penetrating and powerful. It is compelling. The knowledge that comes in the form of such prose is useful; it enables us to do things and it enables us to be, to exist, in ways that seem unequivocal and also quite real. In short, these ways of writing are prime resources for producing the subject of modern liberal society, a subject some have suggested is, through and through, masculine.[3]

Given these and related criticisms of realist epistemology in social/human science work, and in ethnography most particularly, some very homely questions might be allowed to emerge at the level of the subject of this work: 'How shall I write?'; and, more disturbing, 'Who or what is this "I" that writes?' And more disturbing yet, 'What is the link between this I and those others about whom I write "the Truth"?' Being able to hear these as serious, productive, and yet playful questions assumes an openness to the position, central to poststructuralism, that rather than the centred and unified image of the liberal humanist subject of modernist sociology, this subject might productively be read as multiple, split, contradictory, and mobile. Of course, this view is offered up as not only 'about' the one who writes but as relevant to all considerations of subjectivity in later modernity; that is, as relevant both to those ethnography seeks to know and to the ethnographer as well. Better yet, it is about the intimate connection between the two.

The conundrum of 'who writes?' and 'why?', given these considerations, can — as some have warned — produce silence. The fear is that the dilemmas these criticisms present to conventional practices of writing and subjectivity bring 'too much' reflexivity which, it is claimed, foreshadows the loss of one's subject(ivity?). Surely, these arguments have enormous implications for the secure or relatively secure selves produced in and through conventional writing practices; for careers as well as for psyches. They can feel not at all playful but actually quite frightening. Still, 'we' seem to go on writing, perhaps in no small part because the alternatives are even more unsettling. We write. And in this writing we reproduce subjects, ourselves as well as others. The challenge of this moment, which might be marked as one of transformation for the human sciences and for the study of knowledge more generally, is *how* this writing might be done differently, so as to open 'the text' and the various elements linked to it.

What we two have been trying to do of late is to write in this space of transformation, a space necessarily of contradiction and incompleteness; a space of fragmentation and uncertainty. There the modernist subject of humanism — more or less the sociologist, the social scientist, the scholar, the intellectual as we have known *him* — still remains, inevitably, an object of desire, along with the writing practices and tropes of realism that bring this subject into being. But there are also attempts, sometimes laughable but sometimes simultaneously productive, to disturb and unsettle this subject by breaking open the seamless and compelling text of social scientific writing.

To call these and similar attempts by some sociologists 'alternative writing practices', while plausible, seems to reiterate the kind of disciplinary naïveté that kept social scientists so long ignorant of 'the subject of modernism'. Such a characterisation begs to know '"alternative" to what and to whom?' For while the homely moves we and others have tried to effect in writing what we insist on calling sociology may well be 'other' to the standards of 'good writing' or 'clear prose' in this and related disciplines, they are hardly strange outside sociology and social science, especially in fiction writing and autobiography.

When we have tried to say what, finally, we are doing in the project of ethnography we have been writing, we often speak about trying both to invoke and use, on the one hand, and to decentre and undermine, on the other, the conventional tropes of this genre; to use them but to use them, if you will, disloyally and with little sustained respect.[4] There is of course a certain disingenuousness here, for we no doubt use them more than we decentre them, and remain quite modernist after all.

In what follows we offer up segments from three different chapters of a book manuscript as examples of what a disloyal and somewhat disrespectful writing form of ethnography might look/read like. We do not suggest these as 'models' others should follow. Nor do we suggest that such forms are stopping places for 'new ethnography', or that such moves should be taken to make the genre 'better' or 'stronger'. Rather, they are of the present and, for us, local moments of our own embodiments as sociologists of late modernity. And as you shall see, the 'we' that has been ('forced' to be) quite untroubled in the text so far quickly comes apart in what follows. It goes, really, to pieces. You may have wondered about or even sensed some of those fragments under the smoother surfaced writing up to now.

Closure/openings/writing

Sweaty and winded, I sink into my seat just as the train begins to move out of Tianjin station toward Beijing and home. The air-conditioning feels so good. On this trip to China I have been able to admit to myself just how much I depend on it to create a private space of comfort.

5 August 1993. So many feelings come at once. We've made a mad dash to number 16, the soft-seat passenger car that always is just behind the engine and freight car, and always furthest from the entrance to the platform. Nancy sits across from me, looking backward as I look forward out the window, wiping her forehead, tears in her eyes.

'What's wrong? . . . Don't be sad.'

'Oh, you know. I hate leaving all our friends behind. It's such a wonderful place. It's such a terrible place. They deserve better. I just want to bring all of them together in one place and live there.'

'Yeah, but in what place? And for whose pleasure?'

We've had this conversation before. The particular quality of these friends and our relationships aside, it always seems to say more about the differences between us and them, and our desire to erase or elide those differences: we, the white, relatively privileged and highly-educated Americans from the United States, and they, the variously privileged Chinese intellectuals whom we have come (again and again) to feel so close to over the course of the past decade. I, the American researcher, they, the Chinese researchers and administrators in the Social Sciences Academy that hosts my 'research visits'; we, the Chinese and American (from the United States) sociologists, they, the people in the families we enter; we, the Chinese, (t)he(y) the foreigner(s); he the younger, less experienced (but in what?), deferential . . . son?, I the older, more experienced (but where? And in what sense?), authoritative . . . father? And we, men; they, women. A growing awareness of the endless play of fantasised similarity and difference in 'our' links to 'China' have made the notion of seeing things clearly seem increasingly quaint. 'It's such a wonderful place. It's such a terrible place.' What place is this, and seen from where?

But today's leave-taking, for me in any case, has a quality that sets it off. Sadness, of course. Most immediately because of the good-bye to LH, to whom, over the course of the research project and our collaboration on this book and other writings, we have become so attached.

'I didn't get to say a proper good-bye to LH.' I feel a catch in my throat and my own tears welling up.

'I know. I hugged him but you didn't.'

'Yes. But I wanted to, you know, and I'm sorry now that I didn't. Men.'

And I am sorry. For, more than ever before, my young colleague and I seem to have grown deeply comfortable with each other. But with only 15 minutes before the train was scheduled to leave as we pulled up in front of the station, and so far to run with our too-heavy bags, it seemed there was no time to linger over a careful good-bye. A quick, firm handshake and look; a 'thank you so much', and then we were separated by walls and corridors, off toward car 16.

The moment brought back memories of other separations from him: after ten months of his and my fieldwork and deepening friendship, we three then stood fighting back tears in the lobby of the Beijing-Movenpick Hotel. 17 July 1991. Once apart, the tears came to each of us and marked again what we had by that time taken to be a special connection. And then later, after seven months of his living with us in 1992 in Des Moines, to 'continue our writing' and give him a chance to see what 'America' was: more tears and sadness. And again in the fall of that year, after less than a month's visit occasioned by his presentation — his first ever in English — at an international conference, punctuated by some misunderstandings and turmoil between us: I wanted him to commit to a Stateside PhD program, with all the personal and family disruption that would entail; he resisted (rejected?). Still sadness at good-bye, but no tears; we each perhaps read relief in the other's eyes then.

That is what I feel now. I am really glad to be going home this time, unlike the many good-byes we have said to Tianjin since 1985 when Nancy and I first came to China. Relief at a successful five-week visit to re-interview the seventeen families LH and I had visited so many times during our 1990–91 project on family caregiving for elderly parents; relief that Nancy and I managed another period of bike riding, bus riding, eating local foods — just living a piece of everyday life in China — with no apparent mishaps or illness. It's a 'developing country', after all. And China is an 'other' place.

And it all seemed physically more demanding this time. Perhaps it was the heat and humidity; perhaps my age — now 50 years — made it harder not to depend on taxis and Chinese hosts for various comforts. Still, there is a particular sort of relief that comes when you begin to 'feel' closure and an ending to a story that has gone on for a good long time. And after all, I had since learned something about the power and pleasure of narrative closure. Perhaps this summer trip was another return to find/enact (the fantasies of) closure. Whatever it is, it feels so good.

The mystique, exoticness, difference that had so intoxicated me when I first came along to China with my wife, when she was hired to teach English in a foreign languages middle school in Tianjin in 1985, had begun to wear thin. What had once seemed so foreign and strange, so impossible for me to know, not to mention write knowledgeably about, was beginning to seem quite familiar. Even my inability to speak and understand spoken Chinese had given way to surprisingly easy talk and hearing, although I still could read only a few characters and write even fewer. I had more or less successfully convinced myself that this latter wasn't absolutely necessary to my research. After all, I was not and never will be a Sinologist. I'm a Western sociologist who has been studying some small part of contemporary Chinese life. And as such, this summer's revisits to the seventeen families we had earlier studied went so smoothly and seemed so easy that the sense of accomplishment I had enjoyed from just getting into their homes and lives two years earlier had faded.

And more researchers studying all manner of Chinese life past and present were coming to China; and more cooperative projects had begun involving 'famous' scholars from 'famous' universities in the United States. It wasn't any longer so strange or unusual to be doing social science research *in China* rather than interviewing refugees in Hong Kong. And I had always felt self-consciously *not* famous and *not* from a famous university. I could hardly even speak Chinese. All of these — I was sure — along with a 'research design' that was probably seen as insufficiently 'scientific' and too 'personal', had kept me from winning the several grants for which I had applied to the major funding agencies on China research in the United States. The more deeply I had gone into this project, the more multiple my positioning as an outsider here — and even there — had become. As I sought to inhabit the margins, I indeed experienced marginality. (But margins always exist relative to, indeed, help to construct, centres. What were those centres?) Sometimes I feel suffocated by this project and these relationships, unable to get free of them and unable to succeed with them. I am not at all sure that I can gain closure, can 'make something' out of it; be the 'hero' of conventional social science (ethnographic) research. Be . . . a man?

There are many more 'foreigners' in China now who have other sorts of profits in mind: to take advantage of, indeed to create, vast commercial markets and/or similarly vast pools of cheap labour in a state only gradually given to controls and regulations to protect people and the environment. The urban landscape had changed, even in the two years since our last leaving. Endless restaurants, stalls, sellers, concerns about money, street-wise beggars, uncontrolled enterprise; cellular phones; MacDonalds, and even Cadillacs. *Caveat emptor!* These are all too familiar. After all, we are Americans, from the United States. China, Tianjin — the strange, alluring, and slightly sinister place — has been had. And part of the relief I was feeling seemed linked to a growing sense that I could have it too. Finally, I was beginning to feel that I could actually write about it.

Zhi zu chang le

It was a beautiful spring day outside, the humid air of Tianjin summer having not yet arrived. The cool, May morning breeze moved softly through the second-floor apartment, with its southern and northern exposures — one face to the sun, *yang mian*, one to the clouds, *yin mian*. The flat was typical of those built in Chinese cities in the decade after Liberation. . . .

A familiar sort of ethnographic beginning this. Detailed description from 'on high' of a place brings the far-away real close to you, the reader. It was — is — there, and so were — are — we, now, in the text. We will take you around. Stay with us. Just like the humid air, cool breeze, brick walls of that solid place, so too will the characters . . . or 'respondents' emerge to tell their truths to us/you.

'Gao *lao*. Please tell us about your illness, about your family, and your work. Give us some introduction, please,' said the younger man softly, as he looked up from his notebook, meeting the old man's eyes with his last words of invitation. The two sociologists were beginning their first interview with Gao Changping, 66, and his wife Huang Yushu, 67. The elderly couple both were well-educated, having graduated as classmates from university in 1948, the year before The People's Republic of China was founded. They had been together a long time; in fact, they were acquainted as children.

Mr Gao is a retired senior banking accountant who suffers several chronic conditions. We visited him and his family from May until July 1991, with follow-up meetings in summers of 1993 and 1996. Mr Gao had begun to receive the services of a sickbed doctor from the cadre sanatorium in the spring of 1987.

Although Gao Changping was on the first list the sanatorium leaders gave us in late fall, when his name came up again in our discussions the following May we almost eliminated him from the last set of interviews. We had already interviewed several relatively privileged families where the patient was a retired senior cadre. When we first met Mr Gao, a week earlier, we even told him that after hearing some details of his illness and caregiving situation we might stop the interviews, because we didn't want to collect the 'same information' we had already obtained from other senior cadres.

As I think about it now, it strikes me how odd that might have sounded to them. The idea that because we had 'collected' information from other men who were relatively privileged in education and employment, we would then have known something fundamental about him; that what he might then tell us somehow would be redundant; would provide us with 'nothing new' for our project. That must have sounded at least strange.

But it is not odd from within the generalising logic of social science. Laihua and I had both learned in school, although separated by some 15 years and 18,000 miles, that we are sociologists, not historians. *They* are concerned primarily with the details of particular and usually important people's actions and 'significant' events. We sociologists, by contrast, are concerned with social patterns; with structures and processes that are pan- or trans-individual. We are concerned with 'the social' rather than 'the individual'; more interested in studying average or typical social types who had no particular names or faces that might distract attention from the form. As good social scientists we were trying to maximise the diversity of *types* of people and situations in our sample (but where do those *types* come from?). In effect, we told Mr Gao and his wife that the interesting thing about them was the extent to which they did or did not share certain 'characteristics' in common with others in similar and different situations.

If Laihua expressed this in Chinese as bluntly as I put it to him in English when we were preparing for our first visit (which I suspect he did not), perhaps they thought it just one more foreign peculiarity. More happily, perhaps they didn't quite understand what Laihua meant, and, themselves a little uneasy at the beginning of this new adventure, chose simply to let it pass. In any case, they said they understood, and so we went on.

The four of us sat in the larger of the two rooms, Laihua and I in armchairs against one wall, separated by a small, glass-topped table; Gao across from us on a sofa with a large white crocheted doily along the back, and Huang to our right, at the foot of the bed they shared. They both wore brightly white shirts that set off their open, alert faces. She of course smiled more readily than he, and right away we noticed that one side of his mouth was slightly drawn, but not so much as to affect the amount or clarity of his speech. Indeed, we came to think of him as one of the most articulate, meticulous, and thorough chroniclers of his illness and family life. And his eyes belied a usually intense, serious face and marked his facility for wit and humour that put us somewhat at ease. Laihua especially seemed to appreciate the way he spoke, the care he took with their language.

Excuse me. I realise I'm disrupting the story a bit by jumping in here, and by bringing up material from one of your earlier visits with my wife and me at our new place, but your description of our old house made me want to say that I really do miss that place. My wife and I lived there for so many years; over forty all together. My two daughters were born when we lived there, and they grew up in those two small rooms. Moving to this new, much larger apartment in late 1991 seemed like such a good idea. It's bigger, and has enough room for one of my children to come and live here when the two of us get so old or sick we can't live alone. And a telephone. We have a telephone now. That makes many things much easier.

You may have noticed that there are no quotation marks around the above paragraph. Now you notice. There are such marks opening the next paragraph. If you ask, 'So. Did Mr Gao actually say the above words to you?' No. But he could have. He might have. And in a collection of various moments, he did. But we in fact made up his little speech. But we in fact made up all of them, including this text itself. Does that make you 'trust' us less?

'Of course, this is a very good place. And my oldest daughter and her husband moved here too, in this same building. But . . . sometimes I ride my bicycle back to that old house and look at our·building and the yard in back. I stop in the park at the corner where we would meet our neighbours in the evenings after supper for a chat. There are so many big trees there that give cool shade in the summer. That was really a good place. I didn't realise it would be so hard to adjust to this new place. It's much less convenient to go shopping for vegetables and food. Here I don't know any of the neighbours, and outside, around the building . . . is a terrible mess.

When you finished your work in the summer of 1991, I was feeling quite good. But before long I got depressed. It's elderly depression — we call it *lao nian yiyu zheng* — I know. I read that book you gave me, Laihua, the one you and your colleague wrote,[5] and I remember the part about how old people sometimes have difficulty passing the period when they first retire. When I read it I thought, 'I have failed to pass that period.' I had . . . and still have a real sense of loss.

Before I retired I didn't think about this — that I would have trouble adjusting to retirement. Remember, you first came to our house just a few months after I had formally retired in January 1990. I just didn't realise. . . . And I haven't dealt well with the move to this new house. Didn't anticipate how the different neighbourhood and environment would affect me, how my relationships with my friends there would change. In fact, everything has changed. But I hadn't expected it. Now, although my living conditions are better than before, I always think about the past.'

'Gao *lao*, I wonder if you worry too much about yourself, your illness, and your situation. Perhaps it would be better if you didn't think so much about these things,' Laihua suggested.

'Yes, you are right. He thinks and worries about his diseases more than other people,' Huang added. 'But it got even worse when he began to focus on being retired and then moving. He was the worst in 1992. Always unhappy. I don't think he laughed once that whole time, even when he watched those crosstalk programs on television.'

'This kind of problem is not unusual back home,' I added. 'Many older people have trouble adjusting to retirement, especially if their work has been an important part of their lives. Big changes also might be more difficult the older we get.' Laihua translated my Chinese for them since they looked slightly puzzled as I spoke. They nodded. Whenever I spoke about 'the United States' I always felt I was conveying weighty truths, even though back home I was critical of precisely that kind of expert positioning. Nonetheless, it seemed a moment during these interviews when I could clear a space for myself and fully occupy it, even though (or perhaps because?) I usually could do it only in English, with Laihua then translating.

'After he came back from the sanatorium, though, he was better. He had begun, I think, to adjust himself to his new neighbourhood. This year has been better,' Huang hoped.

'But there is good news in my family,' Gao went on. 'My youngest daughter just had a baby. She is 36 years old and just had a baby boy. He is two months old.'

'Oh really!?' We both smiled broadly.

'It's very good. Your situation is really good now,' enthused Laihua. 'Your oldest daughter lives in the same building here. Your youngest daughter just had a baby. You can take care of him when he gets bigger. That would be really fine.'

I felt myself pulling away from this sentiment. Was I so optimistic for Gao *lao*? No. But then I myself didn't have any children, so perhaps I was unable to imagine the joy that might come from such anticipations; the prospect that having a grandson could dissolve the frustrations and depression of ageing, illness, and retirement. I thought to myself, this must be one of those games I often see Laihua play; that thinking positive thoughts will make things better or at least keep them from getting worse. Put a good face on it and it will be good. Sometimes his unshakeable confidence in the powers of optimism was a little annoying. Could it be so easy?

'You are right. *Wo zong bu ren tou* — I never recognise my situation for what it is. For example, I didn't see how good my old house really was, so I moved here. I was wrong to move.'

I smiled to myself. This man was still the worrier we had met two years ago. Not given to wild enthusiasms. I appreciated that.

Huang said, with a trace of exasperation, 'You have to face facts.'

'*Zhi zu chang le!*,' Laihua added quickly. 'You'll stay happy if you face facts!'

'Yes!' chimed Huang. '*Zhi zu chang le!*'

I thought to myself, Gao is right. At least with worry and doubt about facts there remains the possibility that the facts one does not like might be changed.

Feeling, duty, care

19 July 1994
Des Moines
Dear LH:

You have been such a good letter writer lately. Many thanks. Your most recent one came the other day. By this time you should have received the chapter on Gao Changping. I am now working on Wang Su Min and family, so have a few things to say about them here.

I have no very clear logic for moving from Gao to Wang, but if there is one, here it is: here we have another story about caregiving and family that involves issues of gender and that focuses on women. I don't mean that Gao's story did focus on women especially, but he does talk about the daughter/ daughter-in-law and son/son-in-law business, and he does have two daughters who have been supportive caregivers (especially *dajie*).

In our Chapter on Gao Changping, we criticise the generalising logic of social scientific investigation. While we affirm that hesitance to see import-ance only in the general or type, it is disingenuous to suggest that we are uninterested in, or in fact do not depend upon, questions of generality here; or that our choice of stories to tell is somehow made without regard for generalities having to do with family life and caregiving practices in 'urban China'. Indeed, we write some of the people and family situations here primarily *because* they are or seem to be contrary to (or consistent with) the 'patterns' of practices linked to the research object 'the urban Chinese family' and its existence in the foremost research literature. And the very production of 'the interesting', in another generalising process that marks but extends well beyond the space of academic social science, relies heavily on irony, highlighting that which appears to be other than what was expected or known.

Questions of form stand forward here again in our attempt to make the very making of a chapter itself an object of some attention. For a chapter's writing must be disciplined. Beyond the more obvious physical para-meters, such as length and subdivision — not to mention the disciplines of linearity,[6] footnoting, type font and size, chapters are supposed to be 'about' something; some 'thing' that gives the words, sentences, paragraphs and pages a coherence beyond their own boundaries. The designation 'chap-ter' is itself a generalising move. And within social science writing, a very typical device for producing such coherence is to 'raise' the mundane details of the 'data' at hand to a more 'general' or 'theoretical' register. Whatever the chapter is about in its particulars, it will be about many and diverse others, different things too. This 'too' is the promise of theory: to reduce complexity and difference to essence; bridge enormous distance; put unseen (or not fully appreciated) similarity into bold relief. There is both a politics and a morality embedded in this move to theory; and, of course, from its place of deployment — the theorising subject — it has been seen as a centring and unifying flow of power.[7]

Writing a 'we' is a similar sort of centring and consolidation. For the instances of this pronoun that you find here imply a shared authorial/ writing position, and thus cover over the gaping, mostly unexplored and no doubt unrecognised spaces that separate the two of us (and this 'us' is of course here written as though it too were a transparent access to two sites of centred consciousness outside this writing). Which of the various and many 'we's' on these pages could easily be broken open to display differ-ence, disagreement; lack of shared understanding when that is precisely what is being implied by the pronoun's use? The smooth and seamless surfaces produced aid 'fast forward' reading. And in this text, the we's are in almost all cases written by the older, 'American professor' rather than by the younger, more deferential Chinese researcher who continues to live and work at the Tianjin Academy of Social Sciences. The former writes a jointly-authored text in which he has written most of the words. The latter received drafts of said text segments, 'we's' written in; a shared position, for the most part, marked and closed. And the text is of course in English, Schneider's rather than Wang's 'native language.'[8]

This reminds 'us' that quite aside from what sort of disorientation and despair the American might have experienced in 'the field', the actual *writing* in 'the project' involves practices that bring into place the orderli-ness and unity — the discipline — that was lacking in that field. Which of the 'we's' here are more Joseph's than Laihua's? Which are more and which less fraught? How might Laihua resist those 'we's' that Joseph 'really wants'? Which 'we's' serve Joseph, located in a North American academic and scholarly world in which the important questions may well turn on issues that have virtually no currency in the professional and/or personal worlds in which Laihua moves? How will Laihua and Joseph be differentially benefited, or harmed, by the publication of this book?

While these surely are not issues peculiar to multi-cultural projects, they take on added importance when authors live in contexts so discrepant not only in terms of what sorts of work and accomplishment are rewarded and how, but also, frankly, in terms of how disapproval and even punishment for intellectual/ideological 'bad judgement' is handed out. Indeed, all the familiar issues dealing with relationships between 'respondents' and 'researchers' discussed in conventional texts on ethnographic methods seem to bear on our 'we', for Laihua and his 'story' become 'data' for this text in a way in which Joseph and his do not.[9]

But perhaps you still want to know why this segment begins with what appears to be a letter. In the process of visiting the families and then writing this book, we talked a great deal of 'what our book is or might be about'. Some of this talk was face to face; some over the telephone; much through letters between Des Moines and Tianjin. Perhaps for some who write books this is a very simple or clear and securely fastened thing: what your book is about. For us this has never been the case. While there are many strands that make up this ambiguity and fluidity — some of which are on display here — one of them is a desire to resist the discipline that comes with what Roland Barthes has called the 'readerly' text — one primarily to be followed, attended to, known, mastered, and 'copied'.[10] (Incidentally, we Chinese have a lot of experience with this sort of text and its power, although Joseph has asked me to say that I have not read this book by Barthes. Or, has he simply written these sentences himself?) The readerly text, then, is an authoritative text; it is offered up as one that contains Truths to be obtained, consumed; capitalised upon. Indeed, the point of the readerly text is to become transparent, so that what is 'really important', this Truth, can come through unhindered. Readerly texts are especially useful in writing realism, by which we mean here 'true stories'.

But Barthes recommends the pleasures of the *writerly* text, wherein readers are regularly encouraged in the very reading to become writers, or, readers/writers. Such a text is full of marked 'seams', 'rough spots', aporias; it makes the reader more rather than less aware of how writing can be a technology for producing closure and smooth, tidy surfaces; the cleaner the better. A criticism of writerly texts often offered up from within the realist genre is that they are 'self-indulgent' and 'get nowhere' because they focus, as it were, too much on themselves.[11] But in the face of readerly smooth surfaces, says Barthes, one is 'plunged into a kind of idleness — he is intransitive; he is, in short, *serious*: instead of functioning himself . . . he is left with no more than the poor freedom either to accept or reject the text: reading is nothing more than a *referendum*'.[12]

In this book we try to leave in some of the seams and messiness, making the 'openness' of the writing more apparent. Sometimes we don't tell you what is happening — who is speaking — in the hope that you will become more consciously a reader/writer of an other (your 'own') text that would be linked to this one. This kind of writing is seen by some as an egregious transgression against responsible scholarship. 'Why draw attention to you?! Given all we need to know about China (for instance, but "the world" would do in this space as well), tell us about what is really important.' And 'China', and 'the Chinese family' are fine examples of important things 'we' want and need to know about (but why?). Some Sinologists and others whose task in life is to study 'China' seem particularly offended by this sort of writerly, sometimes called 'post-modern', text.

But precisely toward writing such a text, our strategy here is to collect four letters we two exchanged during the summer of 1994 that are focused on a familiar dilemma encountered by those who write: 'now that we have finished *this* piece, what shall we do *next*, and *on what grounds?*'

All boxed and bracketed text, along with the footnotes, are additions made after our original letters were written. Consistent with our project, we strive to have it, as it were, 'both ways'. The letters convey our 'truths' about these families while their form and the diverse intersections in them can be occasions to draw attention to the inevitably accomplished nature of the smooth surfaces that a more conventional chapter would offer.

In this family, we have, as I note Laihua's own words in his fieldnotes, 'one of the most interesting and unusual stories' among those that we wrote. . . .

Notes

1. This paper grew out of a presentation at *Knowledge and Discourse '96*, an international conference held at the University of Hong Kong in June 1996. Thanks to Nigel Bruce for his encouragement in the present version; and thanks to the Drake University Center for the Humanities and the Tianjin Academy of Social Sciences for various fundings that supported the project from which it comes.
2. See Lemert (1995), *Sociology After the Crisis*. See also Clough (1992), *The End(s) of Ethnography*.
3. This subject position, although marked as 'masculine', does not require a particular configuration of genitals or body in order to be activated. Moreover, this position remains, feminist critique to the contrary notwithstanding, an object of desire still. And with good reason, for it is a positionality

filled with opportunities for diverse pleasures, all of which should not be denigrated. A fuller appreciation of this requires a fine-grained examination of this diversity, seeking to sort out and critique those bits that help construct stories of domination and oppression as just, as natural, and as the prerogative of particular kinds of bodies (cf. B. Davies (1989) *Frogs and Snails and Feminist Tales*: and (1993) *Shards of Glass*).

4. See discussion in Nichols's (1991) *Representing Reality* of similar sorts of attempts, some as early as the 1920s, in the history of documentary film.

5. Wang and Wang (1990), *Laonian Shenghuo Fangshi Tan Mi*.

6. One of the most helpful discussions of textual linearity — and how to disturb it — can be found in Landow's fine book on hypertextual writing, *Hypertext*. Much of the writing in the book from which these segments is taken is influenced by developments Landow discusses, including some attempts to actually write parts of this text as hypertext.

7. Latour offers up a very clear view of how this writing subject deploys the power of explanatory discourse. See his *The politics of explanation* (1988).

8. 'We' should note that 'we' are publishing in Chinese a considerably more modern text than the present one, in which Wang is the first author. That text, which one of the 'I/eyes' here cannot read, consists of major segments from the total corpus of fieldnotes that another I wrote during the visits 'we' made to the families in Tianjin.

9. In the many computer files associated with this project there is indeed a folder called 'LH's Story', a collection of autobiographical texts Laihua wrote during the time he first visited the United States and lived with Joseph and Nancy Schneider. There is no such file called 'Joseph's Story', at least not that Joseph knows about.

10. See Barthes, *S/Z* (1974).

11. You will have noticed, of course, how readily 'the object' of analysis here, at least in conventional ethnographic terms, disappears or gets sidetracked by other objects.

12. Barthes, *S/Z*, p.4.

5

Producing new Asian masculinities
Allan Luke

*She wondered if this man — who owned a house, car, dishwasher,
VCR, TV, CD, and the complete recordings of the Beach Boys —
even had a single photograph of his mother.*

LAUREEN MAR (1993)

New cosmopolitan identities

In his discussion of 'cosmopolitics', Robbins (1998) describes the vexed
historical relationship between nationalism, 'statism' and identity, a relationship that has become even more complex in the contexts of cultural and
economic globalisation. In an intriguing attempt to capture the dilemma of
the new cosmopolitan, Robbins asks: What is worth 'dying for' beyond the
nation state and its political, military and economic sovereignty?

To answer the question, we must turn to examine new expressions of
cultural identity, of gender, of local affiliation and loyalty. The unprecedented
and ongoing mass migrations of the post-war period have yielded new classes
of people and new genres of identity — diverse and complex transnational
identities that range from those of guest workers, to nomadic intellectuals,
to those of corporate business travellers. At the same time, one of the legacies of postcolonial writing is a radical scepticism towards those orientalist
and essentialist vocabularies for describing diasporic peoples and migrant
populations. This chapter is an exploration of how we might begin to talk —
non-stereotypically, in differentiated and heteroglossic voices — about one
family of emergent identities and affinities: new Asian masculinities.

The legacies of Ellis Island, Snowy River and other early and mid-century
mass immigrations are social scientific codes for naming and talking about
migrations and migrants. Whether through economic, political, cultural or
military upheaval, what were taken by host cultures to be homogeneous
groups of people relocated, experiencing what became predictable cycles of
economic disenfranchisement, cultural displacement and assimilation. They

and their children confronted practical issues of intergenerational language retention and blended cultural identities — the latter typically resolved after several generations through the assumption of new 'nation–state' citizenship and 'mainstream' cultural identity. These explanatory frameworks — whether represented in sociological analyses, contemporary human geography studies, immigration and citizenship laws, or the grids of specification of governmental instruments such as the census — are the products of alternating anti- and pro-immigration, assimilationist/monocultural and liberal/welfarist discourses developed in the United States and the Commonwealth. My point here is that the very categories for talking about migration are discourses of surveillance and control (Luke and Luke, in press).

The economics and 'cosmopolitics' of fast capitalism mark out a change in the social facts and everyday experiences of migration. The complexity of population movement brought on by increasingly accessible and rapid transportation and communications infrastructure, by voluntary and involuntary mass movement of workers in a global division of labour, and the rapidity and potentially transitory nature of their residency, have meant that the early to mid-twentieth century lexicon that we have for describing migrants, travellers, visitors, indeed even 'multicultural' hybrids or 'stateless' subjects is conceptually and empirically limited (Robertson *et al.* 1994). Setting aside for a moment the preferred academic terms of 'border crossers' and 'multiple subjectivities', the question facing social scientists, and perhaps more importantly the very diasporic people that they might study, is at once theoretical and practical: how do we talk about and across identities in ways that do not *a priori* position new forms of difference as subordinated artefacts of minority or diasporic cultures?

While recognising that a significant majority of migrants continue to be positioned in lower socio-economic classes and localities in the countries of the EEC, North America, Japan, Australia and other Asia–Pacific economies — much as their post-war predecessors were — there is also the need to develop narrative descriptions of minority identity that are not victim-oriented, that begin to describe the complexity, the play and the power of new identities of difference within white-dominated cultures, and that supplant the liberal condescension that continues, to cite Bob Dylan's 1960s song, to 'pity the poor immigrant'.

The Asian diaspora — both as cultural phenomenon and as transnational business and corporate network — has been a longstanding object of study. In her discussion of new 'Chinese Cosmopolitans', Ong (1996) discusses the significance of the *guanxi* — or patriarchal/familial bonds — as a guiding cultural and economic principle of transnational Chinese identity and of its new social configurations, relations and identities: the Hong Kong 'astronaut', the 'parachute family' of overseas Chinese communities. Ong concludes that these characteristics constitute an emergent *homo economicus* for a multinational economy. Certainly, the networks and capillaries of these communities would be crucial in tracking the remaking of Asia–Pacific metropolitan environments (see for example Wilson and Dirlik 1995). The migration of business capital from Hong Kong to Vancouver has become the archetype, with other nascent examples including the emergence of a Chinese-Australian population of 20,000 middle to upper socio-economic level migrants from Taiwan, Hong Kong and Singapore in the Brisbane/Gold Coast corridor.

A materialist analysis of new transnational classes is needed to understand how loyalties other than to the nation and the corporation are central to transnational distributions of resources and power. Yet matters of identity are more complex than their economic motivations and contexts. Precisely because of the degree to which identity formation is contingent upon cultural systems of representation such as regimes of consumption and popular culture, media and cinema (Hall and DuGay 1996), there is a danger that these new analyses will lead to economic reductionism, a move potentially as epistemologically limiting as cultural essentialist arguments of a core phenotypical 'Chineseness' (see Wei-ming 1991). Whatever their intentions, descriptions of the emergence of a transnational Asian economic class risk reconstructing the 'Jews of Asia' stereotype. As we begin to question the adequacy of both the monocultural colonialist equation of nation state/race/language/identity (Hall 1992) and the ubiquitous binary 'between two cultures' metaphors of Western multiculturalism (Luke and Luke 1998), a key challenge is to develop a cultural analysis of these complex kinds of identities, and their fields of representation.

As Ien Ang's (1994) remarkable paper 'On not speaking Chinese' signals — the heterogeneity and heteroglossia of 'being overseas Chinese' is far more contingent and strategically powerful than either economic or cultural reductionist arguments suggest. The task of talking about identity is made much easier by three key moves:

- the demonstration that identity does not precede representation, and that socially and textually constructed subjectivities are produced by multiple, complex, and at times overtly competing textual fields of representation
- the documentation of the emergence of complex, multiply hyphenated identities; and
- the evidence that postcolonial, diasporic and minority subjects engage in complex kinds of local reconstruction and blending of available knowledges, texts, discourses, and identity claims.

The description of a diasporic, hyphenated Asian identity would need to consider the representation of gender and sexuality, and on how these cosmopolitan Asian identities are changing intergenerationally in, Ang argues, post-modern conditions of cultural production. My focus here is on the reconstruction of Asian masculinities. My aim is not to attempt to recover a singular kind of new Asian identity, but to explore critically the production of new Asian masculinities in cinema, novels, biography and other narrative forms.

Asians in production

In recent years there has been a flood of movies, books, biographies and documentaries about Asia and Asians. These range from memoirs about China like *Wild Swans* (Chang 1991) to historical cinema narratives like *The Last Emperor* (1997), from the powerful images of revisionist and reformist Chinese cinema (*Raise the Red Lantern* (1992), *Shanghai Triad* (1995)), to the post-modern work of Asian-American film makers like Wayne Wang and Australia's Clara Law, from Hollywood reinventions of the immigrant experience like *The Joy Luck Club* (1993) to the Broadway orientalism of *Madame M.* The filming of *The Chinese Box* (1997) during the handover of Hong Kong to China — in effect a simulacrum of the event through the personae of Jeremy Irons and Gong Li — itself marked the degree to which Asia itself had become worthy of instant commodification for Western audiences (though one wonders if indeed a television mini-series on the Southeast Asian currency crisis would attract a mass audience: stranger things have happened). These portrayals also indicate the resilience of archetypal orientalist themes such as the depiction of Asian women as erotic objects of Western ex-patriots and cultural tourists. They confirm as well the continued marketing logic that Asia and Asians are not viable without an Anglo/American 'A-list' leading man.

Whatever their cultural contexts, motivations and consequences, representations of Asia and Asians have become big business in the US, Australia, Canada, the UK and, to a somewhat lesser extent, Europe. Taken as a corpus, these works vary from prototypes of a new commodification of the orient by the West, to profound attempts to represent and portray cultural histories and lives that have been silent and unmarked in Western literature and cinema. The latter applies specifically to reformist Chinese cinema, but also to recent work from Vietnam (*The Scent of Green Papaya* (1993)), Taiwan (*Eat Drink, Man Woman* (1994)) and other countries.

Perhaps what differentiates this corpus from feminist and postcolonial 'minority discourses' (JanMohammed and Lloyd 1990),[1] is the actual historical coextension and simultaneity of work from diasporic Asian writers — Asian-Americans, Australians, Canadians, Malaysian-Chinese and others — with the new literary and cinematic texts emerging from Asia itself, from China, Hong Kong, Taiwan and other countries. There is of course a set of historical convergences and enabling conditions at work here, including reduced ideological constraints on Chinese and other regional Asian moviemakers, and the valuing of Hong Kong talent and movies (and, indeed, investment capital) in Hollywood, Vancouver and Sydney. That is, a political economy of media and representation has marketed diasporic discourses on Asia as consumable texts for 'western' audiences, and has moved to explore largely untapped Asian audiences and markets.

Unlike the 'first wave' of, say, African-American literature and cinema in the 1960s and 1970s, this work doesn't form a singular message for main-stream, English-speaking audiences. There's no axiomatic or unified political message at work here precisely because of the geographic, cultural and spatial heterogeneity of Asian experiences. The lack of a singular Asian voice or perspective, its range of sources, themes and contents, itself constitutes a statement of the heteroglossia of new Asian identities. These range from archetypal migrant epics² to John Woo's Hong Kong versions of Hollywood action movies (*Broken Arrow* (1996)), and Ang Lee's representation of insular New England (*The Ice Storm* (1997)). Whether these latter works, with no overt 'Asian content' but produced by a particular epistemological and commercial vision, even count as part of the new 'oriental' cinema is, indeed, a matter for further discussion. What is interesting is the extent to which North American critics tend to 'read off' an 'Asian-ness' from what other-wise would be unmarked Hollywood texts, particularly in Ang Lee's case.

If we leave aside these debates for a moment, the works that represent Asian experience begin to constitute a dialogue between Asian experience north and south, east and west, in homelands and diaspora — a dialogue where, Rey Chow (1993) observes, the 'native' is invented and reinvented in claims of cultural authenticity, truth and essence. My point here is that as much as this burst of aesthetic production is evidence of a political economy of representation of Asia and Asians and Asian localities, a formal com-modification of postcolonial and diasporic experience — it also provides an opportunity for the working through and articulation of new narratives of identity. It is a profitable surface for a new Asian self in literature and autobiography.

New Asian masculinities

One of the principal problems of the Hollywood version of *The Joy Luck Club* was its use of Asian males as character foils for the intergenerational relationships of mothers and their daughters. In that portrayal, Chinese grandfathers and younger Chinese–American males alike are portrayed as flat characters whose principal affective resources are a kind of silent and repressed despair and resignation.

In the midst of the explosion of writing and creativity on the Asian diaspora, new perspectives on masculinity and sexuality have emerged. Garrett Hongo (1995), Ben Fong-Torres (1995), Russell Leong (1996), David Mura (1996) and others in the US have begun to write and talk autobiographically about

Asian men caught up in everyday dilemmas and contradictions about sexuality and desire in white-dominated cultures.

The results are not the archetypal romanticised versions of Asian masculinity that we saw in European cinema like *Indochine* (1992) and *The Lover*, both European authored and produced. In the latter, adapted from a Marguerite Duras novel, the unknowability of the Asian male interiority was translated into a mysterious and, to European women, irresistible sexual force. Nor are these new works migrant victim narratives preoccupied with white racism. In this regard they differ in standpoint from the narratives of liberation of African Americans that stretch in historical lineage to the slave narratives, and they differ in standpoint from the quasi-historical, 'roots' narratives of Maxine Kingston-Hong, Amy Tam and others. These narratives of identity have also arisen relatively autonomously from the corpus of work in English-speaking countries on (predominantly white) masculinities, both the critical, pro-feminist work that explores the emergence of 'hegemonic masculinities' (Connell 1987), and the recent men's studies backlash against the epistemic and political claims of second- and third-wave feminism.

The emergent literature on Asian masculinity addresses how Asian men are struggling with identity and image, agency and power in cultures and sexual economies that historically have marginalised them — about how we are to find 'suitable partners' within and across competing cultural communities; how we are to develop a self-understanding of our complicity in both Asian and white patriarchy and sexism, and what this might mean in terms of sexual preferences, practices and ideologies. This is long overdue. And it has raised for a new generation what are potentially liberating and vexing questions about what it is to be Asian and male in White-dominated cultures. So apart from its obvious political economy and textual free play of the new commodification of the Asian male, this work also has turned many of us to reconsider ourselves, our places in White and Asian patriarchy, our desires and our histories.

I was brought up as a 'number one son' in a 1950s Chinese-American household in Los Angeles — with the requisite domestic privilege and patriarchy of that status. The very partitioning and division of space in our 1950s Los Angeles home set up spaces and conditions for intimacy and power differently from that of the other families — Chicano, Jewish, and American — in our neighborhood.[3] Yet much of my self-understanding came from living most of my adult life with and alongside feminists, in my case, my partner, my daughter and my colleagues. Looking back, I am tempted to ask what kind of technology of self-inspection, what kinds of discourses on the self and masculinity were available to us as Chinese-American males. Certainly nobody I grew up with or in my family went to psychotherapy — to even speak to the school counsellor about the inner workings of the family or community would have been unthinkable.[4] Nor did my father leave me with an elaborated code of emotion — offering instead a kind of stoicism as a shorthand for emotion — the emotion our White partners find so lacking, so absent, even where they find a sensitivity for family, a capacity that is almost feminine in mainstream Western categories.[5] So how do we narrate ourselves?

Asian-American men have often struggled to represent ourselves by blending and restructuring the cultures of others — as a very deliberate kind of bricolage of styles and voices. As adolescents, many of us wanted to emulate Black and Chicano musicians, athletes and street dudes. And we joined the counter-culture, as Ben Fong-Torres's (1995) tale suggests, precisely because it appeared to be colour-blind in its Marcusian pursuit of unity, solidarity and liberation — and, not coincidentally, freedom from sexual repression.

Looking in the mirror, we find ourselves without any of the defining characteristics of dominant masculinity — white skin, hairy chests, beards and facial hair, big arms and big muscles. Quite the contrary: we have all the characteristics of something Other, something more feminine in the normative eye of Western sexuality: slender and relatively hairless bodies, differently textured and coloured skin and straight hair. In Western public representations of masculinity we are defined in terms of absence, lack or silence. In this kind of sexual environment, we are invisible — not present, without a place or 'name' in the discourses and practices of white male sexuality. Our faces, bodies and voices appear neither on the media, on the sports fields, in the legislatures, nor in the fashion business.

The issue of Asian masculinity is at play in Clara Law's recent Australian-produced film, *Floating Life* (1996). Law's film focuses on how two generations of a Chinese family cope with displacement to 'The Chinese Diaspora' of Australia and Germany. For Father, moving to Australia is about adjusting to changes in his children and family — changes that include his sons' rebellion and his daughter's mental illness — as much as it is about adjusting to Australian culture, space and place. His Eldest Son is the last member of a Hong Kong family to migrate to Australia, following his sisters, younger brothers and parents. Immersed in a yuppie Hong Kong lifestyle as a participant in the emergent transnational business class, he looks nostalgically at his family house in Kowloon as 'the place where I first ejaculated in 1970 . . . for 3 full seconds of pleasure'. For him, the loss of the 'home' of Hong Kong is something more than cultural shock. He experiences a loss of desire, sexuality and masculinity, his unborn child, and, indeed, his Hong Kong lovers.

Meanwhile, his younger teenaged brothers are having the time of their lives — until their elder sister catches them with cigarettes, condoms, beer and pornography and tosses the boys out of the house. For them, becoming Australian is about experiencing a new, exciting hybrid sexuality and identity in a culture of strangers, both those from their Australian community and within their own family. And, surprisingly, they find more tolerance of their emergent masculinities from their grandparents than their elder sister. In a scene that could have been lifted from *Puberty Blues* (1981), Law portrays them as hybrid Aussie youth, drinking beer, smoking, and talking about girls on the beach. This is indeed a strikingly different image from that of the new cosmopolitan Asian male *qua homo economicus*.

The portrayal of Asian males as sexual beings in mainstream White cultures caught up in complex interethnic worlds of desire and pleasure is new. We needn't look far to find TV and movie images of violent gangs and kung fu fighters, inscrutable businessmen and confused tourists, and occasional portrayals in advertisements, where we might be spotted selling Asian food, tourism, Japanese cars or, in the worst of early-twentieth-century ethnic stereotypes, laundry soap. Yet there are few biographical or fictional representations of Asian males, and even fewer serious portrayals on TV or in the movies. Where we are portrayed as something less than evil or exotic scenery, we may turn up as non-emotive, repressed and desexed props — a critique which was recently raised about *The Joy Luck Club*.

Growing up Chinese-American in the 1950s, the images I saw of myself in public culture were few and far between: the occasional Second World War villain, evil Fu-Manchus (often played by white people in 'yellow-face'), the houseboys and cooks on dramas and sitcoms like *Bonanza* (1959–73) and *Bachelor Father* (1957–62), some of whom were portrayed on TV by my family and relatives. Television and movie portrayals offered us a simple opposition of good and evil masculinity — with the Good Chinaman portrayed as subservient, loyal, trustworthy to white males in power and the Bad Chinaman portrayed as greedy and violent, potentially disruptive of the civil order, if not a Communist (Hamamoto 1994).

At the same time we were saturated by images about what it means to be sexually powerful males in white society: from John Wayne to Elvis, from John Kennedy to Mickey Mantle. We saw nothing in public culture that resembled ourselves, excepting the face-to-face images of our fathers and grandfathers, uncles and brothers. Until I saw Jason Scott Lee onscreen in the 1990s, I hadn't seen a sexualised image of the Asian male that looked real to me, or that looked like me, an image of the kind of boys and men that we might become, who we should hang out with, the kinds of partners, lovers and families we might encounter. We were invisible. We were de-masculinised.

In the interwar and post-war periods, Asian men of my grandfather's and father's generations were often considered something 'less than men' when they ventured out of their immediate neighbourhoods — the experience described in Kam Louie's (in press) analysis of the negation of Chinese men's masculinity when they immigrate to Australia. They were of course patriarchs within Chinese communities. My maternal grandfather was a farmer and butcher in a Chinese farming village in Hawaii; my grandmother, who had 7 children, had her feet bound as a child in China. But like Law's characters, these men's patriarchy and sexism, however oppressive and powerful it might have been within our family, was powerless and meaningless 'outside' in the larger White community. Within White-dominated public culture, the term 'Chinaman' is not a marker of recognition of your agency or wisdom, your desire or strength, but nor is it a marker of your patriarchal power. It is a marker of your vulnerability and invisibility — as a cultural and political being, but also as a sexual being.

Asian women, of course, were and are portrayed as objects of White desire — rarely in relation to us, but always as they might be seen by white men. In both mainstream cinema and the major subgenre of European pornography, Asian women appear as childlike, eroticised figures: as Suzi Wong figures, as concubines and prostitutes, as house servants and mail-order brides. The cinematic and pornographic representation of Asian women thus reads like a textbook case of Orientalism. The complexities of being an Asian working woman, sister, mother and partner in White culture remain altogether hidden from public culture.

Producing a new masculinity

So what kinds of 'men' are we within white homosocial economies and cultures? The contemporary Chinaman, and particularly the overseas diasporic Chinese, is fixed in the popular imagination as a species of *homo economicus*, as the small businessman, corporate broker or, indeed, international economic criminal. We could ask what other kinds of cultural, intellectual and sexual capital we can exchange in the complex economies of governments, public civic institutions, and communities? How do we become objects and subjects of male power? How do we desire and become objects of desire? Who are our 'suitable' and possible partners within such a sexual/social order? And how do we guide generations of Asian boys and men?

The new cinema and autobiographical work provides us with some interesting ways forward. It suggests that there may be some new possibilities for reworking Asian masculinity, precisely because it has been 'left out' of both traditional systems of western patriarchy and fast-capitalist, commodified masculinity in White cultures.

As children, we had a vocabulary for 'talking back' and fighting back: Cantonese names for black devils, for white devils. Asian men historically have developed different strategies for reconstructing maleness. A key strategy has been to blend Asian masculinity and sexuality with that of others through engagement with popular culture. In his autobiography *The Rice Room*, Ben Fong-Torres (1995) talks about finding his sexuality, his relationships with what his parents considered 'suitable' and 'unsuitable' girls through sixties rock and roll and drug culture. He discusses what he learned working and writing alongside African-American and Hispanic social movements — and ultimately, what he was able to return to the Chinese community. For Fong-Torres — who was one of the most innovative 60s writers in the original San Francisco-based *Rolling Stone* group — becoming part of a slightly bent and politically innovative counter-culture was one way of reframing his options, of moving beyond the classical binaries of acquiescence to migrant tradition or American 'melting pot' acculturation. For Fong-Torres and many of us, it was by playing rock and roll or participating in the broad social movements of the 1960s and 70s that we were able to capture a hybrid agency and activism that isn't recognised in a multiculturalist literature that assumes that migrant ethnic identity is 'discovered' through endless searches for nativist identity.

This is nothing new. In our family albums there are 1930s images of my father and other first- and second-generation Chinese migrants with slicked back hair, wire-framed glasses, double breasted suits and flash cars, forays into dancing and big bands. I heard whispers of jazz and 'underground' clubs in interwar San Francisco Chinatown where men and women would go to dance, to drink, to listen to music — reported in Fae Ng's (1992) remarkable novel about growing up in Chinatown, *Bone*. These men didn't have cultural or economic capital but, like Fong-Torres and those of us who grew up in the 1960s, they were bricoleurs and culture jammers before their time. My Uncle and his friends in the 1930s developed innovative forms of movie art and interior design that combined the Hollywood poster art (which they had been commissioned by theatres and studios to undertake), with the erotic designs of Aubrey Beardsley with traditional Chinese painting. Some married women across racial boundaries. My father went to work in the movies and played catcher on a Hollywood softball team. After his work in acting, he became a linotyper and printer, the first Chinese member of the printers' union. These men were striking, rakish images of a new masculinity. As they struggled to break into and out of institutions that excluded them, they were finding new ways of expressing desire, joy, pleasure. Yet these subtexts of identity are the ones that have yet to be told, that didn't surface as objects of mid-century social science.

These themes of blended identities, new bodies, sexualities, 'ways of being' are key themes in recent literature by gay and straight Asian men (such as Leong 1996). In *Where the Body Meets Memory*, Japanese-American writer David Mura (1996) describes the emotional pain of an obsession with pornography, seduction of white women and infidelity. For Mura, engagements with the western technologies of literature, feminism and psychoanalysis offer a way of exploring why and how the 'desire' is formed. He argues that there was a silence in his family about sexuality and desire that he is only now ready to break. While I remain unconvinced that psychoanalysis and western literature hold any generalisable answers to questions about Asian identity and sexuality, [6] Mura's book makes a compelling, contradictory case for the possibilities of reinventing ourselves.

As it was selectively reinscribed in many migrant communities, traditional Chinese masculinity has been equated with family, money and status. Many of my generation grew up with mock-Confucian sayings about judging a man's wealth by his sons. We learned migrant self-defence strategies: that we had to work harder, to prove that we are twice as good as whites. So 'face' was to be found through taking care of our families, marrying and staying within the community, and the visible accumulation of wealth. How we construct our masculinity within these traditions is hardly straightforward, and it was and is fraught with risk, bricolage and experimentation. The explanation that migrants are caught 'between two worlds' — popularised in the multicultural literature — is a crass simplification of the complex paths that many Asian men and women carved out.

Yes, I had been called names, objectified and grown up feeling 'invisible' in White cultures, unable to catch 'her' eye in the bar or at work. Yet as an upwardly mobile post-war male, there was something 'one-eyed' and de-cidedly non-introspective in my response — about wanting to overcome the invisibility by working twice as hard, as my Father had told me, by getting ahead and showing them my worth. This particular 'folk theory of success' of Chinese-American communities made the adaptation of African-American militant strategies of 'talking back' and 'fighting back' feel unnat-ural, inorganic, unsuited to our habitus as Asian males. It was, ironically, through my partner and other White feminists that I learned a vocabulary for describing that invisibility and otherness.

A close colleague who migrated to Australia from China in the 1950s commented to me recently that hidden behind ethnic success stories pushed by the press and by Asian communities, there is a silent text of breakdown, defeat, and disappearance. Stories of divergence and difference, stories of failure, stories of being on the periphery of the diaspora — many of these have yet to be spoken or written.

Many of us found what were for our parents and communities less than 'suitable' trajectories in search of other forms of masculinity and identity, agency and capital. Some of us diverged variously into the social fields of counter and sub-cultures, intellectual and artistic work, and political activ-ism. These domains enabled us to locate and narrate ourselves differently. What Mura, Hongo, Fong-Torres and the teenagers in *Floating Life* tell us is that Asian masculinity is, for better and worse, an unfinished, partially told story. Mura's work illustrates how the discourses and systems for rationalis-ing and developing Anglo-European masculinity are themselves the prod-ucts of centuries of institutional work: the Bildungsroman, psychotherapy, action cinema, sitcoms, the pickup bar, and rugby league are refined genres for framing, classifying and normalising western masculinity.

I began this chapter by arguing for a cultural, as well as economic, analysis of the configurations of the Asian diaspora. The diasporic Asian male is but one of the new cosmopolitan identities produced by globalised economies and cultures. In their discussion of normative discourses of Chinese mascu-linity, Kam Louie and Louise Edwards (1994) describe the *Analects'* stories of *King Wen* and *King Wu*, mythic personifications of male cultural and

martial power. In Western, White cultures — many Asian men are culturally, politically and economically positioned in ways that remediate, reframe
and misrecognise their cognate intellectual and linguistic resources, and which
dissipate or negate their physical energy and sexual desire. Indeed, Bourdieu
(1990) would remind us, capital is not capital unless it is recognised as such
— nor, I would add, does desire count as desire unless it is recognised as
such. In the face of a normative masculinity where we do not appear or exist
— Asian males in the diaspora are left with few simple choices, few immediate models. Unlike our white male counterparts, we have inherited a relatively open place, a gap, a space within which to reconstruct Asian masculinity.

In her discussion of the 'flexible citizenship' of Asian-Americans, Ong (1996)
comments that:

> In Chinese, the word for bridge (*qiao*) puns with the term for overseas
> Chinese (the *qiao* in *huaqiao*), and . . . diaspora Chinese have been quick to
> play on the metaphor of bridging political boundaries in their roles as
> agents of flexible accumulation and flexible citizenship.   (1996: 155)

Here I have suggested that there are other kinds of bridges across gendered
identities and speaking positions that are emerging among cosmopolitan
Asian males, bridges that reframe and reconstruct archetypal Asian and
Anglo-European masculinities. Through our engagement with anti-racist
movements and feminisms, Mura, I and others have come to see the demas-
culinisation of being 'not a white male' as a strength: as a gap, as an opportunity for finding other ways of being and expressing ourselves as men and
partners, as fathers and sons. Precisely because our very self-constructions
must be premised on counter-racist strategies, we can explore new kinds of
masculinities that run counter to traditional male power and sexism.

Acknowledgements

The author thanks Nigel Bruce and Colin Barron for their encouragement and
patience; Carmen Luke, Kam Louie, David Ip for ideas and editorial advice.

Notes

1. Minority discourses are constructed in an unresolved critical relation to
   dominant discourses in the dynamic social relations and political arrangements between dominant and marginalised cultures and communities. They
   may be written in opposition and complicity with these relations of dom-
   ination/subordination.

2. See, for example, Chow's (1996) commentary on *The Joy Luck Club*.
3. See Lisa See's (1995) family history for an accurate description of some of these homes and communities.
4. The degree to which psychologies themselves are discourse artefacts of Western cultures — historical technologies of, say Wundt's or Piaget's or Freud's aristocratic Europe, Reich's interwar Germany, Skinner's industrial America — often escapes those who profess and perform various kinds of therapies as of universal value.
5. For a discussion of Asian and Anglo-Australian women's descriptions of Asian men's attitudes towards family and childbearing, see Luke and Luke (1998).
6. Like Mura and Hongo, my university studies were of canonical English literature, right at the historical cusp of the mid-1960s when American 'minority' literatures were emerging (cf. Hagedorn 1993). This chapter is itself a product of that mimicry (Bhabha 1994).

Social Practices

Introduction to **Part II:**
The dialectic of authentic and inauthentic discourses

How do we know?

(ZHUANGZI; CITED IN HARBSMEIER 1993: 25)

Discourse expresses itself for the most part in language

(HEIDEGGER 1962 [1927]: 400)

Language is *tensed* and is therefore essentially temporal. Language ecology recognises this and asserts the equality of the temporality of all languages. Discourses that represent the 'I' and which recognise the temporal equality of other discourses are authentic, that is, they are true to themselves and to other discourses. In authentic discourses the subjects do the narration and we know the subjects. We know the world from the first-person perspective. This is a defining feature of postmodern discourse.

In the *modern* world we know everything from the third-person perspective. The Other is the defining and defined subject of modern discourse. We 'know' the Other because 'they' tell us, 'they' being missionaries, anthropologists, scientists, teachers. The linguistic turn which Alastair Pennycook discusses in the first paper in this book constructs a very different world. This suggests the ecological world in which 'every language is a world-view and is, therefore, not a mere *tool* for expressing preexisting significations but instead *constitutes* them' (Dastur 1998 [1990]: 71; emphases in original). In this world 'the epistemological project is to show that thinking is possible only in language and, consequently, that every object that can be given to us in experience is capable of existing for us only through language' (Kögler 1996 [1992]: 63). This is the first-person perspective. We know the subject of the narrative because the subject, 'I', is allowed to speak.

In this section we take a tour through the Asia–Pacific region. In the first paper Gu Yueguo and Zhu Weifang tell us about the *guan*-system that underpins the Chinese bureaucracy. This is an authentic discourse. How do we know that this discourse is authentic? Because it contains simultaneously the three times of an ecological world — the past, the present and 'the present that is waiting for our encounter and is normally called the future' (Heidegger 1971 [1959]: 106). We know the *guan*-system because Gu and Zhu construct the spatiality of the Chinese bureaucratic system from the first-person perspective. They are members of the system:

> A lower organization derives its power from its immediate superior one, which in turn is empowered by its immediate superior one, and so on. The ultimate power of the ruling party with the central government comes from its claim that it represents the best interests of its people   (p.100)

This is authentic because it is ecological. The confident, authentic 'I' is speaking now, configuring the whole of the past and anticipating the future.

In the second paper Colin Barron discusses how colonial discourse is realised in the post-colonial age through the media, on television and in print. It is a paradigmatic example of a lack of co-evalness in which 'the colonisers and the colonised do not communicate with each other at the same level of temporality' (p.116). Barron shows how two kinds of colonialists, the former Australian colonialists in Papua New Guinea (PNG) and the neo-colonialist Malaysians working in PNG, construct an atemporal 'black hole into which the time–space of the black actors is compressed. Nothing can escape from a black hole, so nothing can be known about what is in it' (p.134). This is an inauthentic discourse because we do not know PNG when we watch the Australian Broadcasting Corporation's (ABC) news broadcasts on PNG or when we read *The National*, a Malaysian-controlled newspaper in PNG. Papua New Guineans have no future in this discourse. The disturbing aspect of this dominant inauthentic discourse is that it is so seductive that even those formerly subjected to it (the Malaysians) have become entranced by it.

The next two papers in the section display all the aporias when discourses come into contact with one another. Homosexuals in Thailand have never been an oppressed group, so, as Graeme Storer states, 'we should not expect to see a "gay community" as in the West that is founded on a tradition of liberation' (p.147), simply because without oppression, there can be no liberation. But when this authentic discourse comes up against the global phenomenon of AIDS and the consequent pandemic that could ensue, the authentic discourse of Thailand, a country which has never been colonised by the West, is colonised by the global AIDS discourse. In the authentic Thai discourse we have *kathoey*, 'male transvestites and trans-sexuals' who live as women and use female forms of address. In the inauthentic discourse we have 'gays'. One of Graeme Storer's informants expresses the dialectic of authentic and inauthentic discourses:

> *scene from a bar*: . . . Boy is with the only customer in the bar, a *farang* [non-Asian]. Boy looks across the room at one group who are 'camping' it up. Then he turns to the customer and speaks:

Boy: Look at those *kathoey*. I hate them.
Customer: Why do you hate them?
Boy: I don't like gays.
Customer: But I'm gay and I don't behave like that. But I do like having
            sex with men.
Boy: Oh yes, that's okay. I'm the same. (p.142)

Here we see Boy's self-identity changing as he speaks. *Kathoey* become gays and the Thai discourse changes. Boy's aporia about whether he 'knows' himself is voiced more generally by Graeme Storer when he addresses the global AIDS problem. 'I feel that it is important to promote a sense of fellowship among Thai msw [male sexual workers] because it seems that sexual safety is a social process and because peer support may be critical in promoting the motivation and intention central to behaviour change' (p.147).

The colonial discourse of the triads of Hong Kong has always been am-bivalent. 'In the colonial discourse, triads are both like "us" — with their rituals and bonds of loyalty — and typical of "them" — with their hostility to officialdom, opaque rituals and pre-modern social organization' (p.154). Kingsley Bolton and Chris Hutton show how this ambivalence extends into the Cantonese discourse of triads in films:

Mom: Wah, I heard the neighbours saying that you joined a black gang.
      Really? Is that right?
Son: You misunderstand, it's a patriotic society, I joined a patriotic soci-
      ety. It's the Triad Society, Heaven, Earth, Man, Overthrow the
      Qing and restore the Ming.
Mom: I don't know what you are talking about.
Son: Of course you don't! I am a national hero. But, don't tell father.
      (p.161)

Is this an authentic discourse? Does the son 'know' what a triad society is? He combines the Chinese concept of the triads as a patriotic group with the colonial concept of the triads as criminals, into an emerging authentic dis-course. The comic at the end of Bolton and Hutton's paper came out in the same year as the film from which the dialogue comes, 1995. The dialectic of local (Cantonese) and global (English) languages and therefore of temporal-ities and the translation of objects of enquiry into subjects and hence into co-evalness with the readers of the comic is an attempt to bring triads 'out', just as homosexuals in the West come out. In oppression subjects cannot know themselves because the dominant discourse is inauthentic. The comic is further on the way to authentic discourse.

In this section we see the struggle as subjects try to establish co-evalness with the dominant colonial discourses that have taken over their countries.

We see the dialectic of authentic and inauthentic discourses as temporalities meet and change. Only one of the four discourses in this section is authentic, that of the *guan*-system in China, because China is the only one of the four places that has not been colonised, either politically by other countries, as in PNG and Hong Kong, or epidemiologically by AIDS, as in Thailand. As discourses emerge from beneath the dominant discourses, they establish themselves in whatever niches they can, be it sexuality in Thailand or comics in Hong Kong. They are trying to assure that they have a future, but the aporias we can see in the authentic discourses are indicative of the fragility of that future.

In the dialectic between the authentic and inauthentic discourses we can see emerging the dialectic of knowledge and discourse, for only in a dialectic between these two can we have an ecological linguistics. In the papers in this section we can see the danger to the ecological diversity of authentic discourses, which express themselves in language, from the seductive attractions of an inauthentic discourse, which expresses itself in transtemporal ideas.

6

Chinese officialdom (*Guan*) at work in discourse[1]
Yueguo Gu and Weifang Zhu

This paper investigates the discoursal behaviour of individuals in their capacity as *guan* interacting with one another or with non-*guan* participants in administrative meetings. It is very difficult to find a good English term for the Chinese notion of *guan*. In the statement *Ta shi ge guan* (他是個官, meaning 'he is an official'), it can refer to an official as high as the state president or as low as a group leader of three or more people. The English terms like bureaucrat, civil servant, official can be used to translate *guan* in some contexts, but none of them seem to have the all-embracing flavour or connotations of the original. So instead of translating it, the original *guan* will be used. This however will pose no difficulty in comprehension, for the Chinese notion of *guan* will be elaborated below.

The examination of *guan* at work in discourse is, in a sense, a study of the ways power is enacted in discourse. This kind of study resides in the general research framework pursued by scholars like van Dijk (1987a, 1987b, 1989), Fairclough (1989), Bavelas, Rogers and Millar (1985), Kress (1985), Seidel (1985), Fowler (1985), and many others. The focus of our study, however, is less on the relationship between power and discourse at the macro level. Rather it is on the way individuals interact with one another, mainly in the form of talking, in their official capacity as *guan* during the social process of administrative meetings. There are two kinds of social power (see below) currently operating in parallel in China, and there are many cases in which *guan*-individuals are empowered with both. Furthermore, *guan*-individuals vary in rank, and represent the interests of different groups. Our analysis hence will include interactions ranging from the greater power to the smaller power and from the powerful to the powerless.

The data for this paper were collected over the course of three years (1993–1996) in a public institution in Beijing. Altogether 20 administrative meetings of over 30 hours were audio-taped, with the knowledge of the key participants. A database was set up to manage all the necessary details required by this paper. The general information concerning the nature and duration of the 20 meetings is summarised in the Appendix (Table 6.2).

What follows breaks into three main sections. The first presents the Chinese conception of *guan*. The second takes a snapshot of a *guan* in action. The third and last presents a detailed analysis of *guan* at work in administrative discourse.

The Chinese conception of *guan*

Guan and power (*quan*)

In Chinese folk parlance, the function of *guan* is *guan*[2] 管, that is, *guanren* (管人) or *guanshi* (管事), meaning controlling people or overseeing things done. For a *guan*-individual to be able to exercise his/her control, s/he needs *quan* (官, meaning *power*). The utilization of *quan* to exert control over others or situations constitutes the folk notion of *dang guan* (當官的, being an official). Another built-in sense of *guan* in the usage by men in the street is public legitimacy. Those who control others without this legitimacy will not be called *guan*. For example, a gang leader is not a *guan*, but *tou* (literally meaning *head*).[3] In a private business, to take another instance, the owner, although everything is under his/her control, is not *guan* either: s/he is *laoban* (老板, meaning *boss*).

Technically speaking, a *guan* can be defined as a legitimate position allocated by the Chinese socio-political system to enact a proportionate share of power. In the current state of affairs, there are two general types of social power. One is known as *lingdao quan* (領導權, power to rule). That the present ruling party possesses this power is secured by the latest version of the Constitution. The other is *xingzheng quan* (行政權, administrative power, or power to govern). The power to rule comes from 'the barrel of a gun' (Chairman Mao's words). It is not something to be disputed over. It is close to the conception of power by Bacharach and Baratz (1962), criticised as 'the two-dimensional view' in Lukes (1974: 16–20). The presumed conflict, being a life-or-death class struggle, actual or imagined, during Chairman Mao's era between the winning proletariat and the defeated old enemies, now becomes a legitimacy struggle of the ruling regime against the potential 'denialists' both at home and abroad. The power to govern, on the other hand, is close to Dahl's conception of power (1957, 1961), i.e. 'the one-dimensional view' in Lukes' terminology. In the Chinese context, it is subordinate to the first, and not allowed to be otherwise. The first type of power is exercised through the control of national policy-making, that is, those policies that best protect the interests of the rulers and the people. The second is exercised through decision-making, i.e. decisions that are made to solve specific problems: social, economical, educational, diplomatic, military, etc. The policies made by the first type of power serve as guidelines or principles under which problem-solving solutions are considered.

Correspondingly there are two kinds of hierarchical institution or organisation established to execute the two types of power at various levels. Interestingly enough, the two power-enacting bodies normally run in parallel to each other and are co-present at all levels of the power distribution structure. In other words, an institution or organisation under the system is normally managed by two bodies of *guan*, one representing the first type of power, and the other the second, in spite of the fact that Deng Xiaoping called for the separation of the two (Deng 1993: 177). With regard to a *guan*-individual, s/he is supposed to have one type of power only, either the first or the second. In practice, however, it is not uncommon for him/her to have dual power.

Hierarchy of *guan*

Guan is a scalar phenomenon. At the highest end is the party secretary-general, or the state president, and at the lowest an office chief ranking *keji* (科級, literally meaning *office chief rank*). In between, there are four more grades, namely premier, minister, division chief, and department director. Note that there is a further complication, namely within each rank there is a finer distinction between *zheng zhi* (正職, the rank proper) and *fu zhi* (副職, deputy status of that rank). There are grass-root officials such as production team leaders in the countryside, who, although entitled with *guan* by their team mates, are too small to be placed on the ranking scale. The hierarchy of *guan* is reinforced by the dichotomy of domination vs. subordination: those who are higher in rank dominate those lower in rank.

There is one additional dimension to domination, namely inter-institutional and intra-institutional. Given any two institutions, they can be equal or unequal with one dominating the other. Within a single institution there are also departments with equal or unequal status. Given any two *guan*s of the same ranking, they can be unequal due to the fact that one comes from the dominating institution or department.

In the institution where the data were collected, a *guan*-individual has an extra dimension of power, that is, power of expertise. It is a personal power, so to speak, due to the possession of special knowledge. It is now quite fashionable in the arena of Chinese politics to empower an expertise-individual with social power such as political power (the power to rule) and/or administrative power (the power to govern), as clarified above.

In our data the following classes of *guan* are found operating: (a) *guan* with the governing power ranking from *keji* (the lowest, to be referred to as rank 1 hereafter) to *juji* (局級, two ranks above *keji*, as rank 3 hereafter);

(b) *guan* with the administrative power ranking from *keji* (rank 1) to *juji* (rank 3); (c) *guan* with both types of social power ranking from *chuji* (處級, i.e. the rank above *keji*, below *juji*, as rank 2 hereafter) to *juji* (局級, i.e. rank 3); and (d) *guan*-expertise with either of the two types of social power ranking from *chuji* to *juji*.[4]

A *guan*-individual in a power sandwich

It may already have become apparent that the social power of either kind discussed above is not something owned by a *guan*-individual, but by what is called in Chinese *jigou* (機構, institution) or *zuzhi* (組織, organisation). A lower organisation derives its power from its immediate superior one, which in turn is empowered by its immediate superior one, and so on. The ultimate power of the ruling party within the central government comes from its claim that it represents the best interests of its people. From a *guan*-individual's point of view, being an incumbent of an official office, s/he is placed in the middle of a power sandwich: the upper layer is the dominating superior, and the lower layer the subordinate who can also be a *guan* or a plain member of the institution or organisation. A *guan* is thus in a sense both a superior and inferior. (In folk terms s/he is a dragon at one place, and a worm at another.)

Four ways of being a *guan*

Since a *guan* sits in the middle of a power sandwich, his/her discoursal behaviour at administrative meetings is insecure. In this connection Goffman's 'least self-threatening' strategy is quite relevant:

> What the speaker is engaged in doing, then, moment to moment through the course of a discourse in which he finds himself, is to meet whatever occurs by sustaining or changing footing. And by and large, it seems he selects that footing which provides him the least self-threatening position in the circumstances, or, differently phrased, the most defensible alignment he can muster.
> (Goffman 1981: 325–6)

However, in our analysis of *guan*, we need to make finer distinctions concerning the sources of threat a *guan* perceives. The perceived threat may come from above or below, and s/he will act accordingly. In other words, Goffman's moment-to-moment footing is framed by the perceived threat (see the section on '*Bao wusha mao* and footing' below). Four catch-phrases have been coined by the man in the street to capture the four ways (or strategies) a *guan* holds his/her office in connection with the threat perceived.

Zou shangceng luxian (走上層路線)

Literally this means 'walk along the upper line'. It describes a *guan* who takes orders or instructions from the above and executes them to the letter, disregarding the fact that they might be incorrect or inappropriate. S/he can be said to be a Yes-*guan*. One of the motives behind this strategy is self-protection from the potential loss of office as a result of disobedience.

Zou xiaceng luxian (走下層路線)

This is the opposite of the first strategy. Literally it means 'walk along the lower line', referring to a *guan* who tailors the orders or instructions from above to the needs of those under his subordination. S/he even takes his/her own initiative to please them. S/he may turn out to be so popular among the rank and file that s/he becomes a thorn in the flesh of the superior.

Ba mian linglong (八面玲瓏)

Literally meaning 'clever and nimble on eight sides', this captures a *guan* who is so skilful in manoeuvring between his/her superiors and subordinates that s/he pleases everyone. A *guan* may desperately intend to please every-one, but due to incompetence and poor skill, turns out to be a *hunguan* (昏官, meaning muddleheaded official).

Mang zui liu you (滿嘴流油)

The last catch phrase, *mang zui liu you*, literally meaning 'oil spilling over the mouth', depicts a *guan* who abuses his/her power in satisfying his/her personal needs. This type of *guan* is analysed elsewhere (see Gu 1995). The first three types of *guan* are all found in our data.

Guan at work in administrative discourse

A *guan*-individual: many roles in one

Guan in administrative meetings discourse is not a homogeneous role. A *guan*-individual is many roles in one. S/he is a *guan*, specifically a *guan*-superior or -inferior or -equal in a given meeting. S/he may be also a political friend or enemy of a co-participating *guan*. Moreover s/he is a speaker and an audience, and/or chairperson or key speaker. Interpersonally s/he may happen to be a colleague, a former classmate, a neighbour and so on. These roles activate a series of nested frames that affect the discoursal behaviour of the *guan* in question. The multiple roles are sometimes employed by the *guan* him/herself, or by others to gain advantage (see below).

Guan and meeting frames

There are a nested set of frames operating in administrative meetings. Three general frames can be identified: pre-meeting frame, frame of meeting proper, and post-meeting frame.

Pre-meeting frame

This refers to a situation beginning with the initiation of a need for a meeting and terminating at the beginning of the meeting proper. The pre-meeting frame consists of six essential moves: meeting initiation, agenda fixing, decision on participants, choosing a meeting site, meeting notification, and seating. All of the six are *guan*-sensitive in the following ways.

> *Meeting initiation* is normally performed by one *guan*, who will consult his/her superior and his/her equal(s) for a second opinion. If s/he fails to do this, bad feelings are likely to be generated, and the latter's cooperation is likely to be in jeopardy.
>
> *Agenda fixing* is even more sensitive. What is to be put on the agenda, and what is to be left out, is a form of control. Some issues require prior negotiation behind the scenes before they are placed on the agenda. Others, particularly sensitive topics such as one that will discredit a co-*guan*, may be deliberately put on the agenda so that the co-*guan* will lose public confidence, or even find it difficult to maintain his/her post.
>
> *Decision on participants* should be carefully considered. Failure to invite those *guans* whose presence is required by the prospective meeting means their serious disregard, and that the decisions reached at the end of the meeting are likely to be nullified.
>
> *Meeting site* is *guan*-sensitive in the sense that the higher a *guan*'s rank, the better the meeting site s/he deserves.
>
> *Meeting notification* is no less *guan*-sensitive. A high-ranking *guan* should be notified by the personnel who can represent the institution or department in question, or by a *guan* of the same rank, if the meeting organisers cannot afford to risk the high-ranking *guan*'s absence.

Finally, *seating*, i.e. to seat *guan* individuals in a meeting room, is by no means trivial. It is perhaps the most *guan*-sensitive on formal occasions. A meeting room is normally equipped with chairs and tables, that is, with what Goffman (1974: 21) calls 'primary framework' objects. The arrangement of these innocent objects and their use in space and time constitute a 'social framework' (ibid, p.22). There are a set of spatial and temporal terms in

Chinese that metaphorise the social processes that locate *guan*s of various ranks in their due relative positions.

Domination	**Subordination**
shang (上, up)	*xia* (下, down)
qian (前, front)	*hou* (後, back)
xian (前, first)	*hou* (後, later)
zheng (正, central)	*pian* (偏, sideways)

That is, the dominant deserves the prominence of *shang*, *qian*, *xian*, and *zheng*, whereas the subordinate should accept the obscurity of *xia*, *hou*, *hou* and *pian*. For instance, at a post-meeting banquet, the *shangshou* seat (literally upper hand seat) is reserved for the dominant *guan*, and the subordinate will resume the *xiashou* seat (lower hand seat). The dominant walks at the front (i.e. *qian*) of a party, with the subordinate following behind (*hou*). After the declaration of a meeting open, the dominant *guan* will be offered the first opportunity to speak, and the subordinate may add things afterwards. The dominant *guan*s will take the central place (*zheng*) at the top end of a meeting table, while the subordinates will occupy the side (*pian*) seats.[5]

How the *guan*s in our data fared in these six moves will be analysed in the section on power and discoursal rights below.

Frame of meeting proper

This frame consists of three essential moves: opening, settling agenda business, and closing. The opening is a decisive slot — the meeting chairperson formally or informally declares the meeting open. There are some optional slots, depending on the degree of formality of the meeting in question. For instance, the opening declaration of a formal meeting may be followed by music and the chair's presentation of VIPs.

Like the opening, the determinative closing slot is the chairperson's formal or informal declaration of closure. Sometimes, however, the declaration can be flawed: a new or forgotten issue is brought up, and the meeting is hence dragged on until a second closing is made.

Both opening and closing are highly *guan*-sensitive. They are discoursal rights that are open to privileged access only (see below).

Agenda business settlement has slots that vary in correspondence with the types of meetings in question. In our data there are 15 types of meeting. One important difference among them lies in what Goffman calls 'frame space'. In some meetings, participants have more freedom in turn-taking, topic-switching, and time to speak than in others. Pre-determined allocation of speaker role is quite common in formal meetings. Although a slot for a free speaker role is occasionally allocated, it is more a lip-service than a genuine offer. To simplify the real-life complications a little, our 20 meetings are grouped in two general categories with regard to frame space (see Table 6.2, Appendix).

As far as the relation between power and discourse is concerned, the informal meetings with their freer slots are more dynamic than the formal ones, and can be unorthodox at times. This is so because *guan*-individuals have more freedom and space in enacting their share of power in their personal style (recall the four ways of being a *guan*, above).

Post-meeting frame

This refers to a situation beginning at the closing of the meeting proper and ending with all the participants leaving for home. It is a free slot open to negotiation between participants. The following are the activities found in our data: (1) further private discussions of the issues unresolved due to shortage of time; (2) private discussions on off-agenda business, things that participants have failed to put on the agenda; (3) private discussions on things that cannot be placed on the agenda; (4) further arrangements about the actions to be taken to execute the meeting decisions; (5) follow-up minor meetings in break-up groups; (6) entertaining meals; and (7) interpersonal networking, that is, taking the meeting opportunity to renew old friendship, or to make new friends.

One remarkable feature of post-meeting activities is that a post-meeting *guan* behaves less like a *guan*, and more like an individual with non-*guan* capacities, such as a friend, a classmate, a colleague, and so on. This offers one of the explanations of why post-meeting activities can be quite rich. Since the role of a post-meeting *guan* is less well-defined, less *guan*-like, so to speak, some decisions that cannot be made during the meeting proper are reached through post-meeting activities. Here is a dramatic example in our data. In M2, 7 *guan*-individuals, representing the interests of three separate bodies within a big institution, met to solve a dispute over funding allocation. They failed to reach an agreement after a 45-minute heated discussion. But a compromise was struck at the post-meeting lunch table (see the section on clashes of intergroup interests in discourse).

Power and discoursal rights

As pointed out above, the three general frames, pre-meeting frame, frame of meeting proper, and post-meeting frame, all with various moves and discourse slots, are *guan*-sensitive, i.e. power-sensitive. *Guan* status is jealously guarded, and the meeting frames confer discoursal rights that are almost exclusively made accessible[6] to *guan*-individuals in proportion with their ranks, and only occasionally made accessible to non-*guan* individuals.

The six moves in the pre-meeting frame are distributed in our data as follows:

1. meeting initiation — in 20 meetings, all enjoyed by *guan*-individuals;
2. agenda fixing — in 20 meetings, all enjoyed by *guan*-individuals;
3. participant selection — in 18 of 20 meetings made by *guan*-individuals (with two exceptions being regular meetings with participation by default);
4. meeting site selection — in 18 of 20 meetings made by *guan*-individuals (with 2 exceptions being regular meetings at regular places);
5. participant notification — of 20 meetings, 11 by office secretaries, 8 through personal arrangements, and 1 by the *guan*-individual of rank 3;[7]
6. central seats — of 20 meetings all occupied by the superior *guan*-individuals.

These logistics clearly demonstrate *guans*' privileged access to the pre-meeting frame.

There is however one finer detail that we have yet to touch on, namely the relative *guan* dominance at a given meeting. We may recall that the majority of meetings in our data involve more than one *guan* (see Table 6.2, Appendix). The relative power difference is not included in our analysis. Here we need to make a further distinction between having the right to do something and having the authority to endorse the right to do it. A *guan* of lower rank may have the right to initiate a meeting, but this does not mean that he can thus go ahead with it. His initiation may very well require the endorsement of his superior. Similarly, there is a difference between having the right to fix a meeting's agenda, and having the authority to endorse the right to do it. Given a situation that involves a power difference, for example the more powerful vs. the less powerful, or the powerful vs. the powerless, it is almost always the case that while the subordinate may have the right or be given the right to do something, it is the superior who will assume the authority to endorse the right.[8]

In the frame of the meeting proper, eight of the 20 meetings were informal and hence there was no need for a chair position. The chair of all the remaining 12 meetings was occupied by *guan*-individuals. As for opening and closing, they were all made by *guan* individuals without exception.

There are various parameters that affect the occupation of discourse space for agenda business settlement. Take for example turn-taking and the length of a turn. We found that in formal meetings with more or less fixed agendas, the correlation of power with the number of turns and the turn length was fairly straightforward: the higher the rank, the more turns and more time a *guan* would enjoy. The honour awarding ceremony (M8) and the decision-making meeting (M10) are good examples. The former had 22 participants, of which nine had the opportunity to speak. Among the speakers there were 3 *guan* individuals, and the six non-*guan* speakers were award receivers. The turn-taking and the length of turns are summarised in Appendix Table 6.3. Of the three *guan* speakers, the second *guan*, being intra-departmentally lower than the first, presided over the ceremony, and hence was given more turns, but his total speech time was two minutes less than the first. It is also worth noting that the three *guan* speakers occupied 83% of the total discourse time.

The decision-making meeting (M10) had seven participants, all being *guan* individuals. The power relation was hence that between more power and less power. Table 6.4 in the Appendix captures the turn-taking distribution of the meeting. As shown in the Table, the last guan(*) was not qualified for this meeting. He was specially invited to report in person his office work to the committee. The first speaker was the chairman of the committee, who took 51 turns lasting 39.6 minutes, totalling 64.9% of the meeting time. The second was the deputy chairman, taking 32 turns lasting 7.2 minutes. The two *guan* individuals at rank 2 were newly appointed members, and played a marginal role in the decision-making.

There are two general exceptions in formal meetings that affect the straightforward correlation of power with discoursal rights. A *guan* may be invited (1) for the sake of glory and ceremonial significance, and (2) for bargain advantage. Thus though s/he is high in rank, s/he does not enjoy more meeting space than his/her inferiors. The problem-solving meeting (M20) is a case in point. A *guan*-individual with political power at rank 3 was a good friend of another *guan*-individual with 3 types of power (political, administrative and expertise). She offered her help to the other two *guan*-participants of lower rank, whose project needed the endorsement by the *guan* with the three types of power. Her role in this meeting was to use her influence with her friend to gain advantage. Between the two lower rank *guan*-individuals, one had a better knowledge of the project history than the other. These complications explain why she occupied more discourse time than her superiors (see Table 6.5 in Appendix for details).

Bao wusha mao (保烏紗帽) *and footing*

In the section 'Four ways of being a *guan*' above, three types of *guan* were outlined: upper road *guan*, lower road *guan* and eight sides *guan*. In this section we examine these three types in terms of what Goffman called 'footing'. Goffman introduced the footing concept in order to capture the participants' varied involvement in social interaction. Speakers, for example, may assume various footings in relation to their own remarks, by employing specific 'production formats' (1981: 145). With regard to *guan*, they employ varied production formats as least self-threatening strategies. In other words, they perform speech acts in such a way that they protect their own position in accordance with the way they hold their office. Here is an excerpt from the fact-finding meeting (i.e. M7). Zhang, Qiao, Sun, and Wang, representing three branches of one super-institution, were engaged in heated discussion on project funding.

Speaker	Speech	Comments
Zhang	學校要控制它，聯系人太多 The institute wants to keep it under control. Too many applicants.	• Zhang is a typical upper-road *guan*. She wants to please her superior, Sun, by claiming that it is the institute that wants to control the number of applicants. As a matter of fact it is Sun who wants to do so.
Qiao	學校不讓辦 The institute does not allow [me] to continue.	• Qiao is a typical lower-road *guan*. She wants more applicants so that she can get more money for her staff. Her statement is directed to Wang who is the most superior and who supports her position.
Sun	現在不讓辦，那么多 (laugh) Not allow so many classes at the moment.	• Sun reinserts Zhang's statement, which is corrected by Qiao. Sun is a very experienced *guan*: he wants to protect his own skin meanwhile without offending his superior.
Zhang	那太亂乎啦 Otherwise it would be very messy.	• Zhang supports her boss again. Up to now Zhang and Sun spoke as if they were the spokesmen of the institution, and the position was not their personal one. Several exchanges later, they were forced to reveal the true colour of their footing.
Zhang	因為他是后勤校長，他要管房產啊 Because he's the president in charge of estate and welfare, he has to look after accommodation.	• Zhang tries to defend her boss by implying that it is his job that makes him take the present stance. Note also that Sun is not the president, but a vice-president. Zhang slips in a flattering gesture by referring to him as xiaozhang.

Sun	我要管房產，我要管房產，吃喝拉撒睡，英語整個那樓滿著呢 I have to look after accommodation, I have to look after accommodation, eat, drink, piss, sleep, the English building is so full.	• By now it is clear that the previous stance claimed to be that of the institute is in fact his own position. However, Sun attempts to distance himself from the position he adopts by appealing to his job.
Zhang	整個那那樓是給你培訓部，當時還不夠，還要把7號樓騰出來 That another building is all for your training centre. It was first not big enough. Building 7 had to be evacuated as well.	• Zhang lends further support to her boss.
Sun	給的培訓部，但是那樓滿着呢 All for the training centre. But that building is very full.	• Sun echoes his inferior statements.

In our data there was a *guan* with administrative and expertise power at rank 3. He was notoriously incompetent and was trying to please all sides. The more he tried, the less effective he became. Here is an excerpt from the consultation meeting (M4) in which he used three different collective pronouns to switch from one footing to another.

> 請大家想一想，咱們整個學校收費最高的交費最高的是這一批人，但受到重視最少 …… 今后我們的工作要加強。今天大家可交換一下情況，討論，研究一些問題
>
> Please everybody here think about it. In this institute of ours this batch of people pay the highest fees, but they are given the least attention . . . From today on our work should be strengthened. In today's meeting everybody can exchange views and discuss some problems.

He was actually responsible for the poor service provided to those students who paid high fees. He used *dajia* (actually meaning *everybody together*) twice, hoping to submerge himself into everybody who wanted to find a solution to the problem. This may sound quite trivial in the western context which assumes everyone present in the consultation meeting is equal, but it is quite a self-humbling gesture under that particular circumstance. After all, he was a *guan* at rank 3, but he sounded quite prepared to be part of everybody, willing to listen to everybody's opinion. The use of *zamen* (actually meaning *you and me together*) here implies that you (i.e. everybody except the speaker), including me (i.e. the speaker) benefited from the high fees. You together with me, therefore, sit together to discuss a solution to the problem of poor service. This is a very subtle but ineffective way of alleviating his own responsibility for the problem. The use of *women* (meaning *we, us, our*) here means all those officials in charge, thus including those officials attending the meeting as well as the absent ones, but excluding those non-*guan* participants. By saying *jinhou women de gongzuo yao jiaqiang* (今后我們的工作要加強) he sounded as if he was making a commitment on their behalf, with the implication that he was not responsible alone for all the work required to be done, hence he alone should not be blamed for any future failure.

Usurping power in discourse

The statement that the higher the rank, the more turns and more time a *guan* will enjoy captures a general tendency that is no less real than the perception of power by ordinary people. The progress review (i.e. M1) offers an excellent test case. One *guan* (with administrative power at rank 1) was a newly appointed chief secretary of the general office, who was making her public debut at this meeting. There is a household saying that describes a newly appointed *guan*: *xin guan shangren san ba huo* (新官上任三把火, literally meaning 'A newly appointed *guan* will set up three fires'). Probably this chief secretary took the progress review meeting as her first opportunity to set up her first fire. Appendix Table 6.6 summarises the turn-taking distribution of the meeting.

As shown in the Table, her status among the speakers was relatively low (No. 7). She took two turns that lasted more than 28 minutes, totalling 40.7% of the meeting time. She was supposed to report her office work for the last 2 weeks as well as her yearly planning. She took the opportunity to make two requests to the dean, gave four instructions to the four department heads, and even offered her positive appraisal of 15 staff members' performance. Here is a passage from her lengthy appraisal:

> That day, Miss X [did this]. . . . Though things like this are trivial, they reveal the high sense of responsibility everyone here has. This is needed in the future work of each comrade and every work person here.[9] If each of us possesses this sense of responsibility, we shall have no need to worry about our work not being done well. Moreover we all have our own duties; if we all perform them well, our overall work will definitely be done perfectly well.
> 那天xxx … 這些事雖然小， … 體現出我們在座各位 … 高度的責任感，這是我們以后每一個各個同志工作人在工作中都是需要的，如果我們每個人都有這种責任心的話，我們的工作就不愁搞不好，而且我們每個人都有自己的職責，都把自己的些事情做好，我們的整個全盤工作就一定能夠做得很好。

This is one of the typical ways a Chinese *guan* praises his/her inferiors. The pattern goes as follows:

- identify the good deed done by an individual X
- point out the good quality associated with the deed
- observe that everyone present has it[10]
- instruct that everyone should have it because it is conducive to public good.

The chief secretary almost forgot her own status. After all, she was a chief office secretary, and she had no mandate to deliver a public assessment of her colleagues, nor to instruct everyone present how to behave in their future work. Although the *guan* (with administrative and expertise power at rank 2) tried to rescue her by declaring to the meeting that she was acting on his behalf, she still became an object of gossip among her colleagues. Some described her as a usurper of power. Her first fire seemed to get her own fingers burned.

Challenging power in discourse

As discussed above, there are *guan*s of various kinds, such as 'upper-road' ones and 'lower-road' ones. These differences have a bearing on discoursal behaviour of *guan* participants in their meetings. In another problem-solving meeting (M3), a *guan*-individual with three types of power (political, administrative and expertise) at rank 3 is an instance of an upper-road official notoriously known for his incompetence. He chaired a meeting to solve a low performance problem.[11] The whole session was more like a riot than a meeting chaired by an official at rank 3. Although he took 14 turns out of 61, totalling 20% of meeting time, most of his turns were spent in defending his position. He was constantly interrupted and overwhelmed by challenging voices. He finally declared with his hands in the air: *wo touxiang wo touxiang, bie wen wo qian de wenti* (我投降，我投降，別問我錢的問題, lit. 'I surrender, I surrender. Don't ask me for money'). This clearly shows that he was overpowered by those with less power or no power at all.

Clashes of intergroup interests in discourse

A *guan* normally represents the interests of a group of people. In attending a meeting, s/he promotes the group interests at stake. Clashes of intergroup interests sometimes become unavoidable and even get heated. Still another problem-solving meeting (M2) is a good example. There were seven *guan*s representing three branches of one major institution. The power relations among the seven are shown in Table 6.1.

Intra-institutionally Branch C was subordinate to Branch B, which was in turn subordinate to Branch A. In terms of ranking, *guan* M and *guan* Sh

Table 6.1   Meeting M2: those present and their power relations

Super-institution	Ranking		
	Guan with political and admin. power at rank 3	*Guan* with admin. power at rank 2	*Guan* with admin. power at rank 1
Branch A		guan X	guan Z
		guan Y	
Branch B	guan M	guan Cz	
	guan Sh		
Branch C		guan Wf	

Dominant ↑ ⋮ ↓ Subordinate

were higher than the rest, but they could not overrule *guan*s X, Y and Z due to their intra-institutional domination. The crux of the discussion was over Branch A's further funding of the project that Branch C had been implementing over the past five years. The positions were:

Branch A: stopped funding the project, but wanted Branch C to continue on its own;

Branch B: wanted Branch C to call a halt to the project if Branch A's funding ceased; it believed that it would be an ultimate loser if Branch C continued the project on its own;

Branch C: wanted to continue the project even if Branch A's funding ceased, but wanted Branch B to give it a free hand so that it could manage the project in its own way.

The clashes of interest emerged in three remarkable ways. First, it became common that two or three participants often talked at once, with each trying to overpower the other by raising their voices. Second, when it became so noisy, they started to talk in pairs with similar views. And third, Branch B tried to silence Branch C, while Branch C tried to rebel by seeking Branch A's support to dominate Branch B.

Closing remarks

It is our conviction that real-life discourse is part and parcel of social reality. It is not an external means of realising it, but constitutes a piece of it by itself. Social parameters such as power are hence not things that are imposed on discourse, but are discoursal parameters *par excellence*. As the analysis above shows, power in this paper is not an abstract entity. Rather it is substantiated and implemented by *guan*-individuals. They enact their share of power in the way they consider appropriate. We have discussed four general ways, viz. upper-road, lower-road, pleasing on all sides and personal gains. Power means domination and subordination, which is realised in *guan*-individuals' sensitivity to their share in the pre-meeting frame, frame of meeting proper, post-meeting frame, turn-taking, floor-keeping and even usurping others' share of floor time. *Guan*-individuals not only defend their own share of power, but also the interests of the group or branch they represent. This is shown in our analysis of clashes of intergroup interests.

Notes

1. The authors wish to express their gratitude to Norman Fairclough and the editors of this collection for their constructive comments. Of course all the remaining faults are the authors'.
2. *Guan* pronounced in the first tone means an official or officialdom; in the third tone it becomes a verb meaning 'control'.
3. In an informal colloquial context *tou* can also be used in good humour to refer to a *guan*.
4. Note also that expertise power has no ranking system. It varies in terms of prestige.
5. The dominant *guan* can of course choose not to enjoy the privilege of prominence (*teshu daiyu*, 特殊待遇, meaning 'special treatment'). This is normally interpreted as a gesture of *bu jijiao mingli* (不計較名利, meaning 'do not care for personal fame or interest') or *ping yi jin ren* (平易近人, meaning 'place oneself on an equal footing with the inferior'). If the subordinate offers himself that undeserved prominence, it is seen either as a challenge to authority or a gesture of usurping power (see the section on usurping power in discourse).
6. One of the distinctive features of *dang guan* (being an official) is attending meetings (in folk parlance, *dang guande hui duo*). Meetings except those for entertainment purpose or for private business only, such as *wan hui* (meaning 'evening party') and *tan shenyi* (meaning 'talk about business'), are almost exclusive properties of *guan*. If a non-*guan* individual calls for a meeting to discuss public affairs without prior approval by a *guan* in charge, suspicion will arise about his motives.
7. It may appear surprising that such a high-ranking official should do secretarial work. This was because the meeting required the presence of another *guan* of rank 3 from the dominating institution, who would feel belittled should he have been invited by an office clerk.

8. In folk parlance people draw a distinction between using mouth and using legs. It is the more powerful who uses the mouth; and the less powerful or the powerless who use their legs.
9. The translation here is ungrammatical in English, but it is closer to the Chinese original, which is also ungrammatical.
10. This is a device intended to appease those who are not being praised. When an individual is singled out as an object of praise, the remaining company are automatically being made small.
11. For the sake of privacy we cannot give any further details about what is being tackled.

Appendix

Table 6.2   General information about the 20 administrative meetings

Data code	Meeting category	Length (minutes)	No. of participants	No. of *guan-*participants
A. **Formal** (with more or less fixed frame space)				
M1	progress review	70	40	11
M4	consultation	62	14	14
M8	honour awarding ceremony	53	22	8
M9	management policy briefing	63	30	17
M10	decision-making	61	7	7
M12	regular departmental meeting	50	40	7
M20	problem solving	31	4	4
B. **Informal** (with more free slots in frame space)				
M2	problem solving	45	7	7
M3	problem solving	88	12	11
M5	fact finding	56	5	5
M6	steering committee meeting	36	3	3
M7	fact finding	48	7	3
M9	management policy briefing	63	30	17
M11	negotiation	32	5	5
M13	complaints hearing	20	2	1
M14	job evaluation	31	2	1
M15	job evaluation	7	2	1
M16	staff development	16	2	1
M17	investigating cooperation	10	3	2
M18	staff development	28	2	1
M19	negotiating	34	3	1
M20	problem solving	31	4	4

Table 6.3   M8 — honour awarding ceremony

Order of power	No. of turns	Turn length (mins)	Percentage (total 53 mins)
guan (with 3 types of power at rank 3)	1	18	33.9%
guan (with 3 types of power at rank 3)	6	16	30.2%
guan (with admin. power at rank 2)	4	10	18.9%
Non-*guan* award receivers 1–6	1	Av. 1.2	Av. 2.3%

Table 6.4   M10 — decision-making

Order of power	No. of turns	Turn length (mins)	Percentage (total 61 mins)
guan (with 3 types of power at rank 3)	51	39.6	64.9%
guan (with 3 types of power at rank 3)	32	7.2	11.8%
guan (with admin. and expertise power at rank 3)	29	6.3	10.3%
guan (with admin. and expertise power at rank 3)	8	2.8	4.5%
guan (with admin. power at rank 2)	3	2.3	3.7%
guan (with admin. power at rank 2)	1	0.2	0.3%
*guan (with admin. power at rank 2)	7	1.3	2.1%

Table 6.5   M20 — problem-solving

Order of power	No. of turns	Turn length (mins)	Percentage (total 31 mins)
guan (with 3 types of power at rank 3)	54	9.2	29.7%
guan (with political power at rank 3)	24	4.8	15.5%
guan (with admin. and expertise power at rank 2)	29	4.4	14.2%
guan (with political and admin. power at rank 2)	51	11.7	37.7%

Table 6.6 M1 — progress review

Order of power	No. of turns	Turn length (mins)	Percentage (total 70 mins)
*guan (with admin. and expertise power at rank 2)	2	0.7	1%
guan (with governing and admin. power at rank 2)	10	11	15.7%
guans (with admin. power at rank 1)	Av. 2	Av. 6.5	9.2%
guan (with admin. power at rank 1)	2	28.5	40.7%

*He left this meeting early just to attend another meeting.

7

Discourse of silence: Intermeshing networks of old and new colonialists
Colin Barron

Introduction

A defining feature of colonialism is that the colonisers and the colonised do not communicate with each other at the same level of temporality, that is, they are not co-eval (Fabian 1983: 30–32) because the coloniser imposes its temporality on the colonised. One example of this is the ethnographic present of academia, forever locating the colonised in synchronic time. In the everyday world, the temporal disparity between coloniser and colonised is maintained by denying the colonised a voice — denying them participation in the political, educational and commercial fields. In this paper I will describe two cases to illustrate how manipulation of time and temporality by the media constructs discourses of silence which deny a voice to the people of Papua New Guinea (PNG) in both the local and international media.

The first situation is the reporting by the Australian Broadcasting Corporation (ABC) of volcanic eruptions in PNG in September 1994. Despite the extent of the disaster, there were some very positive outcomes for PNG which were suppressed. The second situation is the reporting of forestry and logging issues in the country by *The National* newspaper, based in Port Moresby. The newspaper, one of two daily English-language newspapers in PNG, was established in 1993 by Rimbunan Hijau. Rimbunan Hijau is a Malaysian logging company with about 70% of the logging rights in PNG, and it established the newspaper in order to stifle criticism of logging practices in the country.

Studies of the news media tend to concentrate on bias in the news (see for example Glasgow University Media Group 1976, 1993; Fairclough 1995: 54–69). In this paper I take the notions of time and space to show that, when global actors reduce spatial distance for their international consumers, they distance Papua New Guineans from their times and spaces. Time and space are not given entities. Time is activated when two or more actors interact (Lévinas 1987: 39). Space is not a contentless form, but the material expression of an actor. Time and space combine in time–space, which 'expresses the very nature of what objects are' (Urry 1991: 161). A dynamic version of time and space is Giddens's (1979: 198–233) notion of time–space distanciation. Time–space distanciation 'refers to the processes by which societies are "stretched" over shorter or longer spans of time and space' (Urry 1991: 165). It is used here to analyse how key actors, translators, change the time–space of the actors to create Otherness, that is, social distance, and thus to account for power, resistance, position, deprivation and autonomy, as Urry suggests (1991: 169).

The mechanism by which the translation of the social and natural worlds is achieved to the benefit of the ABC and the logging industry is the actor-network (Callon 1986a, 1986b, 1995; Callon and Law 1995; Law 1992, 1994; Law and Mol 1995). One of the major principles of actor-network theory is that of symmetry, that is, 'it studies the production of humans and nonhumans simultaneously' (Latour 1993: 103). Actor-network theory is a sociology of presence and absence in its concern with which actors are and are not simultaneously enrolled within certain boundaries. It describes the strategies of actors who have a history in a particular network. I am not concerned with a synchronic ethnographic present in which Papua New Guineans are always timeless. Both the cases presented here occurred in real time and at different times. Both have a history that can be traced back to past events and suggest future events. Both cases illustrate the Heideggerian notion of discourse as having 'a specifically *worldly* mode of being' (Heidegger 1996 [1953]: 161/151; emphasis in original). By following the actors, both human and non-human, we can trace how the time–space of Papua New Guineans is defined as a timeless, spaceless Other.

Case 1   The Rabaul eruptions

On 19 September 1994, just after six o'clock in the morning, two volcanoes erupted on the island of New Britain in Papua New Guinea. The two volcanoes, Tavurvur and Vulcan, are situated on either side of Simpson Harbour on the Gazelle Peninsula, one of the South Pacific's finest natural harbours. Just to the north of the volcanoes lies the town of Rabaul, which was almost completely destroyed in a few hours. The inhabitants of Rabaul had very little warning of the eruptions. Only an earthquake on the afternoon before the eruptions gave any warning that the volcanoes were about to come to life. The eruptions activated the evacuation plan which the PNG Government had put into place a few years earlier. About 50,000 people were evacuated from the town and the surrounding areas in a few hours. Despite the severity of the disaster, only five people died. To put the achievement of successfully evacuating the whole town and the surrounding region into perspective, the previous eruption in 1937 caused over 500 deaths.

How did the Papua New Guinean authorities successfully evacuate about 50,000 people with a minimum loss of life? The ABC, which was the only major media organisation to report the disaster comprehensively on the international front, did not tell us. Instead, the ABC exploited the opportunity to reconstruct PNG's mythical past and to translate it back to that past. An important part of the evacuation plan was the upgrading of the airstrip at Tokua, about 30 kilometres south-east of Rabaul, because the authorities calculated that the fallout of ash would be very light or non-existent in that area. This proved to be correct. Rabaul airport was put out of action as soon as the eruptions started as it lies immediately under Tavurvur, and Tokua became the airstrip into which relief supplies and reporters flew and from which people were evacuated. The PNG authorities' correct prediction enabled reporters, including those from the ABC, to get very close to the disaster area, but they failed to inform viewers how this was possible. The disaster thus entered the global network of news, which is how I saw it in Hong Kong.

In return for international dissemination of the disaster, the PNG television company, EMTV, loaned the ABC cameramen and allowed them to use footage in their news programmes taken for the local television network. The ABC had been given a negotiation space (Law and Callon 1995: 289) to project the disaster onto the global network of news programmes. The ABC acted as an obligatory passage point (Callon 1986a: 205–206) for information about the disaster in the international arena because it is the only major western news organisation which has a permanent representative in PNG. The disaster was the first news item on ABC for several days and it remained a news item on ABC for about two weeks.

The ABC exploited its virtual monopoly as an obligatory passage point to construct its own autonomous negotiation space in which the PNG voice was silenced. Not a single Papua New Guinean was interviewed or allowed to speak on the ABC. The ABC reporters sought out Australians evacuated from Rabaul, and the editors in Sydney edited out all the Papua New Guineans from the footage received from EMTV in Port Moresby.

PNG gained independence from Australia in 1975. It was Australia's only colony and thus there are many Australian discourses on PNG. The ABC revived old discourses and intermingled them with some more recent ones within the negotiation space. The ABC first of all created a boundary between their viewers and Papua New Guineans by turning the disaster into entertainment. PNG and Papua New Guineans are objects to be viewed — at a distance. The entertainment value of the eruptions linked theatre and trivialisation. The eruptions were a fireworks display:

SD (ABC reporter): For the third day fireworks around the port of Rabaul two volcanoes to the north and south of the town spewing their deadly ash across the island of New Britain.   (21 September 1994) and theatre:

> The two mountains Vulcan and Tavurvur are continuing to erupt forming
> clouds of ash more than nine thousand metres high a spectacular floor
> show for those able to get close enough peppering the sea just off the
> shoreline a shower of fiery rocks.   (21 September 1994)

Stage and audience: this theatrical metaphor constructs a boundary between
PNG and viewers. PNG was set up to be a spectacle for the entertainment
of Australian viewers, and could provide entertainment for months or years.

> MG (ABC reporter): Oceans away our only access to the disaster could be
> a repeat of the red sunsets that filled the horizon when Pinatubo last
> erupted.   (24 September 1994)

The ABC emphasised the distance between its viewers and Papua New
Guineans by devoting much air-time (about 40%) to long-distance aerial
shots of the destruction of Rabaul. This had the double advantage of keeping
black faces out of Australian living-rooms and compensating for the dis-
appointment of not being able to 'entertain' viewers with lots of dead bodies
in the streets, for there were no dead bodies. The ABC never explained that
there were no dead bodies because the PNG authorities had successfully
implemented their evacuation plan.

The entertainment value of the disaster created interest — a device constructed between viewers and Papua New Guineans so that the latter's voices
could be ignored. Having constructed this boundary, the ABC was then able
to present a series of interrelated discourses to confirm the spacelessness and
timelessness of PNG. The first of these discourses is the most dominant and
longest running discourse on PNG, that of the 'typical' underdeveloped country.

> PH (female Australian plantation manager): Situations where at ts-
> moment there's er Seventh Day Adventist College next door has six thousand
> people to feed and they've only got taro and tapioca to eat and . water's
> running out the water's dirty people are getting diarrhoea and vomiting .
> and they just don't have enough food to feed people fresh food.
> PW (male ABC reporter): In Rabaul itself a dead city choked with ash
> buildings collapsed and reports of looting not just civilians.
> PH: and the police said pull in here . and the fellows the driver said no
> we've got to get the food down . to the camps they said no and they the
> driver said well how much is it going to cost us to get the food out . one
> truck? and the police said no we want the whole lot.
> PW: So the police have taken that food?
> PH: They they've commandeered the food. There's not three hundred
> police in Rabaul. There's no way they can eat three hundred tonnes.
>   (22 September 1994)

The interview was shown on the fourth day of the disaster. It lasted for thirty-five seconds, a long time in television news where the sound-bite rules, and far longer than any of the other interviews conducted during the disaster. According to PH, PNG is 'dirty, disease-ridden, backward, corrupt, inefficient and lawless' — in other words, a picture of the 'typical' Third World country. The interview locates PNG within a particular kind of global discourse about what 'developing' countries should be like and distances it from the 'developed' world. The United Nations told a different story a few days later when the situation was clearer.

> National implementation of evacuation has proven very effective with only 4 dead.

> Army rations distributed to 40,000–45,000 evacuees in evacuation centres. No report of disease outbreak.

> (United Nations: DHA report, 30 September 1994)

The perceived failure of PNG to conform to Australian, and therefore 'civilised', standards of law and order is a regular feature of ABC reporting on PNG. By constantly reporting law and order problems, the ABC denies PNG its own time–space to sort out the problem, a time–space that Australia itself has experienced. Every ABC broadcast on the eruptions featured a segment on the lawless state existing in the disaster area. For example, the day following the interview with the plantation manager, the television screen showed people taking goods from a supermarket.

> With many shops destroyed, looting is easy. Where they're still standing doors are forced open. In some cases it's looting for survival, food for people with no other choice, but there are also opportunists taking advantage of a situation the military and police don't seem able to control.

> (23 September 1994)

The television screen continues the images of policemen standing (apparently 'doing nothing') for several seconds into the next segment to emphasise the point. This is the only occasion when the editors continue the commentary into the next segment during the coverage of the disaster, perpetuating the discourse of absence of law and order in PNG. The ABC contrasts absence of 'civilised behaviour', represented by perceived lawlessness in PNG, with its presence, represented by repeated reports of Australian relief supplies flowing into the country. This contrast of presence and absence establishes two poles, with Australia going to the positive (presence) pole and PNG to the negative (absence) pole.

News items about disasters would not be complete without the human misery story. As Papua New Guineans could not be allowed into the living-rooms of Australians, human substitutes took their place. Abandoned pets, trapped in the mud and ash, provided the 'human' misery story for the viewers:

PW: Misery too for the hundreds, perhaps thousands, of dogs and cats left behind. We found this dog buried in a mud flow, just its head poking out. It had no food or water for four days. (23 September 1994)

SD (ABC reporter): Although the wreckage is everywhere, some pets have survived. [Image of a fluttering parrot tied to a beam]

(25 September 1994)

Human Papua New Guineans disappeared, metaphorically submerged by the ash and mudslides resulting from the eruptions. Pets can be seen in Australian living rooms. Domesticated animals are members of the family and thus may be considered to be co-eval with humans. The Australians did not 'domesticate' Papua New Guineans during their colonial occupation, so they never became co-eval in the way that they attempted to make Kooris (Aborigines) co-eval by fostering them in white families up to the 1970s, ultimately hoping to transform their Koori temporalities into the dominant Western one and to make them disappear by submerging their black genes with white genes.

The ABC acknowledged its role as an obligatory passage point and enrolled the volcanoes into the international news network by highlighting concerns about the environmental effects that the eruptions would produce.

News reader: There are also fears that the steady stream of poisonous gases now being emitted would further damage the environment.

(24 September 1994)

Environmental damage is harder to measure. Sulphur dioxide is being churned out in massive clouds above Rabaul.

MB (Australian geologist): I've seen estimates in the order of 50,000 tonnes of SiO_2 being injected into the atmosphere er SiO_2 is one of the er greenhouse gases.

MG (ABC reporter): Already 42,000 square kilometres of ash have spewed forth.   (24 September 1994)

The global effects of the eruptions had to be balanced, however, with the fact that they took place in a small developing country and could not have a major effect on the world's environment. On the third day of the disaster the ABC reported:

> DE (ABC reporter): On Tuesday the volcanoes were spewing ash and gas ten kilometres up into the atmosphere and so dense was the cloud it showed up clearly on satellite pictures. This is how the same satellite sees the cloud today. It's almost invisible.   (22 September 1994)

But two days later the ABC reported:

> News reader: Thousands of tonnes of ash and magma continue to pour out of two volcanoes and scientists claim a massive eruption could still eventuate.   (24 September 1994)

The dialectic of the entertainment value of the eruptions, with the dramatic images of twin plumes of smoke, one black the other white, billowing out of the volcanoes, and their reduction to a small, local event in environmental terms was a continuous theme.

> News reader: Geologists and climatologists are playing down the long-term ill effects from the eruptions around Rabaul. They say the eruptions, while significant locally, will probably have little effect globally. . . .

> DE (ABC reporter): The future of Rabaul itself is still in the balance. While some scientists paint a gloomy outlook for the town now blanketed by ash, mud and acid, others aren't as pessimistic. They point out that the eruptions around Rabaul aren't anywhere near as large as those round Mount Pinatubo in the Philippines three years ago.
>
>   (22 September 1994)

PNG's position in the global pecking order, behind the Philippines, was emphasised with an intertextual insertion of a mud slide on Mt Pinatubo that took place at the same time as the Rabaul eruptions. This playing down of the global importance of the eruptions was contradicted two days later when the volcanoes were placed firmly within the Pacific Ring of Fire, a major global feature.

> MG (ABC reporter): This eruption was not a complete surprise. Close to one thousand volcanoes lie in the Pacific ring of fire. [Map showing the Pacific Ring of Fire on the TV screen with Vulcan and Tavurvur clearly identified within it]   (24 September 1994)

The vulcanologists with their gases and the ABC reporter with his map locate the volcanoes firmly within the globalised Western scientific temporality of the arrow of time stretching along a single dimension to end at a definite conclusion; Ring of Fire and consecutive, ordered eruptions; cause and effect.

Papua New Guineans were denied access to this temporality. All the expert vulcanologists and seismologists were white. They located the volcanoes within a well-defined, global, scientific space, but the local space was trivialised. The large amount of ash that fell provided a vehicle for this. The ash, several feet deep, brought distant things within reach.

> PW (ABC reporter): To give you some idea of exactly how deep this ash is . this here is an eight-foot high fence . and over here .. this street sign . would normally be well out of reach. What have we got here? Harbour Lane . easy reach so we're about probably about five feet of material here.
>
> (23 September 1994)

The reporter was able to touch the street sign. The ABC did not mention the devastating effect the ash had had on the livelihoods of the people. Most of those who live in the surrounding villages are subsistence farmers, dependent on the land. They lost everything as the ash destroyed their crops and covered the land to a depth of several feet. The local PNG station, EMTV, included extensive coverage and interviews with local people to illustrate just what effect the eruptions would have on the livelihoods of the people of the Gazelle Peninsula. None of this was included in the ABC's programmes.

Land is an actor in the Gazelle Peninsula and has a major role to play in affecting people's lives.

> Land (*pia*) is perceived as an active subject. When ToVetenge talked about the Supreme Court ruling concerning Tokota, he said, 'Our land returned.' More important, land has the power to harm human beings. Somebody who wrongly claimed a piece of land could die. *A pia i panganga* literally means 'the land opens wide its mouth', it can swallow the person who wrongly claims it.   (Neumann 1992: 148)

In return, humans have respect for land and give it names.

> Land, as any Vunamami inhabitant will say, is the most basic element of life. Every plot of land ..., large or small, from beach landing place to uncultivated virgin forest, has its own name, and without knowledge of these names one is lost.   (Salisbury 1970: 67)

The ABC appropriated the land for itself and mobilised it as a little bit of its global space, particularly a global concern for the environment and the contrast between 'lawless developing' countries and 'civilised developed' countries. In return, the ABC moved Papua New Guineans into a spaceless, timeless nowhere; physically by the volcanoes dumping ash on their land;

globally by the ABC denying them access to the airwaves; and silently by the editors in Sydney excising their voices. Every night for several days the clock measured the time to start the news broadcasts. The editors divided the 30 minutes of the news programme into segments, mobilising news about the eruptions into the global media time–space. Once time has been made measurable and divisible, it becomes a neutral technology with a definite direction — 'it flows equably without relation to anything external' (Newton 1989 [1687]: 20). Papua New Guineans were denied entry to this Western, scientific temporality and returned to the mythical timeless nowhere on the other side of discourse that they were perceived to inhabit before the Europeans arrived.

Case 2   *The National*

The National is a daily newspaper that was established in 1993 to fill the gap created when the *Niugini Nius* ceased publication a few years before. It is owned by the Tiong family, which also owns Rimbunan Hijau, a Malaysian logging company that has 70% of the logging rights in PNG. PNG has one of the four last remaining extensive tropical forests. The Tiong family established the newspaper in order to stifle opposition to the practices of the logging companies which have aroused considerable opposition in PNG and overseas. The PNG Government gave the Tiong family a large negotiation space by relaxing the normally strict regulations on the employment of non-Papua New Guineans. Almost the entire management team of the newspaper is Malaysian, totalling over 20 people. Indeed, the PNG Government could stand accused of giving the entire country over to foreigners because 'national' denotes an indigenous Papua New Guinean. Awareness of such a sensitive and controversial name for the newspaper meant that the name was kept secret until a week before the launch (Wood 1999: 178).

The National is one of two daily newspapers in English in PNG. It is, therefore, an obligatory passage point for the transmission of news by print to the educated PNG population. There are three other newspapers; the daily *Post–Courier* (in English), the weekly *The Independent* (in English) and *Wantok* (in Tok Pisin, the only pidgin newspaper in the world). *The Independent* is owned by a consortium consisting of the four major churches in PNG — the Catholic, Anglican, Lutheran and United Churches. It is very active in reporting environmental issues and is very critical of the practices of the logging companies in PNG and elsewhere in the South Pacific. Supporting it are NGOs, such as the Individual and Community Rights Advocacy Forum (ICRAF), which placed announcements in *The Independent* during this period advising landowners of their rights and warning of the destructive effects of logging.

I monitored the coverage of forestry issues in *The Independent* and *The National* for a three-month period, May to August 1996. In this period forestry issues were regular features in *The Independent*, appearing as major articles, sometimes a page in length or more, in ten of the 14 issues. In contrast, *The National* carried three stories on forestry matters in its 70 issues in this period. One of the articles was half a page in length, and that was the article on the controversial issue discussed below.

The monitoring period coincided with a controversial forestry matter. In July 1996 the PNG Government increased the landowner tax on logs to K10 (= US$7.50 in 1996) per cubic metre from K4–5 per cubic metre (K1 = US$0.75 in 1996). The landowner tax is the amount paid by the logging companies to the owners of the land from which they remove the trees. The Finance Minister had announced the increase in the budget in November 1995, but did not impose it until 1 July 1996 when the second part of a loan from the World Bank was due to be paid. One of the conditions of the loan was an increase in the royalties to be paid to landowners in order to compensate them adequately for the loss of resources. The World Bank is concerned about maintaining the sustainability of the forests in PNG and is in conflict with the logging companies, who wish to log as many trees as possible. The Forestry Industries Association (FIA) refused to pay the increase in the landowner tax. The FIA consists of most of the logging companies in PNG, including Rimbunan Hijau, the largest of the companies. The president of the FIA in 1996 was Francis Tiong. He also heads Rimbunan Hijau's operations in PNG.

The Independent carried the story about the FIA's refusal to pay the increased tax on 5 July (pp.3 and 5) and in the same issue carried a full page announcement by the FIA of its decision not to pay the increase and giving its reasons. This included a table to justify its stand and to establish its scientific credibility.

The National did not carry the story until ten days after the FIA had made its decision not to pay the increased tax. It was one of the three forestry stories carried by the newspaper in the three-month period analysed. The president of the FIA, Francis Tiong, told his own newspaper on 11 July:

> We have reached a collective decision that we all are not going to pay the royalty.
>
> There is just no more money.
>
> You think if there is money to be made, we are going to go to this extent to confront the government. The truth is we are losing money. We are going to close down.   (*The National*, 11 July 1996, p.2)

The National reported the story with added support and comment by Jim Belford, the FIA's Executive Officer:

After operating costs, most companies are operating a loss, Mr Belford said.

Additionally, the government may have unintentionally planted a 'kiss of death' on its own much desired, but little realised, dream of having an on-shore timber processing industry.

There are companies out there with the financial background to make a go of major processing but the conditions are not in place, Mr Belford said.

(*The National*, 11 July 1996, p.2)

The National did not include any dissenting views on the FIA's decision. The FIA, through *The National*, had defined the limits of its space and was inviting the Government of PNG to enter its space by establishing the right conditions. *The Independent* offered an alternative space. It carried the story about the FIA's refusal to pay the increase in a box within a long dissenting response from ICRAF (*The Independent*, 5 July 1996a, b). The article outlined why the PNG Government had decided to implement the increase in July instead of in January 1996, as originally stated by the Minister of Forests. The World Bank would have refused to hand over the next instalment of a loan if the PNG Government had not instituted the increase. The ICRAF was very critical of the FIA, the PNG Government and the World Bank.

They [i.e., the ICRAF] further claimed that new policy is really an extension of the colonial system under which landowners are the victims of unequal and inequitable contracts.   (*The Independent*, 5 July 1996a, p.5)

The Independent set out the limits of the FIA's space literally within its own article and at the same time enrolled its readers into the controversy by locating its article around the FIA response to the Government. *The Independent* also carried full-page announcements by the ICRAF to landowners for the following three weeks advising them of their rights and what they had already lost because of the Government's delay in instituting the tax increase. These announcements were in both English and Tok Pisin. *The Independent* carried the story for several weeks, either as a feature or as advertisements informing landowners of their rights. *The National* used silence to create a boundary and to deny Papua New Guineans a voice on the matter. Its publication of the warnings from the FIA of loss of jobs and income was an attempt to win over Papua New Guineans and the Government by attributing to them a common concern with unemployment and inflation. It had no more information about the matter after the single feature article on 11 July. It did not publish the announcements, nor did it publish any letters of protest from readers.

Rimbunan Hijau, which led the attempt at defying the PNG Government, has been generating approximately US$1 billion annually in revenues. It dominates the timber industry in PNG and owns one of the largest timber concessions in the world at Wawoi Guavi in the Western Province of PNG — 474,078 hectares (Ecological Enterprises, 19 November 1996) and was planning to increase this concession to control over one million hectares (Ecological Enterprises, 5 August 1996). The logging companies in PNG had been paying K4–5 per cubic meter as landowner royalties while selling the timber overseas for K150–200 per cubic metre (Ecological Enterprises, 12 July 1996). Its threat to pull out of PNG because it was losing money was a presence–absence ploy made to pressure the PNG Government to confirm its position at the presence pole in view of the dire consequences that would eventuate if there were no logging practices in the country.

The FIA's threat to pull out of logging in PNG was welcomed by the environmental groups that have been cataloguing the logging companies' violations of PNG's timber laws and people's rights.

> PNG's forests are a great source of wealth that is like money in the bank. If the current bad actors don't want to harvest the timbers while providing a fair rate of return; there is a viable local small scale timber industry and other more respectful foreign operators that can bring equitable development. (Ecological Enterprises, 12 July 1996)

The environmentalists' concerns were shared by the World Bank. Both wanted to redefine PNG land and the trees on it as PNG time–space which would provide benefits for many generations. The decision by the PNG Government to increase landowners' royalties was instigated by the World Bank, which threatened to withhold from PNG an instalment of US$25 million of a loan unless it took action to protect its forests and ensure sustainable logging (*The Independent*, 26 July 1996, p.1). Supporting the World Bank was the Australian Government. The PNG Government, however, considered rejecting the World Bank loan and aid from Australia in order not to upset the logging companies which provide thousands of jobs (Ecological Enterprises, 19 August 1996). Also at risk were the considerable links between government ministers and the logging lobby, who 'have the most influential cabinet ministers under its sway' (Ecological Enterprises, 15 July 1996). One result of the Government's increase in landowner royalties was that threats were made against government officials and the World Bank by unknown criminal elements, and the World Bank's office in Port Moresby was placed under guard (Ecological Enterprises, 19 July 1996).

If the World Bank had not given PNG the $25 million loan, the Government would have been even more dependent on the revenues from the logging companies than before, even though, as the Prime Minister Sir Julius Chan stated, the loan represented only a fortnight's wages bill of the public service (Ecological Enterprises, 14 October 1996). Failure to obtain the loan would have jeopardised future loans from the World Bank, and other aid agencies would have thought twice before lending to PNG. These agencies include the International Monetary Fund (IMF), the Asian Development Bank, the Exim Bank of Japan and the Australian Government, who had offered 'a total support for PNG worth over K200 million' (Ecological Enterprises, 12 August 1996). The Prime Minister was not concerned, however, about losing World Bank funding in the future because:

> From minus reserve position two years ago, the country now has more than 350 million U.S. dollars in reserves, more than 60 million U.S. dollars above target.   (quoted in Ecological Enterprises, 19 August 1996)

He was confident that the PNG Government would be able to ride out the storm, and had informed the country that the government had contingency plans drawn up should the World Bank cancel the loan. This may have been said out of bravado rather than with any basis of fact, as an attempt to obtain alternative funding from Malaysia earlier in 1996 had failed (Ecological Enterprises, 25 July 1996).

While the World Bank was seen as a supporter of the forests of PNG, the severe conditions it had placed on the loan, the Structural Adjustment Programme (SAP) (27 conditions according to the Prime Minister (Ecological Enterprises, 19 August 1996)), aroused the opposition of the NGOs. They saw the SAP as causing undue hardships on the people by cutting social expenditure, such as medical services, and resulting in more people joining the ranks of the unemployed (Ecological Enterprises, 19 August 1996).

The threats against the World Bank and the Government paralysed both in their ability to act against the logging companies. The antagonism between the World Bank and the NGOs split the opposition to the FIA and also resulted in no action being taken against the logging companies. The unwillingness of other aid donors to provide loans placed the PNG Government at the mercy of the logging companies.

> Migration and visas, work permits, labor regulations, occupational health and safety are not serious regulatory impediments to loggers. . . . their actions can wreck the Papua New Guinea economy.
>
> (Ecological Enterprises, 25 July 1996)

The FIA was able to enrol the PNG Government into its space through financial inducements, both legal, as in employment of thousands of Papua New Guineans, and illegal, as bribes to ministers. The only official actor able to threaten action against the FIA was the Internal Revenue Commission, which could institute legal action against the logging companies over their failure to pay taxes. At the end of July 1996 any leverage the World Bank may still have had over the FIA was severely reduced when it threatened to cancel the US$25 million loan, reportedly because the Finance Minister verbally attacked the World Bank in Parliament.

Mr Haiveta reiterated that parliament had made a decision to amend the Forest Act and the decision stands, whether the bank liked it or not.

I want to assure the people of PNG that our external position is very strong and we can live without the World Bank if they chose to abandon the [reforms] program.   (*The Independent*, 2 August 1996, p.3)

It would seem that the FIA would get its way and create a state within a state, with 'honest and professional administrators too frightened to speak out' (Ecological Enterprises, 15 July 1996) and the PNG Government unwilling to jeopardise the economy. For two years landowners at Wawoi Guavi

> have tried to have the logging operation suspended based upon environmental and contractual concerns. The PNG Forest Authority has acknowledged that Rimbunan Hijau is in violation of their timber permit; and as such should be issued a show cause letter, demanding compliance or being shut down. However, the PNG government publicly states that it will not enforce its own timber laws because of fear that a shutdown would harm the economy.   (Ecological Enterprises, 19 November 1996)

The PNG Government had turned inalienable land into a global negotiation space. Having gained a large concession, Rimbunan Hijau excluded all Papua New Guineans, including as we have seen the Government, from further action or interest in the land. The trees were cut down and transported overseas to be turned into chopsticks or shuttering for the new skyscrapers of Asia. The people were cleared from the land with minimum compensation, and government directives and laws are ignored. Ancestral land was bulldozed, rivers polluted and promised infrastructure projects were not implemented. Rimbunan Hijau had mobilised an actor that should not be mobilised. Land is inalienable in PNG and by mobilising it Rimbunan Hijau had taken away the time–space that defines Papua New Guineans. They are condemned to a timeless, spaceless existence. Rimbunan Hijau, a Malaysian company, is supported in this by the Malaysian Government. The Malaysian Primary Industries Minister, Data Seri Dr Lim Keng Yaik, remarked:

> As for forest dwellers, they were just head hunters who had to be 'civilised'.

> Why do they want thousands of hectares of forest land? We give them sufficient enough for their hunting.

> (Ecological Enterprises, 18 September 1996)

This view was made in reference to the peoples of Sarawak, but similar official Malaysian views on the relative rights of loggers and Papua New Guineans have been made (see Wood 1999), and they provide the justification for Rimbunan Hijau to take over other people's land. Successful negotiations and contracts can only be carried out with those who are co-eval with you. Papua New Guineans are not considered to be co-eval, therefore their land can be appropriated for other purposes and they have no right to complain. So their voices are not heard in *The National*.

The PNG Government would not enforce compliance with the timber laws because it feared a shutdown that would harm the economy (Ecological Enterprises, 19 November 1996). The land became an extension of the company's homeland, to be exploited as it saw fit. Local workers were paid below the minimum wage set by the PNG Government. Foreign workers were brought in against PNG immigration laws. The logging company created its own mini-state that is not subject to the laws of PNG, supported by corrupt politicians and bureaucrats and complicit landowners. It had alienated land that is inherently inalienable.

For several months from July 1996 onwards the FIA kept up the pressure by running announcements regularly in *The Independent* lauding the benefits of logging to PNG, such as the fact that 13,000 Papua New Guineans work in the industry and the same number work in support companies, and the FIA's commitment to sustainable forestry with figures of the number of hectares planted. Each announcement states 'Forest Industries Association supports sustained forest industry PNG'. It did not run these announcements in *The National*, presumably believing that it had already succeeded in enrolling its readers into its time–space. The FIA was trying to achieve the same success with its crude repetition of announcements and statistics to silence its critics in *The Independent*.

The National appears every day, announcing the date. The editors divide the newspaper into sections, each informing the PNG reading public what is important. By measuring time and dividing it up into quanta, *The National* acknowledges that it is part of the globalised Western temporality. Absence of PNG voices on the logging issue places Papua New Guineans outwith the arrow of time. It refuses to accept that their times are contemporary with those of other reading publics elsewhere in the world and returns them to a past time of ignorance, a common past time, before they were 'discovered' and were in ignorance of the wider world. This attempt at creating a static society and mobilising the times of the people of PNG into a common past time cannot be successful because, as we have seen, other actors such as *The Independent* and NGOs are actively informing them of forestry issues. In 1999 the PNG Government announced a moratorium on all new logging permits in the country. This act of dissidence (Callon 1986a: 219–221) against the FIA is an attempt at closure of the matter by placing its decision beyond question and cancelling the distant time–space created by the FIA by relocating Papua New Guineans in their own time–space.

Discourse of silence

Follow the actors, says Latour (1987). If we do so, we find that the non-human actors — volcanoes, pets, logs — go one way into the global world and ordinary Papua New Guineans go another way into silence. The ABC and *The National* were not acting in consort in denying Papua New Guineans their own time–space, but they do have a common link. Both networks ultimately led to a definite conclusion and in so doing both expressed the Western temporality of the arrow of time. The ABC in its reports exemplified the Western temporality in its scientific mode by the cause and effect of the environmental impact of the volcanoes, and *The National* exemplified it in its economic mode by the transformation of trees into wooden artefacts via logs. Both directed the time–space of Papua New Guineans into a single black hole of silence, where there is no time. The result is the same, an atemporal existence on the other side of discourse into which Papua New Guineans disappear. Nothing can escape from a black hole, so nothing can be known about what is in it. PNG has no way out. Papua New Guineans are excluded from extending their time–space into the global space of the airwaves and even from their own space, their land. The ABC and *The National* translated them back to a mythical past of ignorance and otherness.

The ABC and *The National* abused their category entitlements (Potter 1996: 132–142) as obligatory passage points for the Papua New Guinean voice by constructing a single absolute silence that recalls the European knowledge about Papua New Guineans in pre-contact days, translating Papua New Guineans to the other side of discourse.

> Silence . . . is less the absolute limit of discourse, the other side from which it is separated by a strict boundary, than an element that functions along-side the things said, with them and in relation to them within over-all strategies. There is no binary division to be made between what one says and what one does not say; we must try to determine the different ways of not saying such things, how those who can and those who cannot speak are distributed, which type of discourse is authorized, or which form of discretion is required in either case. There is not one but many silences, and they are an integral part of the strategies that underlie and permeate discourses.   (Foucault 1978 [1976]: 27)

The silence that the ABC and *The National* have created is not the Foucauldian communicative silence that takes place in real time between co-eval actors; a silence that has presence by being detectable and meaningful, but a deep, absolute, atemporal silence. Because the ABC and *The National* denied Papua New Guineans access to their temporality absolutely, there is absolute silence because '[c]ommunication is, ultimately, about creating shared

Time' (Fabian 1983: 31). When the ABC edited out Papua New Guinean voices and when *The National* refused to print criticisms of logging practices, they were engaging, albeit unwittingly, in the same strategy. They were synchronising globalised Western time and manipulating it to place Papua New Guineans in a time which is other than the globalised time of the arrow of time; of cause and result, raw material and product. Their synchronised temporality located Papua New Guineans on the other side of discourse. Papua New Guineans have only a discourse of silence because they have no time; because they have no time they are not in-the-world. Papua New Guineans cannot escape from this atemporal state because they have no future.

Conclusion

The two cases presented here show, firstly, how Western conceptions of time and temporality become global as they are adopted by non-Western societies, and, secondly, the efficacy of Western conceptions of time as an agent of control. By denying Papua New Guineans Western conceptions of time and temporality, actors in the global networks exploit time and temporality to create an absolute silence on the other side of discourse. The mobilisation of Papua New Guineans to one side of discourse and other actors to the other side shows how powerful and effective absolute, divisible Western time is in its ability to simultaneously synchronise and control the knowledge and discourse of large numbers of actors.

8

Interactions between Thai male sex workers and their customers
Graeme Storer

Introduction

The degree to which ingrained sexual roles are challenged in the discussion of HIV and AIDS is a determining factor in the success or failure of safe sex representations (Nelson 1994). In the discourse surrounding HIV/AIDS in Thailand, homosexual practice has been a muted presence (Lyttleton 1995) and Thai male sex workers must respond to and ascribe meanings to HIV/AIDS campaigns largely directed at the 'family man' or heterosexually-active youth. This coyness to openly discuss homosexual behaviours serves to marginalise male sex workers, for in order to acknowledge this group we need to be able to talk openly about both male–male sex and male prostitution.

The sexual network for Thai male sex workers is complex and includes gay and homosexually-active men, *kathoey* (male transvestites and trans-sexuals) and women. The relationship between the sex workers and customers and management is characterised by a lack of personal scrutiny and the workers' ability to negotiate safe sex 'freely' is constrained by the power exerted by the management and customers. Power relations are manifest in terms of class, age and wealth and also in a 'protocol of service' which operates in either the first language, Thai, or a second language, usually English (Storer 1995).

In this chapter, I will draw on a series of in-depth interviews and group discussions with Thai male sex workers and their customers to explore the frames of reference and language used by the respondents in discussing worker–customer interactions. I will be concerned with four related research questions: How are male sex workers and their customers defining risk behaviours? How do the male sex workers and their customers negotiate sex sessions? What are the points of tension in the interactions between the workers, customers and bar operators and how are these discursively resolved? What are the implications for promoting safe sex in the community of men who have sex with men?

Background to the study

Epidemiological data from Thailand indicate that HIV incidence rates may be slowing among young Thai men and that this may be related to an increase in condom use, a decrease in the frequency of sex with commercial sex workers, and an increase in the frequency of sex with non-commercial partners (Mastro and Limpakarnjanarat 1995; Mason et al. 1995). However, similar behavioural changes have not been reported among homosexually-active men. In an early study of homosexually-active men in north-eastern Thailand, Sittitrai et al. (1992) reported high levels of casual sex contact and inconsistent use of condoms in repeated sexual contacts. A more recent study of male sex workers (msw) catering to male clients in northern Thailand reported low rates of condom use and high rates of HIV infection (Kunawararak et al. 1995). In a third study of same-sex behaviour among 2047 Thai military recruits, 6.5% of the recruits reported one or more male lifetime sex partners (Beyrer et al. 1995). Of these men, 97% also had female partners. Compared with men who reported only female partners, the homosexually-active men had a higher number of female sex partners, more female and male sex worker partners, and were more likely to be married. While reported rates of insertive anal intercourse with male partners were high, reported condom use was low (Beyrer et al. 1995). Because of a reluctance to talk about same-sex behaviours (Sittitrai et al. 1992) and because reported same-sex behaviour can vary considerably with data collection techniques (Beyrer et al. 1995), there is likely to be under-reporting of male–male sex. In addition, many of the Thai msw are behaviourally bisexual and their sexual and social networks are complex (Storer 1998). These findings highlight the need to broaden HIV prevention strategies, giving greater emphasis to male–male sex behaviours.

There has been some research with the managers of gay bars in Thailand (Sittitrai et al. 1994), but little has been done with the customers. While the recruitment of customers is problematic, the reluctance to publicly address behaviours relating to homosexually-active men is a major prohibition. In this chapter, I will attempt to redress this issue by focusing attention on the interactions between the sex workers, management and customers and associated issues of power; the way in which sex work is socially constructed; and the effect of legal issues on sex workers and their practice. In order to do this, I will draw on a series of individual and group interviews with Thai male sex workers and their customers to explore the frames of reference and language used by the respondents in discussing worker–customer interactions.

I will begin by discussing issues related to gender and sexual identity in Thailand and the social constructions of male sex work. I will then draw on research data to scrutinise a service protocol operating in the bars. Next, I will map these representations onto a discussion of male–male sex behaviours.

I will then return to the notion of a community of men who have sex with men before discussing the implications of this work for promoting safer sex behaviours among Thai msw and their customers. But first, I will review the methodology of the research informing the discussions.

Methodology

This report is part of an on-going study and draws on a series of in-depth interviews carried out over a twelve-month period (from April, 1994 to March, 1995) with male sex workers working in various bars in Bangkok and with regular male customers of the msw. The customers included Thais and non-Thais, who were either living in Thailand or visiting Thailand. The interviews with the male sex workers were conducted in Thai at times convenient to the workers, usually late afternoons or early evenings in a Bangkok apartment. The men were paid for their time. Interviews were typically one-on-one, though in some instances two friends were interviewed together. This provided a check on whether the informants were shading their responses or not. Some of the informants were interviewed two to four times over the twelve-month period. All interviews were tape recorded. Notes were written up immediately after each interview and the tapes were transcribed into English by the interviewer (referred to as GS in the transcript) within 24 hours. Translations were discussed with English-speaking Thai men. The interviews with customers were carried out at a place chosen by the informants (either in the privacy of their homes or at some neutral venue). In addition, group interviews were conducted with gay-identified Thai men and with *kathoey*. Interviews with non-Thai informants were carried out in English. All informants were given the opportunity to contact the interviewer for a follow-up talk.

The msw informing this study ranged in age from 19 to 28, with the majority between 19 to 22. A total of 24 msw participated in the interviews. In addition, there were twelve customers and five bar operators. The msw were recruited from either inner-city bars in the Patpong area of Bangkok or from suburban bars in the Saphan Kwai area of Bangkok. All names of the informants and venues have been changed to maintain anonymity. The use of italics in the transcripts indicates either a transliteration of the Thai or words borrowed from English. Bracketed dots (. . .) indicate pauses.

A note on terminology: In this chapter, I will use the term homosexually-active men as a category to include all male–male sex behaviours. The term gay will only be used to refer to men who identify as gay. Thai male sex workers, irrespective of their age, are referred to as *dek* (literally child or 'boy'), a term which reflects their younger age and lower status. There is, of course, considerable control exercised in this naming and I will use the term 'boy' only in direct quotation. Otherwise, I will use msw or 'worker'. The term *farang* is used by Thais to refer to a Westerner (non-Asian) and will also be used here. Other non-Thais will be referred to as foreigners. When a customer takes a worker *off* from the bar, he pays a fee to the bar and then a 'tip' to the msw after the session. The term *off* is part of the vernacular of the bars and will be used throughout the chapter.

Gender and sexual identity

A number of demographic studies of msw in Thailand highlight that the majority of Thai msw do not gay-identify (Nopekesorn *et al.* 1991; Sittitrai *et al.* 1992; Kunawararak *et al.* 1995; Narvilai 1994a; Srivatjana 1995). But, as I have discussed elsewhere, gay identification in Thailand is problematic and constrained by a traditional gender role bifurcation and a lack of clarity of terminology (Storer 1999). As issues of identity appear to be significant in understanding occupational practice (Boles and Elifson 1994: 46; de Graaf *et al.* 1994: 287), I will briefly review Thai social constructions of gender and sexual identity and male prostitution.

While it is not immediately apparent what societal sanctions are at work in Thailand on those men who openly admit to sex with men (Sittitrai *et al.* 1992: 22), there is a definite 'reluctance and delay in applying stigmatized labels to oneself' among Thais (Murray 1992: 31). As in other parts of the world, the perception that homosexuality negates or violates family roles can inhibit disclosure of homosexual identity. But the decision not to disclose or the avoidance of disclosure raises a further risk, the risk of discovery (Strommen 1989: 54). To identify oneself as a male sex worker servicing men, a man becomes subject to the discourses which stereotype masculinity and stigmatise prostitution (Browne and Minichiello 1995). This sets up a double prohibition for the male sex worker, the fear that his family will know that he is prostituting himself — with other men. In order to maintain 'image' (*pha-phot*) and 'face' (*naa*), Thai msw hardly ever talk among themselves about sex with their customers. Such performance management (Goffman 1969 [1959]) can inhibit frank discussions about male–male sex and associated risk behaviours. In addition, it becomes difficult to plan and implement interventions aimed at customers when their homosexuality is hidden and casual.

The poverty of vocabulary to describe homosexuality in Thai means that more often than not the language of homosexuality is English (Morris 1994). But while terms like *gay*, *gay king* and *gay queen* have been appropriated into the Thai vernacular, they seem to mean different things to different people. It is the presumption that masculinity and homosexuality cannot co-exist (Robinson and Davies 1991) and the lack of precision in terms to talk about gay identity that enable Thai men to avoid self-categorisation as homo-sexuals and thereby preserve their masculine self-image.

Each of the gay bars in Bangkok has its own culture which reflects a particular market niche. In some instances, this culture does not allow for homosexual identification, especially in bars like the Tulip where customers go to find 'real' men (read muscle men) and where watching the men lift weights is part of the performance. But at a bar like the Superman, it is acceptable for the msw to gay-identify. Noel, an Australian living in Bangkok, describes it this way:

> It is interesting to look at how the culture of a bar defines the boys. For example, the guys at the Big Boy or Tulip all act like 'men' while in Bar Carousel they act gay. In Superman, you can be either. It's a tolerant environment for those boys who are gay.   (Noel, 08/12/95)

Thus, while a number of studies of Thai msw highlight that the majority of the workers do not gay-identify, the findings can be challenged. Questions that ask, *Are you gay?* or *Do you prefer to have sex with men?*, invite denial in a gender-defined system where terms like 'complete' men (*phu-chai tem tua*) or 100% men (*phu-chai neung roi per sen*) retain currency. Sam had this to say about fellow msw who deny their homosexual feelings:

> They can't say that they are men when they sleep with other men and have feelings ... If you're a 100% man, then you can't sleep with another man.
>
> (Sam, 23/01/96)

In the next section, I will discuss how social constructions of male prostitution serve to constrain Thai male sex workers.

Social constructions of male sex work

Though highly visible, both male and female prostitution remain illegal in Thailand, a factor which impinges on sex workers and their practice, as Sam explains:

> When it was over, [the customer] said that I hadn't been any good (. . .) That I hadn't given it everything. Like this, 'I spent my money at the bar already. You can go and get the money from them. I paid 200 baht [about eight dollars] in the bar. Go and get the money from the bar.' (. . .) And he walked out of the hotel. [laughing] I thought: 'What!' One of the other boys probably wouldn't give in. But me (. . .) Whatever. Because if you work like this, there is no law. It was bad luck. Another day and I will look again.

> You can choose either to work within the law and make 100 per day (. . .)
> Or you can work outside the law and make sometimes 2,000 per day. Some
> days, 1,000. Some days, 500. Which one would you choose?
>
> (Sam, 23/01/96)

In a Masters research study, Anan Narvilai (1994a) speciously argued that young men from up-country, either out of curiosity or from economic necessity, are lured into prostitution and that in the process, they become homosexuals (or at least bisexuals). Further, this trend could lead to an increase in the number of homosexuals and an erosion of Thai society. I would make two comments here. first, we need to avoid being seduced by cause and effect enquiry into homosexual behaviours and the notion that '. . . masculinity is a fragile essence, more easily spoiled than maintained' (Murray 1992: 31). Second, it is possible that for some, male prostitution may be a safe entry to a homosexual experience without being labelled as queer. Narvilai's research was apparently prompted by Peter Jackson's work on homosexuality in Thailand (Jackson 1989) as he felt that Jackson had '. . . applied a very Western perspective' to Thai homosexuality (Narvilai 1994b). Unfortunately, Narvilai did not seem to challenge any of his informants' responses and his conventional reading of the research data confuses sexual behaviour with sexual identity, reinforces stereotypes about homosexual behaviours and desires, and does little to serve the needs of Thai msw. Such an ideology of deviance disempowers sex workers (Browne and Minichiello 1995). It would be more useful to realise the central role played by the msw in a complex pleasure economy, and that an extended workforce ranging from the ice men and waiters to pimps and accountants depends on this economy to make a living.

The development policies pursued in the Thai government's successive Five Year Plans for the past several decades have unintentionally separated Thai women and men from a rural subsistence lifestyle (Winichakul 1995: 116–117) and fostered an economic climate that favours sexual exploitation of the female and, increasingly, male body (Lyttleton 1994: 264). Sulak Sivaraksa, a prominent Thai social critic, believes that the Thai intellect has been colonised by a consumer culture (Sivaraksa 1995: 52) in which consumer goods have become symbols of 'modernisation' and the objects of class identification (Charoensin-o-larn 1988: 210). It is this culture of 'wants' and 'needs', along with a lack of regular employment in rural areas, that encourages migration to the major cities in search for work and a 'better' life. But work opportunities for migrant youth with little education are limited. The minimum wage in Bangkok is currently 160 baht (approximately US$4.00) per day. However, a construction worker may start on as little as 100 baht per day, especially if an agent has been involved in recruiting work crews from up-country. A waiter in a restaurant might make as little as 2000 baht ($50) per month with meals thrown in. If we factor in accommodation, daily living costs and transport to and from work, there is little left over, even for those with a 'good' job, as Tam explained:

> Tam has been working at the Mandrake Bar for about two weeks. During the day, he is a goldsmith and works for a jewellery store. The work is relatively light — he goes into work around 9 in the mornings and finishes around 5:00 pm — and he makes 6,000 baht per month: 'But it isn't enough . . . Without extra money, there's nothing to do'.   (Tam, 14/12/95)

Thus, in many cases, working in a gay bar is not a last resort but a pragmatic economic choice, though it would be naïve to suggest that these choices are always made in circumstances of the workers' own choosing. Most msw enter the bars because the work provides them with much more money than they can make in any other job and with a modicum of control over their lives. In addition, bar work doesn't require long working hours (Storer 1995).

A protocol of service

> **Scene from a bar**: It is early evening and the bar is just warming up. The workers are sitting around in small groups talking while waiting for customers. Maen is with the only customer in the bar, a *farang*. Maen looks across the room at one group who are 'camping' it up. Then he turns to the customer and speaks:
>
> Maen   Look at those *kathoey*. I hate them.
> GS[1]   Why do you hate them?
> Maen   I don't like gays.
> GS   But I'm gay and I don't behave like that. But I do like having sex with men.
> Maen   Oh yes, that's okay. I'm the same. (Maen, 04/11/95)

For the msw, a protocol of service demands that he pleases the customer (*ao jai khaek, taam jai khaek*, — to do what the customer wants, to please the customer) and the ability to call on multiple identities is a must. Presentation of the self is all important here and the sex worker engages in a chameleon-like game, adjusting himself to satisfy the service protocol and pull a trick.

There are a number of points of control in the bars and a 'subtle hierarchy' exists, with uniformed doormen and waiters seeing themselves as superior to the male sex workers, and negotiation of the *off* may be constrained before it even begins. In some bars, for example, the workers can cruise the crowd of customers, but in others, they must sit to one side and wait for the *kaptan* (captain) to intervene. In bars operating a call-out service, it is the manager or *kaptan* who takes the phone call and who is in a position to 'favour' certain workers — it is important to be on good terms with the *kaptan*. In certain bars, the owner/manager 'tries out' the workers when they first start in the bar. This is often couched in terms of needing to be able to make recommendations to the customers.

> In other bars, for example, Andy's (. . .) When a boy starts in the bar, he has to pass (. . .) he has to pass the manager first.   (Sam, 23/01/96)

The larger bars in the inner city area pay the workers a retainer for turning up. Superman, for example, pays the workers 50 baht per night (though this is not paid if they are *off*). The workers also get commission on the drinks a customer orders for them and for appearing in the shows. However, an elaborate system of fines means that the workers may end up owing the bar money. If they don't turn up, they are fined 200 baht per evening (or the equivalent *off* fee). Some bars fine the workers if they miss regular health checks or if they do not get enough *offs*. Service payments are due at the end of each month but are usually delayed, a ruse that ensures high attendance and hence a big selection for the customers.

In the next section, I will look at how the msw and customers negotiate the *off* and safe sex behaviours.

Negotiating safe sex

Generally, the workers' knowledge levels about HIV/AIDS were high and they expressed concern about their health and risk at work. However, confusion and misinformation about HIV remained and no distinction was made between HIV and AIDS (see also McCamish and Sittitrai 1996). In addition, the msw from the suburban bars were less aware of health issues and seemed unprepared to negotiate the *off* with their customers compared with those from the Patpong bars. In both groups, decisions about unsafe sex continue to include the perceived ability to 'know' a person's HIV status.

> GS   Have you ever [not used a condom]? (. . .) Sometimes?
> Toon [quietly] With Thais, sometimes (. . .) Sometimes. With farangs, I always do.
> GS   Always. And when you are *off*, who is the one to suggest condoms (.) You or=
> Toon   =I always carry a condom.
> GS   Yes.
> Toon But usually the farangs have condoms.
> GS   When you go with a customer and you don't use a condom (. . .) How do you decide whether or not to use a condom?

Toon You mean with the Thais?

GS   Yes.

Toon Usually, I look at them first. Is he likely to be positive, unlikely to be positive? (*Naa pen mai, mai naa pen mai?*) Like this.

GS   Why don't you want to use the condom?

Toon [quietly] I don't know. I want to use [a condom] but my heart is not in it (*yaak chai tae jai jing mai yaak chai*).   (Toon, 18/12/95)

My first reaction was to try and situate Toon's comments within the Thai value system — 'smooth interaction,' 'image', and 'appearance,' and acceptance 'at face value' (Komin 1990; Morris 1994). But, of course, there were expatriate men who thought the same way — Brad, for example, who told me that he always avoids the thin men (field notes, 11/12/95). On reflection, I would suggest that some gay men have become more interested in safe men than safe sex and the ability to 'know' is a common mis-perception. Perhaps, it indicates how much we would like to believe we have control in this time of uncertainty.

But the bottom line is economics — one still needs to pay the rent — and, as with female sex workers, economic livelihood for a msw may be improved by a willingness to engage in high-risk sexual activities (Sittitrai *et al.* 1992: 2). There is a 'disturbing fatalism' among the workers, and condom use seems to be based much more on feelings than on financial temptation (McCamish and Sittitrai 1996). Although the bars program safe sex by supplying the workers with a condom and lubricant when they are *off*, it is not clear that this safe sex culture is always carried outside the workplace setting (Storer 1995).

Noel In Superman bar there is a lot of unprotected sex going on. I took a boy off recently. He was 20 and just discovering his sexuality. He wanted to sit on me without a condom.

GS   How did you deal with this?

Noel There's another boy in Superman who has his eye on [the young man]. The boys in Superman sometimes get off with each other. I'm going to talk to him and tell him to talk to him about safe sex (. . .) Why is there so much unprotected sex at Superman? It's an older established bar and there have been interventions there in the past. What are the boys saying to themselves? I'm tattooed and therefore protected? My amulets will protect me?

(Noel, 08/12/96)

All of this may appear to be idiosyncratic, but it is a reminder that actual risk behaviour is determined by perceived risk (based on the 'reading' of health messages); signifiers in terms of partner status; and situational determinants such as emotional needs and relationship status. Unfortunately, not all customers see that they have a role to play in promoting safe sex, despite the fact that they bring an 'authority' to the negotiation (through their age, educational background and buying power).

> GS I was wondering if the guys ever talk to you about health issues? If they bring up the subject of safe sex?
> Reg Well, if it's a bar boy then they always carry condoms. The bar gives them lube and condoms. I carry condoms. I always take precautions. But at my age (. . .) we didn't grow up using condoms and I don't really like condoms. It depends what you're going to do of course. I don't use condoms all the time because I don't always have (. . .) how does one say this? Is there a nice way to say this?
> GS Probably not, just say it.
> Reg Yes, well sex is not always anal. Sometimes I just like to cuddle. But if I'm having heavy sex then I'll use condoms. My friend here (. . .) we never do it because he doesn't like insertive sex. But I won't use a condom if I'm having oral sex. I don't do that. For one thing, I don't like the taste of the condom. It turns me off.
> GS Do you think that there is a safe sex culture among the Thai men?
> Reg Well the bars program safe sex through the boys. They supply them with condoms and lube and the boys have regular checks, every week or every month (. . .) I don't know which.
> GS But what about customers? Why not give condoms to the customers?
> Reg [Grimacing] Well I don't know about that.   (Reg, 09/01/96)

Jan de Lind van Wijngaarden's study of msw in Northern Thailand suggested that *farang* men are less likely to insist on anal sex (de Lind van Wijngaarden 1995: 7). Chai confirms this finding:

> With Thai customers it is difficult. They expect us to do everything they want. With *farang* it is easier to agree. Usually the Thais want to have anal sex (. . .) With Thais it is necessary to agree everything before leaving the bar. With the farangs you can just go.   (Chai, 27/12/95)

A possible explanation here is that the msw are less able to negotiate sexual practice with Thais because they are aware of and constrained by Thai social strata. In the Bangkok-Thai language, 'each pronoun not only signifies the status of the speaker but also his or her position within the hierarchy of the entire society' (Charoensin-o-larn 1988: 220). *Pee-norng* (older-younger brother or sister) are commonly used to substitute for 'I' and 'you' and express familiarity. However, they also reinforce an age difference and can thus retain a hierarchical structure implicit in the more formal pronouns. In the following transcript, Sam describes how his customers 'negotiate' the *off*. Note the repetition of *pee* (older brother) and how the customers focus on their personal needs rather than on risk assessment. Sam's response is well rehearsed.

GS   Sam, some of the guys I talked with told me that the customers say things like: 'You don't have to worry. I'm clean. I go to check my blood often. There's nothing wrong with me.'

Sam I've met this many times (. . .) I think that 70% of [my] customers speak like this. *Pee sa-aat. Pee pae condom. Sai laew khorng my kheun. Pee my chorp chak wao. Pee chorp ao. Torng ao sot. Took khon ja poot yaang nee.* [Older brother is clean. I am allergic to condoms. When I put a condom on, I don't get a hard on. I don't like to jerk off. I like to do it. It has to be 'fresh'. They all talk like this.]

GS   And what do you say when that happens?

Sam What I say is, How many people do you have sex with and not use a condom? And if I say yes to you, how do you know I won't say 'yes' to another person. I just have to meet one person who is HIV+ and it will spread to many others.   (Sam, 23/01/96)

Some workers reported that the *farang* are easier to manage than their Thai customers. But with both Thais and *farang*, the negotiation is limited and full of ambiguity and a worker's ability to negotiate safe sex with a customer is influenced by how confident he is and by his language skills. In some instances, not having a common language proves to be an advantage precisely because the negotiation is limited. In other cases, however, it proves to be disastrous, especially if the msw feels obliged to satisfy the service protocol. Lao, who could not speak English, tells about an early experience he had with a *farang* customer:

I met (. . .) a sadist (. . .) I mean, we had undressed (. . .) He turned on the video (. . .) He used KY like an 'injecting' type and he put it in me and then he pushed it in (. . .) He didn't like (. . .) He didn't go (. . .) He didn't go gently. He pushed it right in. Pushed it right in and then bit me here, bit me there. It really hurt. I couldn't stand it. *Okay*, I couldn't stand it but I had to put up with it (. . .) Because he was a customer. If I really couldn't stand it (. . .) If it was a Thai, then I would be angry. I would have to like (. . .) I would have a fight for sure. But this is a *farang* customer. And another thing, I'm worried that the bar will get a bad name. I have to put up with it.   (Lao, 21/12/96)

A final area for concern is the high turnover of men in the bars; many drift in and out of the bar scene for seasonal work or to free-lance (McCamish and Sittitrai 1996). Others move from bar to bar. While new workers are told about the bar rules, they are not given any information about health-related issues and they are unlikely to learn anything from the old hands in the bar.

In conclusion, while a safe-sex culture is presented in the bars, this culture is not always carried outside. A worker's ability to negotiate sex 'freely' may be constrained by the on-going interaction between the protocol of service;

the language of negotiation; and structures of class, age, regionalism, gender and sexuality. There needs to be a stronger bar endorsement for safety that actively supports the msw and the customers need to be more aware of the role they have to play in promoting safe sex practices. Condoms could be given to customers to reinforce this message. Further, health messages displayed in the bars need to be directed at both the customers and workers and should, therefore, be written in English and Thai.

A community of men who have sex with men

In section one, I referred to a community of men who have sex with men. The notion of 'community' is of course ideological and it is still not clear at this point if such a community will define itself in Thailand. On the one hand, gay-identification is constrained by a gender-role stratification that maintains the notion of 'real' men versus submissive women and trans-gender or effeminate men (Storer 1999). On the other, homosexuality has never been explicitly oppressed in Thailand and sanctions against male homosexuality tend to be non-interventionist. Thai gays can show their resistance to restrictive social norms by simply ignoring them (Jackson 1995) and we should not expect to see a 'gay community' as defined in the West that is founded on a tradition of liberation.

Nevertheless, I feel that it is important to promote a sense of fellowship among Thai msw because it seems that sexual safety is a social process and because peer support may be critical in promoting the motivation and intention central to behaviour change (McCamish et al. 1993: 190–194). I am not suggesting a community based only on homosexual identity; to do so would be to consider that competing interests cannot co-exist. Because many of the Thai msw are behaviourally bisexual, responses to HIV and related health issues can be either (in)formed or limited through their attachment to the Thai gay community.

At present, however, there is no stable and embracing pattern of mutual interaction among Thai msw and it would be dangerous to interpret the Thai value of 'smooth interaction' automatically into safe sex or into other support (McCamish and Sittitrai 1996). In general, close friendships are only formed with other msw from the same area, and msw from the north, northeast and south tend to remain apart. In addition, there is a high turnover of workers in the bars. Thus, interventions cannot tap into pre-existing social organisations. But we can take the lead from the women's group, EMPOWER, a non-government organisation that aims to foster self-esteem and personal pride and build solidarity among female commercial sex workers.

One way to begin to organise social groupings among Thai msw would be to build on regional affinities in which regional language differences are significant. Another would be to establish a 'drop in' centre for male sex workers which could open from early evening to late at night, a centre where the msw could seek advice about health management and other work-related issues in an informal setting. My objective, through this research, is to extend the concept of community to include a culture of need and struggle as well as a culture of sexual practice. But first, it will be necessary to promote a wider institutional acceptance for organising Thai msw in this way.

Conclusions and recommendations

Thai msw sociology (as reflected in both language and sexual practice) is not adequately addressed in the Thai HIV/AIDS discourse. In addition to being placed in the context of sexual negotiation and unequal relationships, health messages need to address the decision-making strategies used by the workers for personal risk assessment both inside and outside the workplace. Health messages also need to address both male–male and male–female sex practices. Bar owners need to promote a safe sex culture that goes beyond giving a worker one condom and some lubricant when he leaves the bar. They could begin by displaying explicit messages in the bar supporting safe behaviours, for example: 'Please help the workers to maintain *our* safe sex policy.' Giving condoms to customers with their change would reinforce such a policy. All messages in the bars should be given in both Thai and English to strengthen the idea that the workers and the customers (Thai and non-Thai) have a role to play in promoting safer sex.

The informants in this study were recruited from the inner city bars in the Patpong area of Bangkok as well as bars located in the Saphan Kwai suburb. In general, workers in the suburban bars were less aware of health issues and seemed less prepared to negotiate with their customers. While all the msw had heard about AIDS and all knew that unprotected penetrative sex poses a risk, other detailed facts were sketchy and often confused. Some of the msw knew of the virus but none made a distinction between HIV and AIDS. Not all negotiated the sexual session before leaving the bar and this sometimes led to disagreement later on. Programs to ensure that all msw have the necessary language and skills to negotiate safe sex prior to the *off* should be implemented. Issues relating to self-esteem and life skills that would encourage the workers to see their occupation as a small business should be included in training interventions.

Kippax and Crawford remind us that 'Particular practices (such as un-protected anal intercourse) *always* occur in a wider repertoire of sexual and social activities' and that changing '. . . a particular practice requires the reshaping of the wider pattern of sexuality' (1993: 256–7; original emphasis). Whatever one man says about why he doesn't use a condom when he has anal sex is only half the story and, thus, a biased view (Davies *et al.* 1993: 145). In this research, I have brought together the voices of Thai msw with the voices of their customers. What we have as a result are a set of competing but interdependent discourses: Sam believes he can negotiate with *farang*; Lao tells us that he cannot. Noel actively deals with safer sex issues; Reg does not. If we are to make sense of the realities described by these homosexually-active men, then msw research needs to include the msw, their customers and the bar operators. My research will continue to do this.

Acknowledgements

I would like to thank all the men who gave of their time to inform the research and who agreed to openly discuss their life stories. I would also like to thank Greg Carl (Research Associate at the Thai Red Cross in Bangkok) and Dr Anthony Pramualratna (Thai business coalition of HIV/AIDS) for their comments and advice.

Note

1.   GS refers to the author.

9

Media mythologies: Legends, 'local facts' and triad discourse
Kingsley Bolton and Christopher Hutton[1]

Triad societies and organised crime

The term 'triad' is generally used to refer to the Chinese secret societies involved in organised crime in Asia, Europe and North America. Most frequently, triads are associated with such crimes as drug trafficking, the smuggling of illegal migrants, loansharking, extortion, protection rackets, prostitution, and gambling, but are also represented in a range of semi-legal and legitimate business activities, such as property development, nightclubs, and the entertainment industry. The rhetoric that appears in Hong Kong and internationally on the wealth and power of triad societies is full of contradiction and inconsistency, and anyone seriously concerned with the analysis of Hong Kong triads soon becomes aware of a contemporary hall of mirrors. On the one hand Interpol officials are cited as claiming that 'Hong Kong's triads are the biggest and most powerful organized crime syndicate in the world' (Flynn 1995); on the other, police estimates suggest that only 5–10% of all detected crime in Hong Kong is triad-related. According to Hong Kong police sources, triad activity is not necessarily isomorphous with 'organised crime' in the territory, and some organised crime syndicates involved in specialised crime, such as the heroin trade, may work together with members from several different triad societies.

At present, an estimated fifty triad societies are believed to operate in Hong Kong, among whom the Sun Yee On (新義安), Wo Shing Wo (和勝和), and 14K (十四K) are judged to be the largest. The second-largest (with 60,000 members), yet best organised and most visible of these, is the Sun Yee On (New Righteousness and Peace). Today it is estimated that the Sun Yee On makes hundreds, if not thousands, of millions of dollars from a range of business interests in property, entertainment, foreign exchange, films and the video industry (Dobson 1993). Issues of law enforcement in Hong Kong in particular are complicated by a mythology based on a historical memorialisation of triads, in a fashion comparable to accounts of the Sicilian 'mafia', as a once-patriotic secret society committed to the overthrow of foreign usurpers. In addition, another set of mythologies have applied to academic writings on the subject, where triads have also been depicted variously as masonic fraternities, early revolutionaries, and migrant mutual-aid organisations.

Sociolinguistics and beyond

This paper deals with the discourse of triads as 'myth' and of triads as social reality grounded in 'local facts'. In our thinking about triads we have gone through a dialectic of our own. Initially, we accepted the criminological rhetoric of the triads as a powerful criminal conspiracy, or set of conspiracies. On closer inspection we became sceptical about the whole notion, seeing it as an Orientalist myth imposed under colonialism and then internalised within Chinese society. We saw the colonial criminology written into the law as paradoxically sustaining the triad myth. However, we came to see that this myth is one that is lived out by Hong Kong society today. Simply put, there are people calling themselves triads who engage in illegal activities. We can only call today's 'local facts' myths if we appeal to a more powerful myth, the myth of authenticity.

In earlier papers we have looked at so-called 'triad language' from a sociolinguistic perspective, seeing it as a source of lexical innovation for Hong Kong Cantonese (Bolton and Hutton 1995), and as a product of the scripts played out by police and triads in a quasi-symbiotic 'loop' of interrogation and prosecution (Bolton, Hutton and Ip 1996). A third paper (Bolton and Hutton 1997) looked at the issue of swearwords and sexual taboo words (粗口, *chòu háu*), which are also subject to censorship in television, films, and comic books. In this study we attempt to move beyond sociolinguistics towards a fuller understanding of 'triad' phenomena in the dialectic between mythology and 'local facts'. In conceptualisations of Chinese secret societies there is mythologisation of various kinds, in which triads are conceived of as a unity, a legend, a transcendent force, a global conspiracy. There is also demythologisation, in which the diversity, local identity, and socio-historical fragmentation of the phenomenon is emphasised. Frequently these two discourse strategies are employed together. In Hong Kong, for example, modern triad groups are often dismissed as mere gangsters and criminals, the unworthy usurpers of an original patriotic society, the Triad Society. The attack on the myth of today is supported by the invocation of the myth of yesterday.

Triad legends and historical facts

In their scholarship on triads and Chinese secret societies, modern western historians such as Dian Murray (1994) and David Ownby (1996) have sought to restore triads to 'the social, historical, and cultural contexts that gave rise to them'. This has involved seeing secret societies as 'informal, popular institutions, created by marginalised men seeking mutual protection and mutual aid in a dangerous and competitive society' (Ownby 1996: 1–2). Their view of triad history has emphasised local realities and historical conditions and is suspicious of 'global comparisons' in favour of a sociologically-informed understanding of the underlying social and political conditions that create a need for particular forms of sworn brotherhoods (Ownby 1996: 180).

Much of the impetus to the historical research of the last two decades comes from access to the archives in Beijing and Taipei, and the western writings must be seen in the context of a substantial body of work by Chinese scholars which has drawn on these and other sources (see Chin 2000). These archives reveal the Heaven and Earth Society (天地會) to have been 'a multisurname fraternity that was transmitted throughout South China by an emigrant society', 'a mutual aid society' rather than a revolutionary movement aiming to 'overthrow the Qing and restore the Ming' (反清復明). Images of the society as a loyalist conspiracy against foreign oppression 'tend to be generated on internally generated sources, and, in particular, on its creation myth, the "Xi Lu" legend' (Murray 1994: 2–3). That legend, which is transmitted in various versions, involves heroism on the part of the Shaolin monks in defence of the Qing Emperor Kangxi. Xi Lu (西魯) was the barbarian invader repelled by the monks. Subsequently the monks were betrayed, and they became outlaws, sworn to overthrow the Qing and restore the 'rightful' Ming dynasty to the imperial throne (see Murray 1994 for different versions of the myth). By contrast, the archives reveal the historical origins of the Heaven and Earth Society to have been in Fujian province in 1761 or 1762 in a Goddess of Mercy pavilion in Gaoxi township, Zhangpu county, Zhangzhou prefecture (Murray 1994: 5).

These historians' accounts of 'true origins' clash epistemologically with triad history enacted through ritual; these are incommensurable discourses. We wish to argue here simply that we cannot separate the history of triads from the history of myths about triads. In ritual, timeless myth is re-contextualised or reactualised in a defined sociological and historical space. It becomes 'local fact'. While the notion of triads as proto-revolutionaries and patriots may be a 'myth', it was a myth acted out by Sun Yat-sen (a triad office-bearer) in the overthrow of the Qing dynasty.

Colonial discourse: ambivalent paternalism and the invention of the triad society

In the nineteenth and twentieth centuries colonial scholars (missionaries, administrators, police officials, etc.) produced a large and diverse literature on Chinese secret societies (Bolton and Hutton 2000). Colonial discourse about triad societies was concerned with law enforcement, the business of Empire, as well as with the great mysteries of the origin, history and nature of human beings. The Protestant missionary William Milne, who coined the English term 'Triad society' in Malacca in 1826 (noting also that there was difficulty in ascertaining with certainty the name of the society), wrote that the triadic symbolism of the society reflected the 'Chinese doctrine of the universe' according to which there are three great powers in nature 'heaven, earth and man'. Like many of his successors, William Milne viewed the triad society as having degenerated from a past higher ethical state (Milne [1826] 1845: 59–61). This view of the descent of the triads is echoed down through the different generations of accounts of triads to this very day. There is nostalgia for a lost social order, but also the evocation of an ethically pure ritual state, a lost knowledge that binds the East and the West. In modern media representations, this moral fall is often symbolised by generational conflict and a decision by younger triads to enter the drugs trade.

The Dutch colonial official Gustav Schlegel (1866: ix) likewise looked at the triads within a universal, Masonic world-view. Admiration for the triad ritual reached its apogee in the writings of John Ward and William Stirling (1925–6). The 'Protector of Chinese' William Pickering (1878: 65–66), writing from Singapore, argued that the triads had been politicised by Manchu oppression, not by any desire on their part to take on a political role. Under British rule the situation was different, for the nature of British rule was such as to make rebellion unnecessary. Pickering clearly identified with what he saw as a triad elite and sympathised with them for the poor quality of their recruits, seeing in that elite a potential buffer class between the rabble of the colony and the British.

Colonial policemen-scholars, such as William Stanton (1900) and W. P. Morgan (1960) shared the reverence–denigration ambivalence, but their research was of course carried out with 'applied criminological' motives in mind. Anti-triad polemic is particularly strong in Morgan (1960), who, while not disputing directly the links between freemasonry and the Hung Society, cautions against a too idealistic view of the contemporary scene (1960: xviii–xix). Morgan however is caught in the policemen's dilemma: dismiss the myth, and devalue your own expertise; evoke the threat of triad conspiracy, and be seen to subscribe to the myth of an all-powerful organisation. In Morgan's rhetoric this dilemma is resolved by referring to the danger of a reunited triad society, and in pointing to its current disarray (1960: 92–93). In the colonial discourse, triads are both like 'us' — with their rituals and bonds of loyalty — and typical of 'them' — with their hostility to officialdom, opaque rituals and pre-modern social organisation.

As a footnote, it is worth noting that this 'mythical' notion of triads as erstwhile patriots has taken on a recent twist, with PRC leaders such as Deng Xiaoping acknowledging (in 1984) that 'not all triads were bad' and that many of them were 'patriotic'. There are growing business ties between PRC officials and Hong Kong triads (Dannen 1997a: 19–20), part of the wider process of reconciliation between refugee (and in part triad-associated) 'Old Shanghai' in the Hong Kong élite and the new Shanghai-based leadership in mainland China. As a further twist, it is worth recalling that at the time of the 'June 4' crackdown on the pro-democracy movement in China, some triad groups were allegedly involved in smuggling dissidents out of the PRC into Hong Kong, making them patriots of a quite different kind.

Triad language and the circularity of triad discourse

The issue of triad language emerged as a significant issue within the scholarly and popular works produced by these missionaries, colonial officials and police officers. Works of colonial anthropology often gave detailed accounts of triad ritual, with guides to the secret signs and gestures, and glossaries of triad secret society jargon. In this respect they are comparable to the extensive criminological literature produced in Europe on thieves' cant and jargon.

The term 'triad language' is capable of interpretation in a number of diverse ways. In one sense it can be understood as referring to ritual and esoteric knowledge (based on poems, legends, cryptic writing, secret signs, etc.). In another sense, triad language could be identified as the street slang of teenage gang members. At least one government body in Hong Kong, the Television and Films Authority (the forerunner of the Television and Entertainment Licensing Authority, Hong Kong's *de facto* censor) has attempted to define the term (Hong Kong Government 1978: 2), drawing on the familiar motifs of codes of secrecy, decline and disintegration:

> Triad language is a system of code-words and jargons developed through the years and used by local underworld societies for communication among their own members. The origination of the system dates back to the Manchu Dynasty during which underground organizations were formed to 'overthrow the Manchu Dynasty and restore the Ming era.' Due to the

underground nature of their work, the Triad members gradually evolved a system of communication whereby they could exchange message [*sic*] with no fear of information leaks. During the latter part of the 19th century, the Triad society began to disintegrate and slowly developed into decentralised criminal organisations connected with all kinds of illegal activities. The Triads' vocabulary is hence enriched with the addition of secret code-words and jargons related to their trades.

On close examination, however, the lists of criminal slang and argot provided by generations of authorities on triads turn out to constitute a self-contained and self-reflexive tradition, and items are copied from one list to the next. Writing on a Japanese source on triad writings, Hirayama, ter Haar (1993) points out that much of the Japanese scholar's work was plagiarised from Stanton (1900). Our own examination of the tradition suggests that this practice is endemic among colonial scholars writing on triad vocabulary. Schlegel is extensively plagiarised in Stanton (1900) and Ward and Stirling (1925–1926); and Comber (1961) relies heavily on Stanton.

How triads actually speak, or spoke at different periods, remains a moot point, not least because the question of who is a triad is itself anthropologically moot, but within Hong Kong today the colonial literature on triad ritual and triad language still plays a central part in the legal definition of triad societies, which are explicitly deemed unlawful under the territory's laws. The courts sentence offenders within a framework where teenage miscreants are labelled 'triads', but where the existence of a single, united Triad society is also denied. Triad experts from the police prosecuting teenage miscreants refer to the works of Schlegel, Stanton and Morgan to support their claims of expertise. Within the police force, officers are schooled in triad mythology and are issued with glossaries of triad jargon; but the discourse of triads now encompasses all of this and more, including the media mythologies of popular culture and the hard local facts of the Hong Kong street life.

These definitional uncertainties notwithstanding, one clear instantiation of triad language is in the names of triad ranks and office-holders. In this context, it is important to note the following. The traditional structure of a triad society involves a number of ranks with their numerical codes: Dragon Head (489, 大路元帥), Deputy Leader (438, 二路元帥), Vanguard (438, 先鋒), Incense Master (438, 香主), Fighter or Red Pole (426, 紅棍), White Paper Fan (415, 白紙扇), Straw Sandal (432, 草鞋), Ordinary Members (49, 四九). That said, the current structure of the triad society is much looser. Typically a triad group is led by an 'area commander' (坐館) with other office bearers, especially those of 426 rank. Ordinary members are still known as 49's, but young recruits are now often referred to as (Hanging the) Blue Lantern (掛藍燈籠) members. The status of this 'rank' is controversial in fact and in law.

The making of modern Hong Kong and the triads

In the period of late British colonialism from 1983–1997 (from the Joint Declaration until the 'handover'), the mythology of the Hong Kong success story promoted by the domestic and international media was that of the Asian economic miracle. The standard elements of Hong Kong's success story occur in most accounts: the relocation of Shanghainese industry and money to Hong Kong in 1949; the UN embargo against China dating from the Korea war; the growth of Hong Kong as a financial centre during the 1970s; and the shift to 'China trade' during the 'open door' era of the 1980s when Hong Kong was to account for almost 60% of total utilised capital investment in the PRC (Allen 1997: 192). But beneath the glitter and glitz of this success story there is another story, that of the gritty reality of Hong Kong social history, one which is much less well documented. Among other things the story involves the creation of a refugee immigrant community. In 1945 the population was just 600,000; by 1996 the by-census registered an estimated 6.2 million permanent residents. Successive waves of immigrants from the early 1950s and 1960s led to a rapid increase in the numbers of immigrants from the People's Republic of China. Thus this is also a story of living space, as this refugee immigrant community struggled for room to live in a city that was frequently ranked the world's most crowded.

According to Grant's (1998) analysis, the cultural formation of contemporary Hong Kong culture, like 'contemporary Hong Kong society', took place essentially in the years between the 1967 riots and the 1980s. Cantonese-language television began broadcasting in 1967; and eventually a Cantonese-based popular cinema reasserted itself in the late 1970s, after a period in the shadows of Mandarin cinema in the preceding decade. Cantonese pop music also began to dominate from 1978 onwards (Grant 1998: 12). By the early 1980s the key elements of a popular mass culture were all discernible, but the emergence of this culture, and the correlate of 'Hong Kong identity', were not created in a socio-political vacuum but constructed by 'historically specific formations of political and economic power' (ibid: 20).

The key watershed in the history of Hong Kong triads was the 1956 riots, when many triad members were deported to Taiwan, and the traditional initiation ceremonies disappeared under official pressure. The social history of triads between the 1960s and 1990s is largely unwritten and full of discontinuities, but it is clear that within the newly-created urban space of Hong Kong there was also the entrepreneurial space for triad societies to adapt to rapid changes in the economy. In the 1950s triads were already established in sectors such as fish and vegetable markets, hawkers, and petty criminals. After that date, they moved into the developing sectors of the Hong Kong economy where fast money was available in return for such services as protection, extortion, and loansharking. These new sectors included entertainment, such as night-clubs, karaoke bars, and restaurants; construction sites; minibuses, property sales, interior decoration, and the film industry (Chiu 2000).

In the context of a British colony, the absence of the strong centralising cultural force from China led to a strong local Chinese identity based in Cantonese and the equation of 'Cantoneseness' with 'Chineseness' within Hong Kong. That vernacular Cantonese identity defined itself primarily against colonial 'western' culture, and paradoxically drew authenticity from the availability of an easily identifiable colonial 'other'. Modern Hong Kong also saw the rise of 'realist' media portrayals of triads, often funded by venture capital from triad groups. This context helped create the triad film hero of modern Hong Kong cinema, which is discussed later in this chapter.

Local facts: triads in the press

A full survey of the coverage of triads in the Hong Kong newspapers is beyond the scope of this paper. Suffice it to say that the Hong Kong media make the most of the 'triad angle' to any story. The popular press such as *Apple Daily* (蘋果日報) and weekly magazines such as *Next Magazine* (壹周刊) and *Eastweek* (東周刊) feature extensive coverage of triads, including material from leaked police documents. Such police material also finds itself into Hong Kong comics that deal with triad characters. These comics often include an appendix giving information on triad history, language and ritual. A comic currently being produced by Young Best Development Limited, *Yaumatei, Tsim Sha Tsui and Mongkok* (named after three core urban districts of Kowloon, 油尖旺) regularly features short articles with basic facts about triads, triad lore and the Hong Kong underworld (names of triad groups, triad ranks, triad ritual, typical economic activities, in particular the sex trade), including triad terminology.

Anthropologically speaking, one key element in the triad question is that of ritual culture, including triad ranks. In general, the police and the media and prosecuting counsel tend to talk up the ritual elements of triad culture (to mythologise, in the terms of this paper); in court the defence will attempt to 'demythologise'. This can lead to somewhat surreal court-room exchanges. In one case reported by the *South China Morning Post* (Young 1996), the magistrate had convicted the defendant for triad membership on the basis of his acceptance of an undercover police officer's 'fawning offer to pour a cup of tea', and because he had been observed to call up 70 'brothers' to a dispute in a karaoke bar. The judge in the High Court considering the appeal 'questioned [. . .] whether accepting the tea was proof enough to have sent Lee to prison for eight months'. The exchange between the judge and the defence counsel, Kevin Egan, was reported as follows:

'What does all this mean . . . to pour a cup of tea? If someone said that
to me in my court I'd think he was a bit thirsty', Mr Justice Sears said. Mr
Egan tried to assist the judge while the court waded through descriptions
of triad rituals. He suggested that triad terms such as 'big brother', 'little
brother' and 'follower' had become commonplace. 'I've had solicitors' clerks
call me Dai Lo [Big Brother] Egan, so I don't know if that labels me a
triad', Mr Egan said. He said the use of these terms was part of normal
street jargon, could be heard on Chinese television, and was not proof of
Sun Yee On membership. But Mr Justice Sears admitted he could not
comment because 'I do not watch Chinese television'. In spite of these
doubts, the judge upheld the lower court's decision, on the grounds that
'certain behaviour by Lee had left no doubt that it was a proper conviction'.

One crucial question is the status and nature of triad ranks in modern
Hong Kong, and the picture one gets from the press of the status of the
triad hierarchy and ranks such as '426 Red Pole Fighter' (紅棍) and 'Blue
Lantern' is somewhat confused. For example, in May 1995, *Eastern Express*
reported the jailing of a 'Sun Yee On' office-bearer for recruiting schoolchild-
ren. The case was described as involving a 22-year-old man, 'a Blue Lantern
(ordinary member) with the Sun Yee On triad' who was attempting to 'boost
his underworld influence' (Western 1995). Talk of 'underworld influence'
suggests something rather grander than a small-time recruiter, but the key
question here is this 'rank' of Blue Lantern. One explanation offered by a
defence lawyer in an earlier case had been that 'the term blue lantern derives
from a mainland tradition of hanging a blue lantern in the home when
someone died' (掛藍燈籠). To join, a member had to sever links with his
family or 'die' (死) before he can be reborn as a triad member (*South China
Morning Post* 1994b). The 'classical' term for ordinary member is '49' (四九);
traditionally, Blue Lantern was not a rank at all but a kind of novice associate, certainly not an office-bearer. This definitional dilemma arises most
commonly in relation to triad initiation ceremonies or rituals. In June 1993,
the *South China Morning Post* reported on the trial of seven young defend-
ants convicted of attending a triad initiation ceremony in which 'they had
knelt before an altar, jabbing their fingers with a needle, reciting a poem and
paying $3.60 of lai see [red packet containing a symbolic gift of money]
during the ceremony' (*South China Morning Post* 1993).
    While the media will often take triad titles and terms at face value, there
is also a common journalistic trope of emphasising the 'depressing facts'
behind the triad stories (*South China Morning Post* 1994a). The emphasis on
the biographical realities of young peoples' lives often includes explicit
demythologisation. Chiu (1995) quoted one 19-year-old as summing up his
experiences with: 'Triads are nothing like what you see in the movies [. . .]
What you see are blood brothers swearing loyalty to each other, but in real
life, triads only care about money and how much you can make for them. If

you're willing to be their pawn for life, then you're finished.' Chiu sums up changes in triad recruitment as follows: 'Youths today are merely asked to pay a symbolic $3.60 lai see packet to a "big brother" to become a triad member', whereas, according to the police: 'Years ago, there used to be elaborate initiation rituals like chopping off the head of a chicken, burning yellow papers and taking oaths before a shrine'.

Triads in the movies

The history of criminal involvement in the Hong Kong movie scene is obscure, but it seems likely that triad elements were attracted by the prospects of quick profits as the local movie industry gained steam in the 1980s. Certainly Logan (1995: 122) makes this assertion in his account of the 'heroic bloodshed' movies of that era: '[t]he rapid rise in triad membership throughout the eighties was certainly caused, in part, by the glorification of the gangster in [Hong Kong] Chinese popular culture' and '[t]he heroic bloodshed genre rebounded on the film industry when real-life triads began forming their own small film companies to both make and launder money'.

The most successful of this new breed of moviemakers proved to be Win's Group (永盛電影公司), which has been closely associated with the Sun Yee On triad society. Win's is run by the Heung brothers, Charles Heung Wah-keung (向華強) and Jimmy Heung Wah-sing (向華勝) (Dannen 1997a, b). According to Dannen, Charles Heung is regarded in the industry as a 'good' triad (1997b: 31). Win's have been very successful in attracting talent to their studio, including actors such as Stephen Chiau (周星馳) (the comedy actor), and Andy Lau Dak-wah (劉德華), a Cantopop heart-throb and screen actor. Among the police, not everyone is reassured about the beneficence of Win's, and Dannen (1997b: 32–33) quotes an obviously frightened 'senior police officer' who refused to answer questions on the topic: 'Please understand — the Heungs are a sensitive topic around here. If I disclose information to you about the Heungs, I will be committing suicide. I do not mean that the Heungs will kill me. I mean that my career will be finished.'[2]

The triad film genre, which developed during the 1970s and 1980s, can be traced back to the crime movies of the 1960s, but the heyday of the triad film seems to date from the mid-1980s to the mid-1990s. During this period hundreds of triad movies appeared. They attracted not only some of the best directorial talent available, including Tsui Hark (徐克), Ringo Lam (林嶺東) and John Woo (吳宇森), but also the mega-stars of the local pop music scene, including Andy Lau Dak-wah, and Ekin Cheng Yi-kin (鄭伊健). According to a survey of Hong Kong gangster films (Chan and Lau 1996), Francis Ford Coppola's (1972) *Godfather* was the immediate inspiration for the Hong Kong genre, which began in 1974. Between 1974 and 1980 33 such films were made; sixteen between 1981 and 1985; fifty from 1986 to 1990; and thirty-seven between 1991 and 1995. The total for the second half of the 1990s remains to be seen, but given the current decline of production and the recruitment of action directors Tsui Hark, Lam, Woo, and actor Chow Yuen-fat (周潤發) to Hollywood, it is possible that the best days have passed (Halligan 1998).

John Woo's *A Better Tomorrow* was not the first film in the triad genre, but it set a benchmark for later films, and even today is regarded as a classic of Hong Kong cinema. It was produced by Tsui Hark and directed by John Woo. The film contains few specific references to triad ritual and triad hierarchies, but its treatment of the central scripted element of 'loyalty' and 'brotherhood' has a specifically Hong Kong resonance. The Cantonese terms are *yih hei* (義氣) or *lèuih hei* (雷氣, 'personal loyalty'), often translated as 'righteousness'. In *A Better Tomorrow* (英雄本色), Ho (Ti Lung, 狄龍) is a triad member, whose brother Kit (Leslie Cheung, 張國榮) joins the police force. After an abortive deal with a rival society in Taiwan, Ho is sent to prison and Ho's triad brother Mark (Chow Yun-fat) is crippled. When Ho is released from prison, he attempts to go straight (in fulfilment of a promise extracted by his dying father), but is shunned by his police inspector brother. Meanwhile, the society, now run by the traitor Shing (李子雄), attempts to force him to re-join. Ho and Mark join forces with Kit in a climactic shoot-out with Shing's triads. During the final sequence Mark is able to lecture Kit on the true meaning of loyalty and brotherhood, before his final words 'to be a brother . . .' (做兄弟) are cut off by a hail of gunfire.

Whereas the themes of male bonding, brotherhood, and loyalty (witness *The Wild Bunch* or *Butch Cassidy and the Sundance Kid*) may have a familiar resonance with US or European audiences, *yih hei*, in the Hong Kong context, is a distinct marker of ethnicity. *Yih hei* is a value in Hong Kong not restricted to triads, or males or brotherhood, but is more generally recognised by the mass of ordinary people as an elusive bond of personal loyalty where your friends keep their word in a fabled 'city of broken promises' (Coates 1967); where if you need a quick loan, or a place to stay, you have someone to count on. If you're fortunate, that someone is a brother or sister; but typically you have to look outside the family, and it is only then that you discover who your true friends are. A second element in the script is a pessimistic fatalism that runs through many of the other films of this genre. Movie triads, predictably, are not all bad; and Ho is a typical 'good triad', trapped by social circumstance and loyalties in a criminal underworld where there is no real loyalty or brotherhood. Nevertheless, in spite of the death of Mark (or because of it), the film ends on an upbeat note, with the 'heroic' message that after all *lèuih hei* does exist, and, against all the odds, can survive, even if it demands the ultimate sacrifice.

The question of heroism recurs in *Those Were the Days* (慈雲山十三太保, 1995, directed by Tang Yin-sing (鄧衍成)), based on the 'true story' of triads who had renounced their life as criminals to follow Jesus, which presents a comparatively realistic depiction of triad societies in the 1970s and 1980s. In an early sequence in a small flat in a public housing estate in Hong Kong, Chan explains to his mother his reasons for joining the society:

Mom: 亞華，我聽啲街坊講，話你入咗黑社會
Wah, I heard the neighbours saying that you joined a black gang. Really? Is that right?

Son: 你誤會啦，係國家社團。係三合會，係天，地，人，反清復明呀！
You misunderstand, it's a patriotic society, I joined a patriotic society. It's the Triad Society, Heaven, Earth, Man, Overthrow the Qing and restore the Ming.

Mom: 都唔知你噏乜
I don't know what you are talking about.

Son: 你梗係唔知啦，民族英雄嚟家嘛，不過，千奇咪話俾老豆知喎。
Of course you don't! I am a national hero. But, don't tell father.

Later, a voice-over read by the reformed Chan comments:

有好多人加入黑社會，係因為貪威，有大佬照，講義氣，包冇衰，另外有嘅人加入黑社會，認為佢可以保護倒你，唔駛俾人恰，又唔駛俾人打，冇錯，入咗黑社會，人哋唔會隨便打你，不過，一郁手就劈友。

Many people join the triad society because they want people to be in awe of them. They will have a big brother and talk about loyalty [*yih hei*]. Other people join the triad society, thinking it will protect them, and they won't be bullied by others, and won't be beaten up by others. That's correct, if you join the triad society, other people won't beat you up casually, but if it happens, then someone will get chopped.

While the film shows Chan to be a serious fighter, in this scene the absurdity of appealing to the myth in the context of a Hong Kong housing estate is apparent, as is the contrast between the big talk and Chan's fear of his father's disapproval. Given the fact that the Qing dynasty was overthrown in 1911, Chan is clearly talking nonsense. The triad myth is exposed as anachronistic; this is a demythologising moment in the film.

The theme of heroism is scripted into *The True Hero* (1994, directed by Joe Cheung Tung-cho, 張同祖), starring Simon Yam Tat-wah (任達華) as a reformed triad leader, who turns his back on crime to become a schoolteacher. Included in this film is a stock sequence showing the recruitment of schoolkid members in a housing estate playground. In this sequence, the kids, led by Kit (阿杰) are playing basketball in the playground when a group of young triads attack them. Another group of older triads intervene. The triad 'big brother' intervenes in the fight and immediately challenges the leader of the triad bullies:

Tiger: 死靚仔，夠膽係我嘅場玩嘢？你係邊度呀？
Bastard, how dare you screw around in my territory? Who are you?
Gang 1: 咪郁手呀兄弟，有事慢慢講呀，我哋係新蒲岡？
Stop! Pals, take it easy, we don't want any trouble. We are from San Po Kong . . .
Tiger: 聽唔清楚，新蒲岡邊度
I can't hear! Where are you from?
Gang 2: 新蒲岡 …
San Po Kong . . .
Tiger: 邊度？你，過嚟
Where? You, come here.
[. . .]
Gang 3: 我哋係新蒲岡金毛
We follow Golden Hair from San Po Kong.

This attempt by the younger triad bullies to 'state their allegiance' (響朵) and thereby avoid trouble is rejected:

Tiger: 甩毛我呀聽過，你班冚家剷再係度攪嘢呢，我全部冇面俾，即刻同我躝!
I've heard of 'hair loss'! If you bastards cause trouble here again, I won't give you face. Get lost, now!

Tiger then turns his attention to the schoolkids, and again goes through the 'script' of asking for their triad allegiance, but all he gets is the name of their school:

Tiger: 你係邊度呀？
Where are you from?
Kit's friend 1: 我係培德中學
We go to Pui Tak College.
Tiger: 哈肥仔，唔怪之得你咁契啦!咩叫培德中學呀？
Fatty, no wonder you're so dumb! What the hell is Pui Tak College?

Tiger then offers the kids the chance to join his group and follow him as their big brother. He takes them to a video games centre, where he identifies 'Brother Shui' as his 'big brother' (*daaih lóu*, 大佬) and their 'big brother's protector' (*a gùng*, 阿公): 'Brother Shui is my boss and he is your [big brother's] protector. He always teaches us to have guts and to have loyalty [*lèuih hei*].' In this way, Kit and his friends are recruited as followers in Tiger's organisation. Finally, the teacher has to intervene and see off the 'bad' triads.

This playground scene is a key element in the social organisation of triad recruitment, and this script recurs in police interviews with young triad offenders (Bolton, Hutton and Ip 1996: 285):

Q: Who invited you to join that sort of thing? The so-called triad society thing?
A: At that time we were sitting in Repulse Bay, we chatted and chatted about being bullied, no interest in going to study anymore. Ah G told me to hand over three dollars sixty and then I did. [. . .]
Q: Didn't she tell you, upon handing over $3.60, that upon being bullied, what should you do?
A: Locate the Tai Lo [i.e. state your allegiance, *héung dó*, 響朵]

It is enough in law to have the suspect say that they 'follow' (*gàn*, 跟) a protector and give the name of a triad society for them to be convicted of triad membership. Police interviews are structured so as to get the suspect to make this symbolic statement of allegiance, preferably using 'triad language' (e.g. *héung dó*, 響朵 'state your allegiance', or *gàn daaih lóu*, 跟大佬 'follow a big brother').

By the mid-nineties, the scripting of triad movies had moved away from the stylised epics of the previous decades, and there was an increased emphasis on street gangs, triad paraphernalia and the explicit use of 'triad language'. The prime example of this was a series of five films made in the 1990s based on exploits of a local triad comic-book hero in the comic *Teddy Boy* (古惑仔); these were called *Young and dangerous I–V* (古惑仔). These star Ekin Cheng as the melancholic 'good triad', Chan Ho-nam (陳浩南). In addition, *Teddy Girl* (古惑女) and *Portland Street* (砵蘭街) have also made the transition from comic-book to the screen.

In the early 1990s a debate about the effects of such media took place in the press. Critics of triad comics claimed that they 'tempt young people into joining triad gangs' (Chan 1993); and Wong (1993) reported that the government's Fight Crime Committee was concerned that young people were learning 'triad jargon and poems' from films. Dobson's (1993) exposé of the Sun Yee On cited a Sham Shui Po inspector who put the case more bluntly: 'A number of Hong Kong film stars are in the Sun Yee On . . . It is depressing to watch movies where they play cops fighting triads, because the truth is, in general, that the movie and everyone in it is working for the Sun Yee On. The irony . . . is that the public go to see a movie about good triumphing over evil, yet all the profits from their tickets goes to triads.'

Triads as portrayed in Hong Kong films, or at least 'good' triads, might be seen as representing vernacular Chinese values (loyalty, hierarchy, face, honesty) in a (colonial) world in which the dice are loaded against the ordinary person, the immigrant from the mainland, the streetkid. Significantly, in *Young and Dangerous V* (1998), Chan Ho-nam is shown as unable to read a business contract, signing it with a statement of faith in the personal relationship. As a result he is cheated. The equation of English with a foreign modern world is also emphasised in *A Better Tomorrow*, where in an early scene Mark is greeted in English by one of his boss's foreign business partners and smiles and nods as if understanding. When the foreigners leave, Ho makes a joke about Mark's lack of English. The modern world in which codes of loyalty do not apply is also the world of international business and triads without loyalty but with degrees in accounting. Here the clash of the pre-modern (solidarity, personal relationships) with the modern (law, English) is portrayed in pessimistic terms. The pessimism is reinforced by the frequency of betrayal in triad films, a theme that links the triad media stories to the myth of a lost world of pure (Chinese) 'knightly' values (Havis 1998).

Conclusion

Like the colonial officials before them, modern historians have written into triad discourse their own preoccupations and concerns. In Edward Said's term, these officials were *Orientalists*, looking into an exotic mirror and constructing their own private narratives about the peoples they ruled. These narratives, however, were not merely abstract musings; they evolved in a dialogue of sorts with the subject peoples (particularly the local elites), and were realised in the policies and categories of colonial rule. In this sense they entered the histories of the societies they governed.

Triad language might then be seen as an 'imagined language', a creation of Orientalism, since in a very real sense the Triad Society is a colonial invention; of course, there *were* societies and sects, but the 'Triad Society' label and much of the discourse that went with it was a product of colonialism. But it would be a mistake to consign the dialogue between ruler and subject — however unequal and ultimately punitive — to the realms of colonial fiction, to the past. For the colonial narrative was backed by real power, but one which sought various forms of accommodation with the cultures and peoples with which it was confronted. In this sense the modern historian's polemic is misplaced, for these texts are keys not only to the fantasies of the rulers but — to a degree — to those of their subjects as well. These subjects *qua* subjects lacked the power to resist the inscribing of these mythologies on their body social.

In 1996, the full complexity of this discourse hall of mirrors was brought home to us when we discovered at the back of a triad comic book the material reproduced as Figures 9.1 and 9.2. The circulation of the glossary, Figure 9.2, is restricted; to all intents and purposes it is a 'secret' police document. And yet it has obviously been leaked to the publishers of the triad

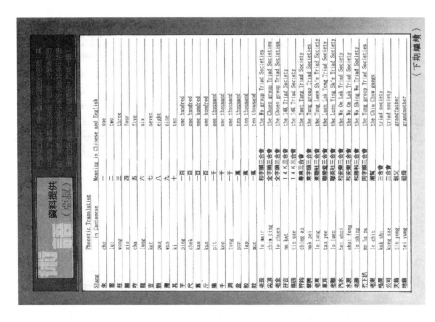

Figure 9.1 The cover of the triad comic, called *The Black Way and the White Way* (黑白道), printed in 1995 (Vol. 2, not dated). **Figure 9.2** A list of triad 'slang', reprinted from a police list, and reproduced on page 50 of this same comic. The source for this list is one of the special glossaries prepared by police triad experts and circulated internally in the police force for the training of officers.

comic, who, if we believe their own publicity, see part of their market as 'bad people' (i.e. triads), triad associates, as well as the local comic-reading public, chiefly young schoolboys. We are now faced with the possibility of an ultimate irony: triads studying police lists, which have been authored in the colonial tradition, in order to master a command of triad language, which police experts continue to study, and the use of which might be cited as proof of membership of a triad society.

The printing of a police triad expert's list of secret language in a triad comic book can stand as emblematic for the history of the triad question. For it is not only the Orientalist lists that are self-reflexive, that plagiarise, but also the 'objects of inquiry' themselves.

Notes

1. The authors wish to thank Ms Katherine Chen for her help in preparing this chapter for publication.
2. Most recently (Li 1998), the Hong Kong Government secretary for Broadcasting, Culture and Sport, Brian Chau Tak-hay, stated that there is 'no evidence' of a serious triad problem in the entertainment business.

Part

III

Professional and Academic Practices

Introduction to **Part III:**
The inspiration of inequalities

Interviewer: *What do you like about acting? Being someone else?*
Or the opposite, going deeper into what you are?

Eric Cantona: *What I like about acting is the very fact of acting,*
playing a part.

(INTERVIEW WITH JEAN-PIERRE LAVOIGNAT JULY 8, 1998)

In this final section of the book, we feature a collection of applied linguistic studies which are largely located in professional and academic practices. But this emphasis on *practices* is not prompted by a nomothetic desire to test out theories — even critical theories. Pennycook takes applied linguistics to task for its reliance on its psycholinguistic black-box emphasis on the cognitive processing of language, on formal semantic systems, but he also criticises more Marxist forms of critical language pedagogy, which tend to impose a deterministic theory of material imperatives on the analysis of discourse. One of the tensions that have emerged in poststructural linguistics has been that between a nomothetic search for language universals, whereby cultural variations tend to be accounted for as forms of 'variable rule', and the more descriptive idiographic approach to understanding difference on its own terms, such as the ethnographic studies of discourse practices. In searching for an alternative epistemological paradigm, it has been tempting for poststructuralist linguists to construct equally totalising accounts of discourse behaviour, to be drawn to the highest common factor uniting the data. More idiographically-driven theorising, such as we see in these papers, seeks to divert energy from the search for explanations to a constructive search for strategies and solutions to practical academic and professional problems.

Many of the papers in this section, then, are studies motivated by a need to address practical social problems. Their ultimate goal is not to arrive at a totalising explanation of behaviour — recent history is strewn with examples of the cost of attempts to impose theoretical models on a community's social and political practice. Many of the contributors are seeking either to better understand the complexities of a particular set of discourse practices, or to better inform a program for action, whether that be pedagogical, clinical or broadly social — for example in contesting gender bias in legal practice (Chng) or in accommodating indigenous literacy practices (Malcolm). They all in their different ways reflect the application of some sustained analysis and interpretation of discourse practices in particular communities, in which those practices extend beyond the purely linguistic, for example (Forey and Nunan) to areas of perceived success, loss of face, professional effectiveness and hierarchical status.

What unites these papers is their respect for the importance of cultural context and their authors' conviction that an understanding of discourse practices needs to extend well beyond a semantic examination of the surface text, of what is said. They are all to some extent concerned with constructions of knowledge, and with hegemonies of one kind or another: Chng with how women are constructed, Hui with how economics and the authority of an economic paradigm are constructed, Forey and Nunan with how language and its role in accountancy practice are constructed — and so on. We see the absence of co-eval relationships emerging in these legal, accountancy, academic and pedagogical contexts, as the 'Western' paradigm casts its roots in strange and fertile terrain, taking on new and initially inauthentic temporalities in a struggle between resistance and accommodation.

Chng Huang Hoon opens this section with an appeal for a multivocal and multidisciplinary perspective on legal discourse. She takes a Foucauldian approach, seeking to show how judicial power resides in language practices which have evolved over time and in particular communities with their own power relationships. In contrasting a nineteenth-century and a recent legal judgement, she shows how courts enact the law by the way in which lawyers and judges construct gender roles and power relations, and employ such constructions in their reasoning. Chng offers an interesting lexical analysis, showing how certain linguistic constructions become a binding precedent of sorts; the doctrine of 'separate spheres' of male and female social and economic roles effectively means legislation needs to discriminate between the type of 'person' the legislation is referring to — as in the nineteenth-century case. In the more recent case, personhood is debated in terms of the point at which — conception, birth, or some intermediate stage of fetal development — a person would begin to have 'rights'. This is crucial for women, as at stake is the priority of a fetus over a pregnant woman's rights over her own body, and *in extremis* over her own life. In the *Roe v. Wade* case, the State of Texas's anti-abortion stance points to a nomothetic orientation, but one which Carol Gilligan suggests has its roots in a masculine disposition to formulating justice in terms of rules, rights and 'ethic of justice', where the moral agent is constructed as an autonomous rational individual. Gilligan counterposes a more idiographic female perspective, which sees moral agents as interdependent and more responsive to the needs of others than to the demands of abstract rules. Gilligan suggests that a female disposition would be to judge each case on its contingencies and context, taking account of all the implications for care and respective responsibilities — not to mention a right to equal treatment before the law. Both the nineteenth-century (Bradwell) and recent (Roe) cases offer evidence of a nomothetic, 'masculine' rhetoric, in which absolutes are sought based on a rational debate over personhood — when does an infant acquire an identity and rights?

Hui Po-keung returns us from a gendered hegemony to a broad cultural one, the East–West theme featured in a number of papers in this book. Hui looks at the hegemonic role of Western capitalist ideology, as instanced by the discursive building blocks that have come to pervade economic discourse, and which he suggests have migrated successfully to Hong Kong, albeit 'with Chinese characteristics'. Hui takes the notions of 'free market', 'free trade' and 'property rights' as emblematic of the interested construction of economic 'truths'. He proceeds to show how Hong Kong Chinese economists accommodate to this Western economic ideology. Hui is especially interested in the culturally hybrid rhetorical style the writers use in their Chinese writing. He shows how these writers give authority to their arguments both by appealing to a martial arts hierarchy or pantheon, and by an almost sycophantic exercise in mutual citation among a tight loop of like-minded economists. Hui argues that their ultimate purpose is to promote the free market paradigm, one which has come to be inextricably associated with Hong Kong's economic success. Hui points to the educational implication of these discourse practices, suggesting that these powerful discursive projections of economics teaching, imbued with appeals to a recognisably Chinese version of knowledge hierarchy and authority, stultify more independent and empirical thought about economics. The inauthenticity — the transtemporality — of this hybrid discourse is seen in the nomothetic, econometric approach to the teaching of their discipline, using a discourse leavened with the entertainment value of a roster of economists-as-kung-fu masters as authorities being invoked to support the underlying thesis.

Forey and Nunan's paper reports the background needs analysis conducted as research into the written discourse practices of junior accountants in Hong Kong. They conducted a questionnaire survey and interviews to gain insights into the attitudes and expectations of junior and senior accountants regarding the communicative skills required of accountants. We see a Hallidayan perspective in their concern to identify the social and contextual demands and influences on the writing practices of the client community. Forey and Nunan found, unsurprisingly, that language and knowledge are taken for granted, the former generally constructed as a medium for the factual transmission of the latter, and 'accuracy' constructed as the chief virtue that would ensure that 'wrong information' would not be transmitted. More surprisingly, they found that written communication in English had taken centre stage in the accountants' working lives: it took up most of their time, partly because it had become the chief and most high-stakes vehicle for demonstrating competence and suitability for promotion. They found that, as Martin suggested (1985: 51), written language is prized above speech. In the Hong Kong context, this reinforces the primacy of English over Cantonese, as proficiency in Cantonese only manifests itself orally, and has no bearing on questions of professional advancement. This is one of the less visible areas of change that will be monitorable as Hong Kong moves into the postcolonial phase of its history. We might wonder how far communication in Modern Standard Chinese will become the dominant vehicle for professional communication in the Hong Kong accountancy workplace.

In Luukka's article, also adopting a Hallidayan social semiotic perspective, we can carry forward some of the issues raised in Forey and Nunan. Luukka looks in more detail at how professional or disciplinary discourses are influenced by the ways of thinking and acting of a community. She extends the discussion from how discourses reflect social practice and relationships to how they actually construct those practices and relationships. While considering the critical discourse-analytic views of Fairclough, she is careful to avoid an over-deterministic view of the way language constructs our lives. To use Halliday's tropes, she opts for a picture of humans as exercising choice as they kick at their chains: 'language offers its user a meaning potential, and using language means making strategic choices'. Her main focus, appropriately in a book featuring a strong representation of papers with a Chinese cultural axis, is on strategies for saving and giving 'face' in the context of the social act of citation and acknowledgement of other people's work in scientific publications. Luukka offers a contrastive linguistic study of hedging and personal reference devices in Finnish and English, comparing written and spoken genres. While there may be an element of individual choice, the functional approach points to an independence of language which places Luukka's perspective somewhere between the nomothetic and the idiographic: there is an attempt to reconcile data across two languages and cultures, and yet there is a respect for respective cultural differences. Luukka insists, for example, that this study of the discourse of an applied linguistic community is indeed an example of 'scientific' discourse, as in the Finnish culture there is no distinction between Science and Social Science.

The last three papers in this section form a continuum. All three are participatory, ethnographic studies made possible by an educational context which allows researchers and researched to interact in a transactional relationship in which the different perspectives of researcher and researched become an acknowledged factor in the research. Plum and Candlin's paper and Malcolm's paper are both concerned with how students in Australia frame their literacies and responses to the demands and requirements of academia, while Malcolm and Goldstein's papers are both concerned with competing literacies in an educational context. In each case the goal is positive educational change, informed by a greater understanding of the particular cultural and discursive characteristics of the target population. Influenced by

Lave and Wenger's situated learning model and by Bourdieu's notion of capital invested in academic literacy, Plum and Candlin's study of how students become psychologists is a contribution to the growing literature on interpretive studies in the analysis of discourse and exhibits the advantages of exploring the dialectic between text and students' voices. They show that the process and product model, or student literacy and student writing in their terms, is much more complex than text-based descriptive analyses of writing suggest. Plum and Candlin disclose the heteroglossic and historic nature of language and discourse in psychology as the students struggle to define writing purposes that are both discipline-internal and discipline-external, 'actively mediated and continually reinforced . . . by the actions and discourses of its ratified members' (p.241) in both academia and the professional workplace.

Malcolm is concerned that higher education institutions in Western Australia are imposing an inappropriate curriculum on Aboriginal students, assuming that a cognate first language among Aboriginal and non-Aboriginal students will entail cognate literacies. He employs a framing approach to analyse literacy events in indigenous Aboriginal culture and in the existing tertiary educational culture. He identifies a principal difference as lying between the contextualised language practices of the aboriginal students and the decontextualised practices of the 'literacy-oriented tradition' of mainstream education in Australia, which he portrays as a kind of transtemporal discursive straitjacket. Hence, a further complication is the one identified by both Barron and Hui, which is the assimilation of 'colonial' cultural practices in postcolonial or neo-colonial societies. Malcolm cites Eggington's observation that urbanised Aboriginal people have assimilated the education system's favoured decontextualised literacy practices. His research identifies the diverse ways in which the negotiation of meaning across different literacy frames is problematic, featuring both accommodation and resistance. For Aboriginal culture to be able to sustain its different literacy traditions, Malcolm suggests the educational authorities should consciously seek to accommodate to those practices, to avoid the current risk of colonising and inevitably assimilating them.

In the final paper in this section, Goldstein is concerned with the possible interethnic/interracial tensions created by bringing into school a home language which is different from that used in the education system. Her research context is a predominantly Chinese-populated school in Toronto, Canada, where the teacher, too, shares the Chinese language of a proportion of the students. Goldstein explores the complex social issues surrounding the choice of language in different situations at school, and the extent to which non-English speakers feel comfortable bringing their home and community languages into their schools. Goldstein advocates the bringing of these linguistic differences out into the open, and making the negotiation of language practices part of the curriculum. As with all the other authors in this section on professional and academic practices, Goldstein is under no illusion that language policy can be effectively transacted in isolation from broader social and economic considerations, not least ethnic stereotypes about Asians and the privileged status of the dominant language — English.

10

The linguistic construction of gender and ideology in judicial discourse
Chng Huang Hoon

Of freedom and constraints: The power of judges

'The natural and proper timidity and delicacy which belongs to the female sex evidently unfits it for many of the occupations of civil life' (Bradwell). With these words, Justice Joseph Bradley argued for the exclusion of Myra Bradwell from practising law in Illinois in 1873. In contrast, a century later, the United States Supreme Court's pronouncement in *Roe v. Wade* proved liberating for a new generation of American women: '[T]he right of privacy . . . is broad enough to encompass a woman's decision whether or not to terminate her pregnancy.' Such displays of judicial power prompted Margaret Michels to write (1988: 229):

> Despite its control over neither 'the sword [n]or the purse,' the United States Supreme Court wields a great deal of power. Through its opinions — its use of language — the Court has affected areas ranging from the fate of snail darters to the power of the executive branch.

The centrality of language in the construction of world views is an idea that can be traced back to the work of Edward Sapir and Benjamin Lee Whorf (Sapir 1963, 1966; Whorf 1956). More recently, Susan Gal makes the link between the linguistic construction of world views and power: 'power is more than an authoritative voice in decision making; its strongest form may well be the ability to define social reality, to impose visions of the world. Such visions are inscribed in language and enacted in interaction' (1991: 197). Dell Hymes goes further by making connections between language and the sources of inequalities between individuals in terms of the constraints on ways of speaking (Hymes 1973). Hymes once said, 'means condition what can be done with them, and in the case of languages, the meanings that can be created and conveyed' (1973: 73).

Following in the footsteps of Sapir, Whorf, and Hymes, my analysis of two samples of judicial discourse will demonstrate the linguistic manifestations of the power of law, and hence, the power of judicial writers. Judicial power is, however, not limitless. Though much power is conferred on judges, in particular Supreme Court judges, as Stanley Fish has argued, even judges must act within the freedom and the constraints of their order (1989: 87ff.). Hence, apart from the textual indexing of power, I will also allude to the varied kinds of constraints on judicial performance.

Judicial power may be seen in the ways in which gender roles are defined in particular periods in American society. The specification in the socio-cultural discourse on what is expected from both men and women in a society, of what are rights and what are privileges, not only testifies to specific ways of constructing gender, but also makes up particular ways of living, and ultimately, ways of constituting and reconstituting the life, history and culture of the community.

The importance of discourse, like the centrality of language, bears repeated emphasis. I agree with Joel Sherzer when he writes that discourse is 'the nexus, the actual and concrete expression of the language–culture–society relationship. It is discourse which creates, recreates, modifies, and fine tunes both culture and language and their intersection' (1987: 296). How the world is represented in discourse is, as Pratt would say, the point 'where discourse and ideology meets' (1982). In the context of discursive representations of world views, a question that needs to be asked is: 'What is the nature of the voices that are privileged in the discourse?' Or as Roman Jakobson (1960: 351) himself once queried, 'what of this universe is verbalised by a given discourse and how is it verbalised?' Since every instance of talk defines its own boundaries of what voices are foregrounded and suppressed, the illusion of the objectivity and homogeneity of texts must be dispelled. Instead, as Pratt has reminded us before, '[w]hen seen as a site of social reproduction and struggle, language cannot be imagined to be unified' (1987: 62), simply because the heteroglossia within texts are often not unified to voice a common cause.

In this paper, then, a point I wish to emphasise is that amidst the freedom and constraints of text production and interpretation, there exist in each text multiple voices articulating differing ideologies. However, in such textual struggles for dominance, the 'reality' is defined by parties with power to determine the meanings in texts and the direction of discourse. Let me begin by saying a few words about the two texts I am focusing on here.

Destiny and rights: Myra Bradwell and Jane Roe

Having passed the Illinois bar exam 'with high honours' in 1869 (Friedman 1993: 18), Myra Bradwell applied for a licence to practise law, but was rejected because she was a married woman. In a subsequent appeal to the United States Supreme Court, the Court upheld the exclusion in its 1873 majority ruling, thus denying Myra the right to an occupation of her choice.

In 1969, Norma McCorvey sought to have an abortion, but she soon learned that under an 1854 Texas statute, abortion was illegal. With the help of two lawyers, Norma's search for a legally sanctioned abortion evolved into the case of *Roe v. Wade* (1973), where it was decided in a majority Supreme Court decision that a woman has a right to decide with regard to the abortion decision and this right is protected under a person's right to privacy. My analysis draws from Justice Joseph Bradley's concurrence in Bradwell and Justice Harry Blackmun's majority opinion in Roe. My analysis will be guided by a multidisciplinary perspective which I will now briefly introduce.

The linguistic construction of gender and ideology: a multidisciplinary perspective

My choice of a multidisciplinary approach to judicial discourse is motivated by my conviction that an understanding of texts can be best achieved by examining a text from multiple perspectives. The value in employing various ideas in my textual analysis lies in what differing points of departure can reveal, and in the process, this kind of multiple complementarities can only contribute to different ways of knowing. Of course, there are times when a multidisciplinary framework may lead to contradictory outcomes. In my opinion, however, even in contradictions, there are valuable lessons to be learnt. For one thing, contradictions in analysis may be indicative of the conflicting voices present in particular discourses, and so the revelation of other voices, otherwise hidden, due perhaps to the limits of singular view-points, is not a bad thing. In addition, I believe that it is in multidisciplinarity that one can arrive at a holistic characterisation of texts, thus resulting in precision in the description of discursive practices and an accuracy in the representation of discourse, community, and history.

I adopt Elinor Ochs's and Michael Silverstein's ideas of indexical relations which connect the 'micro' linguistic resources to the 'macro' constructs of gender and ideology. I also find Robert Benson's semiotic approach to law valuable as it enables me to see judicial performance in terms of freedom and constraints. These are further complemented by the insistence that a community's discourse defines the community's character, an idea I borrowed from Joel Sherzer. Michel Foucault's ideas of power, knowledge, and discourse serve as my guiding philosophy. In my analysis, I have found it useful to adopt Michael Halliday's approach to grammatical relations in texts. All these ideas play a role, in differing capacities, in helping me to grasp not just the meanings conveyed in judicial discourse, but also the politics of judicial text-making. Though what follows is not an exhaustive analysis, it nevertheless provides a glimpse of how judicial discourse can be approached from different perspectives.

Indexing gender and ideology: judicial constructions of how the world should be

The central argument in Bradwell involved an appeal to the doctrine of separate spheres, a doctrine which constructed men and women as belonging to separate domains. As Justice Bradley argued:

> ... the civil law, as well as nature herself, has always recognised a wide difference in the respective spheres and destinies of man and woman.
>
> *Bradwell v. Illinois (1873), 83 U.S. (16 Wall.) 130.*

Man, it was held, 'properly belongs' to the public sphere of the marketplace, whereas woman, by the dictates of her biology, was better confined within the private domain of home and hearth, keeping to her roles as a devoted mother and a dutiful wife. In addition, the definition of personhood constructed by the law is such that women were effectively excluded from public life. The lexical choices made in these respects are presented in Table 10.1, based on Appendix text 1.

Several observations can be made here. The word 'person' is initially used to refer inclusively to both sexes in L[ine] 2, but from L3 downwards, personhood is restricted to 'only men'. From L10, the inclusive chain contains no items, indicating that the use of 'person' to refer to both sexes ceased at that point in the text. Correspondingly, the male and female chains are filled with linguistic items, indexing male and female roles and their domains of operation. For example, the male is said to be 'woman's protector and defender' (L12) and he acts as 'her head and representative' (L16). Due to his 'skill and confidence' (L26), and his 'decision and firmness' (L27), he is said to be qualified to fulfil the 'duties and trusts' placed in a member of the bar. In contrast, the female is characterised as 'incapable' (L17) and 'incompetent' (L18), and she is said to be hindered by 'her condition and sex' (L23) to remain in the private realm of the home. Her role is thus that of 'wife and mother' (L20).

There are four sets of contrast worthy of note here. Firstly, 'nature' is feminised as a woman in 'nature herself' (L11). The connections that resonate in the use of the following phrases, 'nature herself', 'the natural and proper timidity and delicacy [of] . . . the female sex' (L13), and 'in the nature of things' (L14), build up a set of associations that reinforce the inherent and naturalised weakness of woman, which in turn justify her exclusion.

Table 10.1 *Bradwell vs. Illinois (1873)*

Line no.	Male chain	Inclusive chain	Female chain
2		Person, man or woman	Plaintiff, married woman
3	Only men, person (2x), his good moral character		
6		Persons, or class of persons	
7	Members		Females
9		Citizens	Females, women, citizens
10			The sex
11	Spheres [of] man		Nature herself, destinies [of] woman
12	Man, woman's protector and defender		
13	Occupations of civil life		Natural and proper timidity and delicacy, the female sex
14			It, family organisation, nature of things, domestic sphere, domain and functions of womanhood
15	Distinct and independent career, husband		Harmony, identity, of interests, family institution, woman
16	Husband, head and representative		Woman, no [separate] legal existence
17	Husband's consent		Married woman, incapable
18	Duties and trusts, office of any attorney or counsellor		Incapacity, married woman, incompetent
19			[Unmarried] women, duties, complications, and incapacities, married state
20			Paramount destiny and mission of woman, noble and benign office of wife and mother
23			Occupation adapted to her condition and sex
24	Highly special qualifications, special responsibilities		
25		Not every citizen	
26	Nature, reason, experience, skill and confidence		
27	Offices, positions, and callings, men, energies and responsibilities, decision and firmness, the sterner sex		
28		Citizens	

Secondly, while the male is associated with 'duties and trusts' (L18), the female equivalent is cast in terms of 'duties, complications and incapacities' (L19). Similarly, the male occupies the 'office of . . . attorney or counsellor' (L18); but the female occupies the 'noble and benign office of wife and mother' (L20).

Thirdly, no mention is made of the marital status of the male; the female, on the other hand, is either characterised as 'married' or 'unmarried' (L2, 17, 18, 19), both states are, however, treated as problematic. Fourthly, while the male sphere is unqualified when mentioned (L11), the female sphere is qualified as 'domestic' (L14) and is thus marked as private. It is in these kinds of differential constructions that the nature of males and females are cast, thus justifying their separateness and unequal standing. Hence, the male is a full-fledged person with legally sanctioned rights, but the female is restricted by her dependence on her husband (or father) to live by the privileges derived from his social and legal standing. In other words, her biology dictates her destiny, and although her status is legitimated within the family institution, outside the home she has 'no legal existence separate from her husband' (L16).

In contrast, the choice of lexis in the Roe opinion effects a different world view. Three main points can be noted about how lexical choices contribute towards constructing specific arguments in the Roe text.

First, the right to privacy is associated with the concept of personal liberty, and then broadened to include the abortion decision. Second, having established this right to privacy, the Court went on to restrict its scope. Thus, while arguing for the right of a woman to choose, the Court also stressed that this right is not absolute and thus, the state can assert its authority under certain circumstances. Third, the Court denied personhood status to the unborn, stating that the word 'person' applies only 'postnatally'. In these ways of associating concepts and determining semantic scopes, the Court gave its qualified support for choice and dismissed the fetus (prior to the second trimester) as possessing no rights of personhood. It is clear from such a lexical indexing of privacy rights and personhood status that a very different world view from that in the Bradwell case is constructed. The power of language to inscribe the boundaries of individual rights and the power of judges to effect such linguistic constructions are clear.

In both texts, we also see evidence of an unequal distribution of power expressed in terms of subject–verb process relations. Judges assert their power through speaking with a grammar of authority. For example, with the verbal pronouncements, 'we do not agree' (Text 2, L14) and 'we need not resolve the difficult question of when life begins' (L40), Justice Blackmun placed a check simultaneously on the absolute nature of abortion rights and also restricted the scope of the state's case. Such acts of verbal authority are also reinforced by how the Court chose to emphasise the power structures in Court. Hence, the arguments of the plaintiffs are characterised as having

Table 10.2   Text 2 *Roe v. Wade (1973)*

1.	*Privacy*

(i)   *Positive characterisations*
L1:   right of privacy
L2:   guarantee of certain zones of privacy
L3:   the roots of that right in the First Amendment, in the Fourth and Fifth Amendments, in the penumbras of the Bill of Rights, in the Ninth Amendment . . . or in the concept of liberty guaranteed by the first section of the Fourteenth Amendment
L4:   right of privacy; the Fourteenth Amendment's concept of personal liberty and restrictions upon state action . . . the Ninth Amendment's reservation of rights to the people, is broad enough to encompass a woman's decision whether or not to terminate her pregnancy

(ii)   *Negative characterisations*
L13:   the woman's right is absolute
L14:   we do not agree
L15:   Appellant's arguments . . . [are] unpersuasive
L16:   The Court's decision recognising a right of privacy also acknowledges that some state regulation in areas protected by that right is appropriate
L19:   The privacy right involved, therefore, cannot be said to be absolute
L34:   The pregnant woman cannot be isolated in her privacy
L38:   The woman's privacy is no longer sole and any right of privacy she possesses must be measured accordingly

2.	*Personhood*

L23:   the fetus is a 'person'
L25:   personhood . . . the fetus' right to life
L27:   no case could be cited that holds that a fetus is a person
L28:   The Constitution does not define 'person' . . . in so many words
L29:   Section 1 of the Fourteenth Amendment contains three references to 'person'
L30:   it has application only postnatally
L31:   None indicates . . . it has any possible pre-natal application
L32:   the word 'person,' as used in the Fourteenth Amendment, does not include the unborn

only the status of a claim (T1, L2). While such arguments may be dismissed by the Court as 'unpersuasive' (T2, L15), or as having 'failed to meet [the] burden' of proof (T2, L22), the Court reserved for itself the right to be convinced. In addition, Justice Bradley's characterisation of females as 'incapable' (L17), 'incompetent' (L18), and as generally inconvenienced by their married state serve to confine females within a sphere of domesticity. In such expressions of verbal force through the use of relational attributions of litigants, the boundaries that divide the ones in power and those who are not are maintained. As Vicki Schultz stated, '[w]omen's [and men's] interests and identities are fixed "before" the law' (1992: 299) as the court chooses to privilege certain constructions of gender roles and power relations and employs such constructions in their reasoning. The grammatical predication that is employed in the judicial opinions may be said to constitute a discourse of judicial power, a power that is constructed, maintained and perpetuated within the language of the court.

Conley and O'Barr's (1990) work on small claims courts suggests that judges and laypersons approach the law in radically different ways. While the legal practitioners have the tendency to view the law in rule-oriented manners, eagerly translating disputes into relevant legal principles, thus displaying an inclination towards rules of law, the legally untrained persons tend to see the law as an arena for settling personal disputes, stressing not legal principles but relationships. In other words, the layperson approaches the court setting in terms of the relationships which are taken to hold in a society of individuals. Hence, while the legal practitioner tends to think in terms of the legal principles which may be brought to bear on a particular case, the layperson tends to appeal to the court for a satisfactory answer to personal grievances. The result of such a difference in approach and assumptions is that the two parties often come away from the encounter dissatisfied with what is actually achieved in the courtroom. In this light, the parallels that may be drawn from the rule-oriented judge who employs verbal power in his/her discourse on the one hand, and the relationship-based approach adopted by litigants who are also grammatically associated with relational attributions may be said to reinforce the Conley–O'Barr view of the differences that divide the two parties.

Interestingly, in research on gender issues, powerless language is not language used by women *per se*, but is more accurately associated with persons situated in positions lacking power (O'Barr and Atkins 1980). As O'Barr and Atkins have found in their study of language use in the courtroom, the features which Robin Lakoff identified as characterising 'women's language' are more descriptive of what they call 'powerless language' (p.104), a form of language that is associated with the social status rather than the sex of the speaker. In their own words (O'Barr and Atkins 1980: 104),

> we would suggest that the tendency for more women to speak powerless language and for men to speak less of it is due, at least in part, to the greater tendency of women to occupy relatively powerless social positions. What we have observed is a reflection in their speech behaviour of their social status. Similarly, for men, a greater tendency to use the more powerful variant (which we will term *powerful language*) may be linked to the fact that men much more often tend to occupy relatively powerful positions in society.

Drawing on this kind of argumentation, my claim here is that the less powerful form of relational attributions (as opposed to the powerful verbal pronouncements of the judges) the court assigns to laypersons may be said to be a *feminisation* of the powerless situations of litigants, both male and female. Thus not only do lexical choices contribute to particular ways of meaning, at a higher order of linguistic patterning the grammar of power is employed to consolidate the power of the judicial culture.

Moving beyond the level of linguistic structure, we now focus on an intertextual device used by judges to justify their reasoning — the appeal to precedents. As James Boyd White calls it, precedents serve as 'a kind of bridge from one world to the other' (1988: 406). In general, courts observe the principle of *stare decisis* (that is, let the decision stand), which refers to the respect courts show to the rulings of their predecessors. We often find within the judicial text an appeal to cases which have established certain principles of law. Among their many functions, such appeals to precedents serve to reinforce the logic of present decisions, as such appeals show that the court's decision is not whimsical or arbitrary, but instead follows well-defined precedents. However, the constraints placed on judges to observe past traditions are countered by the freedom left to judges to recall whichever precedents he/she deems best for the occasion. This selective use of precedents and the failure to mention others are nicely illustrated in the two judicial opinions studied here.

In his concurrence, Justice Bradley invoked discourses which affirmed both divine and natural laws and placed his emphasis on the doctrine of coverture ('By marriage, the husband and wife are one person in law') and the doctrine of separate spheres ('Man is public; woman is private'). What he failed to mention was that on the same day that he ruled against Myra Bradwell, he also ruled *in favour* of a group of men's right to their choice of an occupation in the famous Slaughterhouse Cases. In his majority opinion, Justice Blackmun appealed to cases such as Botsford and Griswold to lay the groundwork that the right to choose is legitimated by privacy and liberty laws. Due to such differences in the use of precedents, the tone and the direction of the arguments differ markedly in both opinions, and the freedom to go one way or another attests to judicial power in action. However, in such assertions of judicial freedom, it is also true that the constraints on judges are real, and they exert powerful influences on the way judges write.

One such constraint is the pressure to obtain that fifth vote to make one's opinion a part of the majority ruling. In a Supreme Court that is made up of nine justices, each with her or his own agenda and understanding of the law, it is obvious that on any particular issue which the Court confronts, each individual member will have her or his own opinion on the case. For a majority opinion to prevail, there must then be at least five members in the Court in agreement over the ruling in the case. Any justice who finds him- or herself in the minority camp thus has to canvass for support from the other justices. Given such a motivation, it becomes understandable why judges often find themselves resorting to compromise, which may take the form of modifications made to the language (the exact phrasing) or the argument of the judicial opinion. Thus every act of judicial performance, though infused with power, is checked not only by rules of institution but also by the ideologies of fellow colleagues on the bench.

Discussion

To reiterate my points, the choice of lexis made in the production of judicial opinions carves out the universe of discourse in which arguments are embedded. When 'person' indexes only males, then the exclusion of females becomes a logical step in the argument. When privacy is defined in terms of liberty, the scope of the former expands and spreads into the realm of constitutionally-protected rights. Similarly, when the female is constructed as weak and the male as competent, the spheres which males and females occupy are then, by such definitions, separate and unequal. It is through such uses of linguistic terms to index particular domains and gender roles that an argument based on exclusion and inclusion, destiny and rights can be maintained. The ideologies implicated in these different ways of indexing are thus markedly different.

It should also be clear that every act of judicial power is effected in discourse, via discourse. Language is both the tool and the medium where struggles for dominance are sited. In the judicial texts, we see how specific terms are defined and constructed so that the argument emerges as a seamless web of coherence. Just as the grammar biased the power on the side of the Court, the projection of authoritative consistency reinforces and underscores the Court's legitimacy. Shifts in the discourse are effected textually, through definitions and redefinitions of terms, and intertextually, through the appeals to select cases and doctrines, brought about in overt displays of judicial power, in the name of the law.

As discussed above, this power is, of course, not unlimited, for judges act under the cover of law's power as much as within the boundaries of the constraints imposed by the legal and social institutions. But it is in both freedom and constraints that judicial narratives are formed, and hence the final product, the judicial opinion, is not an isolated act of judicial performance, but is a consequence of a long process of negotiation within and among individuals. In Foucauldian terms, we may say that the power conferred on the judiciary enables it to construct particular types of knowledge and inscribe them in the form of judicial discourse, and that the knowledge constructed is a reflection of what that power can do. In the final analysis, however, the power lies *not* in the judiciary, but in language, for the constitutive role that language plays in defining what the world should be is attested by the indelible marks that language leaves behind both in the world of texts and the world that these texts describe even as it creates what is to come.

Appendix

Text 1: *Bradwell v. Illinois (1873), 83 U.S. (16 Wall.) 130*

Concurring opinion of Justice Joseph Bradley (full text, pp.139–142)

I concur in the judgement of the court in this case, by which the judgement of the Supreme Court of Illinois is affirmed, but not for the reasons specified in the opinion just read (L1).

The claim of the plaintiff, who is a married woman, to be admitted to practice as an attorney and counsellor-at-law, is based upon the supposed right of every person, man or woman, to engage in any lawful employment for a livelihood (L2). The Supreme Court of Illinois denied the application on the ground that, by the common law, which is the basis of the laws of Illinois, only men were admitted to the bar, and the legislature had not made any change in this respect, but had simply provided that no person should be admitted to practice as attorney or counsellor without having previously obtained a license for that purpose from two justices of the Supreme Court, and that no person should receive a license without first obtaining a certificate from the court of some county of his good moral character (L3). In other respects it was left to the discretion of the court to establish the rules by which admission to the profession should be determined (L4). The court, however, regarded itself as bound by at least two limitations (L5). One was that it should establish such terms of admission as would promote the proper administration of justice, and the other that it should not admit any persons, or class of persons, not intended by the legislature to be admitted, even though not expressly excluded by statute (L6). In view of this latter limitation the court felt compelled to deny the application of females to be admitted as members of the bar (L7). Being contrary to the rules of the common law and the usages of Westminster Hall from time immemorial, it could not be supposed that the legislature had intended to adopt any different rule (L8).

The claim that, under the fourteenth amendment of the Constitution, which declares that no State shall make or enforce any law which shall abridge the privileges and immunities of citizens of the United States, the statute law of Illinois, or the common law prevailing in that State, can no longer be set up as a barrier against the right of females to pursue any lawful employment for a livelihood (the practice of law included), assumes that it is one of the privileges and immunities of women as citizens to engage in any and every profession, occupation, or employment in civil life (L9).

It certainly cannot be affirmed, as an historical fact, that this has ever been established as one of the fundamental privileges and immunities of the sex (L10). On the contrary, the civil law, as well as nature herself, has always recognised a wide difference in the respective spheres and destinies of man and woman (L11). Man is, or should be, woman's protector and defender (L12). The natural and proper timidity and delicacy which belongs to the female sex evidently unfits it for many of the occupations of civil life (L13). The constitution of the family organisation, which is founded in the divine ordinance, as well as in the nature of things, indicates the domestic sphere as that which properly belongs to the domain and functions of womanhood (L14). The harmony, not to say identity, of interests and views which belong or should belong to the family institution, is repugnant to the idea of a woman adopting a distinct and independent career from that of her husband (L15). So firmly fixed was this sentiment in the founders of the common law that it became a maxim of that system of jurisprudence that a woman had no legal existence separate from her husband, who was regarded as her head and representative in the social state; and, notwithstanding some recent modifications of this civil status, many of the special rules of law flowing from and dependent upon this cardinal principle still exist in full force in most States (L16). One of these is, that a married woman is incapable, without her husband's consent, of making contracts which shall be binding on her or him (L17). This very incapacity was one circumstance which the Supreme Court of Illinois deemed important in rendering a married woman incompetent fully to perform the duties and trusts that belong to the office of an attorney and counsellor (L18).

It is true that many women are unmarried and not affected by any of the duties, complications, and incapacities arising out of the married state but these are exceptions to the general rule (L19). The paramount destiny and mission of woman are to fulfil the noble and benign offices of wife and mother (L20). This is the law of the Creator (L21). And the rules of civil society must be adapted to the general constitution of things, and cannot be based upon exceptional cases (L22).

The humane movements of modern society, which have for their object the multiplication of avenues for woman's advancement, and of occupations adapted to her condition and sex, have my heartiest concurrence (L23). But I am not prepared to say that it is one of her fundamental rights and privileges to be admitted into every office and position, including those which require highly special qualifications and demanding special responsibilities (L24). In the nature of things it is not every citizen of every age, sex, and condition that is qualified for every calling and position (L25). It is the prerogative of the legislator to prescribe regulations founded on nature, reason, and experience for the due admission of qualified persons to professions and callings demanding special skill and confidence (L26). This fairly belongs to the police power of the State; and, in my opinion, in view of the peculiar characteristics, destiny, and mission of woman, it is within the province of the legislature to ordain what offices, positions, and callings shall be filled and discharged by men, and shall receive the benefit of those energies and responsibilities, and that decision and firmness which are presumed to predominate in the sterner sex (L27).

For these reasons I think that the laws of Illinois now complained of are not obnoxious to the charge of abridging any of the privileges and immunities of citizens of the United States (L28).

Text 2: *Roe v. Wade, 410 U.S. 113 (1973)*

Majority opinion delivered by Justice Harry Blackmun (pp.152–159)

The Constitution does not explicitly mention any right of privacy (L1). In a line of decisions, however, going back perhaps as far as *Union Pacific R. Co. v. Botsford*, 141 U.S. 250, 251 (1891), the Court has recognised that a right of personal privacy, or a guarantee of certain areas or zones of privacy, does exist under the Constitution (L2). In varying contexts, the Court or individual Justices have, indeed, found at least the roots of that right in the First Amendment, *Stanley v. Georgia*, 394 U.S. 557, 564 (1969); in the Fourth and Fifth Amendments, *Terry v. Ohio*, 392 U.S. 1, 8–9 (1968), *Katz v. United States*, 389 U.S. 347, 350 (1967), *Boyd v. United States*, 116 U.S. 616 (1886), see *Olmstead v. United States*, 277 U.S. 438, 478 (1928) (Brandeis, J., dissenting); in the penumbras of the Bill of Rights, *Griswold v. Connecticut*, 381 U.S., at 484–485; in the Ninth Amendment, *id.*, at 486 (Goldberg, J., concurring); or in the concept of liberty guaranteed by the first section of the Fourteenth Amendment, see *Meyer v. Nebraska*, 262 U.S. 390, 399 (1923) (L3). These decisions make it clear that only personal rights that can be deemed 'fundamental' or 'implicit in the concept of ordered liberty,' *Palko v. Connecticut*, 302 U.S. 319, 325 (1937), are included in this guarantee of personal privacy (L4). They also make it clear that the right has some extension to activities relating to marriage, *Loving v. Virginia*, 338 U.S. 1, 12 (1967); procreation, *Skinner v. Oklahoma*, 316 U.S. 535, 541–542 (1942); contraception, *Eisenstadt v. Baird*, 405 U.S., at 453–454; *id.*, at 460, 463–465 (White, J., concurring in result); family relationships, *Prince v. Massachusetts*, 321 U.S. 158, 166 (1944); and child rearing and education, *Pierce v. Society of Sisters*, 268 U.S. 510, 535 (1925), *Meyer v. Nebraska, supra* (L5).

This right of privacy, whether it is founded in the Fourteenth Amendment's concept of personal liberty and restrictions upon state action, as we feel it is, or, as the District Court determined, in the Ninth Amendment's reservation of rights to the people, is broad enough to encompass a woman's decision whether or not to terminate her pregnancy (L6). The detriment that the State would impose upon the pregnant woman by denying this choice altogether is apparent (L7). Specific and direct harm medically diagnosable even in early pregnancy may be involved (L8). Maternity, or additional offspring, may force upon the woman a distressful life and future (L9). Psychological harm may be imminent (L10). . . . In other cases, as in this one, the additional difficulties and continuing stigma of unwed motherhood may be involved (L11). All these are factors the woman and her responsible physician necessarily will consider in consultation (L12).

On the basis of elements such as these, appellant and some *amici* argue that the woman's right is absolute and that she is entitled to terminate her pregnancy at whatever time, in whatever way, and for whatever reason she alone chooses (L13). With this we do not agree (L14). Appellant's arguments that Texas either has no valid interest at all in regulating the abortion decision, or no interest strong enough to support any limitation upon the woman's sole determination, are unpersuasive (L15). The Court's decisions recognising a right of privacy also acknowledge that some state regulation in areas protected by that right is appropriate (L16). As noted above, a State may properly assert important interests in safeguarding health, in maintaining medical standards, and in protecting potential life (L17). At some point in pregnancy, these respective interests become sufficiently compelling to sustain regulation of the factors that govern the abortion decision (L18). The privacy right involved, therefore, cannot be said to be absolute (L19). . . .

We, therefore, conclude that the right of personal privacy includes the abortion decision, but that this right is not unqualified and must be considered against important state interests in regulation (L20). . . .

Where certain 'fundamental rights' are involved, the Court has held that regulation limiting these rights may be justified only by a 'compelling state interest,' . . . and that legislative enactments must be narrowly drawn to express only the legitimate state interests at stake (L21). . . .

The District Court held that the appellee failed to meet his burden of demonstrating that the Texas statute's infringement upon Roe's rights was necessary to support a compelling state interest, and that, although the appellee presented 'several compelling justifications for state presence in the area of abortions,' the statutes outstripped these justifications and swept 'far beyond any areas of compelling state interest.' (L22). . . .

A. The appellee and certain *amici* argue that the fetus is a 'person' within the language and meaning of the Fourteenth Amendment (L23). In support of this, they outline at length and in detail the well-known facts of fetal development (L24). If this suggestion of personhood is established, the appellant's case, of course, collapses, for the fetus' right to life would then be guaranteed specifically by the Amendment (L25). The appellant conceded as much on reargument (L26). On the other hand, the appellee conceded on reargument that no case could be cited that holds that a fetus is a person within the meaning of the Fourteenth Amendment (L27).

The Constitution does not define 'person' in so many words (L28). Section 1 of the Fourteenth Amendment contains three references to 'person' (L29). . . . But in nearly all these instances, the use of the word is such that it has application only postnatally (L30). None indicates, with any assurance, that it has any possible pre-natal application (L31).

All this, together with our observation, *supra*, that throughout the major portion of the 19th century prevailing legal abortion practices were far freer than they are today, persuades us that the word 'person,' as used in the Fourteenth Amendment, does not include the unborn (L32). This is in accord with the results reached in those few cases where the issue has been squarely presented (L33). . . .

B. The pregnant woman cannot be isolated in her privacy (L34). She carries an embryo and, later, a fetus, if one accepts the medical definitions of the developing young in the human uterus (L35). . . . The situation therefore is inherently different from marital intimacy, or bedroom possession of obscene material, or marriage, or procreation, or education, with which *Eisenstadt* and *Griswold, Stanley, Loving, Skinner,* and *Pierce* and *Meyer* were respectively concerned (L36). As we have intimated above, it is reasonable and appropriate for a State to decide that at some point in time another interest, that of health of the mother or that of potential human life, becomes significantly involved (L37). The woman's privacy is no longer sole and any right of privacy she possesses must be measured accordingly (L38).

Texas urges that, apart from the Fourteenth Amendment, life begins at conception and is present throughout pregnancy, and that, therefore, the State has a compelling interest in protecting that life from and after conception (L39). We need not resolve the difficult question of when life begins (L40). When those trained in the respective disciplines of medicine, philosophy, and theology are unable to arrive at any consensus, the judiciary, at this point in the development of man's knowledge, is not in a position to speculate as to the answer (L41). . . .

In view of all this, we do not agree that, by adopting one theory of life, Texas may override the rights of the pregnant woman that are at stake (L42). We repeat, however, that the State does have an important and legitimate interest in preserving and protecting the health of the pregnant woman, whether she be a resident of the State or a non-resident who seeks medical consultation and treatment there, and that it has still *another* important and legitimate interest in protecting the potentiality of human life (L43). These interests are separate and distinct (L44). . . .

With respect to the State's important and legitimate interest in the health of the mother, the 'compelling' point, in the light of present medical knowledge, is at approximately the end of the first trimester (L45). . . . It follows that, from and after this point, a State may regulate the abortion procedure to the extent that the regulation reasonably relates to the preservation and protection of maternal health (L46). . . .

This means, on the other hand, that, for the period of pregnancy prior to this 'compelling' point, the attending physician, in consultation with his patient, is free to determine, without regulation by the State, that, in his medical judgement, the patient's pregnancy should be terminated (L47). If that decision is reached, the judgement may be effectuated by an abortion free of interference by the State (L48). . . .

11

The domestication of rhetoric –
Translating Western economic
ideology to Hong Kong
Hui Po-keung

Introduction

'Free markets', 'free trade', and 'private property rights' are said to account for the economic success of capitalism in general, and of Hong Kong in particular. Though not backed by sufficient empirical evidence, these claims are alive and widespread in the local Chinese media. This paper investigates how and why these claims are perpetuated in Hong Kong through the translation and rhetorical strategies of local economists within the context of Hong Kong's historical experience.

Adopting the concept of 'domestication' introduced by Lawrence Venuti and the approach to economic rhetoric developed by Donald McCloskey, this paper analyses a particular genre, 'economics prose', produced by Hong Kong economists, which is then mainly targeted at non-economic-professional, or lay, Chinese readers. The content of this 'economic prose' is largely borrowed from Western mainstream economic ideologies. Hong Kong economists either directly translate or indirectly rewrite Western economic concepts and thoughts into Chinese. Yet in both cases, by comparing their English and Chinese writings, it is not difficult to see that the strategies of their 'translations' (in a broad sense) can be termed as 'domestication'. The art of persuasion that they have employed in their Chinese writings, particularly the use of metaphors of martial arts fiction, as well as the charm of historical precedents and authority, has created a fictional world of economics which attempts to convince their readers of the virtues of so-called laissez-faire economics. Though purporting to convey serious information or 'scientific facts', their 'economic prose' is simply casual articulation which does not encourage readers to engage in any serious evaluation. We need also to add the favoured background that translation of Western economic ideology — as an antithesis to communism — has invoked in the particular geopolitical and historical conditions of Hong Kong. This, of course, makes the spread of negative perceptions of communist China easier to accomplish.

The paper is divided into five sections. First, the relevance and irrelevance to existing capitalism of the claims of free markets, free trade, and private property rights are examined by drawing mainly on the works of Karl Polanyi and Fernand Braudel. In Section II, Lawrence Venuti's concept of domesticating translation and the rhetorical approaches to analysing economic discourses developed by Donald McCloskey are explained. Adopting these approaches, Section III of this paper examines the translation of economic writing into Chinese and discusses the art (or science) of persuasion as used in Hong Kong. A particular genre — 'economics prose' — is selected for analysis as a result of its popularity in Hong Kong society. The following section, Section IV, discusses how the geopolitical and historical conditions of Hong Kong perpetuate this mainstream economic discourse, and finally, Section V is a brief summary.

1   The dominance of Western capitalist metaphors

Despite the appearance of being in opposition, mainstream liberal economists and Marxists have both identified the 'free market' and 'private property' with 'capitalism'. The main difference is that liberals believe the 'free market' and 'private property' have merit, while Marxists believe that they cause more harm than good. Perhaps that is the reason why Marxist economists, notably from the school of analytical Marxism, can share with mainstream liberal economists analytical frameworks such as general equilibrium models and rational choice. At the same time, however, the Marxists remain critical of the conclusions drawn by the liberals (see, for instance, Roemer 1988; Gintis and Bowles 1990).

Economic historians and political economists with a strong historical awareness, however, have pointed out the mistake of confusing 'capitalism' with the 'free market' and 'private property'. Polanyi (1957: 55) for example, argues that the origin of capitalism — in Europe — had never developed a free market before the nineteenth century. Fred Block continues this thesis and has shown that even in the USA, the centre of the capitalist world economy in the twentieth century, the development of free markets is at best partial (Block 1990, 1995). Scholars specialising in East Asian development issues have also demonstrated that free markets were never really the engines behind the rapid economic growth of the newly industrialising states in the region (see Lim 1983; Amsden 1989; Schiffer 1991; Wade 1990).

Nor did free trade play a significant role in the historical development of the world capitalist economy. According to Paul Bairoch, an economic historian, the practice of free trade is at best historical coincidence rather than historical norm. Europe could be characterised as a Free Trade Zone, for only approximately one quarter of a 200-year period between the nineteenth and twentieth centuries. For most of this period, as well as the period from the sixteenth to the eighteenth centuries, Europe is better described as a sea of protectionism or mercantilism (Bairoch 1993: 16–29). And this does not only apply to Europe. From the beginning of the nineteenth to the mid-twentieth century, the USA had among the highest tariff rates of all countries. Although its tariff rates have since been tremendously reduced, other trade barriers such as voluntary export restraints, multifiber agreements and product standardisation requirements have been implemented (Ray 1991: 343, 349–349; Baldwin 1991: 367–369). Similarly, the newly industrialised economies (NIEs) of East Asia are also well known for state intervention in trade (Amsden 1989: 66–70; Wade 1990: 113–148). Indeed, Fernand Braudel, one of the great historians of European capitalism, takes this point to its logical conclusion, and argues that not only should the 'free market' be distinguished from 'capitalism', but the nature of 'capitalism' is in fact 'anti-market' (Braudel 1979: 562; 1982: 433; 1984: 608–622).

Europe, North America, and the East Asian NIEs are areas regarded as the centres of capitalism, yet private enterprises are perhaps over-emphasised with regard to their role in the economy. For instance, in most wealthy European countries and East Asian economies, there has been a large public enterprise sector. These public businesses include steel manufacture, ship-building, petroleum, coal mining, railroads, aero-transportation, electricity, gas, postal service, telecommunication, and banks (Pitelis and Clarke 1993: 16; Wade 1988: 46–7). Japan and the USA, where relatively few public enterprises exist, are probably the two exceptions. But in both countries there are well-developed stock markets and the listed companies are 'collectively owned'. In both countries, the decline of private holding and the increase of institutional holding of stocks have been persistent trends in the post-War period (Blair 1995: 46; Komiya 1990: 161). In Japan, to find out who actually owns a large company is extremely difficult, as most of the large companies are mutually owned (Blinder 1992: 55–56). Moreover, privatisation is not the norm of capitalist economies either. Although the 1980s witnessed a wave of privatisation in many parts of the world, it was more a result of politics — of forcing budget squeezes on to the poor and middle classes — rather than a move to create economic efficiency. Nevertheless, privatisation is not a popular doctrine in most of the rich European countries (Pitelis and Clarke 1993).

The above evidence of the non-private and non-free-market features of the world economy is not difficult for social scientists in general, and economists in particular, to take into consideration. It is surprising how persistent the claims are that the free market, free trade, and private property rights account for the economic success of capitalism. In order to understand how and why these claims have been maintained in Hong Kong, this paper will analyse the translation and rhetoric strategies of Hong Kong economists, as well as the geopolitical context of Hong Kong in which these claims are perpetuated.

2   Domesticating translation and economic rhetoric

Translation has been commonly seen as a translingual practice which transparently and fluently represents something that already exists. Yet since the 1980s, the notion that translation is seen merely as an interlingual process, in which the role of the translator is invisible, has been increasingly challenged.

Among the many critics of the conventional understanding of translation is Lawrence Venuti. 'Transparency' and 'fluency', two canonical criteria set by conventional translation discourse, are characterised by Venuti as a 'domesticating' strategy, which is 'to insure easy readability by adhering to current usage, maintaining continuous syntax, [and] fixing a precise meaning' (Venuti 1995: 1).

According to Venuti, Anglo-American translation practices have long been ruled by domesticating strategies. These strategies have been encouraged by editors, publishers and reviewers because the products of fluent translation 'are eminently readable and therefore consumable in the book market, assisting in their commodification' (Venuti 1995: 16, 21).

Venuti's concept of 'domestication' is not merely confined to the linguistic aspects of translation, although these aspects are certainly critical in the understanding of domestication:

> A fluent translation is written in English that is current ('modern') instead of archaic, that is widely used instead of specialized ('jargonisation'), and that is standard instead of colloquial ('slangy'). Foreign words ('pidgin') are avoided . . . Fluency also depends on syntax that is not so 'faithful' to the foreign text as to be 'not quite idiomatic,' that unfolds continuously and easily (not 'doughy') to insure semantic 'precision' with some rhythmic definition, a sense of closure (not a 'dull thud').   (Venuti 1995: 4–5)

Another aspect of domestication, and perhaps a more important one, is apparently political in nature. A domesticating translation, in Venuti's own words, 'is immediately recognizable and intelligible, "familiarised," domesticated, not "disconcerting[ly]" foreign, capable of giving the reader unobstructed access to great thoughts, to what is "present in the original"' (Venuti 1995: 5). In other words, domesticating translation is able to make reading more comfortable, by presenting ideas and concepts with which readers are familiar. This 'comfortable reading experience' not only emerges from the fluency of the language used, but also from the fact that what is presented in translated texts is concurrent with mainstream doctrines and dominant ideologies, which are, for most readers of the target language, very easy to digest. In short, domestication is the act which reinforces dominant ideologies. As Sengupta (1995: 159) concisely states:

> ... translations often operate under varied constraints and ... these constraints include manipulations of power relations that aim at *constructing an 'image' of the source culture that preserves or extends the hegemony of the dominant group*. In fact, these 'images' construct notions of the Other and formulate an identity of the source culture that is recognizable by the target culture as representative of the former — as 'authentic' specimens of a world that is remote as well as inaccessible in terms of the target culture's self.
>
> (my italics)

While allowing readers to comfortably consume 'foreign cultures', domesticating translation has also reduced the subversive potential of the foreign text.

In contrast to domestication, Venuti proposes 'foreignization' as an alternative translation strategy:

> Foreignizing translation signifies the difference of the foreign text, yet only by disrupting the cultural codes that prevail in the target language ... deviating enough from native norms to stage an alien reading experience — choosing to translate a foreign text excluded by domestic literary canons, for instance, or using a marginal discourse to translate it ... Foreignizing translation in English can be a form of resistance against ethnocentrism and racism, cultural narcissism and imperialism, in the interests of democratic geopolitical relations.   (Venuti 1995: 20)

From this paragraph it is obvious that the concept of foreignization, and hence its oppositional concept — domestication — should be understood in terms of (cultural) politics, instead of mere linguistics.

In the following section I will employ the concept of 'domestication' to analyse the strategy adopted by Hong Kong economists in translating Western economic writing into Chinese. Since their translations (broadly defined) are closely related to their rhetorical strategies in writing these texts, it seems necessary to review briefly the rhetorical approaches to economics, which will also be used as a frame of reference in this paper.

During the course of the 1980s, studies of rhetoric in the social sciences flourished. Now rhetorical approaches have been widely applied in various disciplines within the social sciences, including economics (see for instance special issues on rhetoric in *Economy and Society*, vol. 18, no. 2, 1989 and *Social Research*, vol. 62, no. 2, Summer 1995). In particular, prominent economists Donald McCloskey and Arjo Klamer, among others, have applied these rhetorical approaches to analyse the writings of economists. By closely examining the language of the text, these studies, utilising rhetorical approaches to the social sciences, have yielded significant contributions to our understanding of the art or science of persuasion which social scientists use to persuade their audience.

According to McCloskey, rhetoric does not mean 'a verbal shell game, as in "empty rhetoric" or "mere rhetoric".' Instead, rhetoric, as Wayne Booth defines it, is 'the art of discovering good reasons', or 'in the ancient sense of persuasive discourse' (McCloskey 1983: 482–483 and Nelson *et al.* 1987: 3). The main problem for economists, according to McCloskey, is that they are not sensitive to their own rhetorical practices.

By re-introducing rhetoric, McCloskey tries to persuade his colleagues to be more aware of their own writings in order to rescue economics from falling into the trap of modernism and scientism. Yet McCloskey does not advise replacing 'science' with 'rhetoric'. Instead he believes that rhetoric is an indispensable part of any serious scientific work. For him, 'art is as scientific as science, science as artistic as art' (McCloskey 1995: 224). What is the good of being more sensitive to the rhetoric? McCloskey's answer is: better writing, better teaching, better foreign relations, better science, and better dispositions (McCloskey 1983: 512–515).

It may be true that persuasion 'makes alertness work' (McCloskey 1995: 229). But what makes persuasion work? McCloskey suggests that it is the community of economists who judge what are good economic arguments. Through 'scientific conversations', economists are deciding 'what is a fact, what is a logic, and what is a story' (McCloskey 1993: 140). But how does the community of economists make its judgements?

McCloskey claims that 'overlapping conversations provide the standards. It is a market argument. There is no need for philosophical lawmaking or methodological regulation to keep the economy of the intellect running just fine' (quoted in Stettler 1995: 397). In other words, McCloskey is saying that good scientific arguments are created in a process of market competition similar to that of competition among products competing in the market. Of course, we are arguing in the first place that free market competition is largely a myth. In fact, McCloskey's 'market metaphor' has been criticised by Stettler as supporting 'a laissez-faire theory of economic discourse' which 'can be interpreted as a rhetorical device used to entrench the position of the dominant economic paradigm, under the pretence, of course, that there is fair competition' (Stettler 1995: 397 and 398).

Yet the critiques of McCloskey should not be read as a total dismissal of his analysis of the rhetorical approach to understanding arguments made in the social sciences, and that of economists in particular. According to Brown, for example,

[v]iewing reason as rhetorical has two advantages. First, as a heuristic [device], it facilitates the study of social and political organization as a human product . . . A second advantage of the conception of reason as

social creativity is that it invites an appreciation of alternative types of rationality, each with its own social form and telos. Such an appreciation includes a reflective awareness of the interests presupposed in one's own reasoning, as well as in that of others.   (Brown 1987: 185)

While McCloskey's rhetorical analysis has inspired research on the rhetoric of economics, most of the existing literature on textual analysis of the rhetoric of economics has, however, focused on academic articles and books, research reports, and textbooks. This paper aims instead at understanding the impact of economic discourse on a larger social group by examining the translation strategy and rhetoric used in popular economic writing in Hong Kong. In the next section I select a particular genre — 'economics prose', which is widely received in Hong Kong, for analysis. The writings of a few popular local economists, Steven N.S. Cheung, Hang-chi Lam and Francis T. Lui, are selected. I will examine their translation strategy (domestication) and their rhetorical strategies — how they utilise metaphors,[1] the power of authority, the appeal to commonly-accepted ideology, as well as their prose style of writing.

3   Translation and rhetorical strategies of Hong Kong economists

Cheung, Lam and Lui are three well-known economists in Hong Kong who have helped popularise the pro-free market and private property position.[2] Though they, except for Lam, write many of their academic papers in English, I have selected their Chinese writings for study. This is because most of their English works are written for readers within the international mainstream economic discipline, while their Chinese writings are aimed at local readers. Since the targeted readership of their English and Chinese writings are from two different groups, the ways these authors present their arguments in both languages differ significantly. Generally speaking, their Chinese writings are much more casual than their English academic articles because most of their local readers are not necessarily economic experts, but are drawn from the larger business and academic communities, and indeed, common laypersons as well. This target audience, one can argue, may be more susceptible to the perpetuation of 'free market' and 'private property' myths.

Most writings by Hong Kong economists may not be regarded as translation, if it is narrowly defined. In fact, like other social science disciplines, economics always looks down upon translation practices. Translating an economic text is at best regarded as a secondary scholarly activity, and is certainly not counted on as one deserving professional merit. Yet economists do translate. They translate their own work from one language to another, or they translate other works while quoting them. A more common practice is to adapt or quote indirectly or rewrite economists' ideas written in other languages. If we take a broader definition of translation — as disruption, displacement or producing, rather than reflecting,[3] many of the works written in Chinese by local economists may be qualified as translation.

Let us first look at some of their direct translations. A case in point is the translation into Chinese of Steven Cheung's long article (1982), 'Will China Go "Capitalist?"' The translator, as well as the two people who helped 'improve' the quality of the Chinese translated text, are good friends of Cheung (Cheung 1985: 148). Although Cheung did not translate the work himself, he 'significantly edited' the translated text before it was collected in a book published in 1985, though he claims that those changes are still based on the original translated version which was published in 1983 (Cheung 1985: 150). The following discussion draws on the 1985 Chinese version, which had been proof-read and edited by Cheung.

The most striking difference between the English and Chinese versions of Cheung's book is that he has added two prefaces for the Chinese version. The intonation of these prefaces, especially the first one, is more presumptuous than his English preface. For instance, in explaining why he publishes this long article in Chinese, Cheung glorifies his work by referring to Ronald Coase, a Nobel Prize winner, by saying:

> Professor Coase read the first draft of my paper and discussed it with me on several occasions. He basically agreed with my extension of the Coase Theorem [to China]. No historical precedent is better than Coase in terms of the understanding of institutional operations of an economy. And Coase is also very concerned about the future of China. If he regards this piece highly, how can I disappoint him? Another reason is that I used to send my drafts to my friends for comments. After I sent this article out, several universities put it on their course reading lists, and a petroleum company even reproduced copies and distributed them to its staff. Since it has already become public reading, how can I help not publishing it?
>
> (Cheung 1985: 148; my translation)

Perhaps the reason why Cheung did not write this paragraph in his English preface is that it would look bizarre to Western academics who might find his words wanting in modesty and precision.

It is not difficult to find similar kinds of brazen and exaggerated text in the Chinese version of Cheung's article. Below are a few other examples taken from his English and Chinese versions:

> ... I must here proffer my own *working hypothesis* for the Chinese case, making no claim that it represents a *definitive theory* of institutional change.
>
> (Cheung 1982: 20; my italics)

… 所以我唯有提出自己的理論。我得聲明，這不是有關制度轉變的*唯一理論*。
(Cheung 1985: 157; my emphasis)

But the costs to the producer of discovering consumer preferences, or those to the supervisor of monitoring performance, will be *higher than* under private enterprise. (Cheung 1982: 35; my italics)

可是，生產者要探索消費者的喜好，或督導從屬的費用，卻*遠比*在私有企業下的高。
(Cheung 1985: 178; my emphasis)

… Professor R. H. Coase (an Englishman who taught at Chicago and other US universities) established that, in the absence of transaction costs, a clear delineation of private property rights would lead to the *identical* allocation of resources regardless of how the rights were assigned or distributed. His analysis gave birth to the well-known 'Coase Theorem' which states, in essence, that if all scarce resources are viewed from the standpoint of rights, and if all rights are costlessly [sic] delineated or defined as private or exclusive, then in the absence of transaction costs *the standard theorem of exchange* will operate to bring about the most valuable use of resources.
(Cheung 1982: 36; my italics)

… 高斯教授 (Professor R. H. Coase, 在芝加哥及其它美國大學任教的英國人)指出，在交易費用不存在的情況下，不管產權誰屬，只要清楚界定產權是私有，結果必然是導至最高效益的資源運用情況。他的分析，創立了著名的「高斯定律」。這個理論的要點，是指出從產權的觀點來觀察資源的運用，倘若將產權劃分或界定為私有是不需費用的，那麼在交易費用不存在的情況下，交易取利可保證資源必定會作最有效的運用。

(Cheung 1985: 179; my emphasis)

In the first example, 'working hypothesis' becomes (理論) 'theory' in the Chinese version. And 'a definitive theory' becomes (唯一理論) 'the only theory'. In the second example, 'higher than' in the Chinese version becomes (遠比) 'much higher than'. Perhaps the most note-worthy case is the third example. While the English version maintains that 'in the absence of transaction cost, a clear delineation of private property rights would lead to *identical* allocation of resources regardless of how the rights were assigned or distributed.' In the Chinese version, it turns into '. . . in the absence of transaction cost, a clear delineation of private property rights would *lead to the optimum allocation of resources* (導至最高效益的資源運用)' (my translation). Moreover, in the English version it is only within the framework of 'the standard theorem of exchange' that will 'bring about the most valuable use of resources'. However, in the Chinese version, 'the standard theorem of exchange' is no longer mentioned and it becomes '. . . *profit making exchanges* (交易取利) will guarantee the most effective use of resources.' This difference is significant because 'the standard theorem of exchange' holds only after satisfying several restrictive assumptions and axioms, which are not always realistic.

All these examples, and it is not difficult to find more, are typical of 'domesticating' translations. Written in an impudent and casual style, the Chinese 'translation' not only disrupts the relatively modest and precise tone of the English version, but by providing an easy-to-digest reading, also serves the purpose of persuading readers who are not critical of economic discourses towards a particular way of thought.

Similar examples can be found in Lam's work. For instance, in a newspaper article, Lam (1991)[4] translated the first paragraph of Kenneth J. Arrow's *Social Choice and Individual Values*, (2nd edition, New Haven, CT: Yale University Press, 1963, p.1) as follows:

> In a capitalist democracy there are essentially two methods by which social choices can be made: voting, typically used to make 'political' decisions, and the market mechanism, typically used to make 'economic' decisions.
>
> (Arrow 1963: 1)
>
> 資本主義民主政制有二種方法能作出社會選擇 — 政治事務可通過投票達成，經濟問題則*非由*市場機制完成*不可*。　　(Lam 1991: my emphasis)

The Chinese version, if translated back into English, becomes:

> There are two ways to make social choices in capitalist democratic political systems: political affairs could be dealt with through voting, whereas economic problems *must be* handled through market mechanism.
>
> (my translation and italics)

Such an inconclusive statement is turned into a definite judgement, which is again utilised to support the dominant ideology of 'free market'.

Let us now turn to the rhetorical strategies of some of their other Chinese writings, which can still be regarded, in a broader sense, as translations of western economic ideologies.

A truly fascinating feature of their approach is the use of the popular Chinese genre, 武俠小説 *wuxia xiaoshuo*, or martial arts fiction.[5] In their writings on economic issues they apply terms like 武功 *wugong* (martial arts in general), 招數 *zhaoshu* (martial arts tactics), 內功 *neigong* (inner energy), 武林秘笈 *wulin miji* (magical books from which one learns supreme martial arts). When speaking of other academics whom they support, they refer to them as 大宗師 *dazongshi* (kung fu masters), 世外高人 *shiwai gaoren* (ascetic kungfu masters), or 高手 *gaoshou* (eminent kungfu masters), and so on (see for instance Lui 1995: 10–11, 32–35, 42, 90; Cheung 1991: 26; 1985: 13). They use these metaphors to mobilise the readers' imagination and emotions with reference to the familiar fictional world of Chinese martial arts, so that readers gain an immediate sense of pleasure from reading the work and identify with the context and characters of the fiction imposed on non-fictional socio-economic developments. Fiction and non-fiction, in other words, are blurred.

By using jargon from martial arts fiction (*wuxia xiaoshuo*), the authors furthermore present themselves as *shiwai gaoren* or *gaoshou* (read 'eminent economists') of the fictional world, as though they were living like knight-errant heroes with a higher level of intelligence and 'quality'. By invoking this jargon of martial arts fiction, which carries a slightly facetious tone, they can easily dismiss views differing from their own.

Their writings can be categorised as prose style which is light and pleasurable to read. Their works are relaxed reading, yet they purport to convey serious information or scientific facts. In contrast to heavy and dry academic writings, their casual prose style implicitly encourages readers not to engage in any serious evaluation, since the subject matter itself is no longer serious but has become entertainment. By fusing fiction and 'facts' and presenting their stories like martial arts fiction so popular in Hong Kong, these authors successfully present a fictional world of economics for their readers to persuade them of the virtues of so-called laissez-faire economics.

Another common rhetorical device that is utilised is the creation of authority by describing an economist according to the categorisation of fictional martial arts characters and by fabricating their ranks. When the authors introduce an argument made by an economist, for example, they describe him or her as ascetic kung fu masters (*shiwai gaoren*) or as eminent kung fu masters (*gaoshou*). In addition, they also create professional rankings to bestow authority upon the economists with whose views they agree. For instance, Robert Barro is introduced as a 'top economist' (頂尖的經濟學家), highly ranked as a consequence of the frequency in which his writings have been quoted in other works. Thomas Sargent and Neil Wallace are 'giants' (巨星) of the rational expectations school, and Sargent himself is given the rank of 'number eight' (天下第八). Needless to say, all these 'top economists' are promoters of the free market (Lui 1995: 47 and 86; see also Cheung 1991: 115).

Even lesser-known economists are introduced as top authorities because they are professors of allegedly top schools, or members of known professional organisations. For instance, Lui says of Tom Cooley, Chair Professor at the University of Rochester, that 'if a conclusion is coming out from the mouth of this kind of eminent kung fu master (*gaoshou*), it is of course comparatively reliable' (Lui 1995: 98).

They also attempt to rate each other's status and impress readers by simply mutually complementing and fabricating each other's alleged authority by highly recommending each other's work. For instance, in the preface of his book, Lui writes, 'Professor Gregory Chow is a chair professor of Princeton University, and is a top economist. Mr. Hang-chi Lam of *Xin Bao (Hong Kong Economic Journal)* is surely the number one writer in Hong Kong' (Lui 1995: 12). Chow and Lam in return celebrate Lui as a creative and influential economist, and say in their prefaces that his writings are persuasive, lively, readable, and inspiring.

But they are also skilled at conferring authority upon themselves. Lui, for instance, gives readers his personal opinion of himself and states that 'in my article published in the *Journal of Political Economy*, I proved that under certain conditions, corruption can speed up administrative efficiency . . . [and that] (according to a friend of mine who received his Ph.D from the Economics Department of Chicago, my article had been selected for their course syllabus)' (Lui 1995: 20). Similarly, as illustrated above, Cheung also glorifies his work by referring to his association with a person of international repute, Ronald Coase. After reading these paragraphs, a reader is likely to conclude even prior to reading the entire piece that it is important and truthful and that the author's opinion is of significance. Authority is thus established on egotism, bragging and hearsay.

Yet their translation and rhetorical strategies at best can only explain partially why the aforementioned claims are accepted in Hong Kong. In order to have a more thorough understanding, we should broaden our discussion to include the geopolitical context of the communities in which this interpretation is disseminated as knowledge.

4   The interpretive communities of economic writing in Hong Kong

The practices and structures of academic disciplines are being increasingly acknowledged as an important aspect of knowledge generation (Messer-Davidow *et al.* 1993; Wallerstein *et al.* 1995). As Foucault (1972: 224) points out, disciplinary knowledge is a system of regulation in the production of discourses. Disciplinary knowledge is legitimated and, by and large, is only subject to self-discipline via the regulation of intellectual work. This is done through closed and self-perpetuating mechanisms of distinct disciplinary institutions and practices, such as professional/academic associations, journals and conferences, funding mechanisms and by normalising pedagogic procedures (examinations, grading systems, and writings).

Students trained within this disciplinary setting are likely to be uncritical of the 'common sense' truth associated with the discipline of economics itself. Those engaged in the discipline tend to be moulded by the institutions and practices, and thus come to think and behave like 'economists'.[6] Students of economics, and other academic disciplines as well, are trained not to question the fundamentals of their discipline.[7] In fact, they are told not to 'waste time' justifying their method or theory in any way but just to work with it (Klamer 1987: 170). The 'gatekeeper' in economics is economic rhetoric with its modes of analysis, its concepts and analytical techniques, the problems and agenda it sets for itself and the types of exercises and examinations that are thus generated. In order to publish articles in prestigious journals, for example, one simply must conform to the norms of the discipline through an internal refereeing process which, it turns out, is also a social process in which hierarchical power, relations, and reciprocity factor into the creation of an economist's academic authority.[8] Of course, students of economics are inevitably motivated to also seek a realistic picture of the economy. But since their training is stuffed with dry, and often boring, mathematical models and formalistic arguments, some economists attempt to put a 'human face' on their work by turning to non-academic sources. The success of Cheung, Lam and Lui's writings should be understood in this light. These economic populists have, in Klamer's words, assuaged 'the discomfort of the innocent student by appealing to his common sense' (Klamer 1987: 172). This introduction and translation into casual prose provides readers with an entertainment value fused with allegedly authoritative academic discourse, and has perhaps been the key way in which Western economic myths have been perpetuated in Hong Kong.

The specific geopolitical context of Hong Kong — lying between 'capitalism' (the West) and 'socialism' (China) — has made the spread of negative perceptions of communist China even easier to accomplish. This then has provided a favourable context for the transplantation of Western economic myth as an antithesis to communist power and rhetoric.

In fact, Hong Kong people have long been subjected to cold war ideology in which China and communism have been portrayed as a menacing devil of the world. This view is reinforced by the fact that China is poor (economically speaking), which Hong Kong people can observe at first hand due to their close proximity. The poverty of China has been used as rhetorical evidence to construct a negative image of socialism/communism. The simple fact of China's poverty, in contrast to the increasing standard of living in Hong Kong, has been used as a powerful tool of persuasion by economists which has the popular support of the many Hong Kong people who have migrated from the PRC.

The use of China as a scapegoat[9] to promote the ideology of the free market and private property certainly appears in Cheung's and Lui's writings. When criticising the idea of establishing a Central Provident Fund in Hong Kong, Lui writes, 'as a Central Provident Fund is managed by the government, it can hence be regarded as public enterprise. But the competitive mechanism would obviously be weak. According to *the experiences of China and East Europe*, in the long run, public enterprises are surely inferior to private enterprises. This is clearly observed by everybody' (Lui 1995: 194; emphasis added).

Further, in order to consolidate his assertion that 'historically speaking, only private property and the free market can stimulate production and economic growth' Cheung uses the so-called Fragrant Hills Syndrome to describe the negative impact of the Chinese 'anti-private-property and anti-free-market' system (Cheung 1984: 10–12; see also Cheung 1985: 151–5). The Fragrant Hills refers to a Chinese hotel where the management is regarded as rather inefficient. But this 'scapegoat strategy' can work only when readers have neither the familiarity with, nor the interest in, the complicated historical situations of the countries discussed. It is for this reason that such popularised local economic writing works. Similarly, as their style is designed for more or less casual reading, it precludes the generation of serious thought or critique of historical narration.

5   Summary

I have argued that the perpetuation of 'free market' and 'private property' myths has resulted from the combined forces of the translation and rhetorical strategies of local economists, the system of a self-regulating academic discipline and institutions of knowledge creation, and the geopolitical context of Hong Kong. Local economists, while translating Western economic ideologies, have adopted a domesticating strategy with a particular rhetorical style. The adoption of casual prose and the use of popular fiction in the characterisation of authority figures as a means to present 'scientific' economic arguments dilutes the level of discourse to the point where serious critique is generally avoided, yet allows for the dissemination of the alleged authority of the authors and their arguments to a wider audience. As such their writings have confirmed the dominant discursive values — in this case the perpetuation of a powerful version of free market and private property — in Hong Kong. By further playing on common perceptions that the cause of China's poverty is communism, local economists have been able to popularise their mainstream economic views of the alleged efficiency and wealth-producing effects of the so-called free market and private property.

It is true that a translator 'always exercises a choice concerning the degree and direction of the violence at work in any translating' (Venuti 1995: 19). A translation can never be totally 'faithful', but is 'always somewhat "free" ' and 'always a lack and a supplement' (Venuti 1992: 5–6). However, this does not mean that all translations are equally good or bad. Yet judgement passed on a piece of translation should not be based solely on its linguistic quality, as politics is at least of equal importance. This paper is hence nothing but a study of 'the discursive strategies and institutional structures which determine the production, circulation, and reception of translated texts' (Venuti 1992: 6); or particularly, a study of the politics of the translation of Western economic ideology to Hong Kong.

Acknowledgements

I am grateful to Elson Boles, Lakshmi Daniel, Lau Kin-chi, Law Wing-sang, Pun Wing-chung, the editors of this volume and the anonymous reviewer for their helpful comments. I would like to thank Lau Cheun-wai, Sit Tsui and Wong Tak-hing for their research and technical assistance, and the Lingnan College Research Grants for funding this research.

Notes

1. Economic vocabulary is full of metaphors taken from non-economic domains. A metaphor has the power to link two separate conceptual domains by structurally mapping one to another (McCloskey 1983: 503; 1995: 215).

2. For instance, when criticising the idea in favour of the establishment of a Central Provident Fund (CPF), Lui (1995: 193) writes, '[CPF] violates the [principle of] the common sense of economics — market competition and private property.'

3. According to Niranjana (1992: 8, 81), the term 'translation' in Latin and Greek at once suggests movement, disruption, displacement; and 'translation is always producing rather than merely reflecting or imitating an "original".'

4. I thank Pun Wing-chung for providing this example.

5. Similarly, they also make use of ancient Chinese 'wisdom' for metaphoric pronouncements. For instance, Lui and his colleague's newspaper column is called 烹鮮集 pengxianji which originated from Laozi's phrase 治大國若烹小鮮 zhidaguo ruo peng xiao xian (ruling the country is like cooking a small fish), meaning that you don't want to turn the fish so often as to ruin it. Similarly, do not intervene in the economy too often, i.e. just let the market work! (Lui 1995: 15) However, since this type of metaphor is used less often, I will focus my discussion on their use of martial arts metaphors in what follows.

6. Frank et al. (1993) summarised several studies which show that studying economics has encouraged the development of selfishness.

7. As Strassmann (1993: 152) notes, 'economists are trained by pedagogical methods, such as problem sets, which discourage the questioning of fundamentals . . . While problem sets may seem neutral enough, they teach students to learn and accept a particular form of interpretation . . . [lead] students to view the core material as the valuable and unchallengeable consensus of experts. Indeed, in economics, students quickly learn that it is bad manners to spend too much time questioning the assumptions of a paper . . . such restrictions are used to limit disciplinary membership and define acceptable economic practice.'

8. According to a study, many economic papers are rejected not because of academic merit or demerit, but rather because of social and political considerations (see Gans and Shepherd 1994).

9. Another poor country, India, is also used as another scapegoat. India is presented as a 'corrupted state' in which businesses are monopolised by the government and rich merchants (Cheung 1996: 4–5).

12

The role of language and culture within the accountancy workplace
Gail Forey and David Nunan

Introduction

This paper focuses on discourse practices in the workplace. It is concerned with adults who have well-developed skills in literacy and who are already fully qualified professionals, or who are studying for their professional qualifications. The investigation of written discourse practices will ultimately be utilised to inform the development of pedagogic material for the workplace. At this stage, however, we are attempting to understand the contextual demands and influences affecting written texts within the business world, as suggested by Martin *et al.* (1994),

> What is needed then is a model that shows systematically how text is related to context. This is the kind of model that teachers require . . .
>
> (1994: 236)

The need for a systematic understanding of how the text and context are related in the workplace is raised by Barbara *et al.* (1996), Berry (1986), Brown and Herndl (1986), Williams (1988), amongst others. Underpinning this work is a systemic–functional model of language description and use. This paper, in studying the language of the workplace from a systemic functional perspective, attempts to build upon previous work carried out in this area (Halliday 1985a, 1994). A clearer understanding of the relationship between text and context should yield valuable information for material designers, teachers, trainers and students.

Background to the project

The Communication in the Professional Workplace (CPW) Project was initiated with funding obtained from the Language Fund (a funding body established under the aegis of the Hong Kong Government) for an initial period of 6 months. The research team consisted of David Nunan, who directed the project, two full-time research assistants, Gail Forey and Jassar W. H. Foo, and one part-time (0.5) research assistant, Rae Fossard.

The CPW project sought to replicate and complement a study undertaken by the Effective Writing for Management Project (EWM) initiated and directed by Florence Davies at Bristol University from October 1994 to September 1995. This project surveyed the principal writing requirements of a heterogeneous sample of British middle to senior managers working in a range of organisations, in both the private and public sectors. In the EWM Project the native (first) language of the sample involved was English. The research instruments for the CPW project were based on the questionnaire and interview protocols developed for the Bristol Project.

The data in this paper come from two sources, a questionnaire distributed to members of the Hong Kong Society of Accountants (HKSA), and interviews conducted with individual members of this professional body. During the interviews the informants were asked to bring along example texts they believed were either effective or ineffective. These texts form the initial corpus of authentic texts which will be analysed at a later stage in the Project.

The questionnaire

The questionnaire sought data on the following:

- the type of documents which accountants are required to produce during the course of their work
- the attitudes and views of accountants towards writing in English
- the amount of time invested in the processes of writing
- the problems encountered in the process of writing
- the degree and nature of support and training available.

Two questionnaires were designed; one for junior, and one for senior accountants. Broadly speaking, these two groups can be characterised as follows:

Senior accountants: the group of senior accountants included professional accountants, partners, employers and accountants who work in a supervisory role. This may, in fact, include some people who have been working in accounting for a long period of time, but who have not yet obtained their ACCA/HKSA qualification.

Junior accountants: the second group, junior accountants, refers to accountants who are still studying for their ACCA/HKSA or equivalent qualification, or have been working in accounting for fewer than three years.

From the above characterisation, it should be evident that the distinction between these two groups is not clear cut. Within each organisation, the roles, titles and professional status of an accountant may vary. Consequently, we spent a great deal of time in discussion with contacts in organisations to define, explain and clarify the two target populations. Since separate questionnaires were to be distributed to senior and junior accountants, we needed two identifiable sub-samples within the overall survey.

A second distinction was also made between commercial organisations and public accounting firms. Thus, for the purpose of this paper what is commonly known as the commercial sector and what accountants recognise as the commercial sector can be seen to be different. The distinctions are as follows:

Accountants from public accounting firms refers to those who are practising accountants working in CPA firms (Certified Public Accountants).

Accountants from commercial organisations are all other accountants who are working outside of this field; this would include those working in Government Departments, banks, import and export, and the commercial sectors.

The target population for the study was, therefore, divided into four groups:

• senior accountants from public accounting firms
• senior accountants from commercial organisations
• junior accountants from public accounting firms
• junior accountants from commercial organisations.

The distribution of the sample is as shown in Table 12.1.

Linguistically, 93% of the total population spoke Cantonese as their first language, 5% spoke English as their first language, 1% spoke Putonghua and 1% were speakers of other languages.

Table 12.1   CPW sample distribution for questionnaire

	Public firms	Commercial organisations	Total
Junior	310	236	546 (54.2%)
Senior	282	179	461 (45.8%)
Total	592 (58.8%)	415 (41.2%)	1,007

Table 12.2 Interview sample population

Size of organisation	Public accounting firms		Commercial organisations		Total
	Senior	Junior	Senior	Junior	
Large (> 200 accountants)	6	5	1	1	13
Medium (50–200 accountants)	1	2	2	2	7
Small (< 50 accountants)			5	5	10
Total	7	7	8	8	30

The interviews

In order to obtain more detailed qualitative information, we decided to interview a sub-set of the questionnaire respondents. The interview sample population is outlined in Table 12.2. The aims of the interviews were:

- to expand and develop key issues raised in the survey
- to explore ways in which draft writing is evaluated and edited by accountants
- to discover the criteria used to evaluate effective writing by the informant and his/her organisation
- to identify priority training needs.

These aims led to the development of a set of semi-structured interview protocols.

The sample

In order to differentiate between the responses made by individuals to the survey and responses made by individuals to the interviews, the term 'respondents' will be used to refer to an individual responding to the survey, and 'informants' will be used to refer to an individual responding during the interview.

In the time available and with the assistance of the business community the research team was able to conduct a total of 30 interviews. The interviews took place between 20 December and 4 March, one of the busiest periods for accounting organisations, because during this period 'year ends' are conducted. This placed severe constraints on the number and distribution of subjects available for interview.

In selecting informants, our main concern was to ensure our sample reflected the membership of HKSA. We did this by establishing an initial contact. The initial contact was then asked to select a senior and a junior member of staff whom we would be able to interview. While this raised the possibility of bias, through lengthy discussions with our contact we believed the informants selected would be responsive and receptive to being interviewed. We also believed the effort was worthwhile because the informants provided insights unobtainable by other means (Bhatia 1993: 34).

Outcomes from the project

In this section, we shall set out some of the project outcomes that are pertinent to the themes of this book.

Product orientation to written language

It is interesting, within the context of this collection, to look at the attitude of accountants to language. The view that comes through very strongly is that knowledge and language are givens. Language is a medium for the transmission of given, factual knowledge. The notion of 'constructing knowledge' through discourse would seem to lie beyond the conceptual universe of most of our informants. For these people, accuracy is important because poorly-written documents may result in 'wrong information' being transmitted.

> ... if the kind of letters or faxes I write daily ... are not in good English, this may lead to some sort of misunderstanding between our overseas offices and us. And this unclear ... then we may pass the ... some wrong information to our overseas offices to our clients, and that may cause problem as well. Especially when we are dealing with our clients, if we've done something wrong, even though we are not reporting ... we're not talking on financial statement, but we've written something wrong or not in very good English and passes some sorts of wrong information to them, this may cause us serious trouble.   (Eric)

The public face of the organisation represented by written documents

Another major reason why accurate written English is held to be important is because external communication represents the 'public face' of a firm. If a poorly-written document is sent out, then it will tarnish the image of the firm. As one junior said:

If the report is written in messy English, it'll affect the image of our firm. If we have to communicate with clients in correspondence, if we write in good English, our clients will be impressed. Because all our products are in written English.

(Joseph)

This perception that the image of a firm is conditioned in important ways by the quality of the written product probably accounts for the inordinate amount of time that senior accountants spend in revising and redrafting the work of the juniors. One of the more surprising results from the questionnaire was the amount of time that both seniors and juniors claimed they spent writing. Approximately 64% of junior accountants claimed that they spent 15 hours or more a week writing in English. Of seniors, 49% made a similar claim, as shown in Figure 12.1.

These figures represent the approximate time our respondents estimate they spend on writing in one week. Estimating the amount of time spent on writing in a week may be a difficult task for anyone. For many, writing is an integral part of the working day and it is, therefore, difficult to predict time spent on it. In fact, these figures may be an underestimation. Because

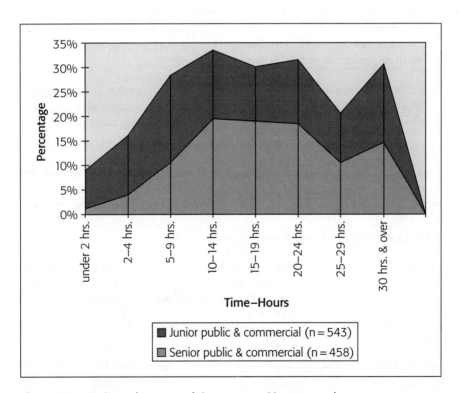

Figure 12.1 Estimated amount of time spent writing per week.

respondents were only asked to include elements of writing where they were physically involved in the writing process, the time estimated by the respondents does not include time spent thinking about writing, researching facts, or discussing with others documents to be written.

Despite this, the findings show that writing occupies a substantial proportion of accountants' working time. An average of 55% of all accountants in our survey spend 15 hours or more a week writing in English. This is a considerable amount of time, especially when one considers that for 94% of our respondents, English is not a first language. However, caution needs to be exercised in interpreting these figures, as they reflect perceptions rather than actual practice. In order to find out exactly how much time and energy is invested in writing, one needs to shadow workplace practices, as, indeed, we shall be doing in the second phase of the project.

In the case of seniors, it would seem that a significant amount of time is spent on redrafting material submitted by junior colleagues. The findings suggest that seniors and juniors believe seniors are generally the only ones who should edit documents, as shown in Table 12.3.

Whether this is an effective use of their time is a matter for individual firms. However, it would seem that an 'audit' or time management study should be carried out by firms to determine whether the amount of time seniors devote to redrafting juniors' work is justified, or whether an alternative scheme can be found. The burden of a person's writing ability is passed on to their senior, as one informant pointed out:

> *Because if someone is not very good at writing the manager has to spend more time with that person to actually go through maybe point by point about how to write something. That means that manager is wasting a lot of time . . .*

> (Emily)

One senior manager, Adrian, who often receives sub-standard documents from others, reported that it would take more time to ask the author to rewrite his or her work than to do it for him or her. This senior manager

Table 12.3 Who should edit juniors' writing?

Person	Who seniors believe juniors should submit their writing to for editing ($n = 461$)	Who juniors submit their writing to for editing ($n = 546$)
A colleague	4.6%	11.5%
Someone senior to you	95.7%	89.6%
No one	0.2%	5.1%

spends much of his valuable time re-writing other people's work, which, understandably, leads to frustration.

> *I find that it's quite frustrating when you have a large team and give certain sections to other people to write with guidelines and then they come back with something that's totally different to what you had asked them to do. And then my weakness then, is not to throw it back at them, but because of pressure of time, I write it myself. I think it's the lack of training on the staff.* (Adrian)

There may be a number of possible reasons for this:

(i)   The senior accountant is ultimately responsible for work produced and wants to ensure that documents circulated internally and externally are accurate and meet the required objective.

(ii) Since the senior accountant must sign off the document before it is finished, he or she will therefore proofread or edit the document prior to its release or completion.

(iii) The senior accountant does not necessarily trust the skills of others.

Numerous informants, both at senior and junior levels, saw the issue in economic terms. They pointed out that if a manager has to spend a great deal of time redrafting poorly written material, this will be an economic drain on the organisation.

Writing skills and the place of the individual within the workplace

In terms of promotion prospects, many informants, both junior and senior, commented on the importance of being perceived as competent in English. Senior informants reported that individual writing skill was one of the main criteria used to appraise an individual's performance, and that the ability to write well was highly correlated with both promotion and popularity. The following quote from an informant sums up the view expressed by many.

> *. . . if they do not possess [writing skills] they cannot fulfil the responsibility satis- factorily. . . . If you are appointed secretary of a meeting, you do not know how to write a report, you do not know how to write an agenda, right? How can you? Even you know how to speak, you know many things about what is the meeting talking about, you cannot write a minute, that means you cannot discharge a duty as secretary of the meeting satisfactorily. All right. This in return, the outcome is that our boss will not consider you as a competent man to do such a post. This is very obvious. Therefore, I think those people, especially my colleague who possess a*

good spoken English skill, or written English, they have an advantage of being consider for promotion.   (Chris)

Several seniors also linked the ability to write effectively with logical reasoning and ultimately with intelligence. One reported that:

I think you have to be a logical thinker in order to write effectively as well because if you think before you write, that save a lot of time. I don't know whether that the other way, I mean you have to be logical thinker before you become an effective writer. I think it's a kind of inter-link, but part of training may be to help them think logically.   (Harold)

Another suggested that, while employees may be intelligent, if they write poorly:

I'll have the impression that they are not as intelligent as they are and they have not understood things clearly because I don't understand what they have written.

(Janet)

The data support Martin's (1985: 51) contention that it is good writers (rather than good speakers) who are privileged in the professional workplace.

The most prestigious users of language become writers not speakers. And written language is prized above speech.   (Martin 1985: 51)

From the data, it is clear that being able to write effectively is much more than an important professional tool, it is a status symbol, along with other personal skills such as the ability to cope with clients, and can have an important influence on an individual's promotion prospects.

New technology and language

The advent of e-mail and the current unavailability of systems for sending messages in Chinese has had a significant effect on workplace practices. Many informants suggested that they preferred to write memos, e-mails and other texts in English because specialist keyboard skills were needed to write in Chinese. Many also added that writing in Chinese was not only mechanically time-consuming, but it also took far greater effort in the amount of thought and concentration needed.

Several informants made the point that with the advent of e-mail, the amount of writing they did had increased significantly. Those who use e-mail also commented on its less formal side.

Like e-mail. I don't draft it, once I typed it, I'd send it straight away. But of course, before you start writing, you must be very careful in dealing with different receivers. Are they your seniors, juniors, or the same rank as yours?

(Beverley)

Feelings and attitudes towards English

The feelings and attitudes of both seniors and juniors towards writing in English was surprisingly positive. The findings from the questionnaire shown in Table 12.4 indicated that 96% of seniors and 95% of juniors were confident about the purposes of writing, and around 90% reported that they had a definite idea of the audience. Almost 90% saw writing as an essential

Table 12.4 Feelings and attitudes towards writing

Statement	Seniors agree (n = 447)	Seniors disagree (n = 447)	Juniors agree (n = 538)	Juniors disagree (n = 538)
Confident about the purpose	96.2%	3.8%	94.6%	5.4%
Definite idea about audience	91.5%	8.5%	87.2%	12.8%
Writing is an essential part of the organisation	88.7%	11.3%	88.8%	11.2%
Excited, it is an opportunity to impress	70.2%	29.8%	63.9%	36.1%
Eager to start / enjoy the challenge	81.1%	18.9%	79.6%	20.4%
Confident about support and advice	76.4%	23.6%	72.5%	27.5%
Strategic about planning time	86.4%	13.6%	79.4%	20.6%
Excited about data collection	47.3%	52.7%	57.9%	42.1%
Unclear about the purpose	5.8	94.2	7.4%	92.6%
Unsure about the audience	8%	92%	13.1%	86.9%
Writing is a distraction from the project	17%	83%	23.2%	76.8%
It's tedious to do	30.8%	69.2%	40.2%	59.8%
Unsure about support and advice	27.4%	72.6%	38%	62%
Concerned about the amount of research required	60.4%	39.6%	73.1%	26.9%
Concerned about finding the time	61%	39%	71.6%	28.4%
Panic at the size of the task	24.9%	75.1%	36%	64%

part of the organisation. Of seniors, 70% saw writing as an opportunity to impress. For juniors, the figure was 64%. Around 80% of both seniors and juniors said that they enjoyed the challenge of writing, and were eager to start.

Thus even though an individual may be placed under pressure and need to perform effectively in writing in order to succeed, writing itself is still viewed in a positive manner by most within the workplace.

Culture of the workplace

It is commonly accepted that culture and communication are inseparable. A number of studies — Westwood (1992), Du-Babcock and Babcock (1995, 1996), Scollon and Scollon (1995) — have highlighted differences in Southeast Asian and Western business communication. In the case of Hong Kong and in multi-national companies where the lingua franca is dominantly English, the members of the business community have to develop adequate English language skills and a basic understanding of the culture of the international business community in order to operate successfully.

As Connor (1996) points out, individuals can be members of several different cultural groups. For example members of the accounting profession in Hong Kong will be members of different cultural communities: the professional accountants' community, probably the international business community, as well as belonging to ethnic, gender and other cultural groups. Connor's argument is similar in many ways to Swales's (1993) notion of discourse communities and speech groups. It is commonly argued that cultural factors associated with a person's L1 influence the production of a second language.

One area of conflict for the members of our study is that a great majority of accountants have Chinese as their first language. In many organisations, the medium of spoken citation is Chinese, while the medium of written communication is English (although there is some evidence in the data that written Chinese is becoming increasingly important). Code and medium switching between Chinese and English, and between spoken and written language, can cause considerable difficulty to many junior accountants.

> . . . *when I am received the explanation from client, in Chinese usually, our conversation is in Chinese, then I have to translate in English. I have to spend much time to translate the Chinese explanation into written English. I find it quite difficult.*   (George)

While code switching from written to spoken language may be a major factor, we believe that cultural differences between Chinese discourse patterns and Western discourse patterns cause an even greater problem.

There are at least two salient factors operating here. Firstly, the basic discourse patterns of Southeast Asian and Western cultures are different. Scollon and Scollon point out that in Southeast Asian texts the main point is expected to appear at the end of a text. The main point is presented in the ultimate position and is introduced by supporting evidence, background information and/or relevant comments (inductive discourse patterns). In Western cultures, on the other hand, the audience expects the main point in the primary position (topic sentence), followed by supporting evidence, background information and/or subsequent comments (deductive discourse patterns) (Scollon and Scollon 1995: 4).

Secondly the level of clarification expected in Southeast Asian texts compared to the Western is very different. Westwood (1992) and Du-Babcock and Babcock (1995) discuss the differences of Southeast Asian cultures which are viewed as 'high-context', compared to Western culture which is 'low-context'. In a high-context culture, relevant information within a text is embedded within the context in which it is set, or it is shared knowledge between the interlocutors. The audience is therefore expected to interpret the message by applying their knowledge of the context and the author to the text. This then supplements the encoded message and makes it complete. However, in a low-context Western culture, it is the author's responsibility to encode a text clearly and to leave nothing to chance interpretation (Du-Babcock and Babcock 1995: 3).

An additional complicating factor appears to be the need for language development in Putonghua. The relationship between English and Chinese in most workplaces is complex, and, according to our informants, becoming increasingly so. The growing significance of Chinese was commented on by a number of informants.

> *We've got a lot of clients in the PRC, where we use Mandarin or in the writing we use Chinese, but still most of our clients are English base. I don't mean that physical base, but the type of language they normally use English. And the financial statements are in English. So we are reporting on those statements, so normally, I should say writing in English is very important still. But if in a coming few years, Chinese becomes more and more important. And the process of learning Mandarin in the moment also . . .* (Eric)

Another informant said:

> *In the past, it seems that English is the only important mean for communication, but now Chinese is also important too. It is changing now, there are a lot of investment in China, so we must communicate with them in Chinese. But we still have to write in English internally.*

When asked how she regarded herself as a writer, this informant reported:

I am a Chinese. I think in Chinese and then translate in English. I couldn't think in English straight away that I'd think it is more efficient.

In order to produce effective documents and to develop worthwhile training materials these fundamental cultural differences should be understood, discussed and manipulated to meet one's aims and objectives. The Southeast Asian factors mentioned above, low-context, inductive discourse patterns and the growing need to communicate both in Cantonese and Putonghua, must then be generally translated (regardless of language ability) to high-context, deductive written discourse, or vice versa when translating from English to Chinese. It is at this stage that an explicit understanding of the culturally different discourse patterns will be of benefit to those involved.

The role of language in the professional workplace

It is clear from this study that effective spoken and written communication is fundamental to the professional workplace. In a real sense, the accountancy firms are fuelled by language. On average, one-third to one-half of an accountant's working day is taken up with the production of reports of various kinds. Not only the content, but also the linguistic accuracy of these reports, is critical to the image and reputation of the firms themselves, and of fundamental importance to the promotion prospects of the individuals within the firms. It is hardly surprising, then, that both firms and individuals place a high premium on the quality of their English, and that both are prepared to invest time and money in improving their competence in English.

The construction of knowledge and discourse within the workplace

The construction of knowledge for the purpose of this paper focuses on the provision made within organisations for formal training, and for informal patterns of learning written English language.

Formal training

From the findings it can be assumed that, in general, organisations do not employ a person or group to be responsible for the development of the staff's writing abilities (43.1%), or if they do, individuals are unaware that such a person or group exists (36.8%). Only 20.1% of the respondents reported that their organisation employed such a person or group. However, 72.3% of seniors and 87% of junior accountants expressed interest in attending a writing course. Such responses and other findings from this project reflect the seriousness of the business community's concern for effective communication.

The informants in the interviews discussed issues and areas they believed should form the focus of training courses. Comments concerning the contents of a course were extremely varied. Many of the informants focused on such technical aspects as grammar, layout and presentation, vocabulary, tone, style, structure, which were all viewed as important features to include within a training programme. Again, many of the informants referred to the need for 'reader-friendly' documents.

Generally, there was a consensus that one of the main purposes of a training course should be to familiarise the members of the course with the variety of documents used in the organisation. The incentive for such familiarisation is to prepare members for documents they will have to write in the future. Talking about the documents he writes now, George, a junior accountant from a large public firm, added that at a senior level '*I will have to write other documents, but I don't know the name*'. Another junior accountant, Julia, simply stated '*give us more practical examples!*'. Claire, a junior accountant from a small commercial organisation, asked for '*more practice with some specific documents that some people usually use in business*'.

From the data collected in the interviews, it can be seen that not only do the informants suggest that exposure to a variety of authentic documents is needed, but the findings also indicate that the informants believe they themselves need assistance in recognising '*what is wrong and what is right*' (Winnie) in their writing. It is suggested by some that a raising of awareness of one's weaknesses will assist in the development of language proficiency. One senior accountant, Harold, stated that writing has been '*trial and error*', adding that training needs to be in the form of feedback:

> *Somebody writes something, you* [the teacher] *better know what's wrong with it, and how to improve it or why you write this way, why you think it's effective. Feedback, immediate feedback, that's the most important thing, I think.*

> (Harold)

Informal patterns of learning

While formal workplace training is important, informal learning is also important. On-the-job support or training appears, as Scollon and Scollon (1995) point out, to be the most common method of learning workplace discourse patterns, and the data from the interviews provides evidence to support this view. For example, when questioned it appears that learning discourse practices tend to be, as one informant put it, a matter of 'trial and error'.

As mentioned earlier, a large percentage of seniors are involved in reviewing and amending the writing of others. The comments made by the reviewer appear to be the main method of learning workplace discourse patterns. However, this is not seen as training by those involved. In the survey a large percentage of seniors (62.3% in commercial organisations and 51.4% in public accounting firms) reported that they did not give on-the-job support or training for writing. Furthermore, even more juniors (74.4% in commercial organisations and 69.8% in public accounting firms) stated that they were not receiving any on-the-job support or training for writing. It would seem that the senior accountants in our survey did not recognise reviewing and amending the writing of others as a method of on-the-job training. However, as one informant stated:

> *Every time when I finish writing, you mean, and let the reviewer to see, to look. I will look at the comments given back to me, about my written English, for example if it is not too long, or not to the point, then the reviewer will mention this, then I will pay attention to this next time. That means I will improve every time I get my document from the reviewer.*   (George)

One senior was quite clear that this is how people learn to write. She explicitly stated that errors are only tolerated within limitations:

> *It's* [learning] *by experience . . . because every day we've got to . . . first time make a mistake, second time make a mistake, but the third time should be no more!*   (Carol)

Other methods of informal learning patterns were mentioned by only a few of the informants. It appears from the findings that very few members are involved in reviewing their own work at a later stage to assess their weaknesses. However, at least one informant saw self-reviews as being of tremendous benefit.

> *Well immediately following the writing I don't think assessment is very impartial. But it's only after a few months that when I'd read it again, that I find that if I were to re-write it may be that document will look very different.*   (Elaine)

It appears that this method of 'trial and error' is a haphazard method of language induction which manifests itself in seniors spending a large amount of time proof-reading, amending, and ensuring these implicit rules are learnt.

Such findings raise questions for further investigation:

- Is the support and training which is being given appropriate and effective?
- Should professional development be provided for seniors so that they can render linguistic support and training on a day-to-day basis as and when required?
- Should notions of language awareness be refined within the workplace, enabling employees to recognise and register when they are receiving assistance?

Where to from here?

Collaboration between the business community, linguists, educationalists and researchers has already achieved a greater understanding of the accounting workplace, and of the existing strengths and future needs of the workers in their various workplaces. Follow-up research in this area promises to prove even more fruitful. The aims and objectives of the next phase of our research are set out below.

Aims
To develop teaching material and teaching guidelines which will help to improve writing skills. The materials developed will be specifically tailor-made for the professional workplace.

Objectives
- To develop a corpus of authentic business texts.
- To base the design of teaching material and teaching guidelines on informed knowledge gained from a systematic investigation of the writing requirements of members of the business community.
- To design material which will improve the written English language proficiency of members of the business community.
- To develop material which will help to bridge the gap between formal education and the professional demands of the workplace.
- To introduce language training support at an early stage of a professional career.
- To pilot, evaluate and refine the material designed.
- To publicly present the findings of CPW's research.
- To provide seminars, workshops and support for teaching/training staff who are involved in language development in the business community.

We suggest that the aims and objectives of this research proposal echo the recommendations (H2-5) made by the Education Commission Report No. 6 (ECR 6). This report recommends that employers should be encouraged to develop suitable language programmes for their employees; that language courses should be made more widely available; and that the government should work closely with employers and educationalists to raise awareness of language proficiency issues and develop programmes which enhance language proficiency.

Summary and conclusion

In this paper, we have presented and discussed some of the data from a large-scale investigation into the writing practices of accountants in Hong Kong.

Data for the study came from over 1,000 questionnaire responses as well as from a series of focused interviews. These data underline the critical importance of effective literacy practices within both public and private accountancy firms. Communicating effectively in writing is seen by both senior and junior accountants as being important both at an institutional and personal level. At an institutional level, a firm's public image and reputation rest largely on the public face of the firm as represented by the documents generated by the firm. For individuals, promotion prospects, prestige and even popularity are closely associated with an ability to communicate effectively in both speech and writing, but particularly in writing.

13

Social and interpersonal perspectives on scientific discourse
Minna-Riitta Luukka

Introduction

Communication is crucial to the work of the scientific community, both
from the point of view of scientific development and an individual scientist.
In fact, scientific discourse is a prerequisite of all scientific activity, and the
only means of legitimising scientific knowledge. For a scientist, participating
in scientific discourse is the only way of finding his or her place in the
scientific community. Only by writing and speaking will scientists be able to
get feedback on their work, earn respect, and establish a reputation in their
community.

Scientific texts are often characterised as impersonal, informative, abstract,
and reserved. Writers hide themselves behind passive constructions and make
use of hedges in presenting their claims. However, texts are produced by
members of a scientific community, and therefore they are influenced by the
social practices, ideals and ways of thinking of a scientific community. They
are a result of the actions of socially situated speakers and writers. Hence,
textual features can be fully explained and become meaningful only when
understood as part of this larger whole.

In this paper, I will try to combine a linguistic micro-analysis with an
analysis of discursive practices of a scientific community and end up describing
linguistic phenomena in relation to the social practices of that community.
My focus is on the interactional and social aspect of the scientific community,
and, therefore, in analysing texts, I have concentrated on interpersonal
characteristics in scientific texts. For me, as for Halliday (for example 1973),
interpersonality means that function of language which expresses a text
producer's attitude towards both content and participants. I aim at finding
answers for the following questions: What are the Finnish means of expressing
the degree of certainty and referring to persons, as considered from a functional and social perspective on the study of language? In what way can
textual features be interpreted as a part of the practice of the scientific

community? What type of interactional rules seem to govern scientific discourse, and how are they realised in texts?

The empirical data consists of five papers read at a Finnish conference of applied linguistics and the published articles that were based on these papers. The spoken corpus was recorded and transcribed. The papers were, as academic presentations usually are, planned in advance but none of the speakers actually read his or her paper aloud. On the whole, the presentations seemed quite informal and spontaneous.

I chose to study scientific articles and papers read in a conference because they represent communicative situations that are significant in the scient ific community, and because such data offers an opportunity for comparing spoken and written discourse. The inclusion of spoken discourse as data is also justified on the grounds that most studies on scientific discourse still deal with written texts only. In choosing data, I tried to ascertain that the written and spoken texts were as comparable as possible. The same persons produced the texts, their topics and purposes are identical, and even the target group is, for the most part, the same.

To date, there has been little research on Finnish academic discourse, and thus one of the aims of my study was to contribute to the knowledge of the use of Finnish in scientific contexts. Another purpose of my study is to develop a functional model for describing the linguistic features under study.

My starting point is the idea that discourses, by which I mean in this case language use, form a part of a more extensive social practice, influenced by the ways of thinking and acting of a community. The relation between discourse and social practice works in two directions: discourses not only reflect social practice and communities, but they also construct them. In this sense, my approach is based on the ideas of social constructionism on the nature of discourse; according to these ideas language use is an activity influenced by society but, at the same time, also exerting influence on, modifying, and giving birth to communities. Language and discourses develop as a part of social activities, and the use of language reproduces and maintains these activities. Discourses are sustained by social institutions since they constitute a rock-like foundation for institutions (see for example Bazerman 1990, Bruffee 1986).

Another starting point of my study has to do with my concept of the nature of language. Also, in order to be able to study language from a social point of view, I have adopted a functional and interactive approach, that language is primarily a means of communication and interaction, not an autonomous system of signs, that is, language is not forms and structures, but rather, functions and meanings realised in a context. Linguistic choices are the result of, and they result in, socially relevant meanings. Theoretically, the present study is thus related to the functional theories of language (Halliday 1978, 1985a, 1985b) and critical approaches to discourse (Fairclough 1989, 1992).

A functional and systemic view on language is based on the idea of language primarily as a social phenomenon and a means of communication. Language is a type of social practice, and therefore linguistic features are always socially motivated. Language is regarded as meaning potential, and language use as the possibilities and choices that a speaker or a writer has at his or her disposal in a communicative situation (see for example Halliday 1978, 1985a, 1985b).

If language is by definition a form of social practice, it is self-evident that discourses are socially conditioned as well. Linguists within critical discourse analysis (CDA) consider discourse as 'language as social practice' (Fairclough 1989: 17) or as a specific form of language use and social interaction, interpreted as a complete communicative event in a social situation (van Dijk 1990: 164). Every discursive event is simultaneously a text, part of discursive practices, and part of social practices. According to Fairclough (1989), text is a linguistic manifestation of discourse, and discursive practices represent the processes of text production and comprehension, and social practices the links of discourses with institutions. Accordingly, the aim of discourse study is to explain how discourses are produced and for which purposes they are used in different communities. The manifestations of discourse, of texts, contain hints about discourse production and interpretation of meanings.

Pennycook (1994: 126) criticises critical approaches to discourse because of the tendency to operate with a problematically static view of both language and society. The model leaves little space for an understanding of the human agency, interpretation, or change. Socially-oriented theories, at their worst, tend to see an individual as a weak-willed, socially-dependent member of his or her community. This is why I have preferred to start with the idea of Halliday and his associates who regard language as meaning potential. Even as a member of a community an individual has freedom of choice, although tacit communal practices, common habits, and shared ideals guide the actions of community members.

Discourse and the scientific community

As far as discourse study is concerned, the approach adopted in the present study requires also that discourse should be analysed as part of a community's practice, guiding principles, and ideals. It is not enough to describe how language is used in a particular discourse situation between individuals; the purpose of research is to reveal how and why discourses are structured in a particular manner in a particular community. According to this approach, even distinct textual features, such as means of modifying the degree of certainty and referring to persons, can be explained and become meaningful only as part of a larger whole.

The general conduct of the scientific community influences scientific communication through discursive practices. In describing these practices, I will concentrate on what 'scientific' means, and how a scientist is able to save his or her social face in communicative situations. I will use the term 'discursive practices' to denote the ways of communication and conventions of language use characteristic of the scientific community. I have described these practices after studying the instructions given in Finnish guidebooks for scientific research and writing, and conducting a number of interviews. In this paper, however, I only summarise my findings and do not analyse the texts of the guidebooks or the interviews in any detail (see Luukka 1995).

While analysing the guidebooks and interviews, it became apparent that the tacit assumptions and ideals embedded in them go back to the so-called Mertonian norms of science. According to Merton (1967), the scientific community is bound together by the so-called ethos of science, by which he means 'an affectively toned complex of institutional values and norms held to be binding the man of science'. These norms form a legitimised system of social values which the community cherishes and strengthens by punishing those who violate the norms and by rewarding those who follow them. Merton describes scientific ethos in terms of four institutional imperatives — universalism, communalism, disinterestedness, and organised scepticism.

Universalism, according to Merton, means that the scientific validity of claims does not depend on the person who puts them forward. Thus, everyone has a right to produce scientific knowledge. Universalism is deeply rooted in the impersonal nature of science. Communalism refers to the fact that scientific discoveries are not considered as private property but something that is generated within the scientific community and that is founded on earlier findings. Thus, the person who conducts the study only has a right to disseminate that information. Members of the scientific community have no right to suppress their findings nor to regard them as their own. Disinterestedness means that the personal interests of a scientist or his or her political, social or moral opinions, for example, must not affect the research process nor the interpretation of findings. A scientist's work is guided by curiosity and desire for knowledge. Organised scepticism also belongs to the basic norms: a scientific finding becomes knowledge only through criticism and testing. Any finding can, at a later date, be brought under suspicion.

Even though the life of the scientific community is, under ideal circumstances, guided by ethical norms, its everyday functioning is, in many ways, less idealistic (see Gilbert and Mulkay 1984, Latour and Woolgar 1979). Competition between the members of the community, power hierarchies, fashionable trends, and pressure for social conformity, for example, influence values and may cause scientists to stray from their ideals. Community members are united by scientific work, but every community made up of people is also a social community. Scientists are not engaged in pure scientific endeavours in isolation from other scientists. For example, according to Becher (1989), a scientist's work is motivated by the need to be recognised and respected by his or her community, which can only be gained through publications, conference papers, and scientific achievements.

Although the main function of an academic communicative situation is not to maintain personal relations, there are, nevertheless, inherent in such a situation similar social expectations as in any other communicative situation. The scientific community is, by nature, a closed community, and anyone seeking admittance has to prove his or her competence. According to Myers (1989), it follows that academic communicative situations tend to be face-threatening. The community gives a definition to science and knowledge, and its members have to contribute to that definition. It also has the power to accept both a study and a scientist into the community, or to refuse their admittance.

Face, that is a person's public self-image (Goffman 1967), is one of the most important concepts of the politeness theory. Brown and Levinson (1987) view politeness as socially-motivated linguistic action which aims at supporting and maintaining each other's face, which is continuously under threat in interaction. The concepts of face and politeness link the language use to the social need to be respected and accepted by others. Politeness strategies are associated with the selection of socially and interactionally appropriate means for achieving communicative goals and creating relationships with other persons involved in the situation.

Within the academic community, the delivery of a scientific paper offers a challenge to members of a discourse community. For example, according to Myers (1989), the authors' claims for their own research and denials of other researchers' claims are face-threatening acts to other members of the community. These threats can be redressed by the use of hedges or by writing or speaking in an impersonal manner. Hedges may be used for 'projecting honesty, modesty and proper caution in self-reports, and for diplomatically creating research space in areas heavily populated by other researchers' (Swales 1990: 175).

In scientific communicative situations, the saving of a writer's or a speaker's own face is, above all, associated with satisfying the criteria of science. Thus, discourse must fulfil the ideological objectives of the scientific community. One can lose one's face by acting contrary to the ideals of science: by presenting self-evident facts, stealing ideas from another scientist, showing imperfect mastery of basic theories or argumentation, regarding one's own achievements as final truths, and by making unfounded generalisations.

Persons reading conference papers or writing articles must also show consideration for the face of their audience by, for example, making positive references to their colleagues' research, by developing their ideas further, and by emphasising the importance of a discipline or a school. Their face will be threatened if a speaker or writer underestimates their knowledge, criticises previous research in an 'unscientific', personal manner, fails to mention research by his colleagues that relates to his own or presents their ideas as his own. As in any other communicative situation, an author has to walk on a tightrope in order to save face.

It seems that interpersonal features, hedging and referring to persons, are clearly related to realising interactive rules and to saving face. Particularly, presenting one's own findings, marketing ideas, drawing conclusions and making suggestions, all require 'face work' that is accomplished by means of hedging and references to persons. On the other hand, interpersonal features are also related to the ideals and ethical rules of science.

Hedging strategies

In this study, I have described the means of modifying the degree of certainty of claims such as emerged from the data. Therefore, I did not, when analysing the texts, start to look for grammatical forms expressing epistemic modality. Instead I sought expressions whose use created an impression that the degree of certainty was toned down, irrespective of the grammatical category to which these expressions belonged. Therefore, my model of description is the *result* of the analysis, not its starting point.

I have classified the means of toning down certainty into two types: reservations and restrictions. These differ in their softening strength as well as in their meaning. The hedges that most clearly express a view on the truth value of the claims are called reservations, which are, broadly speaking, related to epistemic modality. Their basic meaning is: *X is possibly true / certain*. The speaker or writer announces that he or she is more or less uncertain about the truth value of his or her claims.

Reservations are usually expressed with 1) epistemic adverbs (such as *mahdollisesti = possibly*, *ehkä = perhaps*), 2) conditional or potential mood, which in Finnish are expressed with verb endings (such as *sanoisin = I would say*, *tarvinnee = He might need*), 3) modal auxiliaries (for instance *voi = can*, *saattaa = may*) and 4) factitive and unipersonal verbs (like *Oletan että = I assume / suppose*, *Näyttää siltä että = It seems that*). The other type of hedges are called restrictions. They tone down certainty to a lesser extent because the speaker or the writer considers his or her claim true, but restricts its range as regards time (for example *X on usein Y = X is often Y*), quality (*X on tavallaan Y = X is sort of Y*) or generalisability (*Mielestäni X on Y = in my view X is Y*). The basic meaning of restrictive devices is: *X is, with certain restrictions, true / certain*.

Hedging devices also have other functions than indicating the certainty of a claim. For example, the speaker in the following example does not mean that she is unsure whether she will finish her talk by speaking about the consequences of her research — especially as she is, in fact, going to talk about precisely that: *No lopuks mä haluaisin puhua siitä mitä tälläsestä tutkimuksesta vois seurata* 'Well to finish off, I **would** like to talk about what might follow from this kind of research . . .'. Typically, these expressions are used in situations in which speakers announce that they are about to say, claim, assume, or suggest something. They tone down their announcement by using hedging devices that are similar to those used to indicate the degree of propositional certainty. Functionally, they do not show uncertainty about the content of what they say, but, rather, signal interactive uncertainty.

Toning down the degree of certainty of one's claims or conclusions in a scientific text is, above all, related to the principles of organised scepticism and critical nature of scientific knowledge. Scientific findings and truths are not permanent, for even writers themselves can later disagree with their earlier interpretation. Also, writers of scientific articles and speakers in conferences always have to expose themselves to potential criticism. To counter their critics, writers secure their escape route by toning down their claims. A writer may choose to use a hedge in making a claim not because of any uncertainty about the validity of the claim but because of a wish to project an appropriate image of him/herself to the audience.

Example 1 (spoken)
syy miksi tämä jäljentämistehtävä tässä . . . lisää tähän näin paljon tätä selitusvoimaa sillon kun se tuossa ei tehny sitä **johtuu kai lähinnä** siitä että . . . toi jäljentämistehtävä oli heikompi selittäjä **yleensä** mikä **minä luulisin että saattaa olla** tämmönen artefakta joka johtuu **lähinnä** siitä että . . .

the reason why this task here . . . increases this much the explanatory force, whereas elsewhere it didn't, **may be probably due to the fact** . . . that this task was a weaker explanation **in general**, which **I would think might be** an artefact which is **in all possibility** due to . . .

One of the rules of hedging in scientific discourse concerns the choice of whose views will be presented as certain and whose will be toned down. The data of the present study suggest that the findings of previous research were presented with more certainty than one's own hypotheses, findings or conclusions.

Example 2 (written)
Puherytmi, sisältäen painotuksen ja ajoituksen, sekä puhemelodia **ovat** ensimmäisiä asioita, jotka **lapsi kielestä omaksuu**, ensimmäisen ikävuotensa lopulla, jo silloin, kun äänteistöä ei vielä edes ole tai se on hyvin puutteellinen ja horjuva (ks. esim. Crystal 1987: 237).

Speech rhythm, which includes both stress and timing, and the melody of speech **are** the first things, **of language a child acquires**, at the end of the first year, already when the sound segments do not exist, or they are very scarce and faltering (see e.g. Crystal 1987: 237).

Hedging was particularly characteristic in concluding and in explaining one's findings. For example, so-called factual findings, displayed in the form of tables and statistical figures, were always presented without hedging, but conclusions drawn on the basis of these facts were mostly toned down.

Example 3 (written)

Tilastollinen tarkastelu varianssianalyysillä paljasti, että suoritukset **paranivat** vuosien myötä . . . Tulos **on tulkittavissa** siten, että nimenomaan englannin opetuksen alkuvaiheen ääntämis- ja kuunteluharjoituksilla **on merkitystä** suoriutumiselle tässä tehtävässä. Myöhemmällä opetuksella **ei ilmeisesti ole** yhtä dramaattista vaikutusta . . . **Näyttää siis siltä, että** toistamistehtävä on yhteydessä englannin oppimiseen alkuvuosina. **Vaikuttaa myös siltä, että** suoriutumista voidaan parantaa englannin fonologiaa painottavalla opetuksella. **Tuloksista ei tietenkään voida päätellä suoraan, että** tällaisen opetuksen lisäämisellä **välttämättä parannettaisiin** kielen muidenkin osa-alueiden oppimista.

The variance analysis showed that the results **improved** annually . . . The results **can be interpreted to imply** that it is particularly the elementary level pronunciation exercises and listening comprehension practice that **are** relevant for this task. The instruction at a more advanced level **does not seem to** have as dramatic an effect. **It would seem** that the repetition task plays a role in the learning of English in early years. **It also seems obvious that** the results are improved when English phonology is stressed. **Naturally, one can not conclude directly from the results that** by increasing this kind of instruction we **would necessarily improve** the learning of other types of language skills.

Some claims and conclusions are based on generalisations the exact origin of which is not stated. Thus they may result from the writer's own experience or observation that are not founded on the so-called scientific method. These generalisations were characterised by hedges in the form of restrictions that made the claim less definitive and that toned down its force.

Example 4 (spoken)

suomalaisille taas tämä taivutus **ei yleensä** ole mikään ongelma ja kielenhuoltajat **vain harvoin** joutuvat puuttumaan **joihinkin** erikoistapauksiin niin että suomalainen **yleensä** ei ymmärrä katsoa kieltään siitä näkökulmasta kuinka monimutkainen tää taivutusjärjestelmä on

For Finns, this inflection is **not generally** a problem and the language revisers **only seldom** have to consider **some particular** cases, so a Finn, **generally speaking**, is not accustomed to consider his own language from the point of view of the morphological complexity

Thus, scientists are forced to tone down their intrusiveness not only when presenting their conclusion but also when giving a recommendation based on their findings. This is because, in such cases, they claim an expert status. Therefore, it is perhaps diplomatic to express any direct recommendation or suggestion in a less definitive form.

Example 5 (written)

Kun pohditaan vieraan kielen oppimisen aloitusajankohtaa, **olisi syytä** tarkemmin tutkia, riittääkö kolmannen luokan oppilaiden lukutaito vielä vieraan kielen oppimisen pohjaksi. Vaikka lukeminen sinänsä **ei ehkä** englannin alkuopetuksessa **olisikaan kovin** tärkeätä, **voi** toisaalta **osalle** oppilaista vieraan kielen kanssa askarteleminen . . . olla ylivoimaista . . . Tämän tutkimuksen perusteella **näyttää siltä, että** huonosti toimivasta fonologisesta varastosta aiheutuu ongelmia . . . **mahdollisesti** erityisesti uusien sanojen oppimiseen. Tällöin sanojen kirjoitusasusta **voi** muodostua muistiapuneuvo.

When the starting age of foreign language instruction is considered, **it would seem reasonable** to explore whether the reading skills of the 3rd grade pupils are good enough to serve as a basis of learning a foreign language. Although reading as such **may not be very** important in the elementary instruction of English, the foreign language tasks **may** be insurmountable to **some** students. On the basis of the present study **it seems that** a phonological memory that does not function well causes problems . . . **possibly** in learning new words in particular. Then the orthography of words **may** serve as a memory prop.

Naturally, by analysing the means of modifying the degree of certainty it is not possible to find out whether a speaker or writer is, in fact, genuinely uncertain about the truthfulness of his or her conclusions, or whether hedging is only a strategic choice which is used to make it certain that face is mutually saved.

In my data, the proportion of hedges was slightly higher in the written texts. This seems to indicate that writers are somewhat more concerned than speakers about the certainty of the facts they are stating. If there was any doubt about the certainty, writers were cautious and employed modality markers and hedges. Authors favoured hedging utterances such as: 'It is possible that . . .', 'These results seem to indicate that . . .'. Writers modified the degree of certainty mainly with reservations, especially with modal verbs and adverbs. Speakers used weaker modifiers such as hedges, shields and approximators, for example, 'These results in a way indicate that...', 'A is B, at least quite often'. It appears that spoken texts are more vague than written ones in this respect. It is also noteworthy that speakers often used double or even triple modifiers in the same utterance.

Strategies of referring to persons

In describing interactional features in text, the focus is on how persons are referred to either directly or indirectly. References to persons are divided into four categories: 1) Presence of the author, where the author refers, either directly or indirectly, to himself or herself ('In my research I've found that... Next, I will discuss... The results of this study indicate that... The analysis was done in the following way'). The use of these utterances creates an impression of either a personal or an impersonal style of delivery. 2) Presence of the audience, where the author refers — directly or indirectly — to the audience and in doing so, creates an impression of a direct contact with the audience and a conversational atmosphere ('As you all know, A causes B, but you may think that... If you look at this picture, you can see that... In this picture one can see...'). 3) Presence of the author and the audience, where the author refers directly to 'us', himself or herself and the audience, and creates a feeling of togetherness ('As we already know, A causes B... Now we move on and talk a little about B'). 4) Presence of other researchers: these utterances refer to other researchers and their work and incorporate them into the text ('According to Smith (1996)... As can be seen in Smith (1996)... A causes B (Smith 1996)'). By doing this, the authors place themselves in relation to other members of the scientific community and create intertextuality.

One of the special features of the Finnish person system is that in Finnish, personal reference is 'doubled'. Both a pronoun and a personal suffix of a verb are used to indicate person. In the first and second person, the pronoun can be omitted as the suffix indicates the person (*minä istun = istun*: 'I am sitting/ I sit.'). As a result, even if speakers of Finnish want to refer to themselves, they can choose between the more explicit '**Minä** käsittelen seuraavaksi X:ää' (I shall discuss X), or the more implicit form '*Käsittelen seuraavaksi X:ää*', (*shall discuss X). Or if they want to indicate their possessor role they can do it more explicitly, '**Minun** artikkelini käsittelee' (my article deals with...) or less emphatically: '*Artikkelini käsittelee...*' (*article-my deals with...).

Speakers of Finnish have many ways to avoid direct reference to persons. For example, they can use a generic verb form or passive and nominals instead of active verbs. They can also use personal pronouns indirectly, as in choosing the pronoun *we* instead of *I*. The most multi-functional pronoun seems to be the pronoun *we*, since it may also be used impersonally to refer to an unspecified human agent. In this way, the author does not identify any given individual but indicates either anyone or an unspecified group of people. The non-deictic pronoun *one* has no equivalent in Finnish, where a passive or generic verb is used instead.

Obviously, the most frequently-used means of indirect personal reference is the passive. The so-called passive form of Finnish is, however, different from the passive of Indo-European languages. The Finnish passive indicates a state where the agent is in most cases human but unspecified. Accordingly, a sentence like *Mies tapettiin* 'the man was killed' implies a murder. It cannot refer to a traffic accident, for example, in which case one would have to say *Mies kuoli / sai surmansa*, 'The man died'. (For a more detailed description of the Finnish system see Hakulinen 1987, Luukka and Markkanen 1997, Shore 1988.)

On the whole, the proportion of personal references was nearly the same in both written and spoken data. Differences were mainly found in how frequently different persons were made explicit, and how direct the references were. The texts appeared to be fairly 'self-centred', for most personal references were to the writer as 'we' or inclusively to 'us'. Speakers used a direct form of reference in nine cases out of ten possible ones, whereas writers resorted to a direct reference only every second time.

In the written texts, personal involvement was also more implicit: writers never used the first person pronoun but referred to themselves only by means of personal verb endings or possessive suffixes. One of the writers even stated her own personal commitment to and interest in the topic with a passive expression: 'In this study, one was interested in X'. This could be called the ultimate implicitness. Also, there was a tendency to start a spoken utterance with a personal element, as opposed to a tendency to locate it in non-initial position, and thus make it less explicit in the written texts.

The contact with the audience was clearly more explicit and direct in spoken texts: speakers addressed their hearers, asked them to do something, and commented on their possible reactions. For example, 'of course you all know/think that . . .', 'x is very important for you', 'in this picture you can see x' were typical utterances in the spoken data. If the authors wanted to avoid direct address to the audience, they tended to favour expressions that efface the audience, such as generic expressions or passive forms, and avoided using the pronoun *you* ('in this picture one can see . . .'). This was clearly more typical in written texts. However, references to the third person — the other scientists — were more common in the written texts. In addition, creating solidarity by means of *we* appeared to be more characteristic of spoken than of written discourse.

It is to be assumed that impersonalisation is a strategic choice the speaker or writer makes. He or she has the choice of referring to persons (him/herself, the addressee, other persons) either explicitly or implicitly. When choosing to use explicit reference, the speaker or writer is more direct and more open, takes responsibility for his or her opinions, addresses his or her audience directly and creates a conversational atmosphere, refers directly to the source of information, and so on. When implicit reference is chosen, the author is indirect: avoids taking responsibility, highlighting himself, and impinging on the audience. He or she also avoids direct reference to the source of information and speaks in more general and vague terms.

It is not, however, enough only to analyse the means of referring to persons in order to describe the factors that influence use of such reference in the scientific community. The rules of ethics provide an explanation, for example, for the fact that references to the first person are often effaced.

Example 6 (written)

Tässä kirjoituksessa **pyritään** ennen kaikkea tarkastelemaan vieraiden kielten opetusta oppimisen kannalta.

In this article an attempt **will be made** to look at foreign language teaching from the point of view of learning.

The ideal of universalism in science emphasises that it is the knowledge and the findings that are important, not the person who presents them. Similarly, the principle of communalism can explain references to previous research and other scientists.

On the other hand, explanations for impersonality in scientific writing can also be sought from the rules of interaction that prevail in the academic community. Whereas strategies for toning down the degree of certainty are primarily related to saving the speaker's or writer's own face, strategies for referring to persons have more often to do with helping listeners and readers save theirs. It is necessary to take another person's face into account when one is, for example, commenting on and evaluating other scientists' work, drawing conclusions and making recommendations, and thus appearing as an expert. Toning down the definitiveness and force of a claim could also be seen in those cases where the author indirectly criticised or questioned opinions or ways of action that had been previously expressed. In this way, there was no need to name the object of criticism but it could be hinted at by means of an indirect generalisation.

Example 7 (written)

Joissakin suomen kielen helppoa ja mukavuutta rakastavaa ääntämystä käsitelleissä kirjoituksissa **on myös nostettu esiin** suomen vokaalipitoisuus helppouteen pyrkimisen osoituksena ... **Tämä ajattelu** perustuu täydelliselle väärinkäsitykselle ...

In some papers dealing with the easy and lax manner of Finnish pronunciation also the great amount of vowels **has been pointed out** as a sign of a trend towards the ease of pronunciation ... **This argument** is based on a total misunderstanding ...

In addition, emphasising solidarity and treating the listeners as experts is a way of protecting the face of both the speaker and the audience. When considered from an interactive point of view, a scientist's face is most effectively protected if he or she appears as a humble but critical expert who also values the expertise of his or her audience.

Examples 8–10 (spoken)

okei mä lopetan tähän mä ajattelin että **ehkä teillä olis jotakin hyviä ideoita**

okay, I'll finish now, I was thinking **you might have some good ideas**

suomen taivutusjärjestelmä on, **niin kuin tiedätte**, niin se on hyvin laaja ja mutkikas

the inflectional system of Finnish is, **as you know**, it is very comprehensive and complicated

mun omat havaintoni perustuu niihin muutamiin vuosiin jollon mä olen ollut suomen kielen kanssa tekemisissä ja ... tietysti sitten siihen että mä olen foneetikkona öö toki kuunnellut monen muunkielisten puhumaa suomea ja **niinhän te kaikki olette varmasti kuunnelleet ...**

my own observations are based on my experience during the few years I have been dealing with the Finnish language and ... naturally on the fact that I have heard, as a phonetician, how non-native speakers speak Finnish, **as all of you have certainly heard as well ...**

The norms or the maxims that are involved in creating the picture of 'humble servant of science' seem to be different in spoken and written texts. It is difficult to imagine that the following fragments could be found in written academic texts.

Examples 11–12 (spoken)

eli tämmöseltä **tämä pieni ja vaatimaton tutkimus** näyttää jonka tekeminen on ollut tavattoman hauskaa

so this is how **this humble and small research** looks like which I truly have enjoyed doing

niin kuin tosta esipuheesta kuului niin **nyt sitten ei kuulla asiantuntijaa vaan amatööriä**

as was heard in the introduction **one is not going to be listening to an expert, but rather to an amateur**

Conclusions and implications

Adopting a functional view of language as a starting point for analysing discourse has, in the present study, resulted in a model for describing the modification of the degree of certainty and references to persons that differs from traditional linguistic descriptions. The resulting model makes it possible to compare different languages, because, obviously, functions are not language-dependent. The basis for description is to be found in the meaning and function of an expression, not in its form. Therefore, the description will provide a more unified picture of the means that a language has for expressing these meanings. Meanings are created in the interaction between speakers and listeners, or writers and readers. It is possible, for example, that an expression which is grammatically defined as unipersonal, generic, or passive does not, in an interactive situation, actually refer to an unspecified person at all, but to a given and known person.

When the description of linguistic devices starts from authentic discourse in a real community, the means for modifying the degree of certainty and referring to persons described in grammars appear to be intertwined. This occurs particularly with regard to the criteria of accuracy and generalisability as well as the degree of commitment. Accuracy and generalisability are associated with scientific certainty, while vagueness and lack of generalisability go with uncertainty. Both are modified by means of reservations and restrictions used for toning down certainty, but also by references to persons that modify the degree of commitment. In fact, references to persons can be regarded as one substrategy of hedging (see Luukka and Markkanen 1997). While restrictions make a statement vague and tone down the degree of certainty of a claim (for example, 'X is sort of / often / Y'), references to persons can also be used for increasing vagueness ('Some people think that X is Y'). While vagueness, in the case of restrictions, limits the validity of a claim's degree of certainty, in references to persons it concerns the person responsible for a claim's degree of certainty. There is a similar relation between indefinite references to persons and reservations. For example, when a person says 'It is claimed that X is Y' instead of 'I claim that X is Y', he or she evades responsibility for the truth value of the claim. Functionally, the expression operates in the same way as 'X might be Y'.

To sum up, my findings suggest that spoken and written conference papers differ from each other in various ways. Speakers were more personal: they used evaluation and opinion markers more frequently and more freely. Writers, on the other hand, were more concerned about the degree of certainty and used (un)certainty markers. Speaking and writing are different as processes, and this was also evident in their outcome. For example, statements were more vague in spoken texts, and speakers favoured hedges and double-hedges, even though the talks were — to some extent at least —

preplanned. Nevertheless, the most remarkable differences were found in the interpersonal level of discourse. Written texts were clearly more impersonal and monological than spoken ones. Some of these differences can be explained by the differences in communicative situation and the way the texts were produced. However, the texts are similar in many ways. Common interpersonal strategies seem to exist, regardless of the medium, and these can obviously be explained by considering the unifying genre of scientific discourse.

Discursive practices are realised in a text through linguistic features, and thus it is possible to look for explanations for textual characteristics and discursive practices from larger social practices or norms of the community. Communities have their own discursive practices, but these do not form normative systems with strict rules, as practices can always be questioned and are constantly being modified. Nevertheless, community members are aware of these practices which direct, at least implicitly, their linguistic behaviour. In scientific communication, language offers its user a meaning potential, and using language means making strategic choices.

The discursive practices of a scientific community are governed, on the one hand, by the general rules of communication, and on the other hand, by the norms and values of the academic community. It follows that there seem to exist two kinds of discursive practices, namely ethical and interpersonal practices, which in some cases appear even to stand in contrast to each other. In accordance with the ideals of science, a scientist should, for example, have a critical attitude towards previous research, appear as an expert, present his or her own findings as convincingly as possible, and clearly indicate their significance and novelty value. On the other hand, social rules governing interaction and the academic community require him or her to be tactical and face-conscious in expressing these things. One form of linguistic manifestation of these practices is the use of interpersonal features, hedges and references to persons. The strategies of toning down the degree of certainty and referring to persons are part of a scientist's selection of tactical means. In my larger study (Luukka 1995), I analysed both spoken and written textual data, Finnish guide books of scientific writing and interviews of my informants, and the results suggest that scientists observe certain implicit maxims, that may be summarised as set out in Table 13.1.

Regarding scientific text as part of the social practice of the scientific community means that scientific writing cannot be learned nor taught by merely introducing textual structures and formal reference techniques. In order to achieve proficiency in scientific writing, writers must have a thorough knowledge of their field as well as their community, and, through that knowledge, be able to pose essential and interesting research questions, and plan their research in a way acceptable to their community. They must also be able to create proper intertextuality for their texts, be aware of their target group, and know the right way of 'selling' their ideas to that group. In this sense, learning the rules of scientific communication is part of the process

Table 13.1   Discursive practices in the scientific community

Ethical practices		Interactional practices	Linguistic means
Present new knowledge and emphasise the importance of your work and your results	but	do not highlight yourself as a person and do not consider your findings as a final truth	Indirect references to the author, hedges
Build your work upon earlier research, theories and results	and	quote from well-known masters as well as your colleagues	Direct references to other researchers
You can also present your own previous studies	but	do not emphasise that they are yours, mention them only in passing	Indirect references to the author
Do not plagiarise, tell openly whose ideas you are presenting	unless	they are considered as shared knowledge in your discipline. Do not underestimate your audience	Direct references to other researchers or vague references
Be critical and evaluate previous research	but	concentrate on evaluating facts, be tactical and soften your critique	Hedges, vague references
Evaluate your own ideas and findings and consider their validity	but	leave space for further evaluation, do not overestimate their value	Indirect references, hedges
If you present generalisations or opinions without thorough scientific evidence	then	restrict their range of universality or make them vague	Hedges Hedges, indirect references
Propose recommendations and suggestions for further research	but	do not emphasise your expertise or authority	Direct references to the audience and the author (we)
		Create solidarity and refer to shared knowledge and discipline	Direct references to the audience
		Consider your audience as experts	

of enculturation, and can, to a certain degree, be compared to learning a foreign language.

Consequently, the objective of teaching scientific communication is to make explicit the implicit knowledge concerning discursive practices in the scientific community, and to teach how the rules of scientific discourse can be interpreted and used. Instruction should be based on increasing students' awareness of the means of communication and the effects of their use. Instead of offering ready-made models and hints on how to polish a surface text, the instruction should provide writers with strategic courses of action and help them to appreciate the various possibilities of communication.

14

Becoming a psychologist: Student voices on academic writing in psychology[1]
Guenter A. Plum and Christopher N. Candlin

1 Introductory

The central concern of this chapter is an exploration of how undergraduate students in a university department of psychology frame academic writing in response to the writing demands made on them by their department and their tutors, and by Psychology as a discipline; to the writing demands made in other disciplines; to the role of writing in their university work at large, and, more broadly, to the role and demands of literacy and literacies in their university and their subsequent work careers. It offers an additional perspective to that derived from text-based *descriptive* analyses of students' academic writing, or that presented by studies of the lexico–grammatical and discursive structure of disciplinary genres, in that its approach is primarily *interpretive* and ethnographic, exploring students' experiences as they voice how they try to cope with the challenges of academic literacies.

Its methodology owes something to the work of Barton and Hamilton (1998) in their community literacy studies, and to that of Lea and Street (1999) and Ivanic and Weldon (1999) in the field of literacy practices in the academy. It also attempts an *explanatory* account (Candlin 1987; Fairclough 1989), in that it seeks to make connections between the ways that psychology students frame their writing tasks and undertake them against competing understandings of the background of the goals and requirements of their discipline, where this background and these understandings are invested with often-contested ideological positions concerning the purposes and goals of literacy. It discusses the extent to which these purposes can be said to be discipline-internal and contained within the walls of the academy, and the extent to which they are constructed and driven by demands arising from external expectations and requirements of the post-academy world of professional practice. Such expected and required purposes are not abstract, of course, but actively mediated and continually reinforced through the pronouncements, the texts and the practices of the discipline, especially by the actions and discourses of its ratified members, into the membership of which community of practice the students are being guided and recruited.

Access to such specialised literacy practices, as well as the definition of their nature and purposes, is always subject to contestation as some privileged, unequally distributed and inequitably resourced capital (Bourdieu 1991; Foucault 1981 [1970]). Membership of this academic literacy community always involves highly diverse and heterogeneous participants who advance a range of perceptions, beliefs and positions in respect of all features of that community: its goals, its conditions on membership, its discourses, its texts and its conventional practices. While such analyses reveal contested positions within any discipline, these are always personally mediated. Thus charting a range of voiced responses to those positions, as that offered in this chapter, can offer valuable insights into their nature and motivation. Finally, these distinguishing features of this or any community of practice do not exist in some social and historical vacuum. Identities and memberships are always imbricated in chosen forms of language and discursive practices, and to assert the heteroglossic nature of that language and discourse is in the world of high or post-modernity almost commonplace (Giddens 1991). Nonetheless, such heteroglossia is not yet sufficiently well accounted for across a range of professional and other practices. This chapter makes a small contribution to that broader account.

We take the view that the process of educating undergraduate students in any discipline is a gradual and mediated, but not unproblematic, process of *induction* to this membership (Candlin and Plum 1998, 1999; Lave and Wenger 1991). Such a process engages the members of the discipline in framing[2] the discipline in ways which, while natural and transparent to its ratified members, appear not at all so to novices. This framing may be achieved through the licensed practices of the academy — reading, attending lectures and tutorials, writing particular genres — but also by a gradual interactional process of everyday socialisation (Bernstein 1971), not necessarily explicitly focused on literacy practices. Such framing is variably explicit among disciplines, depending on where they might lie on a continuum of professionalisation — ranging from a discipline with a strong vocational orientation being very mindful of the demands of the profession, to a discipline that sees itself engaged in the pursuit of knowledge for its own sake, without a clear career path for students to follow after graduation. Psychology is a discipline with a strong sense of training its best students to become professional (that is, clinical) psychologists, acknowledging a role for relevant professional associations in its own practices, for example through adopting the American Psychological Association's *Publication Manual* (1994) as the standard for its publications. Psychology engages in more explicit framing than other disciplines, compared in our experience, say, to Computer Science (see Gollin 1998).

For tertiary students in psychology — or those *'doing* psychology' to use the student vernacular[3] — this means acquiring and learning to apply existing knowledge by the use of particular skills, adding to its sum, perhaps, and collectively these knowledges and skills come to represent what it means to practise psychology, inside and outside the university. Literacy is central to these processes. All 'doing of psychology' involves literacy practices to the extent that we may say that the practice of psychology is accomplished through the practice of literacy. Attending to student voices provides insights into how students frame their tertiary studies, including themselves as subjects and their discipline, and how, in this personal reflective process, students see themselves being framed by others, most notably by the institution and its teaching staff, especially in relation to, and through, their writing. A key feature of such reflection is the degree of diversity between individuals on some issues and unanimity across entire groups of students on others.

2   Issues in academic writing

In this chapter we address four key issues of concern to both students and teachers:

1   Student literacy — the functions and purposes of students' academic writing
2   Academic writing practices across disciplines
3   Modelling of academic writing in Psychology
4   Student writing — the role of teachers in students' learning to write.

We make a distinction here between student literacy and student writing. The distinction is analogous to that often drawn between *product* and *process*, with the practices and modelling of academic writing being involved in both. Student literacy is commonly seen as a product or outcome aimed at by both tertiary teachers and students, especially if expressed as a model of academic writing, while the act of writing is seen as the process engaged in by students in producing this product. However, it is not uncommon for both teachers and students to consider good writing to be capable of being produced as if it were a product, a misunderstanding Bizzell (1992: 175) derides as 'this fantasy of instant text production'. An alternative perspective is to see literacy and writing as phenomena lying on a continuum differing in both abstraction and generality. Following Swales (1990), literacy, at one end of such a continuum, can be seen as a set of *sociorhetorical practices* which allow members of, for example, the academic 'discourse community' (or *sociorhetorical community*) to make connections among different academic disciplines and subdisciplines on the one hand, and among the worlds of university, work, leisure, and life in general on the other. Literacy in this sense is a kind of *intertextual* knowledge arising out of a discourse community's members' sociorhetorical practices. Adapting Street (1995), we may say that literacy here is a *noun* arising out of a *verb*. Writing, at the other end of the continuum, may then be considered the realisation of such literacy, enacting literacy whenever writing is being done. Particular models of good academic writing in a given discipline mediate between literacy (seen as a product or property one may have or possess) and writing (seen as a process or activity one carries out), and as such are neither product nor process, but rather imply both.

Focus group discussions[4] with undergraduate students sought to address the functions of literacy in students' university studies. Issues were raised either explicitly by using 'literacy' as a keyword or implicitly by using 'writing/academic writing' as keywords. Some students found it difficult to address issues of literacy directly, however expressed, preferring to locate their experience of such issues in practical terms concerned with the writing process, that is, indirectly and implicitly. Their difficulty in discussing these seemingly dichotomous issues reflects to some extent the difficulty the tertiary student has in writing both *in* and *for* the academy, a process equivalent to 'inventing the university' in Bartholomae's memorable phrase:

> . . . he has to invent the university by assembling and mimicking its language while finding some compromise between idiosyncrasy, a personal history, on the one hand, and the requirements of convention, the history of a discipline, on the other.   (Bartholomae 1985)

It is also probably the case that many of the students taking part in these focus group discussions were 'basic writers' in the sense of Bizzell (1992: 7), following Shaughnessy (1977), i.e. 'beginners, newcomers to a complex discursive world with whose ways of using language they were relatively unfamiliar'. Further, issues of confronting and understanding the capital (disciplinary, economic, social, political, cultural) invested in academic literacy (Bourdieu 1990, 1993; Bourdieu and Passeron 1990), and the barriers attendant on access to such capital, may also account for many of the difficulties experienced, and much of the frustration evident in students' discussions of literacy and writing.

A further perspective on these difficulties is provided by the work on 'cognitive apprenticeship' contained in Berkenkotter and Huckin (1995). Their account of a student's induction into the writing appropriate to a graduate program draws particularly on the two concepts of *legitimate peripheral participation* (Lave and Wenger 1991) by newcomers in a discourse community, focusing on its sociorhetorical practices, and the *conversations of the discipline* (Bazerman 1994), focussing on 'the issues and problems that are currently under discussion within the community' (Berkenkotter and Huckin

1995: 118). While such concepts have some clarificatory value, our contention is that in practice, our undergraduate students, at least, lack much opportunity (both qualitatively and quantitatively) for 'peripheral participation' in the discourse community of psychology and 'conversations' with psychologists, to acquaint them adequately with the current sociorhetorical practices of their discipline, and thus the appellation 'apprenticeship', which is often drawn on, may not at all be appropriate (see Candlin and Plum 1999 for further discussion).

Writing issues raised in the focus group discussions were wide-ranging, from the manner of carrying out writing tasks to the problems encountered, the input made into the process, the support given, and students' own suggestions for support. In the context of this chapter and the focus of this book, we are concerned principally with how writing is defined, and in terms of what expectations of performance, and with two related issues: the nature and degree of input and support by the department and/or the tutor, and the feedback by markers, both in terms of comments and grades, rather than with the actual activities involved in the writing of the assignment. Students not unexpectedly responded very readily to such practical issues, and collating and comparing their observations allows us to gain some understanding of the larger issues surrounding the discursive practices of disciplinary literacy where students were often hesitant in addressing these more directly.

A complication arises here in that there appeared to be quite different levels of receptiveness to such issues between +ESB and −ESB writers (see endnote 4 on student focus group membership categorisation), partly related to students' writing ability, and partly to their willingness to discuss practical issues. It is often asserted that English for Academic Purposes (EAP) writing classes (typically, though not exclusively, taken by −ESB students) 'emphasize linguistic and rhetorical forms more than content whereas in other courses the emphasis is reversed' (Leki and Carson 1997: 40, referring to Bridgeman and Carlson 1984) and, furthermore, that such −ESB students show a keen interest in such writing issues even when they report that their teachers are not bothered by grammatical and spelling problems in their writing in content-focused courses (Leki and Carson 1994). Related to −ESB students' markedly different evaluation of writing issues, compared to that of their teachers in content-focused courses, is the issue of the nature of the feedback received by +ESB vs −ESB students, specifically (i) whether teachers provide different feedback depending on whether the student writer is perceived to be either +ESB or −ESB, and (ii), whether there is a systematic difference between +ESB and −ESB students in their own evaluation of feedback. (See Ferris *et al.* 1997 for a discussion of some of the issues of feedback to L2 students and an account of their study of teachers' feedback in an L2 composition class.) Differences in students' receptiveness to the raising of writing issues by their teachers and markers must therefore be expected, and how these in turn may affect how they will discuss these issues. Finally, the assumption made by academics that good writing is something which they 'know when they see it' (Leki 1995) suggests a lack of shared (and explicit) judgement criteria, in terms of which to grade assignments and provide appropriate (and useful) feedback. This further disadvantages −ESB students by adding an element of unfathomable variability in their interpretation of markers' judgements. Indeed, the multi-faceted complexity of issues faced by −ESB writers of academic English (and by their teachers, both of EAP and of content-subjects), as demonstrated, for example, in the wide-ranging collection of papers edited by Belcher and Braine (1995), alerts us to the likelihood that there will be significant if subtly expressed meaning differences between the observations of +ESB vs −ESB students.

3   Students framing academic writing

We introduce in relation to each of the four issues to be discussed a small selection of student views in subsections headed *Student voices*, augmented by others in the discussion and summarised as keywords. The quotations are identified by the course unit from which the focus group was drawn, for instance PSY105, and by ±ESB (English-Speaking Background or Non-English-Speaking Background) and ±WWE (With or Without Workplace Writing Experience) of the speaker's characteristics if known, or of the focus group in which the speaker participated if not; see endnote 4 for further details. Wordings indicative of the students' framing of the issues under discussion are italicised, for example *outsiders* as in 'You can't get *outsiders* to look over your work.' Such key wordings, drawn from the complete corpus of student observations, are often highly metaphorical and appear to function as framing devices for issues within the topic in question. The listing of these *Keywords* is followed by a *Discussion*, again drawing on data from the complete corpus. Quotations used in discussions are identified by any or all of the following: (i) year of study, (ii) whether of English or Non-English Speaking Background (±ESB), and (iii) whether having work-related writing experience (±WWE), provided that information has value in distinguishing views held by different 'types' of students. Again, this information either pertains to the individual speaker if known or to the focus group in which the speaker participated. Discussion of each issue draws on the four-way interpretation of framing proposed by MacLachlan and Reid (1994) mentioned in endnote 2 above.

Student literacy — the functions and purposes of students' academic writing

Framing student literacy in terms of students' social roles raises difficult issues for many students, especially immediate school leavers, because their school experience has linked academic writing closely to the assessment of writing skill and subject mastery. Where such students have been employed, or are concurrently members of a non-tertiary workforce, they are more likely to frame writing for its personal educative value, beyond mere assessment.

Student voices

The articles are full of difficult terminology. You really have to be a *professional* to understand what they are saying. (PSY104/ESB/±WWE)

They're probably *testing* how much we ourselves can *interpret* from information, not just *spoon-feed* or *regurgitate*. (PSY105/±ESB/±WWE)

At high school, writing is more *straightforward* — satisfy requirements and do the right steps; if fulfilled, you get a really good mark. At uni, fulfil requirements and you get an average mark; you have to go beyond requirements to get a good mark. (PSY222/±ESB/±WWE)

I find we *waffle* at university — it's less *precise* than the workplace. (PSY222/±ESB/±WWE)

It's implied that the ability to *write reports* and *express yourself* is going to be essential in *professional life*. (PSY306/±ESB/±WWE)

I'm not sure tutors are set up to do literacy feedback as such. They want to cover the subject matter and the rest is a side issue for them, even though the department wants us to be able to *communicate properly*. (PSY306/±ESB/±WWE)

Keywords

argue, argument, background, communicate properly, concisely, constraining, construct a sentence, criticise, cut us down, debate, describe, disciplined, dogmatic, draw a conclusion, evaluate the evidence, evidence, expertise, express one's own ideas, express yourself, fact, gaps, guidelines, individual interpretation, interpret, lot of information, memorising, outsiders, parroting, picky, precise, professional, professional life, psychological mould, psychology fold, publication, put a letter together, reasoning, regurgitate, replicate, report studies, reports, reproduce, scientific research-type papers, sit on the fence, small amount of words, spoon-feed, standard, straightforward, strict setting out, stringent, structure, style, substantiated, succinct, testing, waffle, write a report

Discussion

The function and purpose of academic writing is predominantly framed as learning something new and different — learning how to write research papers and scientific reports at university — rather than generally becoming (better) writers in life. This contrast is exemplified by second and third year students' views of writing as being geared to perhaps eventually *writing those reports* or to *express yourself*... [as something] essential in *professional life*, rather than just being able to *put a letter together* or *construct a sentence*. These two functions are contrasted in the framing of school writing by a first year +ESB/–WWE student as *12 years of parroting and merely memorising*, on the one hand, and the framing of workplace writing by a second year student as being more *precise* on the other. These framings of student experiences are largely extratextual — they recognise cultural differences between school and university, and to a lesser extent between university and workplace. Such framing may be potentially positive in that recognising genre differences is self-empowering, but it can also be negative in that students are put 'in more danger than others of being alienated from their communities by mastery of academic discourse' (Bizzell 1992: 194).

In terms of its specialist function and purpose at the university and in Psychology in particular, academic writing is principally framed as learning to be *critical*, that is, as learning to marshal evidence, evaluate it, and mount and sustain an *argument*. Third year students comment that, in their first year, they were expected to critique four different articles and saw this as training in constructive criticism and being able to challenge and evaluate studies. They felt that an important requirement was the ability to look for gaps in arguments, 'maybe even looking for *gaps* in your own to make sure that someone can't come in and attack your *argument* and say "but you haven't supported it by this" '. In their study of student writing and faculty feedback in the UK in 1995/6, Lea and Street (1996) also found that

> The twin concepts of 'structure' and 'argument' came to the fore in most [student] interviews as being key elements in student writing.
>
> (Lea and Street 1996: 5)

These observations accurately reflect the position of the Psychology Department in its materials for first year students, one which ranges from the nature of psychology to the 'doing' of psychology:

Extract 1

Aims of the unit

... Psychology as a science involves the discovery of that knowledge through the special methods that researchers use to study behaviour and experience. Psychology as a profession involves, for example, the application of that knowledge to promote human welfare through the particular techniques that practitioners use to assist people. Thus, psychology involves a body

> of knowledge, research to obtain knowledge, and the application of that
> knowledge. (PSY104 & PSY105: Introduction to Psychology I & II (Yr 1,
> Sem 1 & 2), Unit Study Guide)

This duality of acquiring/producing and applying knowledge is of course
mirrored in the duality of science/researcher and profession/practitioner,
both involving 'thinking critically':

Extract 2

Defining and understanding arguments

In studying Psychology, there are two broad goals to be met, firstly, to
help you acquire knowledge about psychology, and secondly, to help you
learn to think in a critical way about this knowledge. . . . Critical thinking
is the key to understanding psychology. But what is critical thinking? It is
an active and systematic process based on logical approaches. Critical thinking is based on arguments, and how these arguments are understood and
evaluated. An introduction to critical thinking, the purpose of this tutorial
is to introduce the <u>concept of an argument</u> and to <u>resolve the argument
into its component elements</u>. That is, to give a detailed structural analysis
of arguments. (*emphasis in original*) (PSY104: Introduction to Psychology I
(Yr 1, Sem 1), Tutorial Guide)

The almost singular focus on critical thinking and the ability to construct a
cogent argument as tools for the acquisition of knowledge by the student
and as 'the key to understanding psychology', may also be seen as the key to
how the discipline understands itself. See here also the discussion in Candlin
and Plum (1999) of the concepts *argument, conciseness* and, among others,
critical thinking, and the injunction by O'Shea (1993), quoted approvingly in
the same Tutorial Guide:

Extract 3

> . . . Psychology essays and reports are expected to show critical, rational
> analysis of data and methods and to be presented in a literary manner. In
> both forms of writing you need to read and to present an argument, rather
> than just regurgitating (sic) existing information (O'Shea, 1993). (PSY104:
> Introduction to Psychology I (Yr 1, Sem 1), Tutorial Guide)

This framing of academic writing as learning to evaluate and critique evidence is seen as a developmental process, with third year students noting differences in university expectations between first and third years. 'Now [in third year] they expect you to have enough *expertise* and *background* to try and know where the failings [in the literature] are'.... 'You can't just *regurgitate* what you've read'. In third year more extensive reading was required, more references were needed, and following strict guidelines, essays needed to be more structured, more coherent, better organised and written more succinctly. The paradox of learning to think for oneself while following strict guidelines, especially in the writing of lab reports, where there was to be 'no room for *individual interpretation or discussion*', occasions interestingly intercultural variation in their evaluation. While a first year −ESB student considered that following strict guidelines made writing tasks easier, a fellow +ESB student found it more difficult since '*constraining*'.

While with hindsight at least this developmental path is clear to third year students, first year students appear less certain of what is expected: 'Are we supposed to be *describing* or *criticising*?' Although aware that 'regurgitating' information is negatively sanctioned, they lack any clear understanding of the characteristics of these different functions of *restating, summarising, describing, evaluating, critiquing, analysing*, all of which constructs have their place in academic writing, though neither equally so, nor similarly highlighted, in all contexts or disciplines. Further, while students and staff both embrace *argument*, and its companion construct *structure*, as keys to successful writing in psychology, and to some extent useful in life beyond the academy, like Lea and Street's respondents (Lea and Street 1996) our focus group participants were equally unclear what the components of such a successful argument were, or what their underpinnings might be. They further note disparities between authoritative understandings of the term(s) as expressed in tutorial comment on student work, and the 'explicit' statements in the guidelines.

> ... even though staff generally had a clear belief in these concepts as crucial to their understanding of what constituted a successful piece of writing, they had difficulty in describing what were the components of a well argued or well structured piece of student work. More commonly, they were able to identify when a student had been successful but could not describe how a particular piece of writing 'lacked' structure. This suggests to us that what makes a piece of student writing 'appropriate' is more rooted in issues of epistemology than with the surface features of literary form that staff often have recourse to when describing their students' writing. That is to say, underlying assumptions about the nature of knowledge affected the meaning given to the terms 'structure' and 'argument'. (Lea and Street 1996: 5)

The most discipline-specific framing of academic writing occurs in the second year 'stats' report. Its purpose is to assess students' ability to present plausible figures for an 'imagined experiment', intended to reflect awareness of what was realistic in a 'real' psychology experiment, and, according to a second year +ESB student, to display thereby evidence of one's belonging to 'the *Psychology fold*'. The link between writing as 'the doing of psychology' and writing 'as gate-keeping to psychology' is thus made overt. Students clearly grasp that being able to write like a psychologist is a requirement for becoming one (Candlin and Plum 1999).

This assertion that there exists a '*Psychology fold*' and that students are being 'put into a *psychological mould*', is complemented by the notion of the '*outsider*', where writing in psychology is framed as incomprehensible to those not already inducted into the specific sociorhetorical practices of the discipline/profession. Students unerringly identify this notion as an obstacle to their learning to write successfully, as they cannot call on outsiders to read and comment on their own work before submitting it for marking. At the same time, when they note approvingly that the department '*wants us to be able to communicate properly*' it remains unclear whether *properly* refers to such specific practices, or to writing ability more generally construed. Notwithstanding this confusion and lack of explicitness among constructs and purposes, we should note that by the third year students had come to claim their self-evident value, despite their equally evident imprecision. 'If you do go into research, you know the *structure* and how to write *concisely* and those kinds of things. In terms of essay writing, it's been good in terms of making sure your thinking is well *substantiated* and *argued* and that each claim you make has to be backed up by *reasoning and evidence*.' Evidence of a kind for a successfully completed induction, or at very least, of a leap of faith, one might argue.

Practice of academic writing across disciplines

From their first day in the academy, most students (with the possible exception of some part-time students) concurrently experience the academic writing practices of different disciplines (Psychology, English, Statistics, Accounting, etc.), which may also be part of different intellectual traditions (Humanities, Social Sciences, Science, Economics, Engineering, etc.). There is much evidence now to show that there are significant epistemological differences both among disciplines and also among 'strands' of disciplines, but also increasing evidence of considerable and concomitant hybridisation of language and interdiscursivity (Hyland 2000, Bhatia and Candlin 2000, *inter alia*).

The problem posed for students is that even when provided with guidance as to the expectations in any one discipline, or across several disciplines, they nonetheless have to work out by trial and error how the practices, conventions and expectations of adequacy of academic writing are both alike and different in their different fields of study. Further, as we show above, they must also cope with the challenge of a plurality of discourses within a 'single' discipline, such as psychology, and with the confusingly similarly-labelled genres and discourse types across disciplines, where the putative constancy of constructs like 'argumentation' and 'problem/solution' betray in fact considerable difference both in their description and their interpretation (Johns 1991). In our example in Psychology, we find also, and not at all surprisingly, that the students shift from framing academic writing to framing the discipline itself — in other words, academic writing in Psychology comes to stand for the discipline of psychology, a stance fully in accord with the view that the doing of psychology is accomplished through the doing of writing.

Student voices

> In psychology you have to be more *careful* what you say — in sociology they give you more *space* to develop your own *opinion*. (PSY104/±ESB/±WWE)

> The style of reporting and discussion is different in psychology from science subjects — it's *non-conclusive*. (PSY105/±ESB/±WWE)

> If I used the *science system of referencing* in another subject, I'd be marked down. (PSY222/±ESB/±WWE)

> Having to learn a different referencing system for different disciplines is very *annoying*, it's *ludicrous*. They all think theirs is the best and the only way. We're supposed to be at uni and the faculties are *acting like children* as far as that kind of thing is concerned. (PSY222/±ESB/±WWE)

> Psychology is more *facts-based* and so it's like a perusal of, or an overview of all the empirical research and all the *facts*, and then, I guess, a little *conclusion* about what you've looked at and what it seems to be telling you. There's not so much *in-depth reasoning processes*, more just *evaluating*, kind of thing. (PSY306/±ESB/±WWE)

> There's more *room* for a lot of *personal things* probably in other disciplines. (PSY306/±ESB/±WWE)

Keywords

acting like children, annoying, careful, come to/draw a conclusion, criticising, describing, essay formula, evaluating, facts, facts-based, in-depth reasoning processes, keep asking questions, ludicrous, meticulous, non-conclusive, opinion, pedantic, personal things, questions, radical difference, room, science system of referencing, space, straight-to-the-point, whiz

Discussion

Students appear to frame academic writing in psychology quite differently from writing in those other disciplines they are familiar with, from the humanities to the social sciences to the natural sciences, seeing major differences. These they interpret qualitatively, for example, 'having to be more *careful* what you say', and technically, for example, using the '*science system of referencing*'. While referencing functions as an intratextual framing device in both written assignments and the articles students read, the emphasis placed in psychology on adhering precisely to a particular *style* of referencing leads them to frame psychology intertextually, generally, as science. Within this there is, however, some variation in students' perception in that we attest an example of two students with contradictory views on the nature of psychology, one claiming psychology to be '*non-conclusive*' ('unlike other science subjects') and another categorising psychology as a discipline which encourages students to come to a conclusion ('unlike philosophy'). More significant perhaps is their evaluation of the stance of psychology intertextually by reference to other disciplines. Like the majority of their fellow students in our focus groups, their framing of psychology as science is achieved through a negative comparative framing with the more open-ended style of inquiry and written discussion they claim to be the hallmark of other disciplines, typically those in the humanities but also in the social sciences.

Academic writing in psychology is especially identified as existing on a different plane from other disciplines — more factual, less personal, more focused on technical aspects, less on creativity, frequently comparing Psychology negatively with other disciplines. Modes of referencing stand out as the key distinctive feature in such comparisons, practices in psychology being referred to by some third year students as '*pedantic*', compelling them to be especially '*meticulous*' in presenting references, far more so than, for example, in the humanities. A shibboleth, perhaps, but one which for many respondents frames and marks off psychology.

Such disciplinary identification through modes of negative comparison is by no means the whole story — Psychology is a very popular subject with entering undergraduate students, many working very hard indeed to become members of the select ten percentile graduating into the Honours stream with the further chance of enrolling in the Masters' programme. Why then such negative framing of academic writing in Psychology compared with other disciplines, and what are its implications for the process of enabling students' writing development?

One reason may lie in the contrast between the explicitness with which expectations of academic writing are conveyed by the department — something clearly interpreted by students as a kind of prescriptiveness they resent but may only resist at the cost of poor grades — and the success with which the department motivates or explains these expectations, that is, the models and practices advocated in guidelines, tutorials, and marking practices. Comparisons among different disciplines drawn by students in the focus group discussions show that they appear to prefer less in the way of explicitly stated expectations, and by implication, at least, more in the way of acceptable variation in their writing.

Modelling of academic writing in Psychology

Psychology stands out among disciplines in its provision of models of academic writing, through departmental guidelines and tutorial teaching, but also through teachers' advice on matters of genre, subject content, style (presentation, including issues of correctness of spelling, grammar), rules to be observed (such as in respect of the citing of sources, of referencing, etc.) and sanctions against breaches of such rules (for example for plagiarism), the input provided (such as handouts for assignments), the personal support offered (for example tutor's advice), guidelines for marking, markers' feedback and, ultimately, the grades awarded. Although such a list of modelling devices and modes of practice may suggest explicitness, much in fact remains implicit, such as encouraging students by a process of consensual hegemony (Gramsci 1931–1933) to take up such models even without explicitly invoking them. An additional and crucial issue confronting both Psychology students and their tutors is whether such models exist to foster the skills needed to *practise* psychology — at university and in the professional world after graduation — or, more narrowly, to develop in them an awareness and knowledge of psychology as an academic discipline. This is an increasingly significant issue for students and tutors in many disciplines with clear professional connections, for example, in law and in medicine, as Candlin, Bhatia and Jensen (2000) identify.

In this section we characterise such modelling in relation to three categories: generic structure, style, and content, categories which are to some extent reflected in the marking sheets used in two of the three course units in Psychology which use them (PSY104, PSY306), with generic structure addressed implicitly, and style and content explicitly.

Generic structure

The concept of generic (text) structure as reflected in the teaching in Psychology of both report and (to a lesser extent) essay writing to students draws (we infer) on the functionally-informed work on narrative by Labov and Waletzky (1967). To this is added work on genre seen as a socially-motivated, goal-oriented and staged process, with clear cognitive implications (Martin, Christie and Rothery 1987; Swales 1990; Bhatia 1993), together with a strong focus on the individual as writer, as in Berkenkotter and Huckin (1995). Academic writing is seen by both students and tutors as a genre to be consciously learned and developed.

Student voices

We had tutes on *argument* and *evaluation* so that's what they expected I suppose. (PSY104/±ESB/±WWE)

We were told to *follow the format* of the previous report [partial lab report done as first assignment] and to *present our results graphically*. (PSY105/±ESB/±WWE)

Our tutor produced a very detailed *fact sheet* for the assignment and said, 'This is *how you write* this report'. (PSY222/ESB/±WWE)

The tutor gave us written *guidelines* and *examples*, including a summary on *how to write reports* and *how to set them out*. (PSY222/±ESB/±WWE)

We were given a *sheet on essay writing*, the same one as in first year, which recommended O'Shea [O'Shea 1993], which is our *bible for essay writing*. (PSY306/±ESB/±WWE)

In one third year course we were presented with a *plan* and had a discussion of the first essay before we wrote the major essay. That was quite *pedantic*, quite *constricting*. (PSY306/±ESB/±WWE)

Keywords

abstract, analyse, argue (the) case, argument, bible (for essay writing), concise, constricting, criticise, depth, detailed fact sheet, difficult to construct, discussion, evaluation, (supported by) evidence, examples, follow format (of previous report), guidelines, how you write (this report), how to write (reports), how to set (them) [reports] out, how to write/structure an essay, introduction, models, outline, pedantic, plan, support (your) position, present (our) results graphically, procedures, sheet (on essay writing), strong (about a point)

Discussion

Students frame issues of writing particular genres — the essay (PSY104/306/ 315) and the report (PSY105/222) — primarily in circumtextual terms of following guidelines, models, procedures and rules, as conveyed through departmental pronouncements 'surrounding' their writing. At the same time, students frame writing intratextually by attending to the structural detail of each genre conveyed in such pronouncements, by recognising the signposting of generic stages such as *abstract, introduction*, etc. Unmistakably, students frame such writing as something that is to be belittled (*bible, pedantic*) and dismissed as coercive and authoritarian imposition of rules (*how to set out/*

follow/write). That they are not too wide of the mark is suggested by O'Shea's injunction in its opening statement:

> The bible for writers in psychology is the *Publication Manual of the American Psychological Association* (APA), usually referred to as the *APA Manual*.
>
> (O'Shea 1993: ix)

and confirmed by Bazerman (1987) in his critique of the APA *Publication Manual* as a model of scientific rhetoric which codifies the behaviourist ascendancy in psychology from the 1920s to the 1960s:

> With the article [in psychology] primarily presenting results, constrained and formatted prescription, authors become followers of rules to gain the reward of acceptance of their results and to avoid the punishment of nonpublication.
>
> (Bazerman 1987: 139)

At the same time, some students make it clear that they appreciate the advice and guidance given, with others asking for more, or more explicit information on how to meet generic expectations. Some course units make such information available as part of their teaching (PSY104/105), while others refer students to books on writing in psychology, or simply to the '"standard" report writing format', with 'additional information . . . available in the Library SR collection'. At issue here are students' responses to such advice — is it because it helps their assessment or because it helps them to learn how to write appropriately generically? Observations of four different tutors teaching report writing revealed not only that they adopted a range of approaches to explaining and motivating its preferred generic structure but that they failed to motivate the functions of such genres, and we feel that this may point to an explanation for some of the negative framing of academic writing by students.

Parallel ambivalence concerning the functions of generic structure is to be found in the course unit marking sheets. Issues of text structure are not addressed there explicitly, implying that students may not receive appropriate feedback. It is impossible to know, for example, to what extent a marking category such as 'Logically developed argument', which certainly has implications for a successful generic structure in both essays and reports (Stuart-Smith 1998), can be related in practice by markers to issues of text structure. Similarly, the marking category 'Legible and well set out work' may also invoke such issues but without a guarantee that all markers will interpret it in this way.

The problem in teaching and learning to write generically, that is structurally, appropriately is that while it is fairly simple to make a particular genre explicit via lexicalisation of the genre and/or its discrete stages (moves), for example by naming a piece of writing a 'lab report' and its stages (moves) 'method', 'design', 'results', etc., it is far less simple to signal local generic structure via (typically) grammatical realisations of what are variously referred to as 'boundary' or 'misplacement markers' (Schegloff and Sacks 1973), 'frames' (Sinclair and Coulthard 1975), or 'discourse markers' (Labov and Fanshel 1977, Schiffrin 1987). Most difficult of all, however, is the teaching and learning of the text-wide patterning of lexicogrammatical choices realising a genre (more correctly its obligatory and optional stages in a particular order as it is these which imply the genre as a whole), since these function by being chosen with a probability for the generic stage that is greater than chance.

Style

Style is a concept more easily invoked than illustrated, let alone taught. Psychology does not shy away from touching upon issues of style in its materials, and even addresses them in some of the marking sheets in use under the heading 'Style and spelling' (PSY104, PSY306). However, it should be noted that both style and generic structure are not only the last categories listed on these marking sheets but that they are explicitly given least importance in PSY306 by being shown under the subheading '(c) Other aspects', following '(a) Minimum Requirements' and '(b) Major criteria for marking'. The problems inherent in any discussion or teaching of style make the question asked in this section, namely how do students come to frame issues of style, all the more interesting and important.

Student voices

At high school you get *outlines* . . . at uni, if they're so *picky* they should say *what they want*. They are looking at *how you say it* and *not what you're saying*, so they have to tell you. (PSY104/±ESB/±WWE)

It's not a particularly *friendly terminology* that you use, the *phrasing* is quite *stilted*, therefore I'm trying to be careful not to do *run-on sentences* and things. (PSY104/ESB/+WWE)

They're really *stringent* and very *picky* with regard to grammar, spelling and vocabulary. (PSY222/±ESB/±WWE)

A list of what should be included and excluded was nothing but a list of *pet hates* rather than guidelines. Basically it was forcing me to write in a *style that wasn't my own*. (PSY222/±ESB/±WWE)

I tend to write in a *simple style* because that's been commented on. (PSY306/±ESB/±WWE)

They don't want your *opinion*, they don't want 'Is' ... And that's an attempt to create an *air of objectivity*, which isn't there because you're writing the paper and that isn't acknowledged. (PSY306/±ESB/±WWE)

Keywords

air of objectivity, communication, concise, consistent and flowing, continuous and smooth, down pat, easier to read, expression, flow, friendly terminology, how you say it, language, lost style (of creative writing), opinion, outlines, pet hates, picky, run-on sentences, simple style, something special (about the way you've said something), spelling, stilted phrasing, stringent, style that wasn't my own, way you deliver it [content], what they want, (not) what you're saying

Discussion

Style is primarily framed circumtextually, students reacting to both teachers' input into the assignment before writing it, and markers' feedback written on it when it is returned. While some students frame issues of style in positive terms, most frame them negatively, raising important questions about how style itself is framed by the discipline for the students in the first instance.

The most positive framing is expressed in terms which either simply assert the importance of style, e.g. a third year student claims that '*expression is important*', or which describe the characteristics of the style implied to be desired by Psychology by adopting the modalisation 'should', for example 'your writing <u>should</u> be *consistent and flowing*', 'your ideas <u>should</u> be *continuous and flowing*', and so on. While in linguistic terms the style attributes most commonly mentioned would correspond to concepts of cohesion and coherence essential to supporting a text's structural organisation (Halliday and Hasan 1985), for students, style follows the advice issued by Psychology as essentially a quality of writing that merely adds polish to content. Indeed, the dichotomy set up between content and style — in the words of a second year student 'What matters is the content and possibly *the way you deliver it.*' — invites just such framing. The danger of this disassociation is clearly shown by the third year student who, in saying that 'I feel that I didn't get my arguments and points across well enough, but I do have my spelling, grammar and structure *down pat*', is claiming success as a 'stylist' yet admitting to failure as a writer of psychology — hardly what the teachers in Psychology are hoping to achieve, one would suppose.

If one way to frame style is in terms of language attributes (*flowing, continuous, spelling, grammar*, etc.), another is to frame it in terms of relative complexity on a scale ranging from *'simple style'* (student's) to one that is *'easier to read'* to *'something special'* (desired of students by Psychology) to one characterised by *'(un)friendly terminology'* and *'stilted phrasing'* (Psychology's). Yet a third kind of framing of style is generic in orientation, juxtaposing *'creative writing'* (student's) with a style unnamed yet clearly incompatible with creativity, 'a *style that wasn't my own*' or that has led to the student having *'lost that* (creative writing) *style'*, in other words, a style fostered by Psychology [report writing] which has replaced that style brought by the student to the university.

This movement from framing style as an attribute of a student's academic writing describable in lay linguistic terms, and approvingly so, to one that poses a student's 'natural' writing style (*simple, creative*) against psychology's 'imposed' style (*difficult, spuriously objective by 'creating an air of objectivity'* via the personal pronoun system) stands against the intertextuality and hybridity of discourses, genres and styles characteristic of, and indeed demanded by, societies in stages of high or postmodernity (Giddens 1991). The negative framing of style has the further consequence that students frame teachers in Psychology rather than the style of the discipline of psychology. Teachers are seen as unreasonable (*'picky, stringent'*) and obsessed with minor and unimportant issues (*'I mean what's spelling for God's sake?'*), or, more troubling, as being more concerned with 'the *language*, the *communication*' than the content of students' writing, with '*how you say it* and not what you're saying'. A student's comment that 'A list of what should be included and excluded was nothing but a list of *pet hates* rather than guidelines' merely echoes what the list in question says in its heading: 'Common report errors to avoid because *they drive tutors nuts*' (emphasis added).

However useful some of the items listed as desirable (or to be avoided) by the discipline may be, what Psychology engages in here is that kind of generalised, interpersonally loaded framing which leads its students to frame issues of style in similarly unfocused terms, rather than, for example, helping them to explore the much more interesting and significant issue of how styles of writing need to accommodate both different audiences as well as distinct genres of particular disciplines, and to reflect variabilities in particular authorial stance (Hyland 2000).

Content

Students frame the issue of content, that is, the display of subject knowledge in their academic writing, circumtextually in the special sense of responding to teachers' input and markers' feedback. Content is the only issue covered explicitly, and in a variety of ways, in all the marking sheets used in Psychology, thus potentially providing students with both detailed in-text and more summary end-of-text feedback. Students also frame content issues extratextually, drawing on their own general knowledge of academic disciplines, and, at least among more senior students, of the particular discipline of psychology itself.

Student voices

> How are we meant to 'elaborate our ideas' [tutors' advice] if we don't have *enough words* to do it? [reference to word limit] (PSY104/±ESB/±WWE)

> It's only first year and we can't be expected to *be up there with the latest research*. (PSY105/±ESB/±WWE)

> You have to indicate a *really good understanding* of the topic; you have to illustrate a *rich understanding* of concepts. (PSY222/±ESB/±WWE)

> What matters is the *content* and possibly the way you deliver it. (PSY222/±ESB/±WWE)

> I thought it'd be more like, I mean, based on all the research, facts and empirical evidence that have been found, you'd have to then give your *opinion* on what would be the most likely explanation. (PSY306/±ESB/±WWE)

> You have to come up with *novel ideas* of your own or try to *pick holes* that haven't been picked before. (PSY306/±ESB/±WWE)

Keywords

> be up there with the latest research, can't say anything without citing, content, easy to pick it [answer] out, enough words, how much you can actually put in of what you think, novel ideas, opinion, pick holes, really good understanding, rich understanding, use it for an argument, vast range of interpretations, (what matters is the) content

Discussion

Students appear to frame the required display of content mastery in conflicting, if not paradoxical terms. On the one hand, they feel obligated to demonstrate a personal if not unique understanding of issues, requiring an *'opinion'* to be voiced; on the other they need to qualify such opinion through a sustainable argument. How much personal opinion is permissible perplexes students, not fully grasping how to balance a so-called 'objective' critical stance with one that is nonetheless theirs alone and capable of demonstrating their understanding of the issues. Students do not all come to the academy appreciating distinctions between unsubstantiated personal opinions — more or less blunt assertions without supporting evidence — and carefully argued positions. In consequence, students frame the position taken by Psychology as a teachers' failing, seeing them as either confused themselves or confusing them. A safe path is to play back to teachers the injunctions in lectures, tutorials and textbooks, stating as neutrally as possible an intellectual position and the argument supporting it.

The key problem which then arises for many students is the demand on them to modulate their own personal, private, voices through the rigour of institutionalised, public rhetoric. The importance of getting this modulation right is particularly emphasised in academic writing in Psychology. Students construe it often however as Psychology making unreasonable demands compared with other disciplines, reinforced by the regular insistence by the discipline that academic writing in psychology is distinctive.

Student writing — the role of teachers in students' learning to write

This role is enacted through two main means: (i) input and support from lecturers/tutors, and (ii) feedback provided by markers. Input here includes materials, advice and information provided for the writing of assignments, while support refers to problem counselling, usually after assignments have been returned. Marker feedback includes both comments and grades awarded as indicators of writing success or failure.

Input and support provided by teaching staff

Student voices

One tutor said 'you should have some *intellectual habits*' but we haven't developed these yet. (PSY104/±ESB/±WWE)

She [tutor] said, '*show basic knowledge and understanding*, follow the little book [Smyth 1994], and keep to the word limit'. (PSY104/±ESB/±WWE)

We're told to look at journals as models but they vary so much. And they're superior to our standard of writing, and don't report details *the way we have to do*. (PSY222/±ESB/±WWE)

We don't know their marking criteria, and there are no model papers in the Library Reserve, so we can't really judge own work objectively; we don't really know *what to aim for*. (PSY222/ESB/±WWE)

They won't explicitly tell you unless you really *plague* them and *beg* them. (PSY306/±ESB/±WWE)

Everyone was falling apart trying to come to grips with what was required and the lecturer said in class, 'all I want you to do is just think about linking hypotheses, just describe them and relate them to the studies'. Yeah, and it was very *vague*. (PSY315/±ESB/±WWE)

Keywords

basic knowledge and understanding, beg, easier, intellectual habits, plague, shorter, more simple/not (gonna be) too simple, stifling, try to test something, vague, want, (the) way we have to, what they expect, what to aim for

Discussion

From the voices of the students, it appears that input and support are evaluated problematically, some pointing to lack of explicitness, others that what is enjoined is some stifling conformity. Teachers are clearly to be damned if they do and damned if they don't. The more interesting question to be asked is how such input and support is framed by the discipline as supporting the kind of writing it believes is defining of its purposes and how students respond to this expectation. It can hardly be an accident that in a discipline which so assiduously models the practice of the discipline for its students to the point of appearing unreasonably prescriptive, the majority of those students have perhaps unrealistic expectations of what can in fact be spelled out for them.

Feedback provided by markers: grades and comments

Student voices

In high school, they praise the good parts. Here they *cut you down* and don't really offer any alternatives so you don't know how to improve it. (PSY104/±ESB/±WWE)

You know where you *got* the marks but you don't know how you *lost* them. (PSY104/±ESB/±WWE)

That *variability in teaching* exists across the board in Behavioural Sciences and to me that's a problem because these people [markers/tutors] are the *gatekeepers* to the profession for us and, you know, if they are postgrad students or whatever and they have several agendas in being here, well, I'm certain to be the last of the priorities. (PSY222/ESB/±WWE)

When our tutor talked about some of the things they had been expecting after the assignment was returned, it came as a very big *surprise* for a lot of people what they were looking for. (PSY222/±ESB/±WWE)

I'm not sure tutors are set up to do *literacy feedback* as such. They want to cover the subject matter and the rest is a side issue for them, even though the department wants us to be able to communicate properly. (PSY306/±ESB/±WWE)

I got an F and I get Bs regularly, so that was an absolute shock for me, it was *crushing*. I've gone off to a psychologist about this because it crushed me. It's *serious*. (PSY315/±ESB/±WWE)

Keywords

aggressive, badly enough/really badly, big beef, brief, broad approach, build on, constructive criticism, confidence, crushing, cut you down, deserve, difficult to read, direction, disappointing, effort, fair, gap, gatekeepers, got/lost, guide, hard to judge, help, helpful, honest, instructive, job well done, just at the end, literacy feedback, looks very pretty, open slate, positive comments, reads nice, right, scathing, serious, should have done this/should not have done that/should-not-haves, standard, sticking to the regulations, surprise, understanding the process, unknown quantity, vague instructions, variability in teaching, variance

Discussion

Although marker feedback is predominantly framed by students in terms of being *'useful'*, *'instructive'*, *'confidence-inspiring'*, *'helpful'*, and providing *'guidance'*, many, though not all students, either asserted that feedback was inadequately specific to be of much use in improving their writing, or that it simply did not constitute *'constructive criticism'*. This latter evaluation interestingly, if unhelpfully, mirrors the model of academic writing fostered by Psychology, which stresses critical thinking and sound argumentation.

Some third year students felt that markers' comments were generally critical and that *'positive comments'* were *'rare'*, with only few comments indicating a *'job well done'*. Others claimed that the comments, positive or negative, would not have enabled them to improve in that they were *'vague'*, and unspecific. In one student's words 'There was nothing that I could really *build on'*.

This general lack of positive feedback is also borne out by Daiker's study (1989), showing that praise for writers' work by college composition teachers in the United States is rare, despite a long line of research studies on writing which emphasise the importance of encouragement, especially to apprehensive or anxious writers likely to expect failure on the basis of past experience. Worse still, the students' claim that there is not sufficient constructive criticism provided is compounded by their observations that feedback is often marked by negative affect, with some markers considered *'aggressive'* by first year students, and some comments called *'scathing'* by second year students. The importance of the role of affect, both positive and negative, in marker feedback appears to be quite obvious to students, if not to markers.

The most significant theme running through the observations on marker feedback and marking practices in general is that the students claim not to understand why they received a particular grade for their assignment. One clue why this sense of bewilderment at their mark is so widely felt is to be found in the observation that 'there's no real *standard'* applying to a given assignment. This observation is in itself interesting since it presages a view of academic writing as a product akin to an industrial product for which one might reasonably be expected to be able to accord a product rating against some set criteria. In the absence of such criteria, it came as little surprise to us that in response to the question whether their mark or grade had met their own expectations, exceeded them or had fallen below them, students from all three years produced the full range of possible responses. Bourdieu's linguistic marketplace (Bourdieu 1993) is clearly alive and well in that writing cost and feedback benefit appear to stand in some market economic relationship, invoking an 'economy of tertiary writing' (Candlin and Plum 1999). The issue then becomes the extent that students can accurately place a value on writing characteristics. That some have learned to do so is reflected in the comment of one third year student who noted that poor marks often accompanied descriptive rather than analytical responses, adding that if they didn't analyse, they ought to expect penalties.

That the evaluation of marker feedback varies considerably between students is of course not surprising, although it does seem clear from our accounts that feedback on, and correction of, so-called 'surface' errors is met with a degree of resistance. In this respect our students differ from a significant group of students in an interview study of ESL writers' reactions to feedback by Radecki and Swales (1988), where students wanted both substantive comment *and* correction of surface errors.

In sum, we may say that the extent to which the most important indicators of success or failure in academic writing, grade and marker comment, are likely to be appreciated by students in terms of evaluation of their work and in terms of some subsequent operationalisability, will be influenced by the degree to which the modelling of academic writing *prior to* the writing of the assignment matches that provided via grade and feedback. It is interesting that another important factor in this matter of matching is whether the marker of a particular student's assignment is also the student's tutor, or at least a tutor or lecturer in the course unit. In units with very large enrolments it is common practice for casual markers to be employed, often postgraduates, who are not otherwise involved in the teaching of the course. In such circumstances, students' natural tendency to write personally 'for a known tutor' may be frustrated, and they may fall back on some general context-independent 'elaborated code' only to find that this style also fails to match the aspired-for, if unclear, standards set by the discipline.

4   Conclusion

One consequence of adopting the ethnographic approach of this chapter is the ever-present danger of losing the wood for the trees — so many voices with so many themes — and the difficulty of identifying key constructs and issues that can then be matched and taken further by parallel research studies. At a risk, then, of reductionism, the following two key constructs and issues seem to us at least to arise from the data. We are bolstered in this selection by a recent extensive and very powerful analysis of the relationship between the worlds of writing in the academy and in the worlds of work provided by Dias *et al.* (1999), and an overt engagement of our study with theirs will help clarify our position here.

Duality and confusion of purpose in student writing

Dias *et al.* argue that the genres of student writing are:

> characterized by an inherent and inevitable duality. On the one hand, such writing is 'epistemic' — in the sense of enabling students, through discourse production, to take on stances toward and interpretations of realities valorized in specific disciplines. At the same time, another fundamental activity of the university is sorting and ranking its students, and scripts are produced as ways of enabling such ranking

This duality is clearly manifest in the voices of our students in psychology, as is the sense (see Toulmin 1958) that psychology poses distinctive epistemic demands.

Dias *et al.* refer further in their study to the work of Willard (1982) who distinguishes between disciplinary fields that are instrumentally oriented and those that are epistemically oriented, and, following Willard, they suggest a distinction between university writing which is epistemically focused — that is, learning how to use language as an occasion for the display of learning — versus workplace writing that is practically focused — that is, purposeful and problem-oriented. The problem for our students is that not only is this distinction unclear — as for example in the genre of the lab report — but also that the understanding of what is meant by *epistemic* varies: is it the display of personal knowledge as a mark of learning or is it more the sense of making a contribution to the knowledge of the discipline? As we have seen, this distinction and this dual purpose is by no means clearly maintained by either tutors or students and there exists, in consequence, considerable confusion concerning what the purposes of student writing actually are.

Participation and apprenticeship

Dias *et al.* draw heavily on Lave and Wenger's construct of 'legitimate peripheral participation' (Lave and Wenger 1991) and Rogoff's parallel construct of 'guided participation' (Rogoff 1990) as a way of explaining and differentiating writing and learning in the academy and in the workplace, seeing the latter construct as leading into the former in the shift from learning in the academy to learning in the workplace, but distinguishing them in arguing that while the latter has learning as its primary goal, the former sees learning as something that is 'incidental and occurs as part of participation in communities of practice' (Dias *et al.* 1999: 188). Although Dias *et al.* reformulate both constructs, Rogoff's as 'facilitated performance' and Lave and Wenger's as 'attenuated authentic participation', we would be even more cautious, and in two respects: firstly, the evidence from our research is that although considerable guidance is provided to facilitate learning to write (and writing to learn) in the academy, this is by no means as carefully structured as Dias *et al.* would appear to believe (1999: 191), having much in common with the 'improvisatory quality of learning opportunities' they see as distinctive of the workplace. As our students make plain, 'noise' is not removed from their learning trajectory, and partly for our second reason. This concerns the purposes of writing in psychology and the conflict between writing seen as an exercise *sui generis* and writing as seen as evidence of a gradual incorporation of the student into the community of psychologists. That this sense of participation and apprenticeship is by no means clear to the students is evident in this chapter, as is the lack of the normal conditioning factors for such apprenticeship (see Candlin and Plum 1999; Gollin 1998). In that sense, our academy bears more resemblance to the unclarity of writing purposes characteristic for Dias *et al.* of the workplace. They argue, further (p. 191), that the workplace is distinguished from the academy by its 'improvisatory quality of learning opportunities'. While it is true that learning through writing is structured in the academy, one should be careful not to overplay the perceptions of students of that structuring. Organised it may be, but *perceiving* the organisation as leading to a clear set of staged learning objectives is another, and it is here that there is yet considerable cause for uncertainty among our students. Finally, there has to be caution on the matter of mentor–learner roles. While it may be the case in some workplaces that learning mentorship roles are unclear to workplace novices, this does not mean that in the academy such roles are crystal clear to students. In fact, as our data make plain, there is still considerable uncertainty as to what the roles of tutors are, or may be, vis-à-vis students, causing the latter considerable concern in terms of where assistance, and what kind of assistance, may be found, and when.

In sum, it would appear that sharp distinctions between the writing world of learning and the writing world of work MAY BE more difficult to sustain than one might imagine, and that insofar as worlds of learning, as in the case of psychology as a discipline, are conditioned in part by the precepts and required competencies of the world of work, these distinctions will inevitably blur. Further, as students themselves, as in our data, may or may not have previous workplace writing experience, these worlds constantly engage AND CONTEND in the everyday perceptions and practices of students, either in relation to their past writing experiences, or in relation to those of their past *and* their future. It is this regular indeterminacy that leads us to prefer an analysis which, driven by voiced experience, seeks to explore how all aspects of the writing process in the academy, the positions, perceptions, actions and attitudes of its members, are variously framed and conditioned and constantly the subject of different and changing valorisations.

Appendix: Focus group discussions

Initial discussion

1   Elaboration of categories used in Information and Consent Form:
    • ESB / NESB
    • Work-Related Writing Experience in English — yes / no
2   Transition question:
    Is there any difference between your past writing practices and what was expected of you now in your assignment?
3   Key questions:
    • Have you encountered any problems doing your assignment?
    • If you think about the different kinds of input into your assignment, what were the most important sources?
    • Did your lecturers / tutors express any expectations they had regarding good / successful / academic writing?
    • What were the processes you followed in doing your assignment?
4   Ending questions:
    • What do you consider the most important issue in considering your writing skills as they are now or might need to be in the future?

Moderator gives brief preview of content of Follow-up focus group discussion: reflecting on marker's comments, fulfilment or not of your expectations in respect of writing requirements, etc.

Follow-up discussion

1   Did the mark you received for your essay meet your expectations?
    • If not, was it higher or lower?
    • Can you explain the discrepancy?
2   Do you have a sense of having met/not met expectations in respect of the
    university's/discipline's writing requirements?
    • in your teacher's terms?
    • in your marker's terms?
    • in your own terms?
3   Had your lecturers / tutors expressed any particular expectations of good
    / successful / academic writing?
4   What do you see as the function of what you were expected to do in
    your course/in Psychology (more generally) / at the university (most
    generally)?
5   Do you have any sense of different literacy demands being made in
    different disciplines?
6   Do you have any sense of the role of literacy in your university career /
    your subsequent / current work career?
7   What do you consider the most important issue in the development of
    your own literacy skills from here on?

Notes

1. This chapter draws principally on research carried out at the Department
    of Linguistics at Macquarie University, Sydney as part of a four University
    project (Macquarie University, Sydney; Curtin University of Technology,
    Perth; Edith Cowan University, Perth; and the University of Western Aus-
    tralia, Perth) funded by the Australian Research Council, entitled *Framing
    student literacy: cross-cultural aspects of English communication skills in university
    settings*. Its immediate source is one of the four Macquarie University project
    reports, entitled *Doing psychology, doing writing: student voices on academic writ-
    ing in psychology*. The authors would like to thank their fellow researchers
    on the Macquarie project: Ruth Busbridge, Mary Cayley, Sandra Gollin,
    Erik Johansen, Virginia Stuart-Smith and Sue Spinks for their contribu-
    tions to the ideas and work of the whole Macquarie project, to Jean Brick
    and Jennifer Thurstun who helped the project team with conducting focus
    group discussions with student groups, and to Mary Cayley and Erik
    Johansen, in particular, for assistance with coding, transcribing and helping
    shape the interpretations of the data included here. Finally, we acknowledge
    with gratitude the help of the many students who participated in these
    focus groups, and to their tutors for allowing research credits to students
    for their participation.

2. MacLachlan and Reid (1994) identify four types of framing in relation to academic literacy practices, which we find useful for this chapter: *extratextual* framing (world and specialised knowledge which is brought to bear by participants on a literacy task); *circumtextual* framing (participants' contextualisation of texts in terms of appearance and apparatus); *intertextual* framing (participants' ability to place texts generically, and in a series); and *intratextual* framing (signposts and markers that guide participants through texts).

3. The phrase 'doing psychology' neatly reflects the view of the contextual theory of register and genre developed by Martin and others in Sydney (Martin 1984, 1992, 1996; Plum 1996, 1988; Ventola 1987) that fields of social activity, including psychology, are constructed through their activity sequences. Compare also the characteristic ways in which conversational analysts and ethnomethodologists (Garfinkel, Sacks, Schegloff and many others) refer to people 'doing complaining', 'doing teaching', 'doing being a doctor', 'doing being ordinary/puzzled', etc.

4. The student data were gathered from 80 students in focus group discussions with 28 groups of students in five undergraduate courses in first, second and third year psychology courses. The discussions were moderated by project members, working with an outline of questions to scaffold the discussion. 16 of the discussions were initial ones, held while the students' assessable written assignments were with their markers, 11 were follow-up discussions held after assignments had been returned. 5 groups could not be reconvened for such a follow-up session. Discussions varied from 45 to 90 minutes, and all discussions were audio-taped and selectively transcribed. Numbers in the focus groups ranged from 4 to 7, distributed unevenly across the course units, from N:31 in PSY 104 to N:4 in PSY 315. More females than males participated, and fewer mature students (post early 20s) than students who had come to university straight from school. Gender and age were not, however, factors on which the project concentrated, and these have not been separately identified in the discussion. The Macquarie University project did, however, distinguish between English-speaking background (ESB) and non-English-speaking background students (NESB) as this Australian government-initiated categorisation (now abandoned) was signalled in University (Commonwealth government) registration and was initially deemed potentially valuable in the context of the overall four university project, though it was subsequently rejected as problematic in the Australian context of long-standing multilingual migration. Since students in the focus groups had, however, been asked to self-identify as ESB or NESB, we retained that in the identification of focus group membership. More relevant to the study was the designation of students who had work-related writing experience (+WWE) or not (−WWE). This distinction cut across the mature-age versus immediately post-school student body. The distinction was motivated by the views of academic staff in Psychology as being potentially significant. Overall, focus groups were partly structured to be either +ESB or −ESB, and +WWE and −WWE in the populous PSY 104 course (see below) but could not be maintained in other courses because of small numbers.

15

Fixed and flexible framing: Literacy events across cultures[1]
Ian Malcolm

Higher education in Australia and literacy

Culturally based differences in higher education

Universities in the present day have been subject to increasing pressure to reduce dependency for funding on governments, to guarantee to their stake-holders that they are quality providers, to relate their offerings to the needs of the global marketplace, to follow the example of industry in the way in which they manage their affairs and to welcome competition from all comers. This changing university culture is not limited to one country: parallel changes are taking place all over the world, and the changes are forcing universities to look beyond the boundaries of their immediate communities for partner-ships, for solutions to their problems and for markets. The move towards an international student market is now well advanced in Australia, although the policy of admitting overseas students on a full paying basis to Australian universities is only ten years old.

The widescale entry of international students into Australian universities has brought a new dimension into the higher educational experience. The incoming students, whose homes are for the most part in Asia, are bringing new traditions of study, new concepts of knowledge and new forms of dis-course into their host institutions. Concepts of education which for many years had been normatised within Australian universities have come into question. With education becoming increasingly client-driven, institutions have had, for their own survival, to consider whether or not they need to learn new discourses appropriate to their increasingly new clientele.

Two years ago at Edith Cowan University a research project was carried out under funding from the university's Student Equity Committee to discover whether or not students of non-English speaking background were being treated with equity in their experiences in the university. Ethnographic tech-niques were employed to gather data from lecture and tutorial rooms and to inquire into the views of students of all backgrounds and of their lecturers.

This project resulted in the publication of a report entitled Worlds Apart, in which it was shown that there were vast differences separating local and overseas students in their conceptions of crucial communicative events taking place in the university, and vast differences also separating the official self-perception of the university from the actual perceptions of the students who were enrolled in it (Malcolm and McGregor 1995). The report resulted in the commissioning of a staff development programme to be made available through the computer network to alert staff to some of the things they need to be aware of with respect to cultural differences affecting the expectations of overseas students in university settings (Rochecouste 1996).

An Australia-wide study of student outcomes reported on by the Department of Employment, Education and Training at the end of 1995 (Taylor et al. 1995) compared the progress of students on a number of criteria. One of the findings of this report was that student progress differed significantly according to cultural and linguistic difference. It was found that the progress rate was 87% for students who spoke English at home, 82% for students from non-English speaking backgrounds and 67% for Aborigines and Torres Strait Islanders. These findings suggest that Aboriginal and Torres Strait Islander people may well be the group most disadvantaged by the cultural inflexibility of the higher education system.

The Framing Student Literacies Project

An opportunity to investigate this situation arose in 1995 with the initiation of a widescale study of tertiary literacy which was funded by the Australian Research Council. This study, which was developed at the initiative of Professor Ian Reid of Curtin University, set out to provide a comprehensive description of the literacy expectations of universities and the ways in which students meet them or fail to meet them. By involving teams in four universities, working in a coordinated way, the study set out to cover a wide range of disciplinary areas, levels of study, and student cultural and linguistic backgrounds. Edith Cowan University undertook, as a part of this project, to investigate the ways in which Aboriginal students participate in the literacy events of the university. This investigation has been conducted at Edith Cowan University where it has involved the entire consenting Aboriginal student population and the staff who work with them. In keeping with the wider project, the Aboriginal investigation has employed the research approach of *frame analysis* as a means of interpreting the communicative practices observed. It has been found necessary, however, to extend the descriptive apparatus of frame analysis and to propose a distinction between *fixed* and *flexible framing* in order to account for the data. It is the object of this paper to describe the procedures employed and through them to provide for the first time an account of the ways in which Aboriginal students manage their participation in the various literacy events of higher education.

Framing and contextualisation in higher education literacy research

The literacy event

In order to study literacy practices in their wider social context, the concept of *literacy event* has been used by a number of scholars. Perhaps the best-known use of the term is by Heath (1983), who adopted it from Anderson, Teale and Estrada (1980), who had defined it as 'any action sequence, involving one or more persons, in which the production and/or comprehension of print plays a role' (1983: 59) and extended its use to incorporate not only *reading events* and *writing events* but *social interactional events* which involve 'talking — and interpreting and interacting — around the piece of writing' (1983: 386). Heath argued that the ways in which written language is talked about are carefully regulated in literacy events and she implied that the literacy event could be considered a subset of the *speech event.*

Literacy events typically occur in schools, although they may also have their reflection in practices which take place in the home and in the community (Heath 1983; Breen *et al.* 1994). In higher education the use of language related to existing or intended writing is so fundamental as to be virtually inseparable from most of the communicative events which go on.

It is an assumption of the project being carried out at Edith Cowan University that the reception, integration, expression and review of communication based on the written word essentially constitutes the study cycle around which the life of the university student revolves (see Table 15.1). The *reception* of the written word typically takes place on an individual basis as the student is involved in reading, computer searching or taking notes in lectures and seminars. It takes place in a group context where students listen to lectures, seminar presentations or media presentations (though these may, of course, also be received individually). Brainstorming in student groups, although apparently totally oral, may often also involve mediation of the written word.

The heart of the study cycle occurs when the student is involved in a process of *integration* of that new learning which has been accessed through such reception processes into his or her existing knowledge. This involves such individual activities as note taking, summarising, preparing assignments, preparing for tests and revising one's lecture notes. It also takes place in such group activities as tutorials, small group interactions, collaborative project work and making oral response to material which has been presented by other students.

The third stage in the cycle is that which involves the *expression* of what has been learned. Individually, students may carry this out by producing assignments, sitting for examinations and carrying out individual research. On a group basis, they may present seminar papers, report on research or

Table 15.1 The Tertiary Study Cycle: embedding of the written word in literacy events

	Individual activity	Group activity
Reception	Reading – before lectures – during lectures – after lectures Computer searching Taking notes in lectures and seminars	Engaging in brainstorming groups Listening to lecturer presentations Listening to media presentations Listening to student presentations
Integration	Study – reading – note taking – summarising Preparing assignments Preparing for tests and exams Revising lecture notes	Participating in tutorials Participating in small group work Carrying out collaborative projects Responding to other students' presentations
Expression	Producing assignments Sitting for exams Carrying out individual research	Presenting seminar papers Carrying out collaborative research Reporting on research

Review	Reading and responding to the
	  marked work
		Receiving and responding to
		  lecturer oral evaluations

collaborate in research. All of these expressions of learning are typically subject to evaluation by lecturers and often by fellow students.

Finally, there is the *review* stage, where the student considers the evaluation which has been given of what he or she has expressed. This involves, for example, reading and interpreting what has been written on essays, or receiving and responding to feedback given orally by the lecturer.

All these activities, based as they are on the written word, may be characterised as literacy events and as such they may be analysed within a common sociolinguistic framework.

Framing

The work of MacLachlan and Reid (1994) on frame theory has been drawn on to provide a common theoretical basis for the studies contributed by all four universities to the collaborative project. In the case of the Edith Cowan University team, an attempt has been made to apply frame theory to a wide range of literacy events (as described in the previous section), whereas in the other universities the focus has been predominantly on student reading or writing. MacLachlan and Reid's work has been carried out within the framework of earlier studies, for example, by Goffman (1974), Gumperz (1982) and Tannen (1993) which postulated that messages are typically accompanied by internal or contextual cues which guide the receiver into adopting the appropriate frame within which they may be meaningfully interpreted, and as mentioned in the previous chapter, they have in particular identified four kinds of framing which readers need to employ: extratextual, intratextual, circumtextual and intertextual (MacLachlan and Reid 1994: 2–5).

Frame theory has been found particularly appropriate in accounting for communication incompatibilities which occur across cultures. For example, Tannen (1993) reports on Watanabe's finding that the Japanese, when providing reasons, do so in the frame of storytelling, whereas the Americans tend to do so in the frame of reporting. Likewise in her own research, Tannen showed how, in responding to the same film, Greek viewers operated from a 'film-interpreter' frame but Americans from a 'film-viewer' frame. Similarly, frame theory has provided a useful basis for examining communication incompatibilities which occur in institutional settings between professionals and clients. Tannen and Wallat (in Tannen 1993: 57–76) demonstrated how, in a medical interview, frame shifts on the part of the paediatrician were accomplished by register shifts. They also showed how the frames of the professional and of the client may make conflicting demands. Ribeiro (1996), describing the interaction between a psychiatrist and her patient in a discharge interview, showed what she described as a 'struggle' between the professional framing, which the psychiatrist wished to maintain, and the personal framing which the patient wished to introduce, in anticipation of moving into a non-professional setting. Research by Emmott (1994) applying frame theory to the analysis of narrative discourse has given evidence that frames may change in two ways: either by *frame shift* (where the author brings about a complete scene change) or by *frame modification* (where the reader has to adjust to one element within the frame changing, as in the case where one character is no longer there).

Contextualisation

A third concept which has been found important in the work to be described is that of *contextualisation*. It has been argued by Denny (1991: 66) that 'Western thought has only one distinctive property separating it from thought in *both* agricultural and hunter–gatherer societies — decontextualisation.' Decontextualisation, in this sense, is defined as 'the handling of information in a way that either disconnects other information or backgrounds it' (1991: 66). Western thought, it is argued, has progressively moved away from contextualisation towards decontextualisation since classical Greek times, supported by the growth in literacy. Denny cites research evidence that traditional Australian Aboriginal children are more inclined to contextualised thinking than are their more Westernised counterparts or white Australian children (1991: 68). In a related argument, Bain (1992) has claimed that white speakers are tolerant of a greater level of abstraction from direct experience than are Aboriginal speakers. Aboriginal speakers show a tendency to avoid abstractions like 'motherhood', which do not retain any direct link with the senses.

Literacy, and the approach to the expression of experience which it favours, may, then, be in conflict with ways of thought and expression which are preferred by Aboriginal speakers. This is certainly argued by Gray (1990: 107), who sees it as the cause of many of the learning difficulties experienced by Aboriginal children in schools. Gray, further, has made the connection between the 'contextualized' or 'concrete' language of the Aboriginal students' oral tradition and the 'decontextualized' language used in the 'literacy-oriented tradition' which the school supports (1990: 108). Eggington (1992: 93), in similar vein, has referred to the incompatibility which may exist between traditional Aboriginal people and their urbanised cousins who have 'crossed over to a high literate culture. . . . These people see things through literate-culture eyes and are often seen as betraying traditional aboriginal values.'

The kind of struggle Ribeiro referred to between professional and everyday approaches to the framing of an interaction may also characterise the encounters of professional educators with Aboriginal students, in both school and university settings. The struggle may indeed be intensified in such settings because it also involves a cross-cultural dimension and a contest between an oral-based culture which demands contextualisation and a literate culture which demands decontextualisation.

The Edith Cowan Project

Aims and approaches

The project which began at Edith Cowan University in 1995 has been attempting to identify and describe a range of literacy events in which Aboriginal students are engaged, to examine the patterns of student and lecturer participation, to apply an analysis on the basis of frame theory to the events studied and to draw inferences from this analysis as to the ways in which the effectiveness of higher education for Aboriginal students may be improved.

The research team, consisting of an applied linguist, a half-time graduate research assistant and consultants with an Aboriginal community base, has been guided by a steering committee composed of Aboriginal staff members of Edith Cowan University and the University of Western Australia. The approach to data gathering has been ethnographic, and the research assistant has (with permission) acted as a non-participant observer of literacy events involving Aboriginal students on a discontinuous basis over more than 12 months. The data gathered have been in the form of field notes, supplemented by informal interviews with both staff and students and questionnaire responses. In addition, material written by Aboriginal students for assignments and examinations has been gathered.[2,3]

Framing and frames

For the purposes of this research, the term framing has been used to refer to *the activity whereby participants in a communicative event reciprocally exhibit and interpret anticipated norms for the conduct of that event.* Framing is typically provisional throughout the course of the communicative event as participants adjust or change frames. It has not been found possible or useful to identify and describe a set of frames, although it is assumed that, at any given point in time, for each participant, a frame exists, in the sense of *an idealised working pattern or schema for a communicative event, or part thereof, which serves as a guide for one's participation in that event.* What interests us in this research is the process of framing, or, perhaps more accurately in Ribeiro's terms, the 'struggle' between competing frames.

Contextualisation and frame shift

The contextualisation/decontextualisation opposition has provided an important additional dimension to the analysis. Contextualisation can be considered at two levels in literacy events: first the linguistic, where we are concerned with the context dependence, or otherwise, of the *language*, and second, the social, where we are concerned with the context dependence, or otherwise, of the *event*.

It has been found that where framing appears to be contested in the context of higher education for Aboriginal students, there has always been a tension between one frame (that of the Aboriginal student) which favours the contextualised use of language and the other frame (that of the higher education system) which favours the decontextualised use of language.

We have also observed a struggle between contextualisations occurring at the level of the literacy event. The literacy events we have been observing are contextualised within the higher education setting. Another way of putting this is to say that the higher education setting provides the frame within which they may be appropriately understood and negotiated. At the same time, the Aboriginal students may be observed to be engaged at times in attempted *re-contextualisation* of the events so that they may be negotiated in the same way as other events with which they are more familiar. This is, of course, another way of saying that they are engaged in a frame shift.

The relationship between the contextualisation of language and the contextualisation of literacy events may be summed up by saying that decontextualised language is contextually appropriate in the *higher education* frame, whereas contextualised language is contextually appropriate in the *indigenous* frame. There is, then, an ongoing negotiation of frames between student and staff member and the currency in which the negotiation takes place is language. A bid to introduce contextualised language into the literacy event is a bid to shift or modify the frame.

Fixed and flexible framing

In contexts such as have been observed in this project, the framing of the literacy event is often problematic, in that the Aboriginal students and the lecturers are actively (though not necessarily consciously) engaged in maintaining their own respective frames, which are, at least to some degree, mutually incompatible. The lecturers are employing frames which relate back to the higher education experience, and the students are employing frames which relate back to the experience of their community life. These contrasting frames entail the employment of different linguistic varieties, speech use features and content, which serve as *frame markers*.

Discourse (even written discourse) is, of course, essentially interactional and governed by sequencing rules which anticipate consistency with respect to the use of a particular register or variety, the observance of certain speech or writing conventions and the maintenance of topic. Generally, this is not a problem. One participant initiates communication in accordance with a given frame and the other participant (or participants) recognises the frame markers being employed, identifies the frame and follows suit, maintaining compatibility of variety, pragmatic features and topic.

However, when discourse has been initiated in accordance with a frame which is not shared, or not completely shared, by those who are expected to maintain it, problems arise. Will the receivers of the communication abandon their pre-existing frame for the one which has been summoned up by the frame markers employed by the first speaker, will they, by employing contrasting frame markers in their discourse, contest the choice of frame which the first speaker has made? And if they do this, how will the first speaker respond?

These questions have been found to be highly relevant to the interpretation of the discourse which characterises literacy events involving Aboriginal students in higher education. In order to account for the phenomena which we have observed, we have found it necessary to identify two approaches which may be taken to the framing of such events. *Fixed framing* is the framing activity which displays resistance to frame change or modification on the basis of evidence of contrasting frames being held by other participants; *flexible framing* is the framing activity which displays openness to frame change or modification on the basis of evidence of contrasting frames being held by other participants. Where communication takes place between parties not sharing the same frame, one side or the other will need to employ flexible framing if communication is to proceed harmoniously.

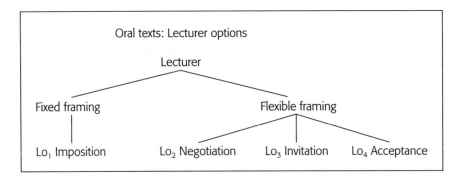

Oral texts: Lecturer options

Lecturer

Fixed framing   Flexible framing

Lo_1 Imposition Lo_2 Negotiation Lo_3 Invitation Lo_4 Acceptance

Figure 15.1   The lecturer's options in an oral-based literacy event

In fact, what we have observed is that in some events frames appear to converge and in other events fixed framing on the part of one side (for example the lecturer) occasions some degree of frame shift on the part of the other (such as the student). Often in the latter case, it seems that the frame shift reflects a desire on the Aboriginal students' part to take over the decontextualised language of the higher education system and *recontextualise* it, that is, give it content or discoursal features which tie it to a particular, known context.

It is possible, along the lines just described, to provide an account of the data showing the framing of literacy events by both lecturers and students, with respect to both oral and written events/texts. In order to demonstrate the ways in which fixed and flexible framing operate within the discourse we need to show the options separately for lecturer and for student (these being essentially a mirror image of one another) and also separately for oral and written texts. This has been attempted in Figures 15.1, 15.2 and 15.3, with Lo and So referring to oral language options which may be taken by lecturer and student respectively.

Figure 15.1 represents the lecturer's options in an oral-based literacy event, which could be, for example, a lecture, a tutorial, an interaction with a small group or a one-on-one counselling encounter. The diagram represents the options open to the lecturer at a given point in such an event, since we are concerned not with *frames* but with *framing*, which takes place on an ongoing basis and is constantly being monitored with respect to the feedback received. If the lecturer is employing fixed framing, there is no option open to the student but to conform to the frame that is imposed or else opt out of the event (for example by leaving the room). Fixed framing (see Example 1 below) occurs where the lecturer takes no account of the fact that the student may be framing the event differently but simply presumes the compliance of the student within the frame which has been set up. If the lecturer employs flexible framing, he or she shows openness to frame modification or shift on the basis of student feedback. This may be shown in three other ways, as set out below: by *negotiation*, where there is a readiness to discuss and possibly modify framing determinations, *invitation*, where the lecturer offers the option of determining the frame to the students, or *acceptance*, where the lecturer accedes to an initiative on the part of a student, or students, to modify or shift the frame. The abbreviations Lo, So and Sw refer, respectively, to lecturer oral, student oral and student written options within the literary events.

Example 1: Lecturer Fixed Framing (oral event): Lo₁ Imposition

Lecturer: *What I want you to do now is* move into pairs and talk about the first one and what can you learn from each other. You might not think it's signif- icant but these first ideas are going to direct your research . . . so just 5 minutes . . . and some noise, *I want to hear some ideas.* (ULS 22.4.96, p.1).

Example 2: Lecturer Flexible Framing (oral event): Lo₂ Negotiation

Lecturer: (referring to assignment preparation) So you know all about this.
Student: It's just putting it in those English words.
Lecturer: No, *just write as though you were talking to me, or writing a letter.* 'Dear T., I want to tell you about . . .' (AEW Block Release, pe, p.46)

Example 3: Lecturer Flexible Framing (oral event): Lo₃ Invitation

Lecturer: Okay, so see what you come up with and *if you want to take yourself off to a corner of the room you can.* (Orientation Course, Oct '95)

Example 4: Lecturer Flexible Framing (oral event): Lo₄ Acceptance

Student: It's about how to collect stuff.
Lecturer: *What sort of stuff do you collect?* (AUOC Statistics class, Oct. '95)

Figure 15.2 represents the options students commonly take in an oral-based literacy event. The anticipated option is for the student to engage in flexible framing and to conform to the pattern for the event which has been set up by the lecturer, if necessary by frame shift. The data we have gathered show that, at least in a passive way, most of the Aboriginal students do this (though discourse turns tend to be minimally filled). This framing activity we call *acceptance* (Example 5). On the other hand, the student may engage in fixed framing and oppose an alternative frame to that which may have been adopted by the lecturer. This may be done in an overt way, by some kind of metacommunicative exchange, in which case we call it *contestation*, or it may be done implicitly by performing acts which are appropriate to another frame, in which case we call it *counter-framing*. In each case, the acceptance

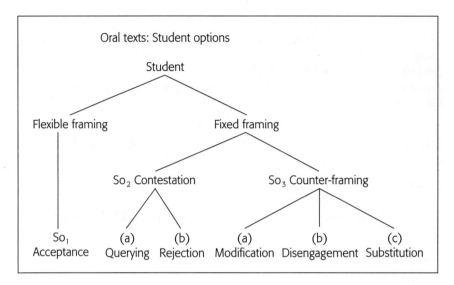

Figure 15.2   Student options in an oral-based literacy event.

or non-acceptance of the lecturer's frame is actualised in linguistic or prag-matic frame markers which are either supportive or unsupportive of decontextualised communication. Contestation of the lecturer's frame may take the form of *querying* its requirements (Example 6), or of *rejection* of them (Examples 7, 8, 9). Counter-framing may be expressed by acts which *modify* (Examples 10, 11), suspend, i.e. *disengagement* (Examples 12, 13, 14), or completely bypass the framing expectations set up by the lecturer (i.e. *substitution*, Examples 15, 16).

Example 5: *Student Flexible Framing (oral texts):* **So₁ Acceptance**

Lecturer: What you need to do is focus on the question . . . What you have to get out of the Castles article is the laws about immigration in Australia, N. *Student*: I understand what a summary is *but I don't understand what I have to do. I don't understand in text and end text referencing.* *Lecturer*: Don't worry for now, we'll talk more about that later . . . (Orientation Course bh 10.8.95).
(Here the student's acceptance of the lecturer's framing is shown in her seeking clarification of the requirements.)

Example 6: *Student Fixed Framing (oral texts):* **So₂ Contestation (a) Querying**

Lecturer: The answers are in the back. *Student*: (gasp)

Student: *So why do we do it?*
Lecturer: No, the question is, 'Why has the lecturer put the answers in the back?'
Student: *So we can find the answers?*
Lecturer: No, so you can check your understanding. (Orientation Course, Oct. 1995).

Example 7: Student Fixed Framing (oral texts): So_2 Contestation (b) Rejection

Lecturer: (reads a paragraph)
Student: *Now you're going quick again.*
Lecturer: What? Sorry (rereads) (Orientation Course, ULS 29.4.96, p.2)

Example 8: (second example of So_2b)

Lecturer: It says pedagogical. Do you know that word?
Student: *I don't like that word. I don't use it.* (AEW Block Release, February 1996).

Example 9: (third example of So_2b)

Lecturer: (refers to an assignment which required students to obtain library information)
Student: *I didn't do that. I couldn't find it.*
Lecturer: You couldn't find it? Why didn't you ask?
Student: *Nup. It's too shame.* (Orientation Course ULS 6.5.96).

Example 10: Student Fixed Framing (oral texts): So_3 Counter-Framing (a) Modification

Lecturer: What words would you be looking for N?
Student: *(no response)*
Lecturer: What words would you be looking for?
Student: *(no response)*
Lecturer: We went through this last week.
Student: *(no response)* (Orientation Course, ULS, 29.4.96, p.2)
(Here the student achieves a modification of the discourse pattern by not taking the offered turns).

Example 11: (second example of So_3a)

Student: (discussing assimilation policies) . . . they were concerned with the children learning European ways so the children were taken from their

parents. *I don't know how you would feel about having your children taken away.*
Lecturer: Yes, there was an obsession about colour, breeding out colour.
(AEW Block Release mg 30.5.95, p.9)

Example 12: *Student Fixed Framing (oral texts):*
So₃ Counter-Framing (b) Disengagement

Lecturer: (asks for a response from a student whom the other students have been joking about for her frequent responding)
Student: *I'll probably balls it all up now* . . . (Orientation Course, ULS, 29.4.96, p.2)

Example 13: *(second example of So₃b)*

Lecturer: There's no board in here.
Students: Over there.
Lecturer: Oh, I'm left handed. A white board is terrible to use.
Student 1: *We all have our problems.*
Student 2: *That's bad organisation. Check your chalk and duster every day.* (AEW Block Release jr 24.7.95)

Example 14: *(third example of So₃b)*

Student: For us it's a long time between courses. Like, I did Science first in 1991 and now I'm doing Science again years later. *It's a long time between drinks* (laughs) (AEW Block Release rb 24.7.95).

Example 15: *Student Fixed Framing (oral texts):*
So₃ Counter-Framing (c) Substitution

Lecturer: What do we mean by gender inclusive curriculum?
Student: *It's sort of having them involved like, you know, all of them are involved.* (AEW Block Release pr 31.5.95)

Example 16: *(second example of So₃c)*

Lecturer: I thought you were going to stay over there?
Student: *I thought I'll join this mob.* (AEW Block Release Feb '96).

Communication cannot proceed if both parties continue to employ only fixed framing. A symmetry is maintained as fixed and flexible framing options are taken up on alternate sides. Figure 15.3 attempts to convey this.

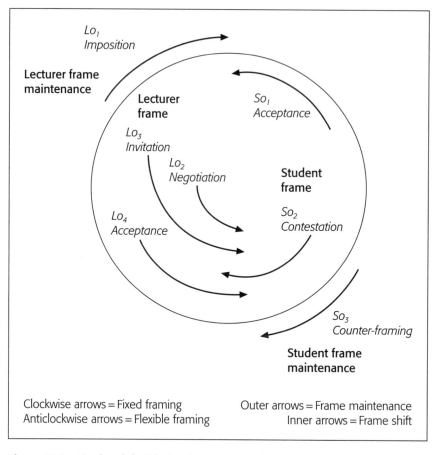

Figure 15.3   Fixed and flexible framing: patterns of reciprocation.

In written literacy events, the same principles appear to apply, although the data analysed up to this point are less extensive than in the case of oral literacy events. The options taken in the data so far analysed are summarised in Figure 15.4, with Sw referring to writing options which may be taken by the student.

The student, when writing, will either employ fixed framing, in which case he or she will carry over principles from contextualised communication domains into the domain of higher education, or else he or she will employ flexible framing and shift frames to follow the conventions of higher education. In the case where flexible framing is employed, the resultant text will demonstrate *acceptance* (see Examples 17, 18). Where fixed framing is employed the writing will demonstrate *counter-framing* and will either modify the higher education frame applying to the text concerned (i.e., *modification,*

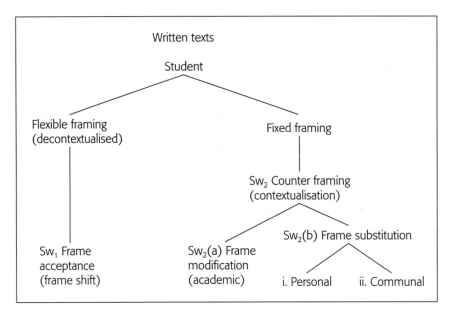

Figure 15.4 Student options in a written literacy event.

Example 19), or will substitute an indigenous frame for it (i.e., *substitution*, Example 20). We have observed two different cases of substitution, one employing a personal and one a communal frame.

Example 17: Student Flexible Framing (written texts): *Sw₁* **Frame Acceptance** *(Extract from an essay)*

The need to carry out European work and stay alive dispersed groups and left little time for Aboriginal culture and tradition which was later to decline. The rituals of ceremonies which played a major part in earlier years became infrequent and the singing and dancing skills gradually declined, although they were not entirely lost. Young people were accused of losing interest in their heritage. (Orientation Course student)

Example 18: *(second example of Sw₁ with non-Aboriginal topic)*

The Oral Language Development Curriculum has been designed to assist children to effectively use the 'language of school'. To be successful, children must be able to control the specialised 'language of school'. School language is no better or worse than other means of communication, its only difference is that children do not encounter this language in everyday interaction. For example 'All eyes to the front' or 'Are we all sitting up straight and holding our pencils correctly'. (AEW 3rd year student)

Example 19: *Student Fixed Framing (written texts):*
Sw₂ Counter-Framing (a) Frame Modification (academic)

(In the last sentence of this paragraph there is a frame shift bringing about personalisation and contextualisation.)

In Nyungar culture its important to allow brothers and sisters (extended family) be involved with the child, responsibility is given to other children to take care of babies from an early age. The strong relationships formed can help the baby to develop at a faster rate because the baby can imitate and learn from the other children. I think one of the reasons that Aboriginal babies walk sooner is because they are encouraged by older children to whom they have regular contact with (daily). (AEW 1st year student)

Example 20: *Student Fixed Framing (written texts):*
Sw₂ Counter-Framing (b) Frame Substitution

(The frame substitution in this essay fragment begins in the last sentence of the extract.)

After all the studying of the word culture, I still can't define the word culture. The dictionary says 'developed understanding of literature, art, music, etc; type of civilisation;

I'm still not sure of my own culture so I will just have to talk about my life so far. Let's see, I was born on the 12th of March 1977, in the small wheat-belt town of K... (Orientation Course student)

Example 21: *(second example of Sw₂b, this time in the form of a Kura, or yarn)*

We took off for home. Opportunity had come our way again. Charged up boys, meant easy pickins for us kids, we were always able to skab some dosh which would be pooled to buy fish, chips, scallops and Coke next day. (Second year student)

Example 22: *(third example of Sw₂b)*

After the telling, there are calls of 'bullshit' from all quarters until someone said 'Stuff this let's go to the [placename] for a charge.' Agreement was instantaneous and unanimous. (Second year student)

Example 22 illustrates how the student may switch between frames for aesthetic effect in the course of a piece of creative writing.

Implications

The investigation which has been reported on here supports the view that the conventions of literacy, as expressed in the literacy events of higher education, are culture-specific. They are, in particular, geared to a culture which is adapted to the use of second-level abstractions and which does not insist on immediate contextual relevance in communication. As such, these conventions attract resistance from students who come from culturally different backgrounds, especially where their cultures are heavily influenced by oral traditions.

It has been pointed out by Olson and Astington (1990: 708) that the evolution of a literate mode of discourse has taken place in Western culture over an extended period, perhaps a millennium. The encounter of Aboriginal society in Australia with literacy began only 200 years ago and until recently was not pervasive. It is understandable, then, that we can find ready evidence of Aboriginal students in the early years of higher education approaching literacy events in a distinctive way.

Through the application of frame theory, we have highlighted the fact that Aboriginal students and their lecturers may bring quite different expectations to the literacy events in which they jointly participate, and sometimes maintain the symmetry of the oral and written texts they create with difficulty.

The number of Aboriginal students in higher education in Australia is rapidly increasing (Ward and Pincus 1992) and there will be a growing need in future to come to terms with the communication problems which universities pose for them. For this to happen, further research will be needed to account for the distinctive way in which they frame literacy events and to explore ways in which universities may accommodate to them. Such research would potentially have application in many cross-cultural higher education settings.

Notes

1. The research reported on in this paper was carried out with the assistance of a Large Research Grant of the Australian Research Council. The overall project was under the coordination of Professor Ian Reid of Curtin University of Technology. Other collaborating research teams were headed up by Professor Christopher Candlin (Macquarie University) and Dr Susan Kaldor and Mr Michael Herriman (University of Western Australia). The views expressed in this paper are solely those of its author.
2. Many Aboriginal students of Edith Cowan University have kindly consented to have their interactions observed and their written submissions analysed. To them and their lecturers (all of whom will remain anonymous) the author expresses sincere thanks.
3. The writing of this paper has been materially assisted by Judith Rochecouste, who gathered all of the data on oral texts and some of that on written texts and who has been actively engaged in helping to refine the analysis.

16

Teaching and learning in Cantonese and English: Multilingual classroom practices and equity in education
Tara Goldstein

Sometimes for the problem-solving or the probability-stuff, you know, you know me, right? I think in Chinese ... In English, I often have to spend, like, fifteen minutes [to understand a problem], right? But in Chinese, I ... like ... six minutes or five minutes, I can, I can figure out [the problem]. It's really easier.

(ROSE,[1] A CANTONESE-SPEAKING HIGH SCHOOL STUDENT
TAKING A MATH CLASS IN METROPOLITAN TORONTO IN THE SUMMER OF 1994)

Educational planning for second language students cannot be single-minded or predetermined. It must be responsive to diversity among children and change within children. It avoids 'back to the basics' if basic means the same for all. And it incorporates and takes advantage of the social, intellectual and personal resources students have acquired in their homes and communities.

(FRED GENESEE (1994), SECOND LANGUAGE EDUCATION RESEARCHER
AND TEACHER EDUCATOR AT McGILL UNIVERSITY IN MONTREAL)

Students' first languages play an important role in the classroom, in the school program as a whole, and in communication with the home.

(*LANGUAGE FOR LEARNING POLICY*, BOARD OF EDUCATION FOR
THE CITY OF NORTH YORK (1995) IN METROPOLITAN TORONTO)

. . . [W]hen I give basic concepts, when I give instruction to the class, I always use English. When I talk to students I always use English unless they are stuck. Then in private I will explain it to them in the language they prefer.

(Edith Lam, a Cantonese, Mandarin and English-speaking high school teacher teaching a math class in Metropolitan Toronto in the summer of 1994)

Introduction

This is a paper about teachers and students working in languages other than English in classrooms and schools where English is the language of instruction. As can be seen from the remarks quoted above, there was increasing support in the 1990s for the use of a variety of languages in Canadian classrooms and schools that serve multilingual communities. This support is centred around the desire to better serve students who do not use the language of school instruction as a first language for academic and social success at school.

In his introduction to *Educating Second Language Children: The Whole Child, the Whole Curriculum, the Whole Community*,[2] Fred Genesee (1994) tells us that researchers and educators have been arguing for a long time that the academic success of children is influenced by their linguistic and social backgrounds. Importantly, as Genesee explains, there has been an evolution in thinking around the relationship between language use and success or lack of success at school. Early theories focused on the relationship between language skills and academic success. In explaining the disproportionate lack of academic success among children from minority linguistic and sociocultural groups, these early theories focused on the children's 'deficient' (majority) language skills (see, for example, Bernstein 1972). Language deficits were understood to be symptomatic of underlying cognitive deficiencies that hampered the children's achievement in school. Such cognitive deficiencies were explained as the result of deficiencies in the quality of the social relationships and intellectual climate in the children's homes.

Critics of this position have pointed out that the language skills of language minority children are not deficient but are as complex and rule-governed as those of children from middle-class majority groups (Labov 1969). Critics have also noted that the patterns of language use and the cognitive abilities characteristic of middle-class language-majority children and their families were being used to judge the competence of other children and their families, as if middle-class ways of using language were the only or best way and an absolute basis for assessing others.

Taking such critiques seriously, subsequent views of the issue characterised the backgrounds of children from minority groups as simply 'different' from those of children from the majority group. Such differences, it has been argued, pose academic problems for these children because the schools they attend are based on and reflect the backgrounds of the dominant social group. Although advocates of this position do not characterise the children as 'deficient', they do view them as ill-prepared for schooling that emphasises predominantly middle-class, majority ways of doing things. As Genesee (1994) points out, this perspective of 'difference' is problematic as it has all too often been used euphemistically by some educators and policymakers as a substitute for 'deficit'.

More recent research in a variety of social and cultural communities has revealed that children from language minority backgrounds have often had linguistic and cultural experiences during their pre-school years that have been enriched by the home culture, the dominant group culture in which they live, and the multiculturalism and multilingualism that can result from contact and interaction between minority and majority groups in a pluralistic society. In Genesee's words,

> . . . far from being impoverished, deficient, or merely different, the out-of-school experiences of second language children are immensely rich and complex. As a result, they acquire rich funds of knowledge that they bring to school.   (1994: 7)

Moving from the realm of educational theory and research to the realm of educational practice, Genesee goes on to say that (1994: 7)

> [i]t is foolish to advocate educational programs that seek to remediate or compensate for non-existent developmental deficiencies in language minority children, as the earlier deficit view prescribed. And it is wasteful to talk about minimising differences between the homes of language minority children and mainstream schools if this means ignoring the capabilities and knowledge that language minority children bring with them to school. To the contrary, the developmentally sound and 'pedagogically optimistic' approach (to use Diaz *et al.*'s term, 1986) is to encourage development of the home language and culture both in the homes of language minority children and, where possible, in their schools, and to use the linguistic, cognitive and sociocultural resources that language minority children bring to school as a basis for planning their formal education.

It is in the light of such thinking that cutting-edge school board language policies in Canada, such as the *Language for Learning Policy* from the North York Board of Education in Metropolitan Toronto, have been designed. Policy makers at the North York Board, who serve a linguistically diverse community,[3] consider all languages and varieties 'equally valid forms of thought and communication' and, as can be seen above, acknowledge that students' first languages have an important role to play in school. The Board's language policy, which was developed with the participation of classroom teachers, is intended to guide the everyday decisions and practices of administrators, teachers and students as they work together towards developing language and learning skills at school. Each school and subject department within the North York Board of Education is required to develop a 'statement of action' related to the *Language for Learning Policy*. This statement of action will become part of each school's 'school plan' and will be reviewed annually by school staff (Board of Education for the City of North York 1995).

Working towards equity in education

In addition to being seen as a 'cutting-edge' response to evolving North American thinking in the field of second language education, North York's language policy can also be seen as part of a larger effort to ensure that principles of 'equity'[4] are observed in North York schools, which, as mentioned earlier, are becoming increasingly racially, culturally and linguistically diverse. This effort has been facilitated by initiatives put forward by the provincial Ontario government who (1) in 1992 amended the province's Education Act[5] to require all school boards in Ontario to 'develop and implement antiracism and ethnocultural equity[6] policies' and (2) in 1993 produced its own policy document entitled *Antiracism and Ethnocultural Equity in School Boards* to provide guidelines for school boards around policy development and implementation plans (Ontario Ministry of Education and Training 1993).

Policies and implementation plans, to have been put in place by October 1995, address ten major areas: (1) board policies, guidelines, and practices; (2) leadership; (3) school–community partnership; (4) curriculum; (5) student languages; (6) student evaluation, assessment, and placement; (7) guidance and counselling; (8) racial and ethnocultural harassment; (9) employment practices; and (10) staff development. Of particular interest to this paper is what the Ministry's expectations are within the area of 'student languages'. The following quotation from the 1993 Antiracism and Ethnocultural Equity policy provides us with an idea of how the Ministry understands both the role language plays in learning and the roles different kinds of language practices play in setting up second language children for success.

> Language is a tool for learning, and access to education depends on language competence. Language proficiency underlies success in most, if not all, curriculum areas. All students, therefore — including those with a first

language other than English or French — must be enabled to acquire competence in one or both of Canada's official languages [English and French] ...

... Teachers in all curriculum areas should recognise the importance of the language the student already speaks. Competence in the first language provides students with the foundation for developing proficiency in additional languages, and maintenance of the first language supports the acquisition of other languages.

The first language also serves as a basis for emotional development and provides a vital link with students' ancestral heritage. Multilingualism enhances students' intellectual functioning and the ability to communicate, as well as their career opportunities ....

(Ontario Ministry of Education and Training 1993: 14)

The links between the Ontario Ministry's guidelines for ensuring equity in education and the North York Board of Education's *Language for Learning Policy* are clear. Here are the 'core assumptions' about language for learning that underpin the policy:

- Language, culture and identity are closely linked. A program that recognises, respects, and values students' racial, cultural, and linguistic backgrounds, as well as the varieties of language, helps them to develop a positive sense of self and motivates them to learn. All students need opportunities to think critically about the social values and status assigned to different languages by various groups in our society and to explore issues of bias and stereotyping related to language and culture.
- First language-literacy is important for second-language learning. It helps students to grasp key concepts more easily and influences general academic achievement.
- For many children, the teacher is the most important model of language. All teachers in culturally diverse settings are cultural and linguistic informants, mediators, explainers, and instructors.
- All languages and varieties of languages are equally valid forms of thought and communication. Canadian Standard English is the language of instruction in North York.
- Students' first languages play an important role in the classroom, in the school program as a whole, and in communication with the home (Board of Education for the City of North York 1995).

In order to implement polices like the North York Board's *Language for Learning Policy* into everyday school practices, principals, department heads and teachers need to make decisions about what kind of language practices they want to promote in their schools. In order to make these decisions, they need to ask a number of questions, for example:

(1) What does it mean to 'incorporate and take advantage of the social, intellectual and personal resources students have acquired in their homes and communities' (Genesee 1994) so that schools can set up second language students for success and work towards meeting equity goals?

(2) What does it mean to acknowledge that 'students' first languages play an important role in the classroom' in schools where 'Canadian Standard English is the language of instruction'? (Board of Education for the City of North York 1995).

(3) Does it mean that students should be encouraged to use a variety of languages to complete classroom learning activities?

(4) Does it mean that teachers who are able to use languages other than English should be encouraged to do so in their classrooms?

(5) If so, when? Under what circumstances?

(6) What issues arise when teachers and students create multilingual classrooms in schools where English is the official language of instruction?

(7) Who is accommodated and who benefits when teachers and students use languages other than English in their classrooms? Who isn't accommodated and who doesn't benefit?

(8) How is the goal of working towards equity in education supported when teachers and students create a multilingual classroom? How might the multilingual classroom create inequities?

These are the questions that are at the heart of this paper and I would like to address them by discussing an ethnographic study that looked at how a group of high school students in Toronto used both Cantonese and English to set themselves up for success in their math class and how their teacher used a set of multilingual teaching practices to accommodate the group's linguistic strategy for learning.

Teaching and learning in Cantonese and English

In the summer of 1994, research assistant Veronica Hsueh and I spent about five weeks observing, recording and talking to students in Edith Lam's math class to find out how native Cantonese-speaking high school students chose to communicate with each other in a classroom where the language of instruction was English. The eleven Cantonese-speaking students from Hong Kong (nine male and two female students) who were enrolled in Mrs Lam's summer math-class had been living in Canada for varying lengths of time and had varying proficiency in the use of Cantonese and English. They were all bilingual to some extent.

Two sets of language practices seemed to be in use among the Cantonese speakers. One — larger — group of students (nine of the eleven) spoke Cantonese among themselves and reserved the use of English for relationships with non-Chinese students and those (often second-generation) Chinese students who did not speak Cantonese at all or who did not speak it well. The other — smaller — group of students (two of the eleven) used English not only with those who did not speak Cantonese (at all or well), but also among themselves.

In sociolinguistic terms, it can be said that the uses of Cantonese and English in Mrs Lam's classroom created a 'language boundary' (see Heller 1988a, b) that split the Cantonese-speaking student body into two groups. The first group consisted of students who *maintained* the boundary between membership in their own linguistic community and membership in the wider school community by speaking Cantonese among themselves and reserving the use of English for relationships with outsiders (which included Chinese students who did not speak Cantonese at all or well). Students in the second group *levelled* the boundary by using English not only with outsiders, but among themselves as well. In this paper I will focus on the language practices of the first — larger — group of students who chose to use Cantonese among themselves.

Using Cantonese to access friendship and assistance

The five weeks we spent observing and talking to Mrs Lam and her students revealed that one of the reasons students used Cantonese among themselves had to do with gaining access to friendship and assistance that was needed to achieve the high marks that would play a role in their getting admitted to college or university. The math course the students were taking was an 'OAC' course, meaning that students who passed the course would receive an Ontario Academic Credit for completing it successfully. The completion of six OAC credits — and high marks in OAC courses — is required to gain admission to post-secondary educational institutions.

Having 'friends' in the classroom (whether they were intimate companions with whom students socialised outside the classroom or acquaintances/ classmates with whom students only socialised inside the classroom) was related to the goal of getting a high or passing mark in several ways.

First of all, 'friends' explained things that students didn't understand, for example, an explanation the teacher had given of a math concept or the reason an answer to a math problem was not correct.

A second reason why 'friends' were important to students' academic success had to do with the way 'friends' encouraged each other to contest (what they perceived to be) an unfair or incorrect mark the teacher had given them on an assignment quiz or test. This is illustrated in Exchange A. In this exchange, Lawrence was trying to figure out why Mrs Lam had taken three marks off an answer he had given to one of the problems on a quiz. He didn't think his answer was completely wrong and wanted to ask Mrs Lam to reconsider the mark she had given him. Eddy and Cindy were helping Lawrence figure out why his answer was not completely wrong when Cindy realised that Eddy had also correctly answered one of the questions that had been evaluated as partly incorrect. In this exchange, each Cantonese speaker's original Cantonese utterances have been translated into English and appear in *italics* to indicate that they were actually uttered in Cantonese. Any additional information needed to make the meaning of the speaker's words clear to the reader appears in brackets ([ ]) within or right after the translated or English utterance. Words that appear in **boldface** are words that were originally uttered in English. As can be seen by reading the exchange, the only English words uttered by the Cantonese-speaking students are words which were associated with the math problems the students were talking about and words which are associated with the English name of the math teachers teaching summer school.

Exchange A

Lawrence: *I really don't understand it. I only have two parts wrong. How could someone take away three marks? I didn't think too lowly of her* [And I thought so highly of her].

Eddy: *She thinks lowly of you.*

Lawrence: *I don't know.*

Cindy: *How come you only have half a mark for your* **bonus question**?

Lawrence: *Yeah, that's what I don't understand. It's not that I don't know* [the right way to do the problem]. *Where did I lose nine marks? There are only two parts here, that is the* **A** *and* **B relationship** *one.* **A** *and* **C** *are wrong, no.* **A** *and* **B** *are wrong, but* **C** *is correct.*

Cindy: (looking at Eddy's answer which was also evaluated as being partly incorrect) *Heh, heh, heh. Your last question should be right.*

Eddy: *Me?* [Mine?]

Cindy: *You.* [Yours.]

Eddy: *I told her. She said she's not going to talk it over with me. I don't know how to do it* [how to explain to her why my answer is partly right and why she should change the way she marked the answer] *Forget it.*

Lawrence: *Never mind* (laughs).

Eddy: *Yesterday, I asked the* **afternoon Finite** [math]*teacher. He said I should have some marks, that I shouldn't have lost a mark.*

Lawrence: *Did you find it?* [Did you find a way to explain to Mrs Lam why your answer is partly right?]. *Even you can't find it?* [Even you can't find a way to explain why your answer is partly right?] *I really don't know what to do.*

Negotiating a mark in a second language was not always an easy task for the Cantonese-speaking students in Mrs Lam's class. As will be mentioned later on in this paper, Mrs Lam insisted that those students who wanted her to change a mark she had given them on a test or assignment had to submit a written statement in English as to why they should receive more marks. This insistence on the use of English — intended to provide students with opportunities to practise their negotiating skills in English so that they could negotiate marks with monolingual English-speaking teachers — meant that students needed to be able to articulate exactly why their answers were (partly) right and why they should receive more marks for their responses. Making a case for more marks was easier when your 'friends' also thought that you deserved more marks (*Your last question should be right*) and when your 'friends' could help you articulate why you deserved more marks (*Did you find it?* [Did you find a way to explain to Mrs Lam why your answer is partly right?]. *Even you can't find it?* [Even you can't find a way to explain why your answer is partly right?] *I really don't know what to do.*)

The third way having 'friends' was important to succeeding academically in Mrs Lam's math class had to do with the way 'friends' advocated for each other in the classroom. Our fieldnotes show that students helped each other gain access to the teacher's attention so students could ask the teacher to re-explain a math concept, find out why an answer to a math problem was not correct, or contest a mark the teacher had given them on an assignment, quiz or test.

Friendship and talk in Mrs Lam's classroom

Initiating friendship (whether it was intimate friendship or collegiality) and developing or nurturing friendship was related to the way people talked to each other in the classroom. Once a friendship had been established, the students were able to ask each other for help and assistance in the ways described above. Talk that was associated with making 'friends' was governed by certain sociolinguistic rules. It took place in different languages that varied according to who was involved in the interaction. Talk at the two tables[7] dominated by Cantonese speakers almost always occurred in Cantonese. The students at these tables exclusively used Cantonese to gain access to friendship and assistance. At one of the tables, there were four Cantonese/ESL speakers and one Korean/ESL speaker. At the other table, there were four Cantonese/ESL speakers and one Hebrew/ESL speaker. At both these tables, the Cantonese-speaking students worked together to solve math problems, while the non-Cantonese-speaking students almost always worked alone. When the non-Cantonese-speaking students needed assistance, they usually asked Mrs Lam. Occasionally, they worked with one of their non-Cantonese-speaking table-mates in English.

In sociolinguistic terms, the use of Cantonese at these two tables functioned as a symbol of solidarity and friendship. Cantonese was (often uncon-
sciously) associated with the rights, obligations, and expectations 'friends'
had of each other. As mentioned earlier, 'friends' explained difficult concepts
to each other, helped each other work out assigned classroom tasks, encouraged each other to contest a mark on an assignment, quiz or test they
perceived to be unfair, and helped each other gain the teacher's attention.

Benefits associated with Cantonese and costs associated with English

As a language associated with achieving both social success (having 'friends')
and academic success (getting high marks),[8] Cantonese was associated with
social and academic benefits for the majority of the Cantonese-speaking
students in the math classroom. These were benefits that were not associated
with the use of English. In fact, the use of English was risky as it could
jeopardise the access to friendship and assistance that was so important to
academic and social success in school.

Cantonese-speaking students reported that fellow Cantonese-speaking
students would consider them 'rude' if they spoke to them in English and
that they 'shouldn't talk in English', they 'should talk in Cantonese'. When
asked why it was rude to speak in English, Rose told us that some people
think that you're trying to be 'special' if you speak English or that you like
to 'show off your English abilities.' Max confirmed this when he told us that
a Cantonese speaker who uses English with another Cantonese speaker is 'a
show-off'.

The association of using English with 'showing off' is an important one.
To understand the reasons behind this association we need to look at English
as the *language of dominance, the language of power* (Grillo 1989) in the school
system: students get evaluated and pass or fail courses by demonstrating
what they have learned in English. Cantonese-speaking students who are
first-generation immigrants to Canada speak English with varying levels of
proficiency. This means they have varying levels of power at school. When
Cantonese-speaking students use English with fellow Cantonese-speaking
students they are demonstrating the power they have and are therefore
showing off their linguistic achievement in the same way people show off
their material or educational achievements (which are also symbols of power).
The use of English with other Cantonese-speaking students in the classroom,
then, is associated with social and academic risks for many of the Cantonese
speakers. Students who depend on 'friends' for assistance with academic
activities cannot risk being considered rude or a show-off. The use of English
may cost them their friendship with their Cantonese-speaking friends. While
the use of Cantonese is a linguistic strategy that is associated with academic

and social resources at school, the use of English is a linguistic strategy that is associated with costs.

In trying to understand the reasons why Mrs Lam's students might associate the use of English with showing off, it is also interesting to consider the status and meanings given to English in Hong Kong, the country from which the students emigrated. In an article that focuses on English language teaching in Hong Kong schools, Angel Lin (1996) explains that English is currently valued by the Hong Kong elite not only as a reflection of British colonial power, but as a means of maintaining Hong Kong's privileged position in world markets, and as a means of access for individuals to economic and educational resources in English-speaking countries as well. These values associated with English also help explain why speaking English may be associated with power and 'showing off' in Mrs Lam's classroom.

It is important to note that the students in Mrs Lam's class were able to use their linguistic resource of Cantonese to enhance their understanding and learning of math because of their teacher's support of languages other than English in her classroom. This support is very much tied to Mrs Lam's vision of what it means to work as a teacher in a multilingual, multicultural, multiracial community. In a presentation we gave together at the 1995 Ontario TESL (Teaching English as a Second Language) Conference, Mrs Lam told our audience that she saw the encouragement of multilingualism in group work as a way to encourage positive contribution from ESL students; to enhance their social skills; and to promote mutual respect and self-worth that, in turn, could enhance 'responsible participation' and 'racial harmony' in the multilingual classroom (Goldstein Hsueh and Lam 1995). As will be discussed in greater detail below, Mrs Lam's vision of multilingualism as a means of encouraging classroom participation and racial harmony at school is not unproblematic. While her support of the use of languages other than English did, indeed, encourage the participation of the Cantonese (and Mandarin) speaking students in her class, it is important to ask the question whether particular kinds of multilingual classroom practices encourage the participation of *all* students in the classroom or only some of the students in the classroom. As well, Mrs Lam's own use of Cantonese and Mandarin was perceived by a student who didn't speak Cantonese or Mandarin as a means for advantaging Chinese students over non-Chinese students in the classroom. The perception that Chinese students have such an advantage when the teacher uses their languages in the classroom can work against the development of racial harmony.

Using Cantonese to teach

As just mentioned, Mrs Lam not only encouraged her students to use languages other than English in her classroom, she herself sometimes used Cantonese and Mandarin when she taught. These multilingual teaching practices accommodated the Cantonese and Mandarin speaking students' linguistic and cultural learning practices and added to the likelihood of the students' succeeding. Importantly, Mrs Lam's use of different languages in the classroom was governed by rules associated with the various roles she played as a teacher.

It seemed that Mrs Lam played three social roles in her role as teacher in the math class. The first role was that of 'teacher'. The second was that of 'helper'; the third was that of 'counsellor'. In her role as teacher, Mrs Lam established her authority as the leader of the class. In this role, she took attendance, sent students who were late to class to the office to get a late slip, formally presented the math concepts to be studied that day, assigned classroom and homework tasks, wrote quizzes and tests, evaluated students' assignments, quizzes and tests, and dealt with students' questioning or contesting of the mark she had given on them. Students who wanted Mrs Lam to reconsider a mark she had assigned to their work had to write her a note in English explaining why they thought they had earned a higher mark. In this role of teacher, Mrs Lam exclusively used English to all the students in her class, regardless of whether they were Cantonese and Mandarin speakers or not.

In her role as helper, Mrs Lam visited from one student table to another during 'classroom practice' activities and assisted individual students with problems they were having with the tasks she had assigned them. In this role, Mrs Lam used English with non-Cantonese and Mandarin speakers, but would use Cantonese and Mandarin with those students who used these languages among themselves 'if they are stuck' (that is, having difficulty completing a task).

Finally, in her role of counsellor, Mrs Lam provided academic and personal counselling to those students who she felt needed support. The type of counselling she provided to students during the five weeks we visited her classroom included academic advice about working harder in school (to a student who she felt was not working to his full potential and achieving the high marks he was capable of achieving) and career advice about going to university (to a student who was trying to make a decision about when and where to go to university). Mrs Lam also told us that she was speaking regularly to a student who was working through family issues at home. In this role of counsellor, Mrs Lam used English with non-Cantonese or non-Mandarin speakers, but used Cantonese with Cantonese speakers and Mandarin with Mandarin speakers.

Mrs Lam's use of Cantonese and Mandarin in her roles as helper and counsellor can also be seen as a symbol of solidarity and collegiality. As a Cantonese and Mandarin speaker herself, she is also bound by sociolinguistic obligations to use Cantonese and Mandarin when she works with Cantonese and Mandarin-speaking students who are 'stuck' on a math problem or need support with an academic, career or family issue. This use of Cantonese and Mandarin in the roles of helper and counsellor contrasts with Mrs Lam's use of English in the role of teacher, which is symbolic of her authority as the class leader and evaluator of students' work.

Benefits and tensions in the multilingual classroom

Unsurprisingly, the multilingual teaching and learning practices that characterise Mrs Lam's classroom were considered to be very helpful to the Cantonese (and Mandarin) speaking students in the class. Rose, who spoke Cantonese as a first language and had been a student in Toronto for four years, told us the fact that Mrs Lam used Cantonese in the class made 'a big difference' to her as a student since it was much easier for her to work out a math problem in Cantonese than it was to work it out in English (see Rose's quote at the beginning of this paper). Max, who also spoke Cantonese as a first language, said the fact Mrs Lam used Cantonese was 'great for us because sometimes [it's] hard to communicate, like using English to, like, to express our ideas or opinions. And if she, like, understands Cantonese, it's good for us.'

However, the benefits Rose and Max talk about are not gained without a concern for the 'Canadian students' who do not speak Cantonese and who may feel alienated or angered by the use of languages other than English in the classroom. Max suggested that even though Mrs Lam is good at Mandarin, Cantonese *and* English, 'maybe the Canadian students don't feel very well, sometimes . . . Canadians are multicultural and they know that, but they don't prefer that situation'. Max also told us that this concern had had an influence over his own language practices with Mrs Lam. Whenever there were English-speaking students within hearing distance, he accommodated *their* linguistic practices by speaking to Mrs Lam in English.

As mentioned earlier, Max's concern that the use of Cantonese and Mandarin in the classroom might alienate or anger non-speakers of those languages was substantiated in our interview with another student in the class who was not Chinese and did not speak Cantonese or Mandarin. Theresa, a white student who was born outside Canada and had learned English as a second language and spoke it with native-like proficiency, told us that she got frustrated when she asked the teacher a question about a math problem or a math concept and the teacher didn't understand her and wasn't able to explain the problem or concept clearly. When she heard Mrs Lam helping students in Cantonese or Mandarin she said that she felt as though they had 'more advantage' than she did.

Underlying this perception of the Cantonese and Mandarin speakers 'having more advantage' was the assumption that the reason that the teacher understood the students' questions was because the questions were asked in the teacher's first and second languages (rather than English which is the teacher's third language). Similarly, the reason that the teacher's explanations were clearer when she explained problems to the Chinese students was because she was able to use her first and second languages.

What Theresa had not examined here was the possibility that her difficulty with understanding the teacher and having the teacher understand her had to do with issues around her own learning. Earlier in our interview, Theresa had spoken candidly about the difficulty she was having focusing on her academic work and completing assignments outside of class time. However, what also needs to be recognised is that Theresa *perceived* herself to be less advantaged than the Cantonese and Mandarin speakers in the classroom. While only one out of the ten non-Cantonese and Mandarin speaking students in the math classroom told us that she felt disadvantaged when the teacher provided assistance in Cantonese and Mandarin to some of the Chinese students, both Mrs Lam and her Cantonese-speaking students know it is important to address the issue of feeling linguistically advantaged or disadvantaged in the multilingual classroom. Max's strategy for managing interethnic/ interracial tensions that arise as a result of multilingualism in a classroom where the official language of instruction is English, was to accommodate the English-speaking students by speaking English to Mrs Lam whenever they are within hearing distance. Mrs Lam's strategy was to use English in the role of teacher and reserve the use of Cantonese and Mandarin for when her students were in need of remedial or extra help or when her students sought her out for counselling on academic and personal issues. Neither of these linguistic strategies, however, prevented Theresa from feeling disadvantaged in the math classroom.

At this point of the discussion, I would like to return to the question of what it means to incorporate the linguistic resources students have acquired in their homes and communities into our secondary classrooms and schools. We have seen that it means acknowledging that the use of languages other than the official language of instruction can create interethnic/interracial tensions in the classroom. This means that teachers like Mrs Lam who acknowledge the important role that students' first languages play in their classrooms and who can use these languages to support their students' learning need to think through how they are going to deal with these tensions.

One way of beginning to deal with issues of interethnic/interracial tensions in the multilingual classroom is by talking about them in a direct, forthright manner. Teachers who have linguistic resources that — when used — can benefit individual students in their classrooms, might wish to talk to their students at the beginning of the year and initiate a discussion concerning language practices in the classroom. Language practices, like other classroom practices (for example rules for leaving the classroom, evaluation practices in the classroom), can be discussed and negotiated with students.

That being said, it is important to point out that negotiation around classroom language practices occurs in a larger educational, political and economic context. My colleague Judy Hunter (1995) tells me that she has overheard conversations among anglophone students that suggest that there is strong resentment of Cantonese-speaking students because of (1) the favourable stereotypes teachers seem to have of them (see Maclear 1994 and Nakanishi and Nishida 1996 for a discussion of how Asian students are stereotyped as the 'model minority'); (2) their membership in privileged economic classes; and (3) their perceived social exclusiveness. Teachers who want to initiate a discussion/negotiation of multilingual classroom practices need to take such resentment into account and understand that multi-lingualism is not unproblematically beneficial in our economically stratified multilingual society.

Not having undertaken such a discussion/negotiation in my own class-room, I am uncertain about how easy or how difficult it is to talk about language practices in the multilingual classroom. I am also uncertain as to how successful such discussions/negotiations are in setting up classrooms in which *all* students feel that they are being set up for success. Recently, we have begun to hear a lot about the benefits of 'action research' and 'teacher research' projects in the field of language education (see for example, Cochran-Smith and Lytle 1993; Crookes 1993; Richards and Lockhart 1994). It seems that action and teacher research projects around questions of negotiating language practices in multilingual classrooms are very much needed and would provide educators with some grounded data on how to work more effectively with second language high school students.

Notes

1. The names of the students in this study have been changed to maintain their anonymity.
2. The 'second language children' described in this volume are children who have learned a language or languages other than English during their pre-school years, who are living in predominantly English-speaking commun-ities or countries and who are being educated primarily through English. In this paper I will use the phrases 'second language children' and 'second language students' to talk about children and students who have learned and used a language or languages other than English not only during their pre-school years, but during their school years as well when they resided in countries and/or attended schools where English was not the language of instruction.
3. To get an idea of how linguistically diverse the community is (and how challenging it is for North York teachers to assist students in developing language and learning skills), consider the following profile of North York students which is included in the 1995 *Language for Learning Policy* document:

- 49% are female; 51% male
- 58% were born in Canada
- 22% have a mother and/or father born in Canada
- for Grades 9 to OAC, students born outside of Canada outnumber those born here by 58% to 42%
- 6% of students have arrived in Canada from a non-English-speaking country or the English-speaking Caribbean within the last year
- in 52% of students' homes, English is the primary language
- 41% of kindergarten students have a language other than English as their primary language.

4. See note 7 for an explanation of what is meant by 'equity'.
5. Education Act, R. S. O. 1990, Chapter E.2, section 8, subsection 1, paragraph 29.1 (July 1992 edition).
6. According to the Ontario Government's 1993 *Policy on Antiracism and Ethnocultural Equity in School Boards* (Ontario Ministry of Education and Training 1993), 'antiracism and ethnocultural equity' refers to equitable treatment of members of all racial and ethnocultural groups and the elimination of institutional and individual barriers to equity. 'Race' is a social category into which societies have divided people according to such characteristics as skin colour, shape of eyes, texture of hair, and facial features. 'Ethnocultural' refers to a person's cultural heritage in the broadest sense. It can include national affiliation, language and religious background. There may also be ethnocultural groups within racial groups.
7. Students in Mrs Lam's classroom sat at tables in groups of five, six, seven and eight.
8. In talking over this particular point with my colleague Judy Hunter, Hunter commented on the potential problems that may be associated with students 'working for grades' instead of 'working for learning'. Students working exclusively for high grades to get into university may value getting a high mark on an assignment or test over learning the material covered in the assignment or test. The valuing of high marks over learning may clash with the values of those teachers who believe that understanding a set of concepts and practice in problem-solving are more important than getting a high score on an assignment or test. It may also lead to divisiveness among students who hold different values around learning and/or who compete with each other for high grades. Such conflicts, which could impact on the academic success students experience in school as well as the goal of working towards racial harmony that is discussed later in this article, did not occur in Mrs Lam's classroom. However, they are potential conflicts that I need to ask questions about as I undertake further study of Chinese students' language practices in Canadian schools.

Coda

Intercultural communication and ethnography: Why? and why not?
Ron Scollon

Knowledge through discourse

My introduction to anthropological linguistics and along with it to ethnography came just a little over 40 years ago in the form of a lecture by Kenneth Pike. As a teenager I was enthralled by the idea that by a process of systematic sampling, careful inference, and then testing through use, an adult could learn a language in a speech community of strangers using no intermediate translating language. Pike's field methods for what was once called 'reducing a language to writing' were what got me into linguistics in the first place and the excitement of discovery against imposing discursive odds is what keeps me doing my work these many years later. What I will talk about in this paper are the broader relations between the discourses of linguistic and ethnographic research work on the one hand and the institutional placement of this work on the other. What I am particularly interested in doing is sketching out a fairly simple thesis based on a rough survey of my own research: you can't rock a boat that isn't already pretty shaky.

When I finally got around to a bit of fieldwork of my own, twenty years had passed and I had narrowed the scope of my interest from whole languages of disappearing Amazonian tribes to the appearing language of a one-year-old child in the altogether more hospitable fieldwork environment of a relative's home in Hawaii. My doctoral dissertation was entitled 'One Child's Language from One to Two: The Origins of Construction'. I thought when I began the project that I was studying phonology. It was only later that I realised the contribution I had to make was in the area of discourse.

The phonological problem is determining when a child acquires full phonological forms of words, English words in this case. When a child says ʃi ʃð ʃi ʃðʃ ʃuʔ what has the child said? If the child is holding up a shoe, one might assume the word is 'shoe'. But which of the utterances is 'shoe', all or just the final instance? If this sequence is preceded by [mam mama mam mama] should this be understood as 'mama, mama, mama, mama, shoe, shoe, shoe, shoe, shoe'? or perhaps just as 'mama', 'shoe'? While there are many issues at stake here which have been better treated elsewhere, the main point I was able to make in that research was that up to this point in the history of studies of child language (at that time — the 70s — often called psycholinguistics) this child would be scored as having said two independent words, 'mama' and 'shoe'. The rest was normally treated as non-utterance and discounted.

Two things were being discounted. One of them was that the child was making a considerable effort to get these words said, but more importantly I think, in this same effort the child was trying not just to say words for the benefit of the phonological analyst, but to put together a bit of discourse. She was saying to somebody, 'This is mama's shoe!' and was fully expecting a response to this bit of interesting news.

This discovery of mine about her mama's shoe was that even before there are any utterances which could be considered classical 'two-word' syntactic constructions, there are rather significant discursive utterances which build upon social interactions between the child and others. This led me to argue that by opening up the analytical lens to include all of these utterances through more ethnographic data collection, in this case continuous tape recording and photography, one could then see that, in fact, there was good evidence that discourse pre-dates syntax in the development of human language.

This 'discovery' of mine came from my methodology, which was ethnographic to a considerable extent, certainly exceptionally ethnographic for what was thought to be a study of phonology. I had tape-recorded everything on a SONY TC110A, the first of the cassette recorders. I had simply transcribed everything said by everyone caught within the microphone's range as a way of seeing where these minuscule utterances of a one-year-old child fit into the broader picture. Each page of transcription on the back of line-printer computer sheets had a column for each speaker and one for the context. Thus the child's attempts at 'mama's shoe' came out as a vertical sequence of separate utterances. For convenience I called them 'vertical constructions'; that is, they were one-word utterances which came in a sequence which together produced a meaningful discourse. I am pleased to see that a number of recent textbooks on child language development now use the term 'vertical construction' without the inconvenience of citing my research. This is likely to be my only contribution to the archives of the discourse of language acquisition.

This was all very exciting to me. As soon as I got my dissertation past the committee, I set about seeking a publisher. One was found and all went well until the problem of the title of the book came up. I wanted to call the book *The Acquisition of Discourse* as that's what I thought it was about. I felt that the main point I had demonstrated was that the acquisition of discourse precedes, not follows, the acquisition of words and sentences, and that it was discourse in the fully socially-interactive sense of the word that I meant —

infants talking to others — which lay at the foundation of language development. The publisher didn't like *The Acquisition of Discourse*. 'Discourse' was an obscure word, nobody knew what it meant, and worse, it wasn't a real field of study like phonology, syntax, or language development. I needed something zippier. Ultimately we settled upon *Conversations with A One Year Old: A Case Study of the Developmental Foundation of Syntax* (Scollon 1976). Syntax was the big word in America six years after Chomsky's *Aspects of a Theory of Syntax* and it had to be somewhere in the title. I put it last.

Thus with my first book I learned a significant lesson: when the publisher wants to change your title, watch out. The first review which came out considered the book possibly a useful contribution except for one thing, the title. The reviewer said the book should have been called *The Acquisition of Discourse*.

You will be certainly tired by now of 'What I did on my dissertation' and I promise to get away from the subject quickly. I have used this to introduce my main point. My dissertation in book form was relatively successful, 'vertical construction' has been adopted by some as a commonsensical trade term within the field, and the ethnographic procedures I used in my fieldwork have become common. Can I be considered a founder of contemporary studies of children's language? Hardly. When the book was released I was already off in the far north of Canada doing fieldwork on the personal history narratives of elderly Chipewyan Indians. Whatever little success my dissertation work enjoyed depended on a broader discourse of which I was at the time entirely ignorant. My work was helpful to others who were trying to carry out a disciplinary revolution.

At almost the same time M. A. K. Halliday, for example, was starting to publish his studies of Nigel, arguing that it was the functional use of language which preceded the development of more elaborate linguistic systems. Elinor Keenan (now Ochs) was studying the development of her twin boys and as a student of Dell Hymes was taking a broad *ethnography of communication* perspective in that study. At Berkeley a group including John Gumperz, Dan Slobin, and Susan Ervin-Tripp were developing the field guide for the ethnographic study of language acquisition. In other words, throughout North America and to some extent within the scope of UK linguistics in the work of Halliday there was a broad movement toward looking closely and ethnographically at how humans become users of language.

This wave of studies had various motives. In the US, certainly the two most compelling motives were on the one hand to wrest the study of language learning away from the psychologists and on the other to try to smarten up the Chomskian anti-learning concept of linguistic structures. The famous footnote in *Sound Patterns of English* somewhere around Chapter Eight that says all of this theory depends upon the assumption of the *instant acquisition of language* was enough to send more than me back to the drawing boards. At least I hadn't learned any of my languages instantly and I doubted that many others did. As to the interest in stealing a bit of the psychologists' turf, it's worth noting that the foundational generation of ethnographic researchers into child language included many students of the psychologist Roger Brown's project at Harvard — Courtney Cazden, Dan Slobin, David McNeill, Ursula Bellugi (Klima), Jean Berko (Gleason) were all part of that first seminar in which Brown hoped to apply Chomskian linguistics to the study of the acquisition of language.

While I would love to think that my work shook the linguistic study of language acquisition to its foundations, it was only my ignorance of what others elsewhere were doing at the time that led me to believe that my own work was so original. I had picked it up in the air somewhere, caught the discursive microbe, added two words of my own, 'vertical construction', and gone on my way.

A contrasting case: Fort Chipewyan, Alberta (Canada)

Those who know Kenneth Pike or his work will know that he has laboured his many years as a missionary, first for the Wycliffe Bible Translators and then later for what was called the Summer Institute of Linguistics. He was also a Professor of English and a Professor of Linguistics. At one time he was the only person to hold two separate professorships in two different departments at the highly respected University of Michigan. I have not been a missionary, nor have the linguists who have most influenced me in more recent years. I went to Fort Chipewyan because of Professor Li Fang Kuei.

Li Fang Kuei arrived at the University of Michigan from China in 1925. He had come to America because he wanted to learn modern linguistic field methods to put into service in the study of the ethnic minority languages of China and of Thailand. In a phenomenal academic career Li completed his American four-year degree in linguistics in one year at the University of Michigan under Carl Darling Buck, graduating in 1926. In 1927 he completed his Master's Degree under Edward Sapir at the University of Chicago and then in 1928 his PhD, also under Edward Sapir. At that time Sapir and Bloomfield in alternate years taught Indo–European and 'American' linguistics. By 'American' linguistics they meant at that time Athabaskan in the case of Sapir or Algonkian in Bloomfield's case. Thus Li Fang Kuei by chance of arriving when he did at Chicago studied American linguistics under Sapir and Indo–European under Bloomfield. While a paper he'd written for Bloomfield in dialects of Middle English had been accepted by Bloomfield as his doctoral dissertation, he'd already had another paper he'd written for Sapir on Mattole, a California Athabaskan language, accepted as his doctoral dissertation. It was a matter of two days' timing that made Li an Athabaskanist and a Sapirian linguist rather than an Indo–Europeanist and Bloomfieldian.

Helping Li to pass his time while the calendar caught up with the University of Chicago's residence requirement of two years, Sapir sent Li Fang Kuei to Fort Chipewyan in Northern Canada to 'collect data' on this rather pernicious Northern Athabaskan language. While this research is in itself an interesting story, one point is pertinent to my argument here. Sapir had previously sent another linguist, J. Alden Mason, to study the Chipewyans. When Mason came back and presented his work to Sapir, then at the National Museum of Canada in Ottawa, for a variety of reasons Mason ended up being declared incompetent and essentially banned from doing research in any of the areas in which Edward Sapir exerted influence. Thus, J. Alden Mason became known for his research in Latin America, an area in which Sapir had no interest.

Li Fang Kuei went to Fort Chipewyan in 1928 for about 8 weeks in the summer. During that short period he collected a tremendous number of field notes — some 1800 file slips of verb paradigms and a dozen notebooks of dictated narratives told by a person named Francois Mandeville. When I met Professor Li in 1972 and began my apprenticeship with him at the University of Hawaii he had not published more than a short sketch of Chipewyan phonology; the rest of his notes had been carried with him for more than 40 years, to and around China and back, during which time, for reasons embarrassing to go into here, he had not done further work on Athabaskan (he had been teaching introductory Mandarin — ma, ma, ma, ma — for decades at the University of Washington as the only academic work he could get within the US). Professor Li passed his Chipewyan work on to me. Thus I went to Fort Chipewyan with both Li Fang Kuei's work in hand (I had edited and translated his collection of Chipewyan narratives) and with my sense of how to do ethnographic work. I wasn't alone in this work. I was accompanied by Suzanne Scollon who was also a student of Li Fang Kuei, though she studied Thai linguistics with him, not Athabaskan.

What we found at Fort Chipewyan was not unlike what I found with my little SONY TC110A in studying a one-year old child: if you broaden the scope of what you can record, you change the nature of the phenomenon you can report on. The result of our study at Fort Chipewyan (Scollon and Scollon 1979) was to argue that rather than saying that the language 'Chipewyan' had been dying out over the past 50 years (Li's data compared to ours), perspectives on linguistic analysis had changed over this same period of time from Sapirian structuralist historical phonology to Gumperzian ethnography of communication. The language we observed in actual use was very much like the actual language used at the time Li had been in Fort Chipewyan, but what had changed was our field methodology. Rather than taking dictated texts from a paid informant, tape recordings of normal day-to-day talk produced a 'language' that appeared to be dying.

I was concerned when I returned to Hawaii that our 'findings' might be construed to be an attack on the published findings of Li Fang Kuei. When

I presented these findings to him and asked him what he thought, he said if I read a certain paragraph in his 1933 paper on Chipewyan I might find something of interest. There in that paragraph I found the suggestion, indirectly hinted at, which confirmed what we had found at Fort Chipewyan. I asked Professor Li why he hadn't written about this over these many years. His answer was that at the time he had written, his teacher, Sapir, was still living and he didn't feel he could contradict him in writing. Later he'd been occupied with other matters.

As still relatively young Americans we thought that we could certainly break out of this feudalistic pall of silencing and write about it, and so we did. Our book *Linguistic Convergence: An Ethnography of Speaking at Fort Chipewyan, Alberta* (Scollon and Scollon 1979) is where we said our piece. Unlike my dissertation in book form, *Linguistic Convergence* didn't do so well. I once applied for a job at UC Berkeley's Linguistics Department. As part of the application I gave a copy of the book to the head of the department. A few years later another friend found this copy of the book, inscribed to this person, for sale in Moe's bookstore, a second-hand bookstore in Berkeley where academics sell off the stuff they've accumulated but never intend to read.

Why did the very minor point about 'vertical construction' succeed and the somewhat more significant issue of the 'Chipewyan language' fail? Of course, there are many reasons. One obvious reason is that until we had written our book, every person who knew anything about Chipewyan from a formal linguistic point of view knew it from Li Fang Kuei's 1928 fieldwork. Everything they had encountered in the field in those intervening 50 years they had considered language loss. People weren't speaking Chipewyan like they used to speak it. This fitted well within a general sense of how it was going with North American indigenous languages. There was an ideology to cover the story. What we had to say was that 'the Chipewyan language' was a construct jointly managed by Francois Mandeville and Li Fang Kuei during one summer in 1928. Nobody before or after ever spoke this language. The only ideological position within which to construct this concept was one of collusion between 'informant' (almost in the police sense of the word) and linguist (as imposer of outside, maybe colonising, power). To accept what we had to say meant to accept that both Li Fang Kuei and Edward Sapir had erred in their understanding of language in the speech community of Fort Chipewyan.

To put a bit of the record straight here. I have mentioned that J. Alden Mason was sent by Edward Sapir to do fieldwork at Fort McMurray and Fort Chipewyan when Sapir was running things at the museum in Ottawa. He went, did his fieldwork, and reported back to Sapir. Edward Sapir, as much as I respect his linguistic and anthropological work, I must say suppressed the findings of this fieldwork. He did not deposit them in the museum, he kept them at home. Later on when he came upon Li Fang Kuei, he passed them on to him saying that he thought this was inferior fieldwork. Li, perhaps recognising another inferior fieldworker, passed those records on to me. I found in J. Alden Mason's fieldnotes the same 'language' we found when we were at Fort Chipewyan in 1976 and 1977. To put it clearly, there was a view of the 'language' Chipewyan which had been successfully suppressed for 50 years. We had inherited both the original fieldnotes of Mason and Li but also collected our own view which coincided with theirs. We did the only thing we could do. We returned the Mason fieldnotes to the National Museum of Man in Ottawa (as they had sponsored the original fieldwork) and we published our *Linguistic Convergence*.

While *Conversations with a One Year Old* fell into a discourse community hungry for any ethnographic and functional studies of language development, *Linguistic Convergence* dropped into a discourse in which Edward Sapir reigned supreme, the classical phoneme was considered the zenith of linguistic success in at least Americanist studies, the concept of languages converging was anathema, and our own mentor, Li Fang Kuei, remained for most linguists an unknown speaker of Chinese whose main contribution was his knowledge of the four tones of Mandarin, ma, ma, ma, ma.

Literacy studies

In the first study I have discussed, an ethnographic perspective especially based on a then quite new recording technology allowed me to problematise the taken-for-granted process of transcription of a young child's language. It became clear to me that the process of transforming a child's utterances through literacy was itself a theoretically crucial moment. In the second study at Fort Chipewyan, our methodological procedures of working with transcriptions of naturally-occurring spoken language produced a literate form at variance with the literate form of transcriptions then considered to be 'the language'. By focusing our attention on our own data-construction activities as ethnographers of communication and contrasting them with the data-construction activities of traditional phonologists, we were able to refocus the attention away from the language Chipewyan and onto the work of the field linguist. It was not the Chipewyan language of 1928 and the Chipewyan language of 1976 we were comparing, but the fieldwork of a particular linguist and his informant situated within a particular school of linguistics as of the 20s with our own very particular work within a rather different school in the 70s. It became clear to us that the literate activities by which language is institutionalised within schools of study were the main focus of our general research plan.

With the institutionalisation of literacy as our focus, it was natural then to shift our focus to a direct comparison of literate and non-literate discourse systems. Our book *Narrative, literacy, and face in interethnic communication*

(Scollon and Scollon 1981) was a four-way comparison of literacy and non-literacy. On the literate dimension we compared the process of socialisation to literacy in early childhood to the expected outcome, what we called 'essayist literacy' — the prototype of elegant expression since the Enlightenment in Europe. On the non-literate dimension we compared socialisation to the oral narrative tradition in early childhood to the oral narratives of elderly Athabaskan tradition bearers. At the same time we cross-contrasted the two adult traditions of essayist literacy and the oral memorate and the two early childhood socialisation practices.

In a chapter entitled 'The Literate Two-Year Old' we argued that the characteristics expected in adult literate performance of rationality, role-distancing of the author from the text, and decontextualisation are already present in the behaviour of a child being socialised into this literate discourse system even before the child has begun to read or write. That is to say, while in the first case I had argued that discourse was the foundation upon which syntax developed, in this case we argued that the conceptual patterns which underlie essayist literacy are already taught through processes of socialisation *before* the relatively minor details of learning the symbols of the alphabet. Perhaps the major consequence of this research was that it focused attention away from educational activities within formal school settings onto conceptual and schematic relations between pre-school and out-of-school socialisation and in-school education. To put it quite simply, a child who has learned to decontextualise narratives at two years old needs only to learn the alphabet to be able to do the same thing in school four or five years later. On the other hand a child who has learned to empirically relate all narrative to his or her own personal experience may easily learn the alphabet but be quite mystified by the expectations of school literate activities.

This research was a considerable success and quickly became known within some North American academic circles. Unfortunately, as much as we would like to think our work was highly original and had not only opened up new vistas in understanding processes of linguistic socialisation but, perhaps more importantly, demonstrated the extent to which literacy is a socially constructed phenomenon, we could not make this claim without taking a number of other factors into consideration. Four major streams of development were at work in getting this work recognised, all of them entirely outside our control and to some extent at that time outside of our own awareness:

1) Alaska was rich. Because of the abundance of oil in Alaska, the University of Alaska where we worked allowed us to go to two or even three conferences a year fully supported and without having to trouble with writing or giving papers. We also had unlimited photocopying and mailing budgets by which we could mail around to all potentially interested scholars draft copies of our research as we wrote it. Thus we found ourselves being referenced by colleagues considerably in advance of actual publication.

2) Many other researchers were concurrently making similar claims. Scribner and Cole's work on Vai literacy (1981) had produced a somewhat comparable examination of vernacular literacy and its consequences. Further, Goody's (1977) *The Domestication of the Savage Mind* had just come out. David Olsen's several papers had outlined the essence of the 'essayist literacy' position on decontextualisation. Walter Ong's several earlier essays provided theoretical background and Shirley Heath's 'Trackton' study (Heath 1983) was nearing publication. Foucault's work was being read in English translation. Taken together, this body of work represented a broad-front attack on current assumptions about the nature of literacy and its relationship to schooling in the US. Our work fitted into this pattern quite by accident on our part as our own interests to that time had had nothing to do with issues of schooling.

3) National legislation against discrimination in the schools had produced an industry of research centres, court cases, school materials development, and consultation. The first move to overcome racial discrimination was the integration of schools. Then when minority students didn't notably succeed in integrated schools, rather than addressing directly the issues of racism and social stratification which now seem rather obviously the roots of the problem, the focus shifted to studies of vernacular language. After almost a decade of studies of Black Vernacular English, Hawaiian Creole English and the like and with the results still indicating that minority students were not significantly improving in schools, the focus shifted to the analysis of the structures of school performance — especially literacy itself. As consultants were being called up from wherever they could be found to speak to the subject of school literacy, our work schedule as consultants was virtually ensured, as was the distribution and citation of our research.

4) The appalling treatment of Native Americans in North American schools meant that there were almost no Native Americans legitimated within the system to speak for themselves. At the time our book was published there was only one Native American with a PhD in linguistics within the US. His interests were largely in theoretical syntax as he had been educated at MIT in the Chomsky era. Thus when governmental panels were convened, when research centres were set up, or when court cases threatened and consultants with good academic credentials were needed, we became the stand-in Native Americans. Often we found ourselves in the position of speaking on behalf of Athabaskans and even all Native Americans on these select panels when our Native American colleagues were rejected because of their lack of academic standing.

Taken together these four factors must be understood to underlie the rapid institutionalisation of our Athabaskan research and the still quite surprising sales of that book. Perhaps the book had to have said *something* intelligible and a bit useful — we certainly hope it does — but it is clear from many of the citations we have dug into that those citing it haven't taken the trouble to read the book. If one wanted to say that literacy itself was a socially-constructed phenomenon — what should be an obvious enough insight, one would think — and particularly if one wanted to say that this fact had negative implications for ethnic minorities in North America, one cited Scollon and Scollon 1981 and passed on to the points one wanted to make.

Of course, we had read our own book and took its implications seriously. As we were then working in an educational institution — the University of Alaska — which regularly took in about 15% Alaska Native students as freshmen and regularly graduated fewer than 1%, it seemed to us that our own research might shed some light on why Alaska Native students, from villages in which they themselves were the first members in their culture's entire history to read and write, might be having trouble graduating from our university. We undertook a research project under the title 'Communication and Retention in a Public University'.

As the problem had been defined by the university, Alaska Native students were unmotivated dropouts who were failing to accommodate to the demands of academic life. As the problem was defined by Alaska Native students, in spite of very high levels of motivation, the university was erecting barriers — often literate ones — to their success in the university. Our research indicated that the university was working with a socialisation model of university performance while the students were working with a client model. That is to say, from the university's point of view, one was considered a success to the extent one *became like university staff members*. The basic assumption governing both content of courses and their assessment was that the goal of a student was to become a professional in the field; thus a sociologist would give higher marks to the student who professed an interest in going on for further study, who showed an interest in sociological issues, and who learned to write like a sociologist. The students' assumption, in contrast, was that they were at the university to learn what a sociologist might contribute to their ability to manage a small corporation, as most of them at that time entered the university to go into a business career. This conflict between a socialisation and a client model led to different styles of writing, speaking, and performance in class that teachers regarded as lacking proper training or motivation, and thus Alaska Native students were systematically given lower marks or failed. What they had not learned in their socialisation was to play the literate game of identifying genres and producing them on demand.

When I had submitted the proposal for this research project, as had happened with my first book, the title had been changed. The title I had given the project was 'Communicative Barriers to Success in a Public

University'. This title was changed by the granting agency, a Federal Agency, to 'Communication and Retention in a Public University'. Their argument was that it sounded too contentious and might attract negative attention to our university. When the research was completed, I wrote up a final report (Scollon 1981) and then we wrote another book covering this project and several others which we had done together on the issue of the role of literacy in providing gatekeeping devices in the university institutional structure. Perhaps you will see the drift of my argument by now and have guessed that this book was never published. The publisher's lawyers warned them off. The reason, like that given by the Federal Agency in Washington, was that it might be regarded as incriminating by the university and result in unwonted litigation.

Ethnographic lessons learned

I have made no attempt to clarify what might be meant by the word 'ethnographic' other than to suggest that it means a rather broad perspective on issues and an insistence on contextualising observations. In the set of studies I have quickly surveyed here, three kinds of contextualisation can be teased out:

1) contextualisation of one's data within a broader view of the situations within which the data are collected
2) contextualisation of one's theory as part of the process of data construction
3) contextualisation of one's own research activities within the institutions where one is working.

In our work we have not always found we could keep these separate. Where we have been most successful, our work has been contextualised in the first two senses. That is to say, we have been able to develop a background against which data construction and theory construction have been merged. Where we have come up against a rather unforgiving wall is when we have turned the light of contextualisation upon our own work and so by extension upon our colleagues' work or on the work of the institutions in which we ourselves were employed. However much money academic institutions and granting agencies are willing to provide to studies of social constructionism, there is an underlying positivist assumption that these institutions themselves are instances of pure, rational enlightenment. To switch metaphors, the searchlight of critical analysis provided by these institutions is to be turned only outward upon others who have little choice in the matter. In these cases, one can expect certain rewards, recognition, and acceptance for what one finds.

I can summarise these lessons learned in two statements:

1) If you want to be successful in your work, don't focus your attention on the weaknesses of your own field or your own institution
2) Beware of publishers or funding agencies who want to change your titles.

Intercultural communication

In our research from my dissertation down to the most recent I have tried very hard to avoid the use of the word 'culture'. *A fortiori* 'intercultural' seems to me more problematical. In our *Narrative, literacy, and face*, for example, we set the problems we discussed there as issues in interethnic communication and identity. Our purpose was specifically to highlight the idea that, on the one hand, the concept of culture is too broad to be of practical use but that, on the other, the problems of discriminatory social practices and policies that we analysed were being carried out within and between members of cultural sub-discourses. Athabaskan Indians in Alaska are, after all, Americans. Whatever other interesting characteristics they may display, they wear jeans bought from Sears Roebuck, they listen to Johnny Cash, they eat hamburgers, drink Cokes, watch television, and read magazines about Caucasian, Afro-American, or Hispanic Americans living in Anchorage or Chicago. What seemed significant to us was that this group of people did share among themselves some aspects of common discursive practice, and that that discursive practice was systematically different from what was expected in the social institutions of schooling, health care, justice, and employment as organised by members of other ethnic groups who held the power to define those discursive practices.

There is another problem with the word 'culture'. As Edward Sapir pointed out many years ago in an essay 'Culture: Genuine and Spurious', we tend to see culture as the description of what is exotic, different, or at the very least distant from the observer. What *we* do is normal, what *they* do is cultural. Thus the use of the concept of culture, as valuable as it might be from the point of view of the analysis of symbolic systems of meaning, is inherently off-putting, distancing, and ultimately limiting. To see the broad picture is to obscure the concreteness of daily life.

Recently we wrote a book with the title *Interdiscourse Communication*. Having had the experience I have commented on above, we specifically *contracted* for that title. The central argument of the book is that problems in communication on the one hand and identity on the other most often arise from differences in competing discourse systems. A person as a member of a gender discourse system, a generational discourse system, a professional one, a corporate one and so on is in any situation having to juggle these multiple and often contradictory symbol systems. The central point was that there is no overarching 'cultural' system which defines the whole of one's behaviour or interpretation, and thus communication across discourse systems is not just a matter of communication between different people, but a matter of the individual strategising his or her own identity within a matrix of these multiple and competing systems of discourse. Perhaps you are more familiar with this book under the title which the publisher unilaterally decided to use, *Intercultural Communication* (Scollon and Scollon 1995). We didn't discover the switch had been made until the book was well into production and at that point it seemed quixotic to try to recall it on a point of legal contract.

I have answered the first part of my title question: 'Intercultural communication: why and why not?': 'Intercultural' communication is largely a useless concept. At most it suggests tour-guide helpful hints on how to behave in someone else's country. As a serious theoretical concept, I think it is bankrupt. Why do I use it? All I can say is that I am at the mercy of both my publisher and my institution. My publisher has chosen that title for the book, which is the textbook in a course of that name in my institution. I spend a good bit of my time trying to explain my way out of this discursive blind alley.

As to the second part of my title, 'Ethnography: why and why not?', while I am entirely familiar with the contemporary critiques of ethnography — one thinks of Geertz, Clifford, or Rosaldo — I don't know what else to call research that is based on participant observation, reflective analysis, concreteness in data construction, and narrative recounting, but which is empirical in its attention to particularistic details of daily life and at the same time holistic in seeking to relate these particularistic symbols, images, and events to the contextualising discourses of the societies within which they occur. If it was innocent work, neither distant people nor one's own institutions would get their backs up so quickly when the spotlight is turned upon them. On the other hand, without the contextualising grounding of ethnography, especially in studies of communication, research can easily be reduced to the endless manipulation of arcane codes.

In all of this one should not forget such basic human emotions as fear, anxiety, or depression. When you are living in a backpacker's tent in the Upper Tanana valley of Alaska working to write down the story of 'Smear Face' [Nesdzeegh] as told by Gaither Paul you know you are talking to a person in his seventies. He, along with Andrew Isaac, are the youngest who still speak the language in the fullest variety. Nobody under 45 speaks more than a few words or phrases. The language will pass out of existence when they do. You want to get the story right because within only a few years what you have written will be the only human memory not only of the story of 'Smear Face' but perhaps of the entire language as well. One is afraid of what one might do to this fragile and so important human memory.

When you are living in Hong Kong and working up a discursive analysis of a Xinhua News Agency story in the *People's Daily* you can be pretty sure that an academic article in the sort of journals I manage to publish in won't do much harm to China or the Chinese language. One sees that the fears one has can be more for one's own academic hide than for the language and one's responsibility to it. It might seem that in the first case what is needed is humility and in the second, courage. I would argue that not only does the ethnographer in the upper reaches of the Chandalar River need humility in the face of the loss of a human language, the ethnographer needs courage to keep up the work, even when other colleagues of contesting theoretical persuasion challenge his or her concept of the phoneme. By the same token, the discursive analysis of a Xinhua news story needs not only the courage to put forward a claim to understanding in a context of hotly-contested ideological formation, one also needs humility to be prepared for the loss not of a language but one's own analysis.

It is the work of an ethnographer in my view to keep alert not only to the discursive systems of one's studied populations, but also to the discursive power that comes with writing ethnographic description. I hope I have both the courage and the humility it takes to continue to call myself an ethnographer in a world of political transition on the one hand and of the ideologisation of academic discourse on the other.

References

Abu Lughod, L. (1990a) Anthropology's orient: The boundaries of theory on the Arab world. In H. Sharabi (ed.) *Theory, Politics and the Arab World.* London and New York: Routledge, 81–131.

Abu Lughod, L. (1990b) The romance of resistance: Tracing transformations of power through Bedouin women. *American Ethnology* 17: 41–55.

Adam, B. (1995) *Timewatch: The Social Analysis of Time.* Cambridge: Polity Press.

Agonito, R. (1979) *A History of Ideas on Women.* New York: Putnam.

Allen, J. (1997) *Seeing Red: China's Uncompromising Take-over of Hong Kong.* Singapore: Butterworth-Heinemann.

Althusser, L. (1971) *Lenin and Philosophy and Other Essays.* London: NLB.

American Psychological Association (APA) (1994) *Publication manual,* 4th edn. Washington, DC: American Psychological Association.

Amsden, A. H. (1989) *Asia's Next Giant: South Korea and Late Industrialization.* New York and Oxford: Oxford University Press.

Anderson, A. B., Teale, W. B. and Estrada, E. (1980) Low income children's preschool literacy experience: Some naturalistic observations. *Quarterly Newsletter of the Laboratory of Comparative Human Cognition* 2 (3): 59–65.

Ang, I. (1994) On not speaking Chinese: Post-modern ethnicity and the politics of Diaspora. *New Formations* 13: 46–74.

Arrow, K. J. (1963) *Social Choice and Individual Values,* 2nd edn. New Haven, CT: Yale University Press.

Bacharach, P. and Baratz, M. S. (1962) The two faces of power. *American Political Science Review* 57: 947–952.

Bain, M. S. (1992) *The Aboriginal–white Encounter: Towards Better Communication.* Darwin: Summer Institute of Linguistics Australian Aborigines Branch.

Bairoch, P. (1993) *Economics and World History: Myths and Paradoxes.* Chicago: University of Chicago Press.

Bakhtin, M. (1981) *The Dialogical Imagination: Four Essays* (ed. Michael Holquist; trans. Caryl Emerson and Michael Holquist). Austin: University of Texas Press.

Bakhtin, M. M. (1981) Forms of time and of the chronotope in the novel. In M. M. Bakhtin *The dialogic imagination: Four essays.* Austin: University of Texas Press, 84–258.

Baldwin, R. (1991) The new protectionism. In J. A. Frieden *et al.* (eds) *International Economy*. New York: St. Martin's Press.

Barbara, L. *et al.* (1996) A survey of communication patterns in the Brazilian business context. *English for Special Purposes* 15 (1): 57–71.

Barron, C. (1991) Material thoughts: ESP and culture. *English for Specific Purposes* 10/3: 173–187.

Barron, C. (1999) On the way to being an engineer: An analysis of time and temporality in mechanical engineering discourse. Unpublished Ph.D. dissertation, Lancaster University.

Barthes, R. (1972 [1957]) *Mythologies* (trans. A. Lavers). New York: Hill & Wang.

Barthes, R. (1974) *S/Z. An Essay* (trans. R. Miller). New York: Hill & Wang/Noonday Press.

Bartholomae, D. (1985) Inventing the university. In M. Rose (ed.) *When a Writer Can't Write*. New York: Guilford Press, 134–165.

Barton, D. and Hamilton, M. (1998) *Local Literacies*. London: Routledge.

Baudrillard, J. (1983) *Simulations*. New York: Semiotext(e).

Bauman, Z. (1992) *Intimations of Post-modernity*. London: Routledge.

Bavelas, J. B., Rogers, L. E. and Millar, F. E. (1985) Interpersonal conflict. In T. A. van Dijk (ed.) *Handbook of Discourse Analysis*, 4 vols. London: Academic Press, 9–24.

Baynes, K., Bohman, J. and McCarthy, T. (1987) General introduction. In K. Baynes, J. Bohman and T. McCarthy (eds) *After Philosophy: End or Transformation?* Cambridge, MA: MIT Press, 1–18.

Bazerman, C. (1987) Codifying the social scientific style: The APA *Publication Manual* as a behavioristic rhetoric. In J. S. Nelson, A. Megill and D. N. McCloskey (eds) *The Rhetoric of the Human Sciences*. Madison, WI: University of Wisconsin Press, 125–144.

Bazerman, C. (1990) Discourse analysis and social construction. *Annual Review of Applied Linguistics* 11: 77–83.

Bazerman, C. (1994) *Constructing Experience*. Carbondale, IL: Southern Illinois University Press.

Becher, T. (1989) *Academic Tribes and Territories: Intellectual Enquiry and the Cultures of Disciplines*. Milton Keynes: Open University Press.

Belcher, D. and Braine, G. (eds) (1995) *Academic Writing in a Second Language: Essays on Research and Pedagogy*. Norwood, NJ: Ablex.

Benson, R. W. (1988) How judges fool themselves: The semiotics of the easy case. In R. Kevelson (ed.) *Law and Semiotics*, vol. 2. New York: Plenum Press, 31–60.

Benveniste, E. (1971 [1966]) *Problems in General Linguistics* (trans. M. E. Meek). Coral Gables, FL: University of Miami Press.

Berger, C. R. (1985) Social power and interpersonal communication. In M. L. Knapp and G. R. Miller (eds) *Handbook of Interpersonal Communication*. Beverly Hills, CA: Sage, 439–496.

Berkenkotter, C. and Huckin, T. N. (1995) *Genre Knowledge in Disciplinary Communication: Cognition/Culture/Power*. Hillsdale, NJ: Lawrence Erlbaum.

Berle, A. and Means, G. C. (1968) *The Modern Corporation and Private Property*. New York: Harcourt Brace & World.

Bernstein, B. (1971a) *Class, Codes and Control (Vol. I): Theoretical Studies Towards a Sociology of Language*. London: Routledge & Kegan Paul.

Bernstein, B. (1971b) Social class, language and socialization. In B. Bernstein (1971a) *Class, Codes and Control (Vol. 1): Theoretical Studies Towards a Sociology of Language*, 170–189.

Bernstein, B. (1972) A sociolinguistic approach to socialisation: With some reference to educability. In J. J. Gumperz and D. Hymes (eds) *Directions in Sociolinguistics: The Ethnography of Communication*. New York: Holt, Rinehart & Winston, 465–497.

Berry, M. (1986) Thematic options and success in writing. In C. S. Butler, R. A. Cartwell and J. Channel (eds) *Language and Literature: Theory and Practice — A Tribute to Walter Grauberg*. Nottingham: University of Nottingham.

Beyrer, C., Eiumtrakul, S., Celentano, D. D., Nelson, K. E., Ruckphaopunt, S. and Khamboonruang, C. (1995) Same sex behaviour, sexually transmitted diseases and HIV risks among northern Thai men. *AIDS* 9: 171–176.

Bhabha, H. (1994) *The Location of Culture*. London: Routledge.

Bhatia, V. K. (1993) *Analysing Genre: Language Use in Professional Settings*. London: Longman.

Bhatia, V. K. and Candlin, C. N. (2000) Dimensions of professional discourse: New challenges for ESP. Paper presented at the TESOL Annual Convention, Vancouver, March 2000.

Bhutalia, U. (1993) Community, state and gender: On women's agency during partition. *Economic and Political Weekly* (Review of Women's Studies), XXVIII (17): WS12-WS24.

Bizzell, P. (1992) *Academic Discourse and Critical Consciousness*. Pittsburgh: University of Pittsburgh Press.

Blair, M. M. (1995) *Ownership and Control: Rethinking Corporate Governance for the Twenty-first Century*. Washington DC: Brookings Institute.

Blinder, A. S. (1992) More like them? *The American Prospect*, Winter: 51–62.

Block, D. (1996) Not so fast: Some thoughts on theory culling, relativism, accepted findings and the heart and soul of SLA. *Applied Linguistics* 17 (1): 63–83.

Block, F. (1990) *Post-industrial Possibilities: A Critique of Economic Discourse*. Berkeley and Los Angeles: University of California Press.

Block, F. (1995) What if financial markets do not get prices right? Paper presented at the American Sociological Association, Washington DC, August 1995.

Board of Education for the City of North York (1995) *Language for Learning Policy*. North York: The Board of Education for the City of North York, Office of the Director of Education.

Board of Studies New South Wales (1997) *Draft English K-6 Syllabus*. Sydney: Board of Studies NSW.

Boles, J. and Elifson, K. W. (1994) Sexual identity and HIV: The male prostitute. *Journal of Sex Research* 31 (1): 39–46.

Bolton, K. and Hutton, C. (1995) Bad and banned language: Triad secret societies, the censorship of the Cantonese vernacular and colonial language policy in Hong Kong. *Language in Society* 24: 159–186.

Bolton, K. and Hutton, C. (1997) Bad boys and bad language: Chòu háu and the sociolinguistics of swearing in Hong Kong. In G. Evans and M. Tam Siu-mei (eds) *The Anthropology of a Chinese Metropolis*. Honolulu: University of Hawaii Press, 299–331.

Bolton, K. and Hutton, C. (eds) (2000) *Triad Societies: Missionary and Colonial Accounts of Chinese Secret Societies*. Six vols. London: Routledge/Thoemmes Press.

Bolton, K., Hutton, C. and Ip, P. F. (1996) The speech act offence: The linguistics of claiming membership of a triad society (MOTS) in Hong Kong. *Language and Communication* 16: 263–290.

Bottomley, G. (1992) *From Another Place: Migration and the Politics of Culture.* Cambridge: Cambridge University Press.

Bottomley, G. (n.d.) Appropriating Bourdieu in the Australian context. Unpublished paper.

Bourdieu, P. (1990) *Distinction.* London: Routledge.

Bourdieu, P. (1991) *Language and Symbolic Power.* Oxford: Polity Press.

Bourdieu, P. (1992 [1977]) *Outline of a Theory of Practice.* Cambridge: Cambridge University Press.

Bourdieu, P. (1993) *The Field of Cultural Production,* R. Johnson (ed.). Cambridge: Polity.

Bourdieu, P. and Passeron, J-C. (1990) *Reproduction in Education, Society and Culture.* 2nd edn. London: Sage.

Boyd-Barrett, O. and Braham, P. (eds) (1987) *Media, Knowledge and Power.* London: Croom Helm.

Bradwell v. Illinois (1873), 83 U.S. (16 Wall.) 130.

Brantlinger, P. (1990) *Crusoe's Footprints: Cultural Studies in Britain and America.* New York: Routledge.

Braudel, F. (1979) *Civilisation and Capitalism 15th–18th century (Vol. 1): Material Civilisations.* New York: Harper and Row.

Braudel, F. (1982) *Civilisation and Capitalism 15th–18th century (Vol. 2): The Wheels of Commerce.* New York: Harper & Row.

Braudel, F. (1984) *Civilisation and Capitalism 15th–18th Century (Vol. 3): The Perspective of the World.* New York: Harper & Row.

Breen, M., Louden, W., Barratt-Pugh, C., Rivalland, J., Rohl, M., Lloyd, S. and Carr, T. (1994) *Literacy in its Place: An Investigation of Literacy Practices in Urban and Rural Communities.* Perth, Western Australia: School of Language Education, Edith Cowan University.

Bridgeman, B. and Carlson, S. (1984) Survey of academic writing tasks. *Written Communication* 1, 427–480.

Brown, P. and Levinson, S. (1987) *Politeness: Some Universals in Language Usage.* Cambridge: Cambridge University Press. [First published in 1978 as Universals in language usage: Politeness phenomena, in E. N. Goody (ed.) *Questions and Politeness.* Cambridge: Cambridge University Press, 56–289].

Brown, R. H. (1987) Reason as rhetorical: On relations among epistemology, discourse, and practice. In J. Nelson, A. Megill and D. McCloskey (eds) *The Rhetoric of Human Sciences.* Madison: University of Wisconsin Press.

Brown, R. L. and Herndl, C. G. (1986) An ethnographic study of corporate writing: Job status as reflected in written text. In B. Couture (ed.) *Functional Approaches to Writing Research Perspectives.* London: Frances Pinter.

Browne, J. and Minichiello, V. (1995) The social meanings behind male sex work: Implications for sexual interactions. *British Journal of Sociology* 46 (4): 598–622.

Bruffee, K. (1986) Social construction, language and the authority of knowledge: A bibliographical essay. *College English* 48: 773–790.

Butler, J. (1990) *Gender Trouble: Feminism and the Subversion of Identity.* New York: Routledge.

Callon, M. (1986a) Some elements of a sociology of translation: Domestication of the scallops and the fishermen of St Brieuc Bay. In J. Law (ed.) *Power, Action and Belief: A New Sociology of Knowledge?* London: Routledge & Kegan Paul, 196–233.

Callon, M. (1986b) The sociology of an actor-network: The case of the electric vehicle. In M. Callon, J. Law and A. Rip (eds) *Mapping the Dynamics of Science and Technology: Sociology of Science in the Real World.* Basingstoke: Macmillan, 19–34.

Callon, M. (1995) Four models for the dynamics of science. In S. Jasanoff, G. E. Markle, J. C. Petersen and T. Pinch (eds) *Handbook of Science and Technology Studies.* Thousand Oaks, CA: Sage, 29–63.

Callon, M. and Law, J. (1995) Agency and the hybrid *collectif. South Atlantic Quarterly* 94, 2: 481–507.

Cameron, D. (1990) Demythologising sociolinguistics: Why language does not reflect society. In J. Joseph and T. Taylor (eds) *Ideologies of Language.* London: Routledge, 79–96.

Canagarajah, A. Suresh (1999) *Resisting Linguistic Imperialism in English Teaching.* Oxford: Oxford University Press.

Candlin, C. N. (1987) Explaining moments of conflict in discourse. In R. Steele and T. Threadgold (eds) *Essays in Honour of Michael Halliday.* Amsterdam: John Benjamins.

Candlin, C. N. and Plum, G. A. (1998) *Researching Academic Literacies: Framing Student Literacy: Cross-cultural Aspects of Communication Skills in Australian University Settings.* Sydney: NCELTR, Macquarie University.

Candlin, C. N. and Plum, G. A. (1999) Engaging with the challenges of inter-discursivity in academic writing: researchers, students and tutors. In C. N. Candlin and K. Hyland (eds) *Writing: Texts, Processes and Practices.* London: Longman.

Candlin, C. N., Bhatia, V. K. and Jensen, C. (2000) Must the worlds collide? Professional and academic discourses in the study and practice of law. Paper presented at the Fifth International Congress of the European Society for the Study of English, Helsinki, August 2000.

Chan, G. (1993) Comic bad guys attain hero status. *South China Morning Post* January 10, 1993.

Chan, I. and Lau, J. (1996) Gangsters in films. *City Entertainment* no. 449, June 27–July 10 1996.

Chandler, A. Jr. (1977) *The Visible Hand: The Managerial Revolution in American Business.* Cambridge, MA: Harvard University Press.

Chang, J. (1991) *Wild swans.* London: Harper Collins.

Charoensin-o-larn, C. (1988) *Understanding Postwar Reformism in Thailand.* Bangkok: Duang Kamol Editions.

Cheung, S. N. S. (1982) *Will China go 'Capitalist'?* London: Institute of Economic Affairs.

Cheung, S. N. S. (1984) *Mai Ju Zhe Yan (The Words of the Tangerine Seller).* Hong Kong: Xin Bao.

Cheung, S. N. S. (1985) *Zhongquo de Qiantu (The Future of China).* Hong Kong: Xin Bao.

Cheung, S. N. S. (1991) *San an Qing Huai (Passion on China, Taiwan, and Hong Kong).* Taiwan: Yuanliu.

Cheung, S. N. S. (1996) A simplistic general equilibrium theory of corruption. *Contemporary Economic Policy* XIV: 1–5.

Chin, James K. (2000). Secret societies in Chinese historiography. In K. Bolton and C. Hutton (eds) *Triad Societies: Missionary and Colonial Accounts of Chinese Secret Societies*. Six vols. London: Routledge/Thoemmes Press.

Chiu, V. (1995) The $3.60 ticket to the triads. *South China Morning Post* November 2 1995.

Chiu, Y. K. (2000) *The Triads as Business*. London, New York: Routledge.

Chow, R. (1993) *Writing Diaspora: Tactics of Intervention in Contemporary Cultural Studies*. Bloomington: Indiana University Press.

Chow, R. (1996) Women in the Holocene: Ethnicity, fantasy and the film *The Joy Luck Club*. In C. Luke (ed.) *Feminisms and Pedagogies of Everyday Life*. Albany: State University of New York Press, 204–224.

Clough, P. T. (1992) *The End(s) of Ethnography: From Realism to Social Criticism*. Newbury Park, CA: Sage.

Coates, A. (1967) *City of Broken Promises*. London: Muller.

Cochran-Smith, M. and Lytle, S. (1993) *Inside Outside Teacher Research and Knowledge*. New York and London: Teacher's College Press.

Comber, L. (1961) *The Traditional Mysteries of Chinese Secret Societies in Malaya*. Singapore: Eastern Universities Press

Conley, J. M. and O'Barr, W. M. (1990) *Rules Versus Relationships: The Ethnography of Legal Discourse*. Chicago: Chicago University Press.

Connell, R. W. (1987) *Gender and Power*. Sydney: Allen & Unwin.

Connor, U., (1996) *Contrastive Rhetoric: Cross-cultural Aspects of Second-language Writing*. New York: Cambridge University Press.

Corson, D. (1997) Critical realism: An emancipatory philosophy for applied linguistics? *Applied Linguistics* 18 (2): 166–188.

Crookes, G. (1993) Action research for second language teachers: Going beyond teacher research. *Applied Linguistics* 14 (2): 130–144.

Crosby, A. W. (1997) *The Measure of Reality: Quantification and Western Society, 1250–1600*. Cambridge: Cambridge University Press.

Crowley, T. (1990) That obscure object of desire. In J. Joseph and T. Taylor (eds) *Ideologies of Language*. London: Routledge, 27–50.

Crowley, T. (1996) *Language in History: Theories and Texts*. London: Routledge.

Crystal, D. (1987) *The Cambridge Encyclopedia of Language*. Cambridge: Cambridge University Press.

Culler, J. (1976) *Saussure*. London: Fontana.

Dahl, R. A. (1957) The concept of power. *Behavioral Science* 2: 201–5.

Dahl, R. A. (1961) *Who Governs? Democracy and Power in an American City*. New Haven: Yale University Press.

Daiker, D. A. (1989) Learning to praise. In C. M. Anson (ed.) *Writing and Response (Theory, Practice and Research)*. Urbana, IL: NCTE.

Dannen, F. (1997a) Partners in crime: China bonds with Hong Kong's underworld. *The New Republic*, July 14 and 21 1997: 18–26.

Dannen, F. (1997b) Hong Kong Babylon: a reporter looks at the Hollywood of the East. In F. Dannen and B. Long *Hong Kong Babylon*. London and Boston: Faber & Faber, 1–55.

Das, V. (1995) *Critical Events: An Anthropological Perspective on Contemporary India*. Delhi: Oxford University Press.

Dastur, F. (1998 [1990]) *Heidegger and the Question of Time*. Trans. F. Raffoul and D. Pettigrew. Atlantic Highlands, NJ: Humanities Press.

Davidoff, L. and Hall, C. (1987) *Family Fortunes: Men and Women of the English Middle Class 1780–1850*. Chicago: University of Chicago Press.

Davies, B. (1989) *Frogs and Snails and Feminist Tales: Pre-school Children and Gender*. Sydney: Allen & Unwin.

Davies, B. (1993) *Shards of Glass: Children Reading and Writing Beyond Gendered Identities*. Sydney: Allen & Unwin.

Davies, F., Forey, G. and Hyatt, D. (1999) Exploring aspects of context: Selected findings from the Effective Writing for Management project. In F. Bargiela Chippini and C. Nickerson (eds) *Writing Business: Genres, Methods and Language*. London: Longman, 293–312.

Davies, P. M., Hickson, F. L. I., Weatherburn, P. and Hunt, A. J. (1993) *Sex, Gay Men and Aids*. London: Falmer Press.

Deleuze, G. and Guattari, F. (1987 [1980]) *A Thousand Plateaus: Capitalism and Schizophrenia*, trans. Brian Massumi. London: Athlone Press.

Deng, X. (1993) *Selected Readings of Deng Xiaoping, Vol. 3*. Beijing: People's Press.

Denny, J. P. (1991) Rational thought in oral culture and literate decontextualisation. In D. R. Olson and N. Torrance (eds) *Literacy and Orality*. Cambridge: Cambridge University Press, 68–89.

Derrida, J. (1974) *Of Grammatology*. Baltimore: Johns Hopkins University Press.

Derrida, J. (1978) *Writing and Difference*. Chicago: University of Chicago Press.

Diamond, I. and Quinby, L. (eds) (1988) *Feminism and Foucault: Reflections on Resistance*. Boston: Northeastern University Press.

Dias, P., Freedman, A., Medway, P. and Paré, A. (1999) Students and workers learning. In *Worlds Apart: Acting and Writing in Academic and Workplace Contexts*. Mahwah, NJ: Lawrence Erlbaum, 185–200.

Dobson, C. (1993) Sun Yee On incorporated. *South China Morning Post*, October 3, 1993.

Du-Babcock, B. and Babcock, R. D. (1995) An analysis of intercultural organisational communication in multinational corporations. In Daruthiaux, P. (ed.) *Working Papers of the Department of English, Vol. 7, No. 1*. Hong Kong: City University of Hong Kong.

Du-Babcock, B. and Babcock, R. D. (1996) Patterns of expatriate–local personnel communication in multinational corporations. *The Journal of Business Communication* 33/2: 141–164.

Duranti, A. (1997) *Linguistic Anthropology*. Cambridge: Cambridge University Press.

Ecological Enterprises (1996) 12 July: Timber industry refuses to follow PNG law: 'We all are not going to pay the royalty'. 15 July: Loggers campaign over 'kiss of death', meaning having to pay fair royalties. 19 July: Short PNG forest crisis update. 25 July: Recent developments in landholder revenue arrangements. 5 August: Rimbunan Hijau's Wawoi-Guavi timber concession exposé (M. Wood). 12 August: World Bank threatens to withhold loans over forestry changes; and then does. 19 August: World Bank makes an environmental stand, while some question fairness. 18 September: South Pacific forestry and cultural abuses continue. 14 October: World Bank gets its way on forests, to benefit of PNG. 19 November: Rimbunan Hijau timber violations, landowners want shutdown. Madison, WI (all e-mail messages).

Eggington, W. (1992) From oral to literate culture: An Australian aboriginal experience. In F. Dubin and N. A. Kuhlman (eds) *Cross-cultural Literacy: Global Perspectives on Reading and Writing*. Englewood Cliffs, NJ: Regents/Prentice Hall, 81–98.

Eley, G. (1994) Nations, publics, and political cultures: Placing Habermas in the nineteenth century. In N. B. Dirks, G. Eley and S. B. Ortner (eds) *The Nineteenth Century, in Culture/Power/Bistory: A Reader in Contemporary Social Theory*. Princeton, NJ: Princeton University Press, 297–335.

Emmott, C. (1994) Frames of reference: Contextual monitoring and the interpretation of narrative discourse. In M. Coulthard (ed.) *Advances in Written Text Analysis*. London: Routledge, 157–166.

Ervin-Tripp, S., O'Connor, M. C. and Rosenberg, J. (1984) Language and power in the family. In C. Kramarae, M. Schulz and W. M. O'Barr (eds) *Language and Power*. Beverly Hills, CA: Sage, 116–135.

Fabian, J. (1983) *Time and the Other: How Anthropology Makes its Object*. New York: Columbia University Press.

Fairclough, N. (1989) *Language and Power*. London: Longman.

Fairclough, N. (1992) *Discourse and Social Change*. Cambridge: Polity Press.

Fairclough, N. (1995) *Critical Discourse Analysis: The Critical Study of Language*. London: Longman.

Ferris, D. R., Pezone, S., Tade, C. R., and Tinti, S. (1997) Teacher commentary on student writing: Descriptions and implications. *Journal of Second Language Writing* 6 (12): 155–182.

Firbas, J. (1992) *Functional Sentence Perspective in Written and Spoken Communication*. Cambridge: Cambridge University Press.

Firth, A. and Wagner, J. (1997) On discourse, communication, and (some) fundamental concepts in SLA research. *Modern Language Journal* 81 (3): 285–300.

Firth, J. R. (1957 [1950]) Personality and language in society. In J. R. Firth *Papers in linguistics 1934–1951*. London: Oxford University Press, 177–189.

Fish, S. (1989) Working on the chain gang: Interpretation in law and literature. In S. Fish *Doing What Comes Naturally: Change, Rhetoric, and the Practice of Theory in Literary and Legal Studies*. Durham: Duke University Press, 87–102.

Flynn, K. (1995) HK triads said to rule world crime. *Eastern Express*, October 6, 1995.

Fong-Torres, B. (1995) *The Rice-room: Growing up Chinese-American from Number Two Son to Rock 'n' Roll*. New York: Plume.

Foucault, M. (1972) *The Archaeology of Knowledge* (trans. A. M. Sheridan Smith). London: Tavistock.

Foucault, M. (1972–1977/1980) *Power/knowledge: Selected Interviews and Other Writings*, ed. C. Gordon. Trans. C. Gordon, L. Marshall, J. Mepham and K. Soper. New York: Harvester Press.

Foucault, M. (1977) *Discipline and Punish: The Birth of the Prison* (trans. A. Sheridan). London: Penguin.

Foucault, M. (1978 [1976]) *The History of Sexuality, Volume 1: An Introduction* (trans. R. Hurley). London: Penguin.

Foucault, M. (1979) *Discipline and Punish: The Birth of the Prison*. New York: Random House/Vintage.

Foucault, M. (1981 [1970]) The order of discourse. In R. Young (ed.) *Untying the Text: A Post-structuralist Reader*. Boston, MA: Routledge & Kegan Paul, 48–78.

Fowler, R. (1985) Power. In T. A. van Dijk (ed.) *Handbook of Discourse Analysis*. 4 vols. London: Academic Press, 61–82.

Frank, R. H., Gilovich, T. and Regan, D. T. (1993) Does studying economics inhibit co-operation? *Journal of Economic Perspective* 7 (2): 159–171.

Friedman, J. M. (1993) *America's First Woman Lawyer: The Biography of Myra Bradwell*. New York: Harvester Press.

Gadamer, H. G. (1997) *Truth and Method*, 2nd edn. (Trans. Joel Weinsheimer and Donald G. Marshall.) New York: Continuum.

Gal, S. (1991) Between speech and silence: The problematics of research on language and gender. In Micaela di Leonardo (ed.) *Gender at the Crossroads of Knowledge: Feminist Anthropology in the Post-modern Era*. Berkeley: University of California Press, 175–203.

Gans, J. S. and Shepherd, G. B. (1994) How are the mighty fallen: Rejected classic articles by leading economists. *Journal of Economic Perspectives* 8 (1): 165–179.

Gee, J. (1993) Postmodernism and literacies. In C. Lankshear and P. McLaren (eds) *Critical Literacy: Politics, Praxis, and the Post-modern*. Albany, NY: SUNY Press, 271–296.

Genesee, F. (1994) *Educating Second Language Children*. New York: Cambridge University Press.

Giddens, A. (1976) *New Rules of Sociological Method*. London: Hutchinson.

Giddens, A. (1979) *Central Problems in Social Theory: Action, Structure and Contradiction in Social Analysis*. Berkeley: University of California Press.

Giddens, A. (1991) *Modernity and Self Identity: Self and Society in the Late Modern Age*. Stanford: Stanford University Press.

Gilbert, G. N. and Mulkay, M. (1984) *Opening Pandora's Box: A Sociological Analysis of Scientists' Discourse*. Cambridge: Cambridge University Press.

Gintis, H. and Bowles, S. (1990) Contested exchange: New micro-foundation for the political economy of capitalism. *Politics and Society* 8: 165–222.

Glasgow University Media Group (1976) *Bad News Volume 1*. London: Routledge & Kegan Paul.

Glasgow University Media Group (1993) *Getting the Message: News, Truth and Power*. London: Routledge.

Goffman, E. (1967) On face-work: An analysis of ritual elements in social interaction. In E. Goffman *Interaction Ritual: Essays on Face-to-face Behaviour*. New York: Pantheon Books, 5–45.

Goffman, E. (1969 [1959]) *The Presentation of Self in Everyday Life*. London and New York: Penguin.

Goffman, E. (1974) *Frame Analysis: An Essay on the Organisation of Experience*. Cambridge, MA: Harvard University Press.

Goffman, E. (1981) *Forms of Talk*. Oxford: Basil Blackwell.

Goldstein, T., Hsueh, V. and Lam, E. (1995) High marks, credits, and the importance of friends: Speaking Cantonese and English for success in high school. Presentation given at TESL '96 Conference, Toronto, Ontario.

Gollin, S. (1998) Literacy in a Computing department: the invisible in search of the ill-defined. In C. N. Candlin and G. Plum (eds) *Researching Academic Literacies: Framing Student Literacy: Cross-cultural Aspects of Communication Skills in Australian University Settings*. Sydney: NCELTR, Macquarie University.

Goodenough, W. H. (1956) Componential analysis and the study of meaning. *Language* 32: 195–216.

Goody, J. (1977) *The Domestication of the Savage Mind*. New York: Cambridge University Press.

de Graaf, R., Vanwesenbeeck, I., van Zeesen, G., Straver, C. J. and Visser, J. H. (1994) Male prostitutes and safe sex: different settings, different risks. *AIDS Care* 6 (3): 277–288.

Gramsci, A. (1975 [1931–33]) *Quaderni del carcere*, V. Gerratana (ed.) Turin. ed. and trans. Q. Hoare and G. Nowell-Smith (1971): *Selections from the Prison Notebooks of Antonio Gramsci*. London: Lawrence & Wishart.

Grant, J. (1998) Post-industrialism and Hong Kong's autonomy. Unpublished paper, presented at the International Conference on Hong Kong and Modern China, Centre of Asian Studies, the University of Hong Kong, December 2–5, 1997.

Gray, B. (1990) Natural language learning in aboriginal classrooms: Reflections on teaching and learning style for empowerment in English. In C. Walton and W. Eggington (eds) *Language: Maintenance, Power and Education in Australian Aboriginal Contexts*. Darwin: NTU Press, 105–139.

Gregg, K., Long, M., Beretta, A. and Jordan, G. (1997) Rationality and its discontents in SLA. *Applied Linguistics* 18 (4): 539–559.

Grillo, R. D. (1989) *Dominant Languages: Language and Hierarchy in Britain and France*. Cambridge and New York: Cambridge University Press.

Griswold v. Connecticut (1965), 381 U.S. 479.

Gu, Y. (1995) Guanxi and goal-directed discourse. Paper delivered at the Fifth International Conference on Systemic Linguistics and Chinese Functional Grammar in Beijing.

Gu, Y. (1996) Doctor–patient interaction as goal-directed discourse. *Journal of Asian Pacific Communication* 7 (3 and 4): 156–176.

Gu, Y. (1996) The changing modes of discourse in a changing China. Plenary speech delivered at the First International Conference on Knowledge and Discourse at Hong Kong.

Gu, Y. (1997) Five ways of handling a bedpan. *Text* 17 (4): 457–475.

Gumperz, J. J. (1982) *Discourse Strategies*. Cambridge: Cambridge University Press.

Habermas, J. (1992) *The Structural Transformation of the Public Sphere: An Inquiry into a Category of Bourgeois Society* (trans. T. Burger and F. Lawrence). Cambridge, MA: MIT Press.

Hagedorn, J. (ed.) (1993) *Charlie Chan is Dead: An Anthology of Contemporary Asian American Fiction*. New York: Penguin.

Hakulinen, A. (1987) Avoiding personal reference. In J. Verschueren and M. Pertucelli-Papi (eds) *The Pragmatic Perspective: Selected Papers from the 1995 Pragmatics Conference*. Amsterdam: Benjamins.

Hall, S. and DuGay, P. (eds) (1996) *Questions of Identity*. London: Sage.

Hall, S. (1992) Culture, community, nation. *Cultural Studies* 7: 349–363.

Halliday, M. A. K. (1973) *Explorations in the Functions of Language*. London: Edward Arnold.

Halliday, M. A. K. (1977) *Aims and Perspectives in Linguistics*. Parkville, Victoria: Applied Linguistics Association of Australia (Occasional Papers Number 1: Ch. 3, Ideas about language).

Halliday, M. A. K. (1978) *Language as Social Semiotic: The Social Interpretation of Language and Meaning*. London: Edward Arnold.

Halliday, M. A. K. (1985a) *An Introduction to Functional Grammar*. Baltimore: Arnold.

Halliday, M. A. K. (1985b) Systemic background. In J. D. Benson and W. S. Greaves (eds) *Systemic Perspectives on Discourse, vol. 1. Selected Theoretical Papers from the Ninth International Systemic Workshop*. Norwood: Ablex, 1–15.

Halliday, M. A. K. (1994) *An Introduction to Functional Grammar*, 2nd edn. London: Edward Arnold.

Halliday, M. A. K. and Hasan, R. (1985) *Language, Context and Text: Aspects of Language in a Social–semiotic Perspective*. Oxford: Oxford University Press.

Halligan, F. (1998) Nightmare on film street. Hong Kong: *Sunday Morning Post*, January 18, 1998.

Hamamoto, D. Y. (1994) *Monitored Peril: Asian Americans and the Politics of TV Representation*. Minneapolis: University of Minnesota Press.

Harbsmeier, C. (1993) Conceptions of knowledge in ancient China. In H. Lenk and G. Paul (eds) *Epistemological Issues in Classical Chinese Philosophy*. Albany, NY: State University of New York Press, 11–30.

Harding, S. (1982) Is gender a variable in conceptions of rationality? A survey of the issues. *Dialectica* 36 (2–3): 226–242.

Harding, S. (1986) *The Science Question in Feminism*. Ithaca, NY: Cornell University Press.

Harris, R. (1981) *The Language Myth*. London: Duckworth.

Harris, R. (1990) On freedom of speech. In J. Joseph and T. Taylor (eds) *Ideologies of Language*. London: Routledge, 153–161.

Havis, R. (1998) Thriller a cut above the rest. *Sunday Morning Post*, March 8, 1998.

Heath, S. B. (1983) *Ways with Words: Language, Life and Work in Communities and Classrooms*. Cambridge: Cambridge University Press.

Heidegger, M. (1962 [1927]) *Being and Time*. Trans. J. Macquarrie and E. Robinson. Oxford: Blackwell.

Heidegger, M. (1996 [1953]) *Being and Time*. Trans. Joan Stambaugh. Albany, NY: State University of New York Press.

Heidegger, M. (1971 [1959]) *On the Way to Language*. Trans. P. D. Hertz. New York: Harper and Row.

Heim, M. (1999) *Electric Language: A Philosophical Study of Word Processing*, 2nd edn. New Haven, CT: Yale University Press.

Heller, M. (1988a) Introduction. In M. Heller (ed.) *Code-switching: Anthropological and Sociolinguistic Perspectives*. Berlin and New York: Mouton de Gruyter.

Heller, M. (1988b) Strategic ambiguity: Code-switching in the management of conflict. In M. Heller (ed.) *Code-switching: Anthropological and Sociolinguistic Perspectives*. Berlin and New York: Mouton de Gruyter, 77–96.

Henriques, J. *et al.* (1984) *Changing the Subject: Psychology, Social Recognition and Subjectivity*. London: Methuen, 1984.

Higginbotham, J. (1999) Tense, indexicality, and consequence. In J. Butterfield (ed.) *The Arguments of Time*. Oxford: Oxford University Press for The British Academy, 197–215.

Hinkel, E. (ed.) (1999) *Culture in Second Language Teaching and Learning*. Cambridge: Cambridge University Press.

Hobsbawm, E. and Ranger, T. (eds) (1983) *The Invention of Tradition*. Cambridge: Cambridge University Press.

Hoijer, H. (1951) Cultural implications of some Navaho linguistic categories. *Language* 27: 111–120.

Hong Kong Government (1978) *A Preliminary Study of the Use and Control of Triad Language on Television*. Hong Kong: Television and Films Authority.

Hongo, G. (1995) *Volcano*. New York: Vintage.

Hunter, J. (1995) Personal communication.

Hyland, K. (2000) *Disciplinary Discourses*. London: Longman.

Hymes, D. (1964) Introduction to Part III, World view and grammatical categories. In D. Hymes (ed.) *Language in Culture and Society: A Reader in Linguistics and Anthropology*. Bombay: Allied Publishers, 115–120.

Hymes, D. (1973) Speech and language: On the origins and foundations of inequality among speakers. *Daedalus* 102: 59–85.

The Independent (Port Moresby) (1996): (5 July 1996a) PM directs forest minister to endorse new measure, p.5. (5 July 1996b) Landowners to be paid old loyalties [sic]: FIA, p.5. (5 July 1996c) Inability to pay royalty increase, p.28. (19 July 1996) Yupela iwok long lusim K26 million na yupela bai lusim moa, p.22. (26 July 1996) It's time to stand up to the loggers, p.32. (2 August 1996) World Bank will not dictate to parliament: Haiveta, p.5. (8 November 1996): no title, p.13. (15 November 1996): no title, p.14.

Ivanic, R. and Weldon, S. (1999) Researching the writer–reader relationship. In C. N. Candlin and K. Hyland (eds) *Writing: Texts, Processes and Practices*. London: Longman.

Jackson, P. (1989) *Male Homosexuality in Thailand: An Interpretation of Contemporary Thai Sources*. New York: Global Academic Publishers.

Jackson, P. (1995) *Dear Uncle Go: Male Homosexuality in Thailand*. Bangkok: Bua Luang Books.

Jacob, P. G. (1987) Cultural competence in the ESP curriculum. *English for Specific Purposes* 6, 3: 203–218.

Jakobson, R. (1960) Closing statement: Linguistics and poetics. In T. A. Sebeok (ed.) *Style in Language*. Cambridge, MA: MIT Press, 350–377.

Jakobson, R. (1971) *Selected Writings. Volume IV, Word and Language*. The Hague: Mouton.

JanMohammed, A. R. and Lloyd, D. (eds) (1990) *The Nature and Context of Minority Discourse*. Oxford: Oxford University Press.

Johns, A. (1991) Faculty assessment of ESL student literacy skills: Implications for writing assessment. In L. Hamp-Lyons (ed.) *Assessing Second Language Writing in Academic Contexts*. Norwood, NJ: Ablex, 167–179.

Keech, M. (1997) Literacy, culture and difference: Feedback on student writing as discursive practice. In Z. Golebiowski and H. Borland (eds) *Academic Communication Across Disciplines and Cultures*. (Selected Proceedings of the First National Conference on Tertiary Literacy: Research and Practice, Vol. 2), 127–139.

Kippax, S. and Crawford, J. (1993) Flaws in the theory of reasoned action. In D. Terry, C. Gallois and M. McCamish (eds) *The Theory of Reasoned Action: Its Application to AIDS Preventive Behaviour*. Oxford and New York: Pergamon Press, 253–269.

Klamer, A. (1987) As if economists and their subject were rational. In J. Nelson, A. Megill and D. McCloskey (eds) *The Rhetoric of Human Sciences*. Madison: University of Wisconsin Press.

Kögler, H. H. (1996 [1992]) *The Power of Dialogue: Critical Hermeneutics after Gadamer and Foucault* (trans. P. Hendrickson). Cambridge, MA: MIT Press.

Komin, S. (1990) Culture and work-related values in Thai organisations. *International Journal of Psychology* 25: 681–704.

Komiya, R. (1990) *The Japanese Economy: Trade, Industry, and Government*. Tokyo: University of Tokyo Press.

Kress, G. (1985) Ideological structures in discourse. In T. A. van Dijk (ed.) (1985) *Handbook of Discourse Analysis*, 4 vols. London: Academic Press, 27–42.

Kress, G. (1993) Against arbitrariness: the social production of the sign as a foundational issue in critical discourse analysis. *Discourse and Society* 4 (2): 169–191.

Kunawararak, P., Beyrer, C., Natpratan, C. *et al.* (1995) The epidemiology of HIV and syphilis among male commercial sex workers in northern Thailand. *AIDS* 9: 517–521.

Labov, W. (1969) The logic of non-standard English. Washington, DC: *Georgetown Monographs on Language and Linguistics* 1–22.

Labov, W. and Fanshel, D. (1977) *Therapeutic Discourse*. New York: Academic Press.

Labov, W. and Waletzky, J. (1967) Narrative analysis. In J. Helm (ed.) *Essays on the Verbal and Visual Arts*. (Proceedings of the 1966 Spring Meeting of the American Ethnological Society.) Seattle: University of Washington Press.

Lam, H. C. (1991) Editorial. *Xin Bao (Hong Kong Economic Journal)*, September 14, 1991.

Landes, J. B. (1995) The public and the private sphere: A feminist reconsideration. In J. Meehan (ed.) *Feminists Read Habermas: Gendering the Subject of Discourse*. New York: Routledge, 91–116.

Landow, G. (1992) *Hypertext: The Convergence of Contemporary Theory and Technology*. Baltimore: Johns Hopkins University Press.

Latour, B. (1987) *Science in Action: How to Follow Scientists and Engineers Through Society*. Cambridge, MA: Harvard University Press.

Latour, B. (1988) The politics of explanation: An alternative. In S. Woolgar (ed.) *Knowledge and Reflexivity: New Frontiers in the Sociology of Knowledge*. London: Sage, 155–76.

Latour, B. (1993) *We Have Never Been Modern* (trans. C. Porter). Hemel Hempstead: Harvester Wheatsheaf.

Latour, B. and Woolgar, S. (1979) *Laboratory Life: The Social Construction of Scientific Facts*. Beverly Hills: Sage.

Lave, J. and Wenger, E. (1991) *Situated Learning: Legitimate Peripheral Participation*. Cambridge: Cambridge University Press.

Law, J. (1992) Notes on the theory of the actor-network: Ordering, strategy, and heterogeneity. *Systems Practice* 5: 379–393.

Law, J. (1994) *Organising Modernity*. Oxford: Blackwell.

Law, J. and Callon, M. (1995) Engineering and sociology in a military aircraft project: A network analysis of technological change. In S. Leigh Star (ed.) *Ecologies of Knowledge: Work and Politics in Science and Technology*. Albany, NY: State University of New York Press, 281–301.

Law, J. and Mol, A. (1995) Notes on materiality and sociality. *Sociological Review* 43 (2): 274–294.

Lea, M. and Street, B. (1996) Keynote Address. Multiliteracies Conference, Institute of Education, Cardiff, September 1996.

Lea, M. and Street, B. (1999) Writing as academic literacies: understanding textual practices in higher education. In C. N. Candlin and K. Hyland (eds) *Writing: Texts, Processes and Practices*. London: Longman.

Lee. A. (1996) *Gender, Literacy, Curriculum: Re-writing School Geography*. London: Taylor and Francis.

Leki, I. (1995) Good writing: I know it when I see it. In D. Belcher and G. Braine (eds) *Academic Writing in a Second Language: Essays on Research and Pedagogy*. Norwood, NJ: Ablex.

Leki, I. and Carson, J. (1994) Students' perceptions of EAP writing instruction and writing needs across the disciplines. *TESOL Quarterly* 28 (1): 81–101.

Leki, I. and Carson, J. (1997) 'Completely different worlds': EAP and the writing experiences of ESL students in university courses. *TESOL Quarterly* 31 (1): 39–69.

Lemert, C. (1995) *Sociology After the Crisis*. Boulder, CO: Westview.

Leong, R. (ed.) (1996) *Asian American Sexualities: Dimensions of Gay and Lesbian Experience*. New York: Routledge.

Li, A. (1998) 'No evidence' of triad gang problem in film industry. *South China Morning Post*, March 26, 1998.

Lim, Y. C. L. (1983) Singapore's success: The myth of the free market economy. *Asian Survey* XXIII (6): 752–764.

Lin, A. (1996) Bilingualism or linguistic segregation? Symbolic domination, resistance, and code-switching. *Linguistics and Education* 8 (1): 49–84.

de Lind van Wijngaarden, J. W. (1995) *A Social Geography of Male Homosexual Desire: Locations, Individuals and Networks in the Context of HIV/AIDS in Chiang Mai, Northern Thailand*. Chiang Mai: Social Research Institute, Chiang Mai University.

Logan, B. (1995) *Hong Kong Action Movies*. London: Titan Books.

Louie, K. (in press) I married a foreigner: Recovering Chinese masculinity in Australia. In W. Ommundsen (ed.) *Bastard Moons: Writing the Chinese Diaspora in Australia*. Sydney: Against the Grain Publishing.

Louie, K. and Edwards, L. (1994) Chinese masculinity: Theorising *wen* and *wu*. *East Asian History* 8: 135–148.

Lui, F. T. (1995) *Yong Jingji xue Zuo Yangjing (To Use Economics as Eyes)*. Hong Kong: 1 Publishing Co.

Luke, A. (1996) Genres of power? Literacy education and the production of capital. In R. Hasan and G. Williams (eds) *Literacy in Society*. London: Longman.

Luke, C. and Luke, A. (1998) Interracial families: Difference within difference. *Ethnic and Racial Studies* 21: 728–754.

Luke, C. and Luke, A. (in press) Theorising interracial families and hybrid identities: An Australian perspective. *Educational Theory*.

Lukes, S. (1974) *Power: A Radical View*. London: Macmillan.

Lukes, S. (ed.) (1986) *Power*. Oxford: Basil Blackwell.

Luukka, M-R. (1994) Metadiscourse in academic texts. In B-L. Gunnarsson and B. Nordberg (eds) *Text and Talk in Professional Context*. Uppsala: ASLA.

Luukka, M-R. (1995) Puhuttua ja kirjoitettua tiedettä: Funktionaalinen ja yhteisöllinen näkökulma tieteen kielen interpersonaalisiin piirteisiin (Spoken and written science: Functional and interpersonal features of scientific texts). *Jyväskylä Studies in Communication* 4. University of Jyväskylä.

Luukka, M-R. and Markkanen, R. (1997) Impersonalization as a form of hedging. In R. Markkanen and H. Schröder (eds) *Hedging and Discourse: Approaches to the Analysis of a Pragmatic Phenomenon*. Berlin: Walter de Gruyter.

Lyttleton, C. (1994) The good people of Isan: Commercial sex in northeast Thailand. *The Australian Journal of Anthropology* 5 (3): 257–279.

Lyttleton, C. (1995) Messages of distinction: The HIV/AIDS media campaign in Thailand. To appear in *Medical Anthropology* 16: 363–89.

MacLachlan, G. and Reid, I. (1994) *Framing and Interpretation*. Melbourne: Melbourne University Press.

Maclear, K. (1994) The myth of the 'model minority': Rethinking the education of Asian Canadians. *Our Schools/Our Selves* 5 (3): 54–76.

Malcolm, I. G. and McGregor, A. L. (1995) *Worlds Apart: An Investigation of Linguistic and Cultural Factors Affecting Communication Between NESB Students and Edith Cowan University Staff*. Perth, Western Australia: Centre for Applied Language Research, Edith Cowan University.

Malcolm, I. and Rochecouste, J. (1998) *Australian Aboriginal Students in Higher Education*. Perth: Centre for Applied Language Research, Edith Cowan University.

Malinowski, B. (1923) The problem of meaning in primitive languages. In C. K. Ogden and I. A. Richards *The Meaning of Meaning*. London: Kegan Paul, Trench, Trübner and Co., 296–336.

Malinowski, B. (1937) The dilemma of contemporary linguistics. *Nature* 140: 172–173.

Malinowski, B. (1965 [1935]) *Coral Gardens and Their Magic. Volume II, The Language of Magic and Gardening*. Bloomington, IN: Indiana University Press.

Mar, L. (1993) Resistance. In J. Hagedorn (ed.) *Charlie Chan is Dead: An Anthology of Contemporary Asian-American Fiction*. London: Penguin, 296–313.

Martin, J. R. (1984) Lexical cohesion, field and genre: Parcelling experience and discourse goals. Paper presented at Second Rice Symposium on Linguistics and Semiotics: Text Semantics and Discourse Semantics. (February 8–14, 1984), Rice University, Houston, Texas.

Martin, J. R. (1985) *Factual Writing: Exploring and Challenging Social Reality*. Geelong, Victoria: Deakin University Press (republished by Oxford University Press 1989).

Martin, J. R. (1992) *English Text: System and Structure*. Amsterdam: Benjamins.

Martin, J. R. (1996) Systemic functional perspectives on genre, 1 — Modelling genre. Paper given at The Textlinguistic Approach to Genre Colloquium, American Association of Applied Linguistics Conference (AAAL), Chicago, IL, 23–26 March, 1996.

Martin, J. R., Christie, F. and Rothery, J. (1987) Social processes in education — a reply to Sawyer and Watson (and others). *Working Papers in Linguistics* 5. Sydney:

Department of Linguistics, University of Sydney. (Reprinted (September 1987) in *The Teaching of English*. Sydney: English Teachers' Association of New South Wales. Abridged version in I. Reid (ed.) *The Place of Genre in Learning: Current Debates*. (Typereader Publications no. 1.) Geelong, Victoria: Centre for Studies in Literary Education, Deakin University.

Martin, J. R., Christie, F. and Rothery, J. (1994) Social processes in education — a reply to Sawyer and Watson (and others). In B. Stierer and J. Maybin (eds) *Language Literacy and Learning in Educational Practice: A Reader*. Clevedon, Avon: Multilingual Matters.

Martin, J. R. and Plum, G. A. (1997) Construing experience: some story genres. (Special Issue: Oral versions of personal experience: Three decades of narrative analysis.) *Journal of Narrative and Life History* 7 (1–4): 299–308.

Marx, K. and Engels, F. (reprinted 1973) *Feuerbach: Opposition of the Materialist and Idealist Outlooks*. The first part of *The German Ideology*, published in accordance with the text and arrangement of the original manuscript. London: Lawrence & Wishart.

Mason, C. J., Markowitz, L. E., Kitsiripornchai, S., *et al.* (1995) Declining prevalence of HIV-1 infections in young Thai men. *AIDS* 9 (9): 1061–1065.

Mastro, T. D. and Limpakarnjanarat, K. (1995) Condom use in Thailand: How much is it slowing the HIV/AIDS epidemic? *AIDS* 9: 523–525.

McCamish, M. and Sittitrai, W. (1996) The context of safety: Male sex workers in Pattaya. Thai Red Cross Society, Bangkok: Program on AIDS, Research Report No. 18.

McCamish, M., Timmins, T., Terry, D. and Gallois, C. (1993) A theory-based intervention: The theory of reasoned action in action. In D. Terry, C. Gallois and M. McCamish (eds) *The Theory of Reasoned Action: Its Application to AIDS Preventive Behaviour*. Oxford and New York: Pergamon Press, 185–205.

McCarthy, M. (1999) *Spoken Language and Applied Linguistics*. Cambridge: Cambridge University Press.

McCloskey, D. (1983) The rhetoric of economics. *Journal of Economic Literature*, 21 (2): 481–517.

McCloskey, D. (1993) The rhetoric of economic expertise. In R. H. Roberts and J. M. M. Good (eds) *The Recovery of Rhetoric: Persuasive Discourse and Disciplinarity in the Human Sciences*. London: Bristol Classical Press, 137–147.

McCloskey, D. (1995) Metaphors economists live by. *Social Research* 62 (2): 215–237.

McNay, L. (1992) *Foucault and Feminism: Power, Gender and the Self*. Oxford: Polity Press.

Merton, R. (1967) *Social Theory and Social Structure*. New York: Free Press.

Messer-Davidow, E., Shumway, D. R. and Sylvan, D. J. (eds) (1993) *Knowledges: Historical and Critical Studies in Disciplinarity*. Charlottesville: University Press of Virginia.

Meyer, J. W., Boli, J. and Thomas, G. M. (1994) Ontology and rationalization in the Western cultural account. In W. R. Scott and J. W. Meyer (eds) *Institutional Environments and Organizations: Structural Complexity and Individualism*. Thousand Oaks, CA: Sage, 9–27.

Michels, M. M. (1988) Rhetoric and legitimation: An analysis of Supreme Court reversals. In R. Kevelson (ed.) *Law and Semiotics, Volume 2*. New York: Plenum Press, 229–240.

Milliband, R. (1983) *Class Power and State Power*. London: Verso.

Milne, W. (1845 [1826]) Some account of a secret association in China, entitled the Triad society. *The Chinese Repository* 14: 59–77.

Morgan, W. (1960) *Triad Societies in Hong Kong*. Hong Kong: Hong Kong Government Press.

Morris, R. C. (1994) Three sexes and four sexualities: Redressing the discourse on gender and sexuality in contemporary Thailand. *Positions* 2 (1): 15–43.

Mühlhäusler, P. (1996) Ecological and non-ecological approaches to language planning. In M. Hellinger and U. Ammon (eds) *Contrastive Sociolinguistics*. Berlin: Mouton de Gruyter, 205–212.

Mulhall, S. (1996) *Heidegger and Being and Time*. London: Routledge.

Mura, D. (1996) *Where the Body Meets Memory: An Odyssey of Race, Sexuality and Identity*. New York: Anchor Books.

Murray, D. (1994) *The Origins of the Tiandihui: The Chinese Triads in Legend and History*. In collaboration with Qin Baoqi. Stanford: Stanford University Press.

Murray, S. O. (1992) The 'underdevelopment' of modern/gay homosexuality in Meso-America. In K. Plummer (ed.) *Modern Homosexualities: Fragments of Lesbian and Gay Experience*. London and New York: Routledge, 29–38.

Myers, G. (1989) The pragmatics of politeness in scientific articles. *Applied Linguistics* 10 (1): 1–35.

Nair, J. (1993) On the question of agency in feminist historiography. *Gender and History* 6 (1): 82–100.

Nakanishi, D. and Nishida, T. (eds) (1996) *The Asian American Educational Experience: A Sourcebook for Teachers and Students*. New York/London: Routledge.

Narvilai, A. (1994a) Interview: Young men following in their sister's footsteps. *Bangkok Post: Outlook* XLIX (183).

Narvilai, A. (1994b) Phuchai kai tua (Male sex work in urban cultures). Summary of an academic conference on urban cultures. *Urban Communities and their Transformation in Bangkok and its Environs* (7–8 December). Sirinthom Anthropology Centre, Silapakorn University, Bangkok (in Thai), 55–70.

The National (Port Moresby) (6 June 1996) Sustainable, selective logging 'beneficial', p.6.

The National (Port Moresby) (11 July 1996) FIA refuses to pay K10 royalty, p.2.

Nelson, J., Megill, A. and McCloskey, D. (1987) Rhetoric of inquiry. In J. Nelson, A. Megill and D. McCloskey (eds) *The Rhetoric of Human Sciences*. Madison: University of Wisconsin Press.

Nelson, S. D. (1994) Wear your hat: Representational resistance in safer sex discourse. *Gay and Lesbian Studies in Art History* 27 (4): 285–304.

Neumann, K. (1992) *Not the Way it Really Was: Constructing the Tolai Past*. Honolulu: University of Hawaii Press.

Newton, Isaac (1989 [1687]) Newton's Scholium on absolute space and time. In J. Earman *World Enough and Space-time: Absolute Versus Relational Theories of Space and Time*. Cambridge, MA: MIT Press, 20–26.

Ng, F. (1992) *Bone*. New York: Doubleday.

Nichols, B. (1991) *Representing Reality: Issues and Conceptions in Documentary*. Bloomington, IN: Indiana University Press.

Niranjana, T. (1992) *Siting Translation: History, Post-structuralism, and the Colonial Context*. Berkeley: University of California Press.

Noble, D. (1979) *America by Design: Science, Technology and the Rise of Corporate Capitalism*. Oxford: Oxford University Press.

Nopekesorn, T., Sungkarom, S. and Somlum, R. (1991) HIV prevalence and sexual behaviours among Thai men aged 21 in northern Thailand. Program on AIDS. Bangkok: Thai Red Cross Society, Report # 3.

Nowotny, H. (1994 [1989]) *Time: The Modern and Post-modern Experience* (trans. N. Plaice). Cambridge: Polity Press.

O'Barr, W. M. and Atkins, B. K. (1980) 'Women's language' or 'powerless language'? In S. McConnell-Ginet, R. Borker and N. Furman (eds) *Women and Language in Literature and Society*. New York: Praeger, 93–110.

Ochs, E. (1993) Constructing social identity: A language socialization perspective. *Research on Language and Social Interaction* 26 (3): 287–306.

Ochs, E., Schegloff, E. A. and Thompson, S. A. (eds) (1996) *Interaction and Grammar*. Cambridge: Cambridge University Press.

Okin, S. (1981) Women and the making of the sentimental family. *Philosophy and Public Affairs* 11 (1), 65–88.

Olson, D. R. and Astington, J. W. (1990) Talking about text: How literacy contributes to thought. *Journal of Pragmatics* 14: 705–721.

Ong, A. (1996) Flexible citizenship among Chinese cosmopolitans. In P. Cheah and B. Robbins (eds) *Cosmopolitics: Thinking and Feeling Beyond the Nation*. Minneapolis: University of Minnesota Press, 134–162.

Ontario Ministry of Education and Training (1993) *Antiracism and Ethnocultural Equity in School Boards: Guidelines for Policy Development and Implementation*. Toronto: Queen's Printer for Ontario.

O'Shea, R. (1993) *Writing for Psychology: An Introductory Guide for Students*. Sydney: Harcourt Brace Jovanovich.

Ownby, D. (1996) *Brotherhoods and Secret Societies in Early and Mid-Qing China*. Stanford: Stanford University Press.

Parakrama, A. (1995) *De-hegemonising Language Standards*. Basingstoke: Macmillan.

Pateman, C. (1988) *The Sexual Contract*. Stanford: Stanford University Press.

Pennycook, A. (1994) Incommensurable discourses. *Applied Linguistics* 15 (2): 115–138.

Pennycook, A. (1998) *English and the Discourses of Colonialism*. London: Routledge.

Pickering, W. A. (1878) Chinese secret societies and their origin. *Journal of the Straits Branch of the Royal Asiatic Society* 1: 63–84.

Pinker, S. (1994) *The Language Instinct*. London: Penguin.

Pitelis, C. and Clarke, T. (1993) Introduction: The political economy of privatisation. In T. Clarke and C. Pitelis (eds) *The Political Economy of Privatisation*. London and New York: Routledge.

Plum, G. A. (1998) *Text and Contextual Conditioning in Spoken English: A Genre-based Approach*. Nottingham: Department of English Studies, University of Nottingham (Monographs in Systemic Linguistics, No. 10).

Plum, G. A. (1996) Systemic Functional Perspectives on Genre 2 — Analysing Genre. Paper given at *The Textlinguistic Approach to Genre Colloquium*, American Association of Applied Linguistics Conference (AAAL), Chicago, 23–26 March 1996.

Polanyi, K. (1957) *The Great Transformation*. Boston: Beacon Press.

Polt, R. (1999) *Heidegger: An Introduction*. London: UCL Press.

Porter, T. (1995) *Trust in Numbers: The Pursuit of Objectivity in Science and Public Life*. Princeton, NJ: Princeton University Press.

Potter, J. (1996) *Representing Reality: Discourse, Rhetoric and Social Construction*. London: Sage.

Poynton, C. (1993) Grammar, language and the social: post-structuralism and systemic-functional linguistics. *Social Semiotics* 3 (1): 1–21.

Poynton, C. (1996) *Language and Difference*. Plenary address to the 21st Annual Applied Linguistics Association of Australia Congress, Sydney, October 1996.

Prakash, G. (1990) *Bonded Histories: Genealogies of Labour Servitude in Colonial India*. Princeton: Princeton University Press.

Pratt, M. L. (1982) Conventions of representation: Where discourse and ideology meet. In H. Byrnes (ed.) *Contemporary Perceptions of Language: Interdisciplinary Dimensions*. Georgetown University Round Table on Languages and Linguistics. Washington DC: Georgetown University Press, 139–155.

Pratt, M. L. (1987) Linguistic utopias. In N. Fabb, D. Attridge, A. Durant and C. MacCabe (eds) *The Linguistics of Writing: Arguments Between Language and Literature*. Manchester: Manchester University Press, 48–66.

Prior, P. A. (1998) *Writing/Disciplinarity: A Sociohistoric Account of Literate Activity in the Academy*. Mahwah, NJ: Lawrence Erlbaum.

Pusey, M. (1987) *Jürgen Habermas*. London: Tavistock.

Radecki, P. M. and Swales, J. M. (1988) ESL Student reaction to written comments on their written work. *System* 16 (3): 355–365.

Ram, K. (1991) *Mukkuvar Women: Gender, Hegemony and Capitalist Transformation in a South Indian Fishing Community*. Sydney: Allen & Unwin.

Ram, K. (1993) 'Too traditional once again': Some post-structuralists on the aspirations of the immigrant/Third World female subject. *Australian Feminist Studies* 17: 5–28.

Ram, K. (1994) Modernist anthropology's 'comparative' project: The construction of Indian identity as tradition. In A. Gomez (ed.) *Modernity and Identity: Asian Illustrations*. Melbourne: La Trobe University Press, 122–158.

Ram, K. (1995) Migrating dances: 'Tradition' and 'innovation' in the work of an Indian dance company in Australia. *Writings on Dance* 13: 35–54.

Ram, K. (1998) Maternity and the story of enlightenment in the colonies: Tamil coastal women. In K. Ram and M. Jolly (eds) *Maternities and Modernities: Colonial and Postcolonial Experiences in Asia and the Pacific*. Cambridge: Cambridge University Press, 114–143.

Ray, E. J. (1991) Changing patterns of protectionism: The fall in tariffs and the rise in non-tariff barriers. In J. A. Frieden *et al.* (eds) *International Economy*. New York: St. Martin's Press.

Reed-Danahay, D. E. (1997) Introduction. In D. E. Reed-Danahay (ed.) *Auto/ethnography: Rewriting the Self and the Social*. Oxford: Berg, 1–17.

Reimer, M. (1988) The social organisation of the labour process: A case study of the documentary management of clerical labour in the public service. University of Toronto PhD dissertation.

Ribeiro, B. T. (1996) Conflict talk in a psychiatric discharge interview: Struggling between personal and official footings. In C. R. Caldas-Coulthard and M. Coulthard (eds) *Texts and Practices: Readings in Critical Discourse Analysis*. London: Routledge, 178–193.

Richards, J. and Lockhart, C. (1994) *Reflective Teaching in Second Language Classrooms*. Cambridge: Cambridge University Press.

Ricoeur, P. (1984 [1983]) *Time and Narrative. Volume 1* (trans. K. McLaughlin and D. Pellauer). Chicago: University of Chicago Press.

Ricoeur, P. (1992 [1990]) *Oneself as Another* (trans. K. Blamey). Chicago: University of Chicago Press.

Robbins, B. (1998) Comparative cosmopolitanisms. In P. Cheah and B. Robbins (eds) *Cosmopolitics: Thinking and Feeling Beyond the Nation*. Minneapolis: University of Minnesota Press, 246–264.

Robertson, G., Mash, M., Tickner, L., Bird, J., Curtis, B., and Putnam, T. (eds) (1994) *Travellers' Tales: Narratives of Home and Displacement*. London: Routledge.

Robinson, I. (1975) *The New Grammarians' Funeral: A Critique of Noam Chomsky's Linguistics*. Cambridge: Cambridge University Press.

Robinson, P. and Davies, P. (1991) London's homosexual male prostitutes: Power, peer groups and HIV. In P. Aggleton, G. Hart and P. Davies (eds) *AIDS: Responses, Interventions and Care*. London: Falmer Press, 95–110.

Rochecouste, J. (1996) *Creating a Community of Scholars* [online tutorial]. Available: http://www.cowan.edu.au/calr/home.html

Roe v. Wade (1973), 410 U.S. 113.

Roemer, J. E. (1988) *Free to Lose: An Introduction to Marxist Economic Philosophy*. Cambridge, MA: Harvard University Press.

Rogoff, B. (1990) *Apprenticeship in Thinking: Cognitive Development in Social Contexts*. New York: Oxford University Press.

Rorty, R. (1987) Pragmatism and philosophy. In K. Baynes, J. Bohman, and T. McCarthy (eds) *After Philosophy: End or Transformation?* Cambridge, MA: MIT Press, 26–66.

Said, E. (1978) *Orientalism: Western Conceptions of the Orient*. London: Penguin.

Salisbury, R. F. (1970) *Vunamami: Economic Transformation in a Traditional Society*. Melbourne: Melbourne University Press.

Sapir, E. (1963) *Selected Writings*. Berkeley: University of California Press.

Sapir, E. (1966) *Culture, Language and Personality: Selected Essays*, ed. D. G. Mandelbaum. Berkeley: University of California Press.

Saussure, F. de (1974 [1915]) *A Course in General Linguistics*, 2nd edn (trans. W. Baskin). Glasgow: Fontana/Collins.

Saussure, F. de (1983 [1915]) *Course in General Linguistics* (trans. Roy Harris). La Salle, IL: Open Court.

Schechner, R. (1985) *Between Theater and Anthropology*. Philadelphia: University of Pennsylvania Press.

Schegloff, E. A. and Sacks, H. (1973) Opening up closings. *Semiotica* 8: 289–327. (Reprinted in R. Turner (ed.) (1974) *Ethnomethodology*. Harmondsworth: Penguin, 233–64.)

Schegloff, E., Ochs, E. and Thompson, S. (1996) Introduction. In E. Ochs, E. Schegloff and S. Thompson (eds) *Interaction and Grammar*. Cambridge: Cambridge University Press, 1–51.

Schiebinger, L. (1989) *The Mind Has No Sex: Women in the Origins of Modern Science*. Cambridge, MA: Harvard University Press.

Schiffer, J. R. (1991) State policy and economic growth: A note on the Hong Kong model. *International Journal of Urban and Regional Research*, 15: 180–196.

Schiffrin, D. (1987) *Discourse Markers*. Cambridge: Cambridge University Press.

Schlegel, G. (1866) *Thian ti Hwui: The Hung League or Heaven-earth-league*. Batavia: Lange.

Schultz, V. (1992) Women 'before' the law: Judicial stories about women, work, and sex segregation on the job. In J. Butler and J. W. Scott (eds) *Feminists Theorise the Political*. New York: Routledge, Chapman & Hall, 297–338.

Scollon, R. (1976) *Conversations with a One Year Old: A Case Study of the Developmental Foundation of Syntax*. Honolulu: University Press of Hawaii.

Scollon, R. (1981) Human knowledge and the institution's knowledge. Final report to the National Institute of Education on grant No. G-80-0185 'Communication Patterns and Retention in a Public University'.

Scollon, R. and Scollon, S. (1979) *Linguistic Convergence: An Ethnography of Speaking at Fort Chipewyan, Alberta*. New York: Academic Press.

Scollon, R. and Scollon, S. (1981) *Narrative, Literacy and Face in Interethnic Communication*. Norwood, NJ: Ablex.

Scollon, R. and Scollon, S. (1995) *Intercultural Communication: A Discourse Approach*. Oxford: Basil Blackwell.

Scribner, S. and Cole, M. (1981) *The Psychology of Literacy*. Cambridge, MA: Harvard University Press.

See, L. (1995) *On Gold Mountain*. New York: Random House.

Seidel, G. (1985) Political discourse analysis. In T. A. van Dijk (ed.) *Handbook of Discourse Analysis*, 4 vols. London: Academic Press, 43–60.

Sengupta, M. (1995) Translation as manipulation: The power of images and images of power. In A. Dingwaney and C. Maier (eds) *Between Languages and Cultures*. Pittsburgh and London: University of Pittsburgh Press, 295–301.

Seremetakis, N. (1994) The memory of the senses, part 1: Marks of the transitory. In N. Seremetakis (ed.) *The Senses Still: Perception and Memory as Material Culture in Modernity*. Boulder, CO: Westview Press, 1–19.

Shapiro, M. (1989) A political approach to language purism. In B. Jernudd and M. Shapiro (eds) *The Politics of Language Purism*. Berlin: Mouton de Gruyter.

Shaughnessy, M. (1977) Some needed research on writing. *College Composition and Communication* 28 (December 1977).

Sherzer, J. (1987) A discourse-centred approach to language and culture. *American Anthropologist* 89: 295–309.

Shevelow, K. (1989) *Women and Print Culture: The Constitution of Femininity in the Early Periodical*. London: Routledge.

Shore, S. (1988) On the so-called Finnish passive. *Word* 39: 151–176.

Silverstein, M. (1985) Language and the culture of gender: At the intersection of structure, usage, and ideology. In E. Mertz and R. Parmentier (eds) *Semiotic Mediation: Sociocultural and Psychological Perspectives*. New York: Academic Press, 219–259.

Sinclair, J. McH. and Coulthard, R. M. (1975) *Towards an Analysis of Discourse*. Oxford: Oxford University Press.

Sittitrai, W., Phanuphak, P. and Roddy, R. (1994) *Male Bar Workers in Bangkok: An Intervention*. Thai Red Cross Society: Program on AIDS, Research Report No.10.

Sittitrai, W., Sakondhavat, C. and Brown, T. (1992) *A Survey of Men Having Sex with Men in a North-eastern Thai Province*. Thai Red Cross Society: Program on AIDS, Research Report No.5.

Sivaraksa, S. (1995) Interview: Illusions of wealth. *Newsweek* 22: 52.

Slaughterhouse Cases (1873), 83 U.S. (16 Wall.) 36.

South China Morning Post (1993) Teenager gets second chance. *South China Morning Post*, June 26 1993.

South China Morning Post (1994a) Triad and error. *South China Morning Post*, October 2 1994.

South China Morning Post (1994b) Man wins key triad appeal. *South China Morning Post*, July 2 1994.

Spivak, G. (1988) French feminism in an international frame. *In Other Worlds: Essays in Cultural Politics.* London and New York: Routledge.

Spivak, G. (1990) The post-colonial critic: Interview with Rashmi Bhatnagar, Lola Chatterjee, and Rajeswari Sunder Rajan. In S. Harasym (ed.) *The Post-colonial Critic: Interviews, Strategies, Dialogues.* New York: Routledge, 67–74.

Srivatjana, P. (1995) Life styles and health behaviour of male prostitutes in Patpong area. Presented at the Third International Conference on AIDS in Asia and the Pacific and Fifth National AIDS Conference in Thailand. Chiang Mai, September 1995.

Stanton, W. (1900) *The Triad Society.* Hong Kong: Kelly & Walsh.

Stettler, M. (1995) The rhetoric of McCloskey's rhetoric of economics. *Cambridge Journal of Economics* 19: 391–403.

Storer, G. (1995) Making choices: HIV/AIDS education and male sex workers. Presented at the Second International Conference on Language in Development. Bali, Indonesia, April 1995.

Storer, G. (1999) Rehearsing gender and sexuality in modern Thailand: Masculinity and male–male sex. In P. Jackson and G. Sullivan (eds) *Lady Boys, Tom Boys, Rent Boys: Male and Female Homosexualities in Contemporary Thailand.* New York: Haworth Press, 141–59. [Also in *Journal of Gay and Lesbian Social Services*, Special Edition (1999), 9, 2/3: 141–59.]

Strassmann, D. (1993) The stories of economics and the power of the storyteller. *History of Political Economy* 25 (1): 148–165.

Street, B. (1995) *Social Literacies: Critical Approaches to Literacy in Development, Ethnography and Education.* London: Longman.

Strommen, E. F. (1989) 'You're a what?' Family member reactions to the disclosure of homosexuality. *Journal of Homosexuality* 18 (1): 37–58.

Stuart-Smith, V. (1998) Constructing an argument in psychology: rhetorical structure theory and the analysis of student writing. In C. N. Candlin and K. Hyland (eds) *Writing: Texts, Processes and Practices.* London: Longman.

Sundara, Rajan R. (1993) *Real and Imagined Women: Gender, Culture, and Postcolonialism.* London and New York: Routledge.

Swales, J. M. (1990) *Genre Analysis: English in Academic and Research Settings.* Cambridge: Cambridge University Press.

Swales, J. M. (1993) Genre and engagement. *Revue de Philologie et d'Histoire.* Fasc.3: *Langues et Littératures Modernes.* AFL 3 *Moderne Taal-en Letterkunde.*

Tannen, D. (ed.) (1993) *Framing in Discourse.* New York: Oxford University Press.

Taylor, C. (1992) Heidegger, language, and ecology. In H. Dreyfus and H. Hall (eds) *Heidegger: A Critical Reader.* Oxford: Blackwell, 247–269.

Taylor, G. *et al.* (1995) *Student Progress in 1993.* Canberra: Department of Employment, Education and Training.

Taylor, T. (1990) Which is to be master? The institutionalisation of authority in the science of language. In J. Joseph and T. Taylor (eds) *Ideologies of Language*. London: Routledge, 9–26.

ter Haar, B. (1993) The gathering of brothers and elders (*Ko-Lao hui*): A new view. In L. Blussé and H. Zurndorfer (eds) *Conflict and Accommodation in Early Modern East Asia*. Leiden: E. J. Brill, 259–283.

Threadgold, T. (1997) *Feminist Poetics: Poesis, Performance, Histories*. London: Longman.

Toulmin, S. (1958) *The Uses of Argument*. Cambridge: Cambridge University Press.

Union Pacific R. Co. v. Botsford (1891), 141 U.S. 250.

United Nations: Department of Humanitarian Affairs. 30 September 1994 (E-mail message).

Urry, J. (1991) Time and space in Giddens' social theory. In C. G. A. Bryant and D. Jary (eds) *Giddens' Theory of Structuration: A Critical Appreciation*. London: Routledge, 160–175.

Vachek, J. (ed.) (1964) *A Prague School reader in Linguistics*. Bloomington, IN: Indiana University Press.

Valdes, J. M. (ed.) (1986) *Culture Bound: Bridging the Cultural Gap in Language Teaching*. Cambridge: Cambridge University Press.

van Dijk, T. A. (1985) *Handbook of Discourse Analysis*. 4 vols. London: Academic Press.

van Dijk, T. A. (1987a) *Communicating Racism: Ethnic Prejudice in Thought and Talk*. Newbury Park, CA: Sage.

van Dijk, T. A. (1987b) *News Analysis: Case Studies in International and National News*. Hillsdale, NJ: Lawrence Erlbaum.

van Dijk, T. A. (1989) Structures of discourse and structures of power. In J. A. Anderson (ed.) *Communication Yearbook 12*. Newbury Park, CA: Sage, 18–59.

van Dijk, T. A. (1990) Social cognition and discourse. In H. Giles and W. P. Robinson (eds) *Handbook of Language and Social Psychology*. Chichester: John Wiley, 163–183.

Ventola, E. (1987) *The Structure of Social Interaction: A systemic approach to the semiotics of service encounters*. London: Pinter.

Ventral, E. (1987) *The Structure of Social Interaction: A Systematic Approach to the Semiotics of Service Encounters* (Open Linguistic Series). London: Pinter.

Venuti, L. (1992) Introduction. In Lawrence Venuti (ed.) *Rethinking Translation: Discourse, Subjectivity, Ideology*. London and New York: Routledge, 57–74.

Venuti, L. (1995) *The Translators' Invisibility*. London and New York: Routledge.

Wade, R. (1988) State intervention in 'outward-looking' development: Neo-classical theory and Taiwanese practice. In G. White (ed.) *Developmental States in East Asia*. New York: St. Martin's Press.

Wade, R. (1990) *Governing the Market*. Princeton: Princeton University Press.

Wallerstein, I. *et al.* (1995) *Open the Social Sciences*. Report of the Gulbenkian Commission on the Restructuring of the Social Sciences. Hong Kong: Oxford University Press (in Chinese).

Wang, H. and Wang, L. (1990) *Laonian Shenghuo Fangshi Tan Mi (The Life Style of the Elderly)*. Tianjin: Tianjin People's Press.

Wang, Y-M. (1963) *Instructions for Practical Living and Other Neo-Confucian Writings* (trans. Wing-tsit Chan). New York: Columbia University Press.

Ward, E. and Pincus, S. (1992) *Aboriginal and Torres Strait Islander Students Update*. Canberra: Department of Employment, Education and Training.

Ward, J. S. M. and Stirling, W. (1925–1926) *The Hung Society or the Society of Heaven and Earth*. Three vols. London: Baskerville Press.

Weber, M. (1968) *Economy and Society, Vol. 3* (ed. G. Roth and C. Wittich). New York: Bedminster Press.

Weedon, C. (1987) *Feminist Practice and Post-structuralist Theory*. Oxford: Basil Blackwell.

Wei-ming, T. (ed.) (1991) *The Living Tree: The Changing Meaning of Being Chinese Today*. Cambridge: Cambridge University Press.

Western, N. (1995) Sun Yee On office-bearer jailed. *Eastern Express*, May 2 1995.

Westwood, R. I. (ed.) (1992) *Organisational Behaviour: Southeast Asian Perspectives*. Hong Kong: Longman.

White, J. B. (1988) Judicial criticism. In S. Levinson and S. Mailloux (eds) *Interpreting Law and Literature: A Hermeneutic Reader*. Evanston: Northwestern University Press, 393–410.

Whorf, B. L. (1956) *Language, Thought, and Reality*, ed. John B. Carroll. Cambridge, MA: MIT Press.

Willard, C. A. (1982) Argument fields. In J. R. Cox and C. A. Willard (eds) *Advances in Argumentation Theory and Research*. Carbondale, IL: Southern Illinois University Press, 27–77.

Williams, G. (1992) *Sociolinguistics: A Sociological Critique*. London: Routledge.

Williams, M. (1988) Language taught for meetings and language used in meetings: Is there anything in common? *Applied Linguistics* 9 (1): 46–58.

Wilson, R. and Dirlik, A. (eds) (1995) *Asia/Pacific as Space of Cultural Production*. Durham: Duke University Press.

Winichakul, T. (1995) The changing landscape of the past: New histories in Thailand since 1973. *Journal of South East Asian Studies* 26 (1): 99–120.

Wong, F. (1993) Film 'triad hero' image sparks alarm. *Hong Kong Standard*, February 16 1993.

Wood, M. (1999) Rimbunan Hijau versus the World Bank and Australian miners: Print media representations of forestry policy conflict in Papua New Guinea. *Australian Journal of Anthropology* 10, 2: 175–189.

Yates, J. (1989) *Control Through Communication: The Rise of System in American Management*. Baltimore: Johns Hopkins University Press.

Young, P. (1996) Triad's appeal rejected despite sympathy on tea. *South China Morning Post*, November 30 1996.

Index (word & phrase)

Index (writer names)